A NOTE FROM THE AUTHOR

This book has been designed for you to use in preparation for the Advanced Placement English Language and Composition exam. In it you will find information about the AP exam, important test-preparation advice, strategies on approaching multiple-choice questions, advice and examples for dealing with the essay questions, and a comprehensive list of terminology typically used on the test. Finally, two practice exams are included for you to hone your skills. Responses are discussed so that you can better understand why some responses are wrong, why some are almost right, and why others are the only possible correct responses.

Those of you who have completed an Advanced Placement course in English Language and Composition are to be congratulated. Not only have you conquered a challenging curriculum and completed many impressive reading and writing assignments, but you have also learned how to manage your time, assume demanding responsibility, and exercise self-discipline. Now you have only to prepare for the AP exam. I hope that this book will help you with this last step in an arduous, but rewarding, adventure.

Best wishes,

Denise Pivarnik-Nova

RELATED TITLES

AP Biology

AP Calculus AB & BC

AP Chemistry

AP English Literature & Composition

AP Environmental Science

AP European History

AP Human Geography

AP Macroeconomics/Microeconomics

AP Physics B & C

AP Psychology

AP Statistics

AP U.S. Government & Politics

AP U.S. History

AP World History

ACT Strategies, Practice & Review

ACT Premier

8 Practice Tests for the ACT

ACT English, Reading & Writing Prep

ACT Math & Science Prep

SAT Strategies, Practice & Review

SAT Premier

SAT Total Prep

8 Practice Tests for the SAT

Evidence-Based Reading, Writing, and Essay Workbook for the SAT

Math Workbook for the SAT

SAT Subject Test: Biology E/M

SAT Subject Test: Chemistry

SAT Subject Test: Literature

SAT Subject Test: Mathematics Level 1

SAT Subject Test: Mathematics Level 2

SAT Subject Test: Physics

SAT Subject Test: U.S. History

SAT Subject Test: World History

AP® ENGLISH LANGUAGE & COMPOSITION

2017–2018

Denise Pivarnik-Nova

KAPLAN

PUBLISHING

New York

© 2017 by Kaplan, Inc.
Published by Kaplan Publishing, a division of Kaplan, Inc.
750 Third Avenue
New York, NY 10017

TABLE OF CONTENTS

About the Author IX

Kaplan Panel of AP Experts x

PART ONE: THE BASICS

Chapter 1: Inside the AP English Language and Composition Exam 3

    An Overview of the Test Structure 3

    How the Exam Is Scored 5

    Getting Your Grades 5

    Registration and Fees 5

    Additional Resources 6

Chapter 2: Strategies for Success: It's Not Always How Much You Know 7

    How to Use This Book 8

    What the Test Requires 9

    How to Approach the Multiple-Choice Section 10

    How to Approach the Essay Questions 14

    Take Control: How to Approach the Test as a Whole 18

    Stress Management 20

    Countdown to the Test 29

PART TWO: DIAGNOSTIC TEST

    Diagnostic Test 35

    Answer Key 65

    Answers and Explanations 66

    How to Make This Book Work for You Based on the Results of Your Diagnostic 91

PART THREE: THE AP ENGLISH LANGUAGE AND COMPOSITION EXAM

Chapter 3: Key Terminology..**95**

    Introduction 95

    Key Terms 95

    Applying Key Terminology 103

Chapter 4: Reading for Understanding.......................**109**

    Introduction 109

    Reading Critically 110

    The How-What Approach 111

    Applying the How-What Approach 113

    Sample Annotations... 115

Chapter 5: The Multiple-Choice Section.....................**117**

    About the Multiple-Choice Section 117

    Reading the Questions 118

    The Types of Questions 120

    Applying the Strategies 125

    Practice Sets.. 130

    Answers and Explanations................................... 137

Chapter 6: Writing the Essays...............................**141**

    A Brief Review... 141

    The Scoring Guide 142

    The Types of Prompts.. 144

    The 3-D Approach... 155

    Applying the 3-D Approach 156

    Practice Set... 165

PART FOUR: PRACTICE TESTS

How to Take the Practice Tests 174

Computing Your Score 175

Practice Test 1 ....**177**

Practice Test 1: Answer Key 206

Answers and Explanations 207

Practice Test 2 ....**235**

Practice Test 2: Answer Key 265

Answers and Explanations 266

PART FIVE: RESOURCES

Grammar Reference Guide **295**

Guide to Usage and Style **315**

Word Roots **337**

Index **345**

ABOUT THE AUTHOR

Denise Pivarnik-Nova is an Advanced Placement English teacher and an independent consultant for the Midwest office of the College Board in AP English and English Vertical Teams (pre-AP). She has been an AP English exam reader for over 16 years and has also taught freshman literature and composition at the college level. In addition to working on College Board publications and other AP prep materials, Denise is a teacher and college advisor at Breck School in Golden Valley, Minnesota. Every summer she facilitates AP English teacher workshops throughout the Midwest.

KAPLAN PANEL OF AP EXPERTS

Congratulations—you have chosen Kaplan to help you get a top score on your AP exam. Kaplan understands your goals and what you're up against—achieving college credit and conquering a tough test—while participating in everything else that high school has to offer.

You expect realistic practice, authoritative advice, and accurate, up-to-the-minute information on the test. And that's exactly what you'll find in this book, as well as every other in the AP series. To help you (and us!) reach these goals, we have sought out leaders in the AP community. Allow us to introduce our experts.

AP ENGLISH LANGUAGE AND COMPOSITION EXPERTS

Natalie Goldberg recently retired from St. Ignatius College Prep in Chicago, Illinois, where she helped develop a program to prepare juniors for the AP English Language and Composition exam and taught AP English Literature. She was a reader for the AP English Language and Composition exam for six years and has been a consultant with the Midwest Region of the College Board since 1997.

Susan Sanchez has taught AP English since 2001 and English since 1980 at Mark Keppel High School, a Title I Achieving School and a California Distinguished School, in Alhambra, California. She has been an AP reader for seven years and a table leader for three. She has been a member of the California State University Reading Institutes for Academic Preparation task force since its inception in 2000. Susan has also been a presenter at the Title I High Achieving Conference and at the Greater Los Angeles Advanced Placement Summer Institute.

Ronald Sudol has been a reader of AP English Language and Composition since 1998, a table leader since 1997, and a workshop consultant since 1996. He is Professor of Rhetoric at Oakland University in Michigan, where he is also Dean of the College of Arts and Sciences.

Part One

THE BASICS

CHAPTER 1: INSIDE THE AP ENGLISH LANGUAGE AND COMPOSITION EXAM

IF YOU LEARN ONLY FIVE THINGS IN THIS CHAPTER . . .

1. The AP English Language and Composition exam is 3 hours and 15 minutes long and includes a 1-hour multiple-choice section (52 to 58 questions) and a 2-hour-and-15-minute essay section (three questions and a reading period).

2. The exam is scored on a scale of 1–5, with 5 being the highest possible score.

3. Kaplan's *AP English Language and Composition* guide will give you a good idea of what will be covered on the test.

4. Having a thorough understanding of the concepts covered in your AP English Language and Composition course will help you conquer the test.

5. Rereading your textbook and class notes isn't always enough. Use this guide to assess your test strengths and weaknesses and practice for the exam. The more you prep, the more confident you will feel on Test Day!

AN OVERVIEW OF THE TEST STRUCTURE

The AP English Language and Composition exam is a 3-hour-and-15-minute exam, designed yearly by the AP Test Development Committee in English. The exam is an opportunity for you to demonstrate that you have mastered skills equivalent to those typically found in introductory college composition classes. A strong performance on the AP English Language and Composition exam can allow you to qualify for credit and advanced class placement during your first year at many colleges and universities throughout the United States and over 40 other countries.

THE AP EXAM

There are two exam sections:

Section I	52–58 multiple-choice questions	1 hour
Section II	1 reading period	15 minutes
	3 essay responses	2 hours
	Total length	3 hours and 15 minutes

In Section I, you will be presented with four or five passages, including a passage pertaining to documentation and citation of sources. These passages will be mostly from nonfiction, and occasionally from fiction. Each piece will be followed by 12 to 15 questions. If the test has five passages, the pieces are shorter with fewer questions than if the test has four passages.

The multiple-choice section contains skills questions that test your ability to analyze passages critically, as well as rhetorically, for style, organization, purpose, and effect. There are also a few factual questions based on the specific given selection, and questions that refer to documentation and citation of sources. Generally, these questions increase in difficulty as you progress through each passage, but that is not an absolute.

Each multiple-choice question has five possible answers. These questions are scored by the College Board and standardized to national norms. There is no penalty for wrong answers, so guessing is encouraged.

Section II consists of three essay questions: prose analysis, rhetoric and argumentation, and synthesis of sources. The prose passage is generally, but not always, nonfiction. Sometimes a double passage requires you to compare and contrast two pieces based on their stylistic and rhetorical development. The argument prompt might be an opinion already written that you must analyze it based on the tasks given in the prompt. However, you might also have to develop an argument of your own on a specific topic, often derived from a quotation. Recent tests have included an argumentative prompt that requires students to explain different sides of a concept, synthesize information, and develop a stance of their own. The Synthesis Essay question will require you to read a collection of related source material and respond to a prompt by writing an essay in support of an argument or analysis.

HOW THE EXAM IS SCORED

Scores are based on the number of questions answered correctly. **No points are deducted for wrong answers.** No points are awarded for unanswered questions. Therefore, you should answer every question, even if you have to guess.

Essays are scored by AP readers who convene each June to assess the essay responses. The multiple-choice section makes up 45 percent of your final score, and 55 percent depends on your performance on the essays.

KEY POINT

All AP exams are rated on a scale of 1 to 5, with 5 being the highest:

5 Extremely well-qualified

4 Well-qualified

3 Qualified

2 Possibly qualified

1 No recommendation

GETTING YOUR GRADES

You can obtain your AP grade report in July. When you take your exam, you can designate which colleges you would like to receive your grade. If you are unsure of your college at the time you take the exam, you may contact the Advanced Placement Program and have them forward your grade when you are closer to making your college decision.

REGISTRATION AND FEES

Registration for taking the exam begins in March of the year you are taking it. If you are not sure when to register, your AP teacher, AP coordinator, and/or your school guidance counselor can help you. If your school does not administer the exam, you can contact the Advanced Placement Program for a listing of schools in your area that do.

At the time of this printing, the fee for each AP exam is $93 within the United States, and $123 at schools and testing centers outside of the United States. For those qualified with acute financial need, the College Board offers a $31 credit. In addition, most states offer exam subsidies to cover all or part of the remaining cost for eligible students. To learn about other sources of financial aid, contact your AP coordinator.

ADDITIONAL RESOURCES

For more information on the AP Program and the English Language and Composition exam, contact the Advanced Placement Program:

Phone: (888) 225-5427 or (212) 632-1780
Email: apstudents@info.collegeboard.org
Website: apstudent.collegeboard.org/home

CHAPTER 2: STRATEGIES FOR SUCCESS: IT'S NOT ALWAYS HOW MUCH YOU KNOW

IF YOU LEARN ONLY FIVE THINGS IN THIS CHAPTER . . .

1. Remember the keys to Kaplan's general test-taking strategies:
   - Pacing
   - Process of Elimination
   - Knowing When to Guess
   - Gridding Carefully
   - Reading and Writing Actively and Critically

2. Know how to manage your stress. You can beat anxiety the same way you can beat the exam—by knowing what to expect beforehand and developing strategies to deal with it.

3. Take Kaplan's Diagnostic Test to learn your test-taking strengths and weaknesses. Knowing these will allow you to focus on your problem areas as you prepare for Test Day.

4. Get organized! Make a study schedule between now and Test Day and give yourself plenty of time to prepare. Waiting until the last minute to cram an entire semester's worth of information is not only unwise but also exhausting.

5. Make a Test Day game plan. Have everything you need to bring to the exam ready the night before. On the morning of the test, make it a priority to eat a good breakfast. Avoid too much caffeine. Read something to warm up your brain. And finally, get to the test site early.

HOW TO USE THIS BOOK

You should be proud of yourself for deciding to take the AP English Language and Composition exam. If you took AP English Language and Composition in high school, or if you have a good foundation in rhetorical analysis, a broad reading background, and strong composition skills, taking the exam can help you earn college credit and/or placement into advanced coursework. Think of the money and time you can save! Taking the exam can also improve your chances of acceptance to competitive schools, because colleges know that AP students are better prepared for the demands of college courses.

PLEASE NOTE

As you work your way through the chapters, you will discover precisely what knowledge and skills you will need to do your very best on the AP English Language and Composition exam. You will learn the most effective way to tackle each type of question, and you'll reinforce your studies with lots of practice questions.

PREP WITH CONFIDENCE!

With Kaplan's proven test-taking strategies, dozens of practice questions, a review of rhetorical analysis and stylistic terms, and guidelines for writing your essay responses, you will be able to take the exam with confidence!

In the following pages, you will find information about the format of the exam, test-taking strategies, and an extensive review of essential topics. Various sections include relevant review questions. These will help you identify your strengths and weaknesses and establish a plan for preparing for the exam. Also included are a full-length Diagnostic Test and two Practice Tests, with answers and explanations following each.

The first thing you need to do is find out what is on the AP English Language and Composition exam. The next chapter of this book presents the overall test structure and a brief overview of its scoring. This book provides you with background information about the test, and it gives you the most effective test strategies to help you score your best.

There is no doubt you have a lot more interesting things to do than go through this study guide. Nevertheless, make a commitment, just until the test, to give yourself every opportunity to improve your test score.

This book will help you focus on language and composition. It provides the key terminology you need to understand both multiple-choice passages and essay prompts. The different types of prose you might encounter on the exam are discussed in this book as well as guidelines for successful multiple-choice testing and essay construction.

KEY STRATEGY

If possible, work your way through this book bit by bit over the course of several weeks. Cramming the week before the test is NOT a good idea; you would probably absorb little information, and that approach is bound to make you more anxious.

Don't fight what is here. Bite the bullet and move forward. There's not that much more time before your test date.

WHAT THE TEST REQUIRES

Although the AP English Language and Composition exam is not a test that one passes or fails, a 3 or higher on the 5-point scale is generally necessary to receive advanced placement, credit, or both from the college of your choice.

DID YOU KNOW?

Many states, such as Minnesota, Texas, and Wisconsin, post the AP test score requirements online or offer them in hard copy (usually from the Department of Education) for the various colleges and universities within the state. These vary from state to state, just as score requirements vary from college to college.

The best way to find out what the test requires is to take the AP Diagnostic Test. This includes detailed explanations for each question. There are sample student responses for each essay question and a commentary from an "AP reader" who will tell you why the response received the score it did. Use the scoring guides provided and these commentaries to get a sense of your own strengths and weaknesses.

The best way to use the Practice Tests is to take them under testlike conditions. Don't just drop in and do a random question here and there. Use these tests to become familiar with the complete testing experience, including pacing and endurance. You may do these tests at any time. You do not necessarily have to save them all until after you have read the whole book. You should, however, try to reserve one of the practices to do near the time of the exam itself. That will give you the best experience simulating the actual exam and its time constraints.

If you have at least looked at the Diagnostic Test, you will see that the AP English Language and Composition exam is a unique test. It does not expect you to memorize specific authors and their works. Instead, it tests your critical and analytical thinking skills; it asks you to understand the ways writers use language to provide both meaning and pleasure for their readers; it requires you to apply concepts and terms to any piece of writing presented; and, most importantly, it necessitates your translating some of this information into multiple-choice selections and written responses. These multiple-choice questions and written responses ask you to make careful observations of textual details, establish connections among their characteristics, and draw from your observations a series of associations and inferences that lead to a meaningful and interpretive conclusion about a passage of writing.

REMEMBER

The more familiar you become with the test as a whole, the better (and more comfortably) you will perform.

IMPORTANT TIP

Use this book to study what types of questions may be on the exam, but also spend time studying the directions and format of the exam.

Your teacher has probably given you bits and pieces of the exam, but because of the usual constraints of a school day's schedule, students often do not have the opportunity to sit down and take an entire exam. Use the Diagnostic and Practice Tests for practice. Go to the College Board AP website or ask your AP English teacher for additional exposure to exams.

After you have experienced taking the entire exam in one sitting (with a 10- or 15-minute break between the multiple-choice and essay sections), you will have a better handle on the test.

HOW TO APPROACH THE MULTIPLE-CHOICE SECTION

The following are must-know hints that will help you tackle the multiple-choice section. We will elaborate on them throughout the book.

READ ACTIVELY

You cannot be passive when reading the passages or the questions in the multiple-choice section. Read carefully but quickly and mark any important words and points. Underline key words and phrases in the question. This will help you focus on just what it is you are looking for in the passage. Be sure to read all the choices. Sometimes more than one response is correct, but only one will be the *best* response.

DON'T FORGET

Some people find it helpful to skim the questions before they read the passage. Although this strategy takes more time, these people find that they are better able to focus when they read and annotate the passage.

SPECIFIC LINE OR WORD REFERENCES

Occasionally, a question will direct you to a particular line or even a specific word within the passage. Find the location but be ready to read a few lines before and after the reference to understand the context. Rarely can you go right to a word and grasp the answer to the question.

CRITICAL WORDS

Read the instructions carefully, paying particular attention to critical words such as *only, except, always, not, never, best.*

Students often find the most difficult multiple-choice questions to be those that ask for "all of the following except." This is understandable because you are used to looking for one correct response among other wrong answers. This is how most multiple-choice questions are set up. In EXCEPT questions, however, all but one of the responses are correct. Pay particular attention to these when you take the Diagnostic and Practice Tests.

PUT YOUR PRIDE ASIDE

Easy questions are worth just as much as more difficult ones. To maximize your score, you need to answer as many questions correctly as possible. Generally speaking, the easier questions are at the beginning of a series of questions following a passage. However, what one person thinks is an easy question might really stump the next person. Do not get too concerned with order of difficulty. Just answer what you can and move on.

PACE YOURSELF!

Pace yourself throughout the school year as you prep for the exam. Try to allow yourself at least 30 minutes nightly to review. Use your textbook, class handouts, and Internet resources for content mastery.

HOW MANY PASSAGES?

The 60-minute time limit includes reading and understanding four or five passages as well as answering the questions that follow. With four passages, the test will have more questions on each passage than it will with five passages. When you open the multiple-choice section, immediately check the number of passages. If there are four passages, estimate an average of about 15 minutes for each passage. If it contains five passages, estimate about 12 minutes.

Don't be too rigid about these timing rules. Some passages will be harder than others. This is often a very individual judgment. A lot of it has to do with your interest in or some prior knowledge about the topic of the passage.

PLEASE NOTE

You can read a passage out of order and answer its questions before returning to what you have skipped. This can get tricky, however, and you *must* be aware of the number of the question and where you are on the scoring grid.

PREDICT AN ANSWER

Before you look at the possible responses, try to think of the answer on your own. That will help you narrow down your choice. It will also help you avoid the temptations of wrong answers that "seem" right at first glance, a favorite trap of the test makers.

IF YOU DON'T KNOW, GUESS!

Scores are based on the total number of questions answered correctly. **No points are deducted for wrong answers.** No points are awarded for unanswered questions. Therefore, you should answer every question, even if you have to guess.

GRID CAREFULLY AND CLEANLY

You will need a No. 2 pencil to fill in the answer sheet for the multiple-choice section of the exam. Bring several sharpened pencils. Your test site may not provide a pencil sharpener. Be sure to erase changes thoroughly and do not allow any stray marks to appear on your answer sheet.

IMPORTANT

If you are able to eliminate at least one wrong answer, make an educated guess. The more wrong answers you can eliminate, the better. Remember, **no points are awarded for unanswered questions** and if you have to guess, you want the odds to be one in three or, better yet, one in two. It's better to guess than to skip a question entirely.

Put a large, easy-to-see mark in your test booklet (not on your answer sheet) when you skip a question. If there is time left after you finish that section of questions, then you should return to any skipped questions and think about them again. Who knows—you may see things differently after you've been away for a few minutes.

REMEMBER

Frequently check to make sure that the number of the question on your answer sheet corresponds to the number of the question in your exam booklet. It is easy to get out of sequence if you skip a question.

BE CAREFUL WITH THE ANSWER GRID

We cannot stress this enough: 45 percent of your score is based on the multiple-choice answers you select on your answer grid. If you know the right answer but mis-grid, you'll receive a low score. So be careful! Don't disdain the process of filling in the "little bubbles" on the grid. Sure, it's mindless, but under time pressure, it is easy to lose control and make mistakes.

Develop a disciplined strategy for filling in the answer grid. Some students find that it's smart to grid the answers in groups rather than one question at a time. As you figure out each question, circle your answer choice in the test booklet. Transfer those answers to the answer grid in groups of five or more (until you get close to the end of the section—then you must start gridding answers one by one).

Gridding in groups also saves time you'd otherwise spend moving papers around, finding your place, and redirecting your mind. Answering AP questions takes deep, hard thinking. Filling out answer grids is easy, but you have to be careful, especially if you do a lot of skipping around. Shifting between "hard thinking" and "careful bookkeeping" takes time and effort.

KEY STRATEGY

Gridding in groups cuts down on errors, because you can focus on one task and do it correctly.

This may not be how you are used to taking tests. If you are not sure of this batching of answers, then try your way—probably recording your answers one at a time after each question. Practice both ways and choose what works best for you.

DON'T SWEAT IT

Never agonize for too long over any one multiple-choice question. If you are not sure of the answer, clearly circle the question in the test booklet so that you can find it readily after you have completed the other questions. Be sure to leave that number unmarked on the answer sheet. You very likely will have time to return to the question before the 60 minutes are up.

HOW TO APPROACH THE ESSAY QUESTIONS

Here's what you need to know and do to succeed on the essay portion of the test.

WHAT DOES THE QUESTION ASK?

Before you begin writing, read and decode the essay prompt carefully. What is it asking? Is there more than one part to the question? Usually there is. Then read the passage and reread the prompt to ensure that you respond to all tasks. In about 40 minutes (average for three essays in two hours), you should study the problem, identify the focus of the question, read the selection, reread the prompt, make a plan, and start writing within 7 to 10 minutes. Remember, the exam will include an additional 15-minute reading period for the Synthesis Essay source material, so use this time accordingly as you prepare to develop your essay. If you are confused about how to start, restate the topic as it is addressed in the question and start writing.

DON'T CRAM!

Mastering the material in AP English Language and Composition will be much easier if you learn it in small chunks rather than cramming the night before the exam!

> ## IMPORTANT
>
> Most AP essay questions ask you to analyze on a two-level system: what did the author do (in terms of main idea, central attitude, or basic response evoked from the reader) and how did he or she do it (examining such elements as imagery, figurative language, diction, syntax, structure, tone, style)? Brainstorm and plan quickly by jotting notes in the test booklet.

READ, READ, AND READ AGAIN

Read the prompt; read the passage; read the prompt again. Make sure you know what you are supposed to do. Often, students will read the prompt and then the passage and jump right into the writing. Doing so often makes you overlook a particular angle of the prompt you might not have noticed upon the first reading. Read, read, and read again. If all of this sounds repetitive, it is. Repetition leads to remembering.

CHOOSE THE EASIEST QUESTION FIRST

You do not have to answer the essays in the order in which they appear. When you open your essay test packet, quickly scan the three choices and begin responding to the question for which you seem to have the most ready response. Beginning with the "easiest" question will help give you confidence and reduce your stress. You are asked to put your responses on pages that are clearly marked with 1, 2, or 3 across the top of the answer booklet. Let's face it—if a reader cannot readily identify what question you are answering by what you have said, then you have a real problem.

READ CRITICALLY

When you read the prompt and the essay, do so with your pen in your hand, ready to underline, circle, and make notations. Mark the prompt carefully, identifying the task it presents and what it tells you to consider while fulfilling each task.

For instance, a prompt may ask you to identify the narrator's attitude through his or her use of stylistic devices and rhetorical structure. When you read the passage itself—whether it be a short piece requiring your reaction or a longer passage requiring analysis—annotate and make notes as you read, looking especially for support that is most relevant to the prompt. This becomes your prewriting.

Many prompts ask you to investigate the language to assess the writer's or narrator's attitude. If this is the case, remember your main task is to explain that attitude with specific examples and support.

ORGANIZE YOUR ESSAY

In responding to the prose analysis questions, it is best to write one body paragraph for each major section of the passage. Generally, let your response flow chronologically with the passage.

If this doesn't work for you, then take the elements you are talking about and let each of them become a major paragraph in your response. Although this is not the recommended method for organizing your answer, it may be the most comfortable for you.

KEEP YOUR QUOTES SHORT

Integrate words and phrases from the passage within your response. A direct quote of more than one or two lines of the text is too much. You need not always write out the actual quotations; sometimes you can simply make a reference to a particular section by giving the line numbers. Keep in mind that the Synthesis Essay question will require you to refer to and cite the sources provided to support your position on the topic.

DISCUSS AND EXPLAIN, DON'T RETELL OR LIST

When writing about a passage, direct your attention to the elements addressed in the prompt. You should be prepared to discuss tone, attitude, point of view, imagery, rhetoric, and the effect of the passage. Avoid the trap of just rephrasing or retelling the passage with quotes. Avoid listing, but be sure to explain and show your thinking.

When responding to an argument, be sure you precisely follow the task(s) in the prompt. Sometimes you are asked to evaluate the success of someone's argument without the opportunity of becoming involved in the topic of the argument. That is difficult to do.

When you are writing an argument, be sure you follow the dictates of the prompt. Make your statement and support it thoroughly, using examples from your experience, your reading, or your observations.

HOW LONG?

The length of your answer is not a guarantee of quality; however, it takes more than a paragraph or two to merit an upper-half score (remember, essays are scored on a scale of 1 to 9). As a rule, five paragraphs—an introduction, three body paragraphs, and a good conclusion—make an adequate essay. This can vary, however, depending

USING QUOTATIONS

Be sure that when you use quotations, the references support your own points. Direct quotations should never be used randomly.

GET TO THE POINT!

Sometimes students are tempted to "wow" AP readers with fancy rhetorical terms. No matter how impressive these terms may sound, they can never replace a direct response to the prompt.

on the length of your paragraphs, your writing style, etc. Also, the cookie-cutter five-paragraph structure may not be the best for developing your ideas or expressing your opinion. It is just a baseline, not an absolute.

USING OUTSIDE REFERENCES

Use examples and support that make sense to the development of your thesis. These do not always have to be from profound resources. Sometimes, especially in the argument questions, more local and sometimes even personal examples are quite acceptable. Use examples with which you are familiar. Don't bring in some obscure piece of history unless it fits the issue and you truly know what you are talking about. If you do not, it will show.

WHAT IF I MAKE MISTAKES?

Those who read and score AP essays are trained to reward students for what they do well, rather than look for little "missing pieces" or tiny errors. They recognize that essays are barely revised first drafts.

DON'T FORGET

If you have made an error that you wish to correct, don't hesitate to cross it out neatly. Either write the correction between the lines, if you can, or if it is a lengthy change, use an asterisk and put the revised information at the end of your essay. You should be writing your essays in ink, so readers expect to see corrected errors within an essay.

LEGIBILITY COUNTS

Be sure to write your essays in blue or black ink. As mentioned above, cross-outs will not count against you. Avoid using a pen that may bleed through the paper; it is best to use a ballpoint. Bring at least two pens. If your handwriting is particularly small, make an effort to make it large enough to be read easily. If your penmanship is bad, do not hesitate to print. Some students find that well-cushioned pens help clarify difficult-to-read handwriting. Just remember that human eyes will be trying to read your response.

KEY POINT

Severe or numerous mechanical difficulties will reduce your score if they hamper communication.

The test booklet has 16 pages—enough to make corrections and additions. Some students whose handwriting is not particularly large find they are most comfortable writing on one side of the page only.

TAKE CONTROL: HOW TO APPROACH THE TEST AS A WHOLE

The AP English Language and Composition exam requires a logical and creative mindset, not only in the subject matter you will be approaching but also in your overall attitude toward the test. Remember the following three basic strategies as you prepare, as well as on Test Day.

QUESTION TRIAGE

In a hospital emergency room, the triage nurse evaluates each patient and decides who gets attention first and who can be treated later. You should do the same thing on the AP English Language and Composition exam.

Practicing triage is one of the most important ways you can control your test-taking experience. It's a fact that there are some multiple-choice questions on the test that most students could never answer correctly, no matter how much time or effort they spent on them. Do not let that alarm you.

The first time you look at a multiple-choice question, make a quick decision about how hard and time-consuming it looks. Then decide whether to answer it now or skip it and do it later.

KEY STRATEGY

- If the question looks comprehensible and reasonably easy, do it right away.
- If the question looks tough and time-consuming but ultimately doable, skip it, circle the question number in your test booklet, and return to it later after you have answered the other questions for that passage.
- If a question looks impossible, skip it until you have time to think it over. Try to narrow down the choices and make an educated guess, if you can. If you can't narrow down the answers, or if you're running out of time, go ahead and guess. No points are deducted for wrong answers so you have nothing to lose if you're wrong. You can always go back and change your answer if you end up with extra time at the end of the multiple-choice section.

For the Synthesis Essay, students have a 15-minute reading period—to read sources, align thoughts, brainstorm, and outline an essay response. Few students need or take the entire 15 minutes for this. Consequently, you may find yourself with five to six minutes of "extra" time.

Use this time to assess and triage all three essay questions. Perhaps question two or three will strike you as a better, more doable place to begin your writing. If this is the case, go for it!

DEVELOP A PLAN OF ATTACK

The best plan of attack is to do each passage as a block. First, you must determine whether you have 15 minutes for each of four passages and their questions or 12 minutes for each of five passages and their questions. Then make a longish first pass through the questions (call it the "triage pass"), doing the easy ones, skipping the impossible ones, and reserving any that look like they might cause trouble. You should actually do this in the test booklet. Then make a second pass (call it the "cleanup pass") and do those questions you think you can answer with some thought. If you have to leave a couple of questions unanswered, do not become unduly upset.

PARAPHRASE

AP English Language passages can be confusing; other times, the questions might not be readily understandable. If any of the material seems intimidating to you, reword it into a form you can better handle. Even if you are not sure of all the words that are being used, make your best guess based on the context.

MARK UP YOUR TEST BOOKLET

This strategy should be employed on both the multiple-choice and essay sections. The secret is to put the passages into a form you can understand and use. For starters, quickly identify the main idea of each paragraph and jot it down, using shorthand, into the margins. Underline key details and circle transition words. This way you make a map of the passage, labeling each paragraph so you understand how it all fits together. This acts as a type of brainstorming/outlining to get you jump-started into answering multiple-choice questions or responding to an essay prompt.

CHECK BACK

Don't hesitate to refer to the passage. Much of the information is too complex to remember accurately, and no one expects you to absorb it all after only one reading. Often, the wrong answers of the multiple-choice section will be "misplaced details"—details taken from different parts of the passage. They are things that don't answer the question properly but that might sound good to you if you aren't careful. By checking back in the passage, you can avoid choosing such devilishly clever wrong choices. And by checking back to the passage and the prompt while you are responding to the essay questions, you will be more likely to write more coherent and accurate responses.

> **LOOK FOR CLUES**
>
> Before you give up on a passage, take a look at the various questions being asked about it. These can sometimes give you clues about a passage's content and meaning.

ANSWER THE RIGHT QUESTION

This strategy is a natural extension of the last. The test makers often include the correct answer to a different question among the wrong choices for question. Keep an eye out for those key words *not* and *except*. Under time pressure, it's easy to fall for one of these red herrings; that is, thinking that you know what's being asked for when really you don't.

If necessary, check the question again before choosing your answer. Doing all the right work but then getting the wrong answer can be seriously frustrating. So make sure you are answering the right question.

KEEP TRACK OF TIME

Pace yourself. Multiple-choice passages will be about 12–15 minutes each, depending on the number of passages you must read. Essay questions should take about 40 minutes each. Remember, you can begin with your favorite or the easiest passage. Watch your time, no matter how much you have to say about it.

DON'T FORGET

Reminders:

- Food and drink are not allowed during the exam. Some locations may permit capped bottled water. Remember that this is a 3-hour-and-15-minute test. Be sure to have a good breakfast before the test—nothing unusual or too greasy. And watch your caffeine intake. Test Day is not the best time to give it up or to ingest it in large quantities if your body is not used to it.
- Never count on there being a clock in your testing room. Bring your own watch, but remember that you will not be permitted to use an alarm or timer settings.
- You may write and underline in your test booklet, but you may not use a highlighter.

STRESS MANAGEMENT

Imagine the countdown has begun. Your date with the test is looming on the horizon. Anxiety is on the rise. The butterflies in your stomach seem to have had too much caffeine. Perhaps you feel as if the last thing you ate has turned into a lead ball. Your thinking is getting cloudy. Maybe you think you won't be ready. Maybe you already know your stuff, but you're going into panic mode anyway. Worst of all, you're not sure what to do about it.

Lack of control is one of the prime causes of stress. A ton of research shows that if you don't have a sense of control over what's happening in your life, you can easily end up feeling helpless and hopeless. So having concrete things to do and think about—taking control—will help reduce your stress. This section shows you how to take control during the days leading up to the test.

IDENTIFY THE SOURCES OF STRESS

In the space provided, jot down anything you identify as a source of your test-related stress. The idea is to pin down that free-floating anxiety so that you can take control of it.

DON'T FREAK OUT

Tame that anxiety and stress—before and during the test.

WHAT STRESSES YOU OUT?

- I always freeze up on tests.
- I'm nervous about the essay (or the argument, or remembering synecdoche).
- I need a good/great score to go to Acme College.
- My older brother/sister/best friend did really well. I must match his/her score or do better.
- My parents, who are paying for school, will be really disappointed if I don't test well.
- I'm afraid of losing my focus and concentration halfway through the test.
- I know I'm not spending enough time preparing.
- I study like crazy, but nothing seems to stick in my mind.
- I always run out of time and get panicky.
- Right now I feel as though thinking is like wading through thick mud.

Now list your own.

SOURCES OF STRESS

_____

_____

_____

_____

Take a few minutes to think about the things you've just written down. Then rewrite them. List the statements you most associate with your stress and anxiety first and put the least disturbing items last. Chances are, the top of the list is a fairly accurate description of exactly how you react to test anxiety, both physically and mentally.

The later items usually describe your fears (disappointing Mom and Dad, looking bad to your peers, etc.). As you write the list, you are forming a hierarchy of items so you can deal first with the anxiety provokers that bug you most. Very often, taking care of the major items from the top of the list goes a long way toward relieving overall testing anxiety. You probably won't have to bother with the things you placed last.

YOUR STRENGTHS AND WEAKNESSES

Take one minute to list the areas in AP English Language and Composition where you have the most skill. They can be general (prose analysis) or specific (rhetorical devices). Write down as many as you can think of and, if possible, time yourself. Write for the entire time. Don't stop writing until you have reached the one-minute stopping point.

STRONG AP ENGLISH LANGUAGE AND COMPOSITION SKILLS

_____

_____

_____

_____

Next, take one minute to list the areas of AP English Language and Composition where you think you are weakest, just plain bad in the subject matter, have answered questions incorrectly, or keep messing up. Again, keep it to one minute and continue writing until you reach the cutoff. Don't be afraid to identify and write down all of your weak spots! In all probability, as you do both lists, you will find you are strong in some areas and not so strong in others. Taking stock of your assets and liabilities lets you know the areas you don't have to worry about and the ones that will demand extra attention and effort.

WEAK AP ENGLISH LANGUAGE AND COMPOSITION SKILLS

_____

_____

_____

_____

Facing your weak spots gives you some distinct advantages. It helps a lot to find out where you need to spend extra effort. Increased exposure to tough material makes it more familiar and less intimidating. (After all, we mostly fear what we don't know and are probably afraid to face.) You will feel better about yourself because you are dealing directly with areas of the test that make you anxious. You can't help feeling more confident when you know you are actively strengthening your chances of earning a higher overall test score.

Now, go back to the "good" list and expand it for two minutes. Take the general items on that first list and make them more specific, then take the specific items and expand them into more general conclusions. If anything new comes to mind, jot it down. Focus all of your attention and effort on your strengths. Don't underestimate yourself or your abilities. Give yourself full credit. At the same time, don't list strengths you really don't have.

Expanding from general to specific might go as follows: If you listed "argument" as a broad topic you feel strong in, you would then narrow your focus to include areas of this subject about which you are particularly knowledgeable. Perhaps you are a debater, and you understand the configuration of successful argumentation—thesis, concession, and presentation using support and detail.

Whatever you feel comfortable about goes on your "good" list. You get the idea—check the time and start writing for at least two minutes your expanded "good" list.

STRONG AP ENGLISH LANGUAGE AND COMPOSITION SKILLS: AN EXPANDED LIST

_____

_____

_____

_____

After you've stopped, check your time. Did you find yourself going beyond two minutes? Did you write down more things than you thought you knew? Is it possible you know more than you've been giving yourself credit for? That means you've probably found a number of areas in which you feel strong.

CONGRATULATIONS!

You just took an active step toward helping yourself. Notice any increased feelings of confidence? Has your stress level decreased, maybe a little bit? Good, enjoy this new confidence.

Here's another way to think about this exercise. Every area of strength and confidence you can identify is much like having a reserve of solid gold at Fort Knox. You'll be able to draw on your reserves as you need them. You can use your reserves to solve difficult questions, maintain confidence, and keep test stress and anxiety at a distance. The encouraging thing is that every time you recognize another area of strength, succeed at coming up with a solution, or get a good score on a test, you increase your reserves. And there is absolutely no limit to how much self-confidence you can have or how good you can feel about yourself.

IMAGINE YOURSELF SUCCEEDING

The next group of exercises is both physical and mental. It's a natural follow-up to what you've just accomplished with your lists.

First, get into a comfortable sitting position in a quiet setting. Wear loose clothes. If you wear glasses, take them off. Close your eyes and inhale a deep, satisfying breath of air. Really fill your lungs until your rib cage is fully expanded and you can't take in any more. Then exhale the air completely. Imagine you are blowing out a candle with your last little puff of air. Do this two or three more times, filling your lungs to their maximum and emptying them totally. Keep your eyes closed, comfortably but not tightly. Let your body sink deeper into the chair as you become even more comfortable.

With your eyes shut, you can notice something very interesting. You're no longer dealing with worrisome stuff going on in the world outside of you. Now you can concentrate on what happens inside you. The more you recognize your own physical reactions to stress and anxiety, the more you can do about them. You might not realize it, but you've begun to regain a sense of being in control.

Let images begin to form on the "viewing screens" on the back of your eyelids. You're experiencing visualizations from the place in your mind that makes pictures. Allow the images to come easily and naturally; don't force them. Imagine yourself in a relaxing situation. It might be a special place you've visited before or one you've read about. It can be a fictional location that you create in your imagination, but a real-life memory of a place or situation you know is usually better. Make it as detailed as possible and notice as much as you can.

Stay focused on the images as you sink further back into your chair. Breathe easily and naturally. You might feel the sensations of any stress or tension draining from your muscles and flowing downward, out of your feet and away from you.

TAKE A MOMENT TO RELAX

Take a moment to relax and check how you're feeling. Notice how comfortable you've become. Imagine how much easier it would be if you could take the test feeling this relaxed and in this state of ease. You've combined the images of your special place with sensations of comfort and relaxation. You've also found a way to become relaxed simply by visualizing your own safe, special place.

Now, close your eyes and start remembering a real-life situation in which you did well on a test. If you can't come up with one, remember a situation in which you did something (academic or otherwise) that you were really proud of—a genuine accomplishment. Make the memory as detailed as possible. Think about the sights, the sounds, the smells, even the tastes associated with this remembered experience. Remember how confident you felt as you accomplished your goal. Now start thinking about the upcoming test. Keep your thoughts and feelings in line with that successful experience. Don't make comparisons between them. Just imagine taking the upcoming test with the same feelings of confidence and relaxed control.

This exercise is a great way to bring the test down to earth. You should practice this exercise often, especially when the prospect of taking the exam starts to bum you out. The more you practice it, the more effective the exercise will be for you.

EXERCISE FRUSTRATIONS AWAY

A surprising number of students get out of the habit of regular exercise, ironically because they are spending so much time prepping for exams. Also, sedentary people—this is a medical fact—get less oxygen into the blood and hence to the head than active people. You can live fine with a little less oxygen; you just can't think as well.

EXERCISE!

Whether it is jogging, walking, biking, mild aerobics, push-ups, or a pickup basketball game, physical exercise is a very effective way to stimulate your mind and body and to improve your ability to think and concentrate.

REMEMBER

Any big test is a bit like a race. Thinking clearly at the end is just as important as having a quick mind early on. Along with a good diet and adequate sleep, exercise is an important part of keeping yourself in fighting shape and thinking clearly for the long haul.

Another thing happens when students don't make exercise an integral part of their test preparation. Like any organism in nature, you operate best if all your "energy systems" are in balance. Studying uses a lot of energy, but it's all mental energy. When you take a study break, do something active instead of raiding the fridge or vegging out in front of the TV. Take a 5–10 minute activity break for every 50 or 60 minutes that you study. The physical exertion gets your body into the act, which helps to keep your mind and body in sync. Then, when you finish studying for the night and hit the sack, you won't lie there, tense and unable to sleep because your head is overtired and your body wants to pump iron or run a marathon.

One warning about exercise, however: it's not a good idea to exercise vigorously right before you go to bed. This could easily cause sleep onset problems.

BUFFER PERIOD

It's not recommended to study right up until bedtime. Make time for a "buffer period" before you go to bed: for 30–60 minutes, take a hot shower, meditate, or simply veg out.

KEEP BREATHING

Conscious attention to breathing is an excellent way of managing test stress (or any stress, for that matter). The majority of people who get into trouble during tests take shallow breaths. They breathe using only their upper chests and shoulder muscles, and they may even hold their breath for long periods of time. Conversely, the test taker who by accident or design keeps breathing normally and rhythmically is likely to be more relaxed and in better control during the entire test experience.

Now is the time to get into the habit of relaxed breathing. Do the next exercise to learn to breathe in a natural, easy rhythm. By the way, this is another technique you can use during the test to collect your thoughts and ward off excess stress. The entire exercise should take no more than three to five minutes.

With your eyes closed, breathe in slowly and deeply through your nose. Hold the breath for a bit, then release it through your mouth. The key is to breathe slowly and deeply by using your diaphragm (the big band of muscle that spans your body just above your waist) to draw air in and out naturally and effortlessly. Breathing with your diaphragm encourages relaxation and helps minimize tension. Try it and notice how relaxed and comfortable you feel.

QUICK TIPS AS YOU PREPARE FOR THE EXAM

- Be sure you know the schedule for the AP exam ahead of time so you can adjust your mental and physical energies accordingly.
- Make sure you adjust any meal schedule to fit with your test schedule. You do not want to go into an afternoon exam without having eaten.
- For the last several years, the AP English Language and Composition exam has been the first exam given on Monday morning of the two-week AP exam schedule.
- Whatever you do, try to get enough sleep the night before the test.
- If something serious interferes with any of the test times, be aware that each test does have an alternative date that you might be able to take under extreme extenuating circumstances.
- No matter what else is going on at testing time, put it out of your mind. Your job, during the three hours of the exam, is to score your best.

QUICK TIPS FOR THE DAYS JUST BEFORE THE EXAM

- The best test takers do less and less as the test approaches. Taper off your study schedule and take it easy on yourself. You want to be relaxed and ready on the day of the test.

- Positive self-talk can be extremely liberating and invigorating, especially as the test looms closer. Tell yourself things such as, "I choose to take this test," rather than "I have to"; "I will do well," rather than "I hope things go well"; "I can," rather than "I cannot."

- Get your act together sooner rather than later. Have everything (including choice of comfortable, layered clothing) laid out days in advance. Most importantly, know where the test will be held and the easiest, quickest way to get there.

- Visit the test site a few days in advance. This is especially important if the site is unfamiliar to you.

- Avoid additional practice or study cram sessions on the day before the test. It is in your best interest to marshal your physical and psychological resources for 24 hours or so. Try to keep worries about the test on the back burner of your mind.

HANDLING STRESS DURING THE TEST

The biggest stress monster will be the test itself. Fear not—there are methods for quelling your stress during the test:

- Keep moving forward instead of getting bogged down by a difficult question. You don't have to get everything right to achieve a fine score. This strategy buys time and builds confidence so you can handle the tough stuff later.

- Don't be thrown if other test takers seem to be working more furiously than you are. Continue to spend your time patiently thinking through your answers; it's going to lead to better results.

- Keep breathing. Improper breathing interferes with clear thinking.

- Some quick isometrics during the test—especially if your concentration is wandering or your energy is waning—can help. Try this: put your palms together and press intensely for a few seconds; then quickly release the pressure. Feel the difference as you let go.

- Here's one other isometric that will relieve tension in both your neck and eye muscles: Slowly rotate your head from side to side, turning your head and eyes to look as far back over each shoulder as you can.

COUNTDOWN TO THE TEST

Is it starting to feel as though your whole life is a buildup to the AP English Language and Composition exam? As the test date gets closer, you may find your anxiety is on the rise. Try not to worry. After the preparation you have done, you are in good shape for the test.

To calm any very-last-minute pretest jitters you may have, here is a sane schedule for the last week.

THE WEEK BEFORE THE TEST

Review the chapters in this book and in your textbook and any notes you have made from this book and/or from your AP English class. Are there major holes in your preparation? If there are, choose a few of these areas to work on—but do not try to overload your mind.

Take a full-length Practice Test. If you haven't done so already, take one or more of the Practice Tests in this book. These are a good practice for the real thing.

TWO DAYS BEFORE THE TEST

Do your last studying—a few more passages, an essay outline, and/or a look through the Key Terminology chapter—and then call it quits.

THE NIGHT BEFORE THE TEST

Don't study. Get together the following items:

- A watch or whatever timepiece you are used to using (turn all the sound off)
- A few sharpened No. 2 pencils for the multiple-choice section and a couple of reliable ballpoint pens (blue or black)
- Erasers
- Photo ID card (sometimes necessary in large testing situations where the proctor does not know you)

Know exactly where you are going and exactly how and when you will get there.

Relax the night before the test. Read a good book; take a warm bubble bath; watch TV. Get a good night's sleep. Go to bed at a reasonable hour and leave yourself a bit of extra time in the morning.

THE MORNING OF THE TEST

Eat breakfast. Make it something substantial but not anything too heavy or greasy. Don't drink a lot of coffee if you're not used to it. Bathroom breaks may or may not be allowed other than the normal break time between the multiple-choice and the essay section of the test. If they are allowed, they will cut into your testing time.

Dress in layers so that you can adjust to the temperature of the test room.

Read something. Warm up your brain with a newspaper or a magazine or even a cereal box. You should not let the test questions be the first thing you read that day.

Arrive at the test site in plenty of time.

DURING THE TEST

Don't be shaken. If you find your confidence slipping, remind yourself how well you have prepared. You know the structure of the test; you know the instructions; you have studied for every type of question.

IMPORTANT

Even if something goes really wrong, don't panic. If the test booklet is defective—two pages are stuck together or the ink has run—try to stay calm. Raise your hand; tell the proctor you need a new book. If you accidentally misgrid your answer page on the multiple-choice section, again, don't panic. Raise your hand; tell the proctor.

Food or drinks are not allowed during the exam. Some test sites may permit capped bottled water. Remember, however, that this is a 3-hour-and-15-minute test. You may want to eat a piece of fruit or have a juice drink or power bar during the short break between the multiple-choice and essay sections of the AP exam.

AFTER THE TEST

Once the test is over, put it out of your mind. Feel free to start thinking about more interesting things than tests. If you have subsequent AP tests to take, now you may start thinking about them.

DON'T FORGET

Even if you walk out of the test room thinking that you blew it, you probably didn't. You tend to remember the questions that stumped you, not the many that you knew.

Part Two

DIAGNOSTIC TEST

Diagnostic Test Answer Grid

Before taking this Diagnostic Test, find a quiet place where you can work uninterrupted for about three hours. Make sure you have a comfortable desk, several No. 2 pencils, and a few ballpoint pens.

The Diagnostic Test includes a multiple-choice section and a free-response question. Use the answer grid to record your multiple-choice answers. Write the essays on the pages provided; use additional sheets if needed.

Once you start the test, don't stop until you've finished, except for a 10-minute break between the multiple-choice and essay sections. The answer key and explanations follow the test.

Good luck!

1. Ⓐ Ⓑ Ⓒ Ⓓ Ⓔ
2. Ⓐ Ⓑ Ⓒ Ⓓ Ⓔ
3. Ⓐ Ⓑ Ⓒ Ⓓ Ⓔ
4. Ⓐ Ⓑ Ⓒ Ⓓ Ⓔ
5. Ⓐ Ⓑ Ⓒ Ⓓ Ⓔ
6. Ⓐ Ⓑ Ⓒ Ⓓ Ⓔ
7. Ⓐ Ⓑ Ⓒ Ⓓ Ⓔ
8. Ⓐ Ⓑ Ⓒ Ⓓ Ⓔ
9. Ⓐ Ⓑ Ⓒ Ⓓ Ⓔ
10. Ⓐ Ⓑ Ⓒ Ⓓ Ⓔ
11. Ⓐ Ⓑ Ⓒ Ⓓ Ⓔ
12. Ⓐ Ⓑ Ⓒ Ⓓ Ⓔ
13. Ⓐ Ⓑ Ⓒ Ⓓ Ⓔ
14. Ⓐ Ⓑ Ⓒ Ⓓ Ⓔ
15. Ⓐ Ⓑ Ⓒ Ⓓ Ⓔ
16. Ⓐ Ⓑ Ⓒ Ⓓ Ⓔ
17. Ⓐ Ⓑ Ⓒ Ⓓ Ⓔ
18. Ⓐ Ⓑ Ⓒ Ⓓ Ⓔ

19. Ⓐ Ⓑ Ⓒ Ⓓ Ⓔ
20. Ⓐ Ⓑ Ⓒ Ⓓ Ⓔ
21. Ⓐ Ⓑ Ⓒ Ⓓ Ⓔ
22. Ⓐ Ⓑ Ⓒ Ⓓ Ⓔ
23. Ⓐ Ⓑ Ⓒ Ⓓ Ⓔ
24. Ⓐ Ⓑ Ⓒ Ⓓ Ⓔ
25. Ⓐ Ⓑ Ⓒ Ⓓ Ⓔ
26. Ⓐ Ⓑ Ⓒ Ⓓ Ⓔ
27. Ⓐ Ⓑ Ⓒ Ⓓ Ⓔ
28. Ⓐ Ⓑ Ⓒ Ⓓ Ⓔ
29. Ⓐ Ⓑ Ⓒ Ⓓ Ⓔ
30. Ⓐ Ⓑ Ⓒ Ⓓ Ⓔ
31. Ⓐ Ⓑ Ⓒ Ⓓ Ⓔ
32. Ⓐ Ⓑ Ⓒ Ⓓ Ⓔ
33. Ⓐ Ⓑ Ⓒ Ⓓ Ⓔ
34. Ⓐ Ⓑ Ⓒ Ⓓ Ⓔ
35. Ⓐ Ⓑ Ⓒ Ⓓ Ⓔ
36. Ⓐ Ⓑ Ⓒ Ⓓ Ⓔ

37. Ⓐ Ⓑ Ⓒ Ⓓ Ⓔ
38. Ⓐ Ⓑ Ⓒ Ⓓ Ⓔ
39. Ⓐ Ⓑ Ⓒ Ⓓ Ⓔ
40. Ⓐ Ⓑ Ⓒ Ⓓ Ⓔ
41. Ⓐ Ⓑ Ⓒ Ⓓ Ⓔ
42. Ⓐ Ⓑ Ⓒ Ⓓ Ⓔ
43. Ⓐ Ⓑ Ⓒ Ⓓ Ⓔ
44. Ⓐ Ⓑ Ⓒ Ⓓ Ⓔ
45. Ⓐ Ⓑ Ⓒ Ⓓ Ⓔ
46. Ⓐ Ⓑ Ⓒ Ⓓ Ⓔ
47. Ⓐ Ⓑ Ⓒ Ⓓ Ⓔ
48. Ⓐ Ⓑ Ⓒ Ⓓ Ⓔ
49. Ⓐ Ⓑ Ⓒ Ⓓ Ⓔ
50. Ⓐ Ⓑ Ⓒ Ⓓ Ⓔ
51. Ⓐ Ⓑ Ⓒ Ⓓ Ⓔ
52. Ⓐ Ⓑ Ⓒ Ⓓ Ⓔ
53. Ⓐ Ⓑ Ⓒ Ⓓ Ⓔ
54. Ⓐ Ⓑ Ⓒ Ⓓ Ⓔ

COMPUTING YOUR SCORE

There is no way to determine precisely what your AP grade will be because:

- the conditions under which you take the Practice Test will not exactly mirror real test conditions.

- while the multiple-choice questions are scored by computer, the free-response questions are graded manually by faculty consultants. You will not be able to accurately grade your own essays.

SECTION I: MULTIPLE-CHOICE

Number Correct ☐ × 1.298 = ☐ = Multiple-Choice Raw Score

SECTION II: FREE-RESPONSE (DO NOT ROUND)

Question 1: (out of 9 points possible) ☐ × 3.0556 = ☐

Question 2: (out of 9 points possible) ☐ × 3.0556 = ☐

Question 3: (out of 9 points possible) ☐ × 3.0556 = ☐

Total Questions 1, 2, and 3 = ☐ = Free-Response Raw Score

COMPOSITE SCORE

Section I Multiple-Choice Score ☐ + Section II Free-Response Score ☐ = ☐ = Composite Score (round to the nearest whole number)

CONVERSION CHART

Composite Score Range	AP Grade
112–150	5
98–111	4
80–97	3
55–79	2
0–54	1

DIAGNOSTIC TEST

Section I: Multiple-Choice Questions

Time—1 hour
Number of questions—54
Percent of total grade—45%

Directions: This part consists of selections from prose works and questions on their content, form, and style. After reading each passage, choose the best answer to each question and completely fill in the corresponding oval on the answer sheet.

Questions 1–14. Read the following passage carefully before you choose your answers.

Although my early life tended to encourage my flirting propensities it did not make me the real heartless coquette, I afterwards became. The flirtations of school life were
(5) harmless, for there was no real love between myself and the parties concerned. When I left school I was just seventeen. Young, gay, rich, happy and thoughtless, without a wish ungratified. I had been accustomed
(10) to admiration all my life, and now I really deserved it. I was rather stylish in my personal appearance, so every one said. Every advantage, that money could give, had been given me, and I do not flatter myself, when I
(15) say I improved my talents. I rode well, danced well, played and sang well, conversed well, and in truth everything I attempted I did well.

Among the first satellites that moved around my sphere, were two young gentlemen,
(20) both handsome, but very unlike in personal appearance and disposition. One was dark as a Spaniard, with eyes and hair as dark as night when the moon and stars have hid their beams under a canopy of cloud. He was very
(25) handsome and talented, yet I could not love the man, for I feared him. Still it amused me to lead him on, intending to tell him every time we met, that his love was vain; but I continued putting it off.

(30) The other—God knows I loved him, if woman is capable of loving. He was fair, very fair, with dark eyes and light hair. His mouth was beautiful, but deceit lurked in each exquisite curve of his lips. An Adonis
(35) was not more perfect in form: and he knew it. He was young in years, yet old in sin. I now sometimes think that he, like Bulwer's Zanoni, had found the true secret of perpetual youth, and that he had lived for centuries, so well was

(40) he versed in the ways of the world, and in each phase of human nature. He often boasted of the many conquests he had made, and said that no woman he chose to captivate could escape loving him. I did not like this speech; but I
(45) loved him. He had certainly many rare traits of character. His generosity was proverbial; he was a warm friend and had the most perfect control over his very high temper. It was not long before we became engaged. He said that
(50) he loved me at first sight; and God knows that his love was more than returned. He called to see me each day, and every night escorted me to some place of amusement. He was very jealous, but I liked that. He was my sun during
(55) the day, and my moon at night. There was a cloud over all my happiness when he failed to come. He was young, ardent, fiery and passionate, and I—I was a fool! The passionate devotion of my heart was lavished upon a
(60) worthless object. I knew nothing of his former conduct or character, as he had come to Macon but recently. Knowing how particular my father was about such things, I employed a friend to visit the town he was from, and
(65) enquire into his past history. Now, friends, bear with pity my sad trial, and paint to your own imaginations how you would feel in such a case.

Within two weeks of marriage, with a man
(70) that you loved with your whole heart and soul, a perfect man, as you thought, imagine how you would feel to hear that he had (Oh God! how can I relate truth as I heard it! but I must or you will never hear with charity my
(75) flirtations) that he had been compelled to leave the town in which he lived, on account of his base seduction of a most beautiful, but poor girl, under solemn promise of marriage. He lived as a husband with her for a few
(80) months, and then deserted her, leaving her to

GO ON TO THE NEXT PAGE ⟶

die alone, in ignominy, and the most abject
poverty. On her death-bed she divulged her
secret to her brother, who traced the seducer
to the city and wounded him in a duel, and
(85) was fatally shot himself. A seducer and a
double murderer, the man I thought free from
guile as an angel in heaven! It was enough to
drive one mad, and I am sure I was crazed for
years.

(90)   He came to see me that night! How my
hand trembles! I can scarcely write to describe
our meeting. I was sitting alone, for I had
refused to receive visitors that night, when he
entered the room.

(95)   'Ah! darling,' said he, kissing me. 'Alone I
see. I am very glad too, for I wanted to see you
with no one near.' How handsome he looked,
with his flushed cheeks, red from his ride in
the wintry wind. 'What's the matter with my
(100) bird to-night? her voice is as sweet as ever, but
it is too sad for me.' 'Ella do let me urge you
to appoint our wedding day a week sooner,
for you are so pretty and sweet, you will tempt
me to'—he did not finish the sentence, but
(105) I understood his meaning but too well. It
was the first time he had ever acted in such
a singular manner, and I saw he was excited
highly by spirituous liquors.

     'Indeed sir,' I answered, 'If I have heard
(110) the truth I am not the first woman who
proved too sweet and pretty for you, and in
whose presence you could not control your
passions.'

     'Who told you that Ella?' he exclaimed,
(115) starting from his seat! 'By all that is sacred if I
find out, he shall not live an hour!'

     'You shall never know,' said I. 'Two
murders are quite enough to doom your
blackened soul, Dudley Earle!'

(120)   How pale he looked, but not with
penitence, it was anger only toward the
person who had divulged his secret. He

remained an hour trying to persuade me
to revoke my decision, and then left me a
(125) heart-broken sad woman, without an object
in life. And then and there I bent my knee,
before the throne of God. (I know now it
was blasphemy) but I was crazy then! and
vowed to revenge myself upon the whole sex,
(130) for the misery one, I then supposed the type
of the species, had wrought in my soul; and
faithfully I kept that vow.

     The Devil aids his own, and he surely
helped me. Even unsought, men would
(135) lay their love at my feet, and their foibles,
rendered harmless by my own self-control,
became my playthings. Often, very often
have I acted in such a way, that I knew would
inflame an even unimpressable man, and
(140) then would send his love back ungratified, to
corrode his very heart. Was that just or right?
No indeed, it was not. It was dangerous to me,
and outrageous to others. But dear reader in
pity for my anguish, and for the long years of
(145) intense mental suffering, forgive me. Never!
believe me, would I divulge this passage of my
life to any one, did I not think that perhaps it
may be a warning to the young, of both sexes.

     Let the young gentlemen always think
(150) and know, that no matter how secret an evil
act may be committed, it will always come
to light, and at the very time you may wish it
to be kept concealed. To the girls: No matter
my dears, how handsome or fascinating a
(155) gentleman may appear, never allow your
affections to become fixed on any human
being, until you know that being worthy.
Often times the veriest serpent wears a
shining coat, most beautiful to look upon,
(160) but the poison of whose fangs will corrupt a
young heart and mar its peace a whole life time.

     From *Confessions of a Flirt* by Mrs. Edward
Leigh (1859)

GO ON TO THE NEXT PAGE →

1. This passage can best be described as

   (A) a process narrative that provides the background of a flirtatious young woman.

   (B) a personal narrative that shows the development of a flirtatious nature.

   (C) a cause and effect essay that explains some unladylike behavior.

   (D) an argument that justifies personal revenge.

   (E) a comparison of two very handsome but very different young gentlemen.

2. The narrator can best be described as

   (A) indulged but sensitive.

   (B) revengeful but trustworthy.

   (C) angry but personable.

   (D) vindictive but personable.

   (E) spoiled but generous spirited.

3. In the context of the entire essay, paragraph 2 provides which of the following?

   (A) It describes the naiveté of a young ingénue.

   (B) It discloses a heartlessness preparatory to her later behavior toward men.

   (C) It gives the reader a poetic description using astronomy.

   (D) It contrasts two very different young suitors and the narrator's behavior toward them.

   (E) It explains the narrator's naiveté in her early years of womanhood.

4. Paragraph 3 utilizes all of the following stylistic devices EXCEPT

   (A) allusion.

   (B) simile.

   (C) hyperbole.

   (D) polysyndeton.

   (E) anaphora.

5. In paragraph 3, the narrator primarily relies upon which of the following sentence structures?

   (A) Simple sentences

   (B) Compound sentences

   (C) Parenthetical sentences

   (D) Fragmented sentences

   (E) Periodic sentences

6. Based on the rest of the passage, the best description of the young man as depicted in paragraph 3 is

   (A) charming and thoughtful.

   (B) sensitive and artistic.

   (C) suave and experienced.

   (D) brave and adventurous.

   (E) modest and mannerly.

7. The last sentences of paragraph 4 (lines 85–89) employ which of the following two characteristics?

   (A) Repetition and exaggeration

   (B) Irony and hyperbole

   (C) Explanation and sorrow

   (D) Simile and metaphor

   (E) Juxtaposition and understatement

GO ON TO THE NEXT PAGE

8. The most likely meaning of the word "singular" (line 107) would be

 (A) remarkable.
 (B) by oneself.
 (C) earnest.
 (D) deceitful.
 (E) duplicitous.

9. The pronoun "that" in line 70 refers to

 (A) his guilty conscience.
 (B) his surprise at her anger.
 (C) the despicable gentleman.
 (D) the murder he committed.
 (E) her sadness over his deceit.

10. The phrase "The Devil aids his own" (line 133) can best be interpreted to mean

 (A) the narrator's prayers were directed to the Devil.
 (B) the Devil only helps out other devils.
 (C) the narrator's evil revenge on men was accomplished with the help from the Devil.
 (D) the deceitful gentleman was like the Devil in his actions.
 (E) without the Devil's help, the narrator might never have learned the truth.

11. Paragraph 11 (lines 133–148) utilizes all of the following rhetorical devices EXCEPT

 (A) alliteration.
 (B) assonance.
 (C) rhetorical question.
 (D) zeugma.
 (E) exclamation.

12. The tone of the last paragraph can best be described as

 (A) sarcastic.
 (B) melodramatic.
 (C) angry.
 (D) injured.
 (E) didactic.

13. The best meaning for the phrase "veriest serpent wears a shining coat" (lines 158–159) is

 (A) wolf in sheep's clothing.
 (B) coal in a holiday stocking.
 (C) garbage wrapped in shiny paper.
 (D) snake in the shiny wet grass.
 (E) reptile clothed in jewels.

14. This story, especially in light of its last paragraph, can best be summed up by the cliché

 (A) "Beware of Greeks bearing gifts."
 (B) "Don't judge a book by its cover."
 (C) "Beauty is only skin deep."
 (D) "Always walk a mile in another's moccasins."
 (E) "Don't look a gift horse in the mouth."

GO ON TO THE NEXT PAGE →

Questions 15–28. Read the following passage carefully before you choose your answers.

The only purpose of being in politics is to strive for the values and ideals we believe in: freedom, justice, what we Europeans
Line call solidarity but you might call respect for
(5) and help for others. These are the decent democratic values we all avow. But alongside the values we know we need a hard-headed pragmatism—a *realpolitik*—required to give us any chance of translating those values into
(10) the practical world we live in.

The same tension exists in the two views of international affairs. One is utilitarian: each nation maximizes its own self-interest. The other is utopian: we try to create a
(15) better world. Today I want to suggest that more than ever before those two views are merging.

I advocate an enlightened self-interest that puts fighting for our values right at the
(20) heart of the policies necessary to protect our nations. Engagement in the world on the basis of these values, not isolationism from it, is the hard-headed pragmatism for the 21st century.

(25) Why? In part it is because the countries and people of the world today are more interdependent than ever. In truth, it is very rare today that trouble in one part of the globe remains limited in its effect. Not just in
(30) security, but in trade and finance—witness the crisis of 1998 which began in Thailand and ended in Brazil—the world is interlocked.

This is heightened by mass communications and technology. In Queen Victoria's time,
(35) reports of battles came back weeks or months after they were won or lost. Today we see them enacted live on the BBC, Sky or CNN. Their very visibility, immediate and in technicolour, inflames feelings that can spread worldwide
(40) across different ethnic, religious and cultural communities.

So today, more than ever, "their" problem becomes "our" problem. Instability is contagious and, again today, more than ever,
(45) nations, at least most of them, crave stability. That's for a simple reason. Our people want it, because without it, they can't do business and prosper. What brings nations together—what brought them together
(50) post–September 11—is the international recognition that the world needs order. Disorder is the enemy of progress.

The struggle is for stability, for the security within which progress can be
(55) made. Of course, countries want to protect their territorial integrity but few are into empire-building. This is especially true of democracies whose people vote for higher living standards and punish governments who
(60) don't deliver them. For 2,000 years Europe fought over territory.

Today boundaries are virtually fixed. Governments and people know that any territorial ambition threatens stability, and
(65) instability threatens prosperity.

And of course the surest way to stability is through the very values of freedom, democracy and justice. Where these are strong, the people push for moderation and
(70) order. Where they are absent, regimes act unchecked by popular accountability and pose a threat; and the threat spreads.

So the promotion of these values becomes not just right in itself but part of our
(75) long-term security and prosperity. We can't intervene in every case. Not all the wrongs of the world can be put right, but where disorder threatens us all, we should act.

GO ON TO THE NEXT PAGE ⟶

(80) Like it or not, whether you are a utilitarian or a utopian, the world is interdependent. One consequence of this is that foreign and domestic policy are ever more closely interwoven.

(85) It was September 11 that brought these thoughts into sharper focus. Watching the horror unfold, imagining the almost unimaginable suffering of the thousands of innocent victims of the terror and carnage, the dominant emotion after the obvious

(90) feelings of revulsion, sympathy and anger was determination.

The guts and spirit of the people of New York and America in the aftermath of that terrible day were not just admirable, they

(95) were awesome. They were the best riposte to the terrorists that humanity could give and you should be very proud of that. I want you to know too that the British people were with you from the first moment, and we will always

(100) be with you at times like those. We are not half-hearted friends and we never will be. But the determination must be not just to pursue those responsible and bring them to justice but to learn from September 11. There is a

(105) real danger we forget the lessons of September 11. Human beings recover from tragedy and the memory becomes less fraught. That is a healthy part of living. But we should learn from our experience.

(110) The most obvious lesson is indeed our interdependence. For a time our world stood still. Quite apart from our security, the shock impacted on economic confidence, on business, on trade, and it is only now, with the

(115) terrorist network on the run, that confidence is really returning. Every nation in the world felt the reverberation of that fateful day. And that has been well illustrated by the role which the United Nations—under Kofi Annan's

(120) excellent leadership—has played since September 11.

So if we didn't know it before, we know now: these events and our response to them shape the fate not of one nation but of one

(125) world.

For America, it has laid bare the reality. American power affects the world fundamentally. It is there. It is real. It is never irrelevant. It can affect the world for good, or

(130) for bad. Stand aside or engage; it never fails to affect.

You know I want it engaged. Under President Bush, I am confident it will be and for good. But if that's what I and many others

(135) want, it comes at a price for us too. It means we don't shirk our responsibility. It means that when America is fighting for those values, then, however tough, we fight with her. No grandstanding, no offering implausible but

(140) impractical advice from the comfort of the touchline, no wishing away the hard not the easy choices, but working together, side by side.

British Prime Minister Tony Blair to the
(145) American citizens following 9/11/2001

15. In opening this speech, Prime Minister Blair engages his audience by immediately

(A) talking about politics.

(B) referring to ideals the masses believe in.

(C) referring to the need for hard-headed pragmatism.

(D) translating values into the practical world we live in.

(E) directing attention to international affairs.

GO ON TO THE NEXT PAGE ⇨

16. The sentence that best expresses the essence of the message of the speech is

(A) "Disorder is the enemy of progress" (line 52).

(B) "In truth, it is very rare today that trouble in one part of the globe remains limited in its effect" (lines 27–29).

(C) "We are not half-hearted friends and we never will be" (lines 100–101).

(D) "American power affects the world fundamentally" (lines 127–128).

(E) "So if we didn't know it before, we know it now: these events and our response to them shape the fate not of one nation but of one world" (lines 122–125).

17. In two parts of this speech, lines 62–65 and lines 122–125, the two-sentence and single-sentence paragraphs are included to

(A) provide a break from the tension of longer paragraphs.

(B) show a reader the syntactical cleverness of the speech writer.

(C) provide syntactical transition to indicate shifts in the focus of the speech.

(D) give the speaker a moment to collect his thoughts.

(E) keep the audience attentive.

18. Throughout the speech, Prime Minister Blair includes all the following pairs of contrasting ideas EXCEPT

(A) engagement not isolation.

(B) ours not theirs.

(C) interdependent not independent.

(D) utilitarian not utopian.

(E) stability not disorder.

19. Blair's use of the words "guts" and "awesome" (lines 92 and 95) can best be described as

(A) informal diction.

(B) an attempt to be humorous.

(C) a slip in his British stuffiness.

(D) a speech writer's error.

(E) a throwback to the speaker's common upbringing.

20. The long sentence in lines 85–91 has its main clause appearing at the end of the sentence. This is known as what type of sentence?

(A) Loose

(B) Rhetorical

(C) Periodic

(D) Compound

(E) Complex

21. Paragraph 14 (lines 110–121) contains all of the following stylistic devices EXCEPT

(A) parenthetical statement.

(B) hyperbole.

(C) metonymy.

(D) personification.

(E) conceit.

22. The major effect of the syntactical structure of paragraph 16 (lines 126–131) makes this paragraph

(A) pointedly powerful.

(B) boringly repetitious.

(C) unimaginatively simplistic.

(D) dramatically stressful.

(E) abruptly brief.

GO ON TO THE NEXT PAGE ⟩

23. In the final paragraph, Blair effectively makes his point by

(A) explaining how Britain will work side by side with the United States.

(B) appealing to responsibility and commitment.

(C) using a series of negatives followed by a positive.

(D) speaking directly to the audience by using the pronoun "you."

(E) reminding the audience that everything comes with a price.

24. The word "riposte" used in line 95 refers most specifically to

(A) a meal.

(B) a request.

(C) a challenge.

(D) a retort.

(E) a retaliation.

25. The sentence, "It can affect the world for good, or for bad" (lines 129–130) utilizes a literary device known as

(A) contradiction.

(B) asyndeton.

(C) assonance.

(D) litote.

(E) zeugma.

26. From the last sentence of paragraph 5 (lines 37–41) we can infer that the speaker's attitude toward this point is

(A) ambiguous.

(B) displeased.

(C) inflammatory.

(D) regretful.

(E) critical.

27. In lines 129–131, the pronoun "it" refers to

(A) September 11.

(B) international involvement.

(C) British solidarity.

(D) American power.

(E) American retaliation.

28. The speaker in the passage can best be described as a person who

(A) is committed to developing independent nations.

(B) is actually more interested in the camaraderie between the United States and Britain.

(C) has an interest in the utilitarian view of international affairs.

(D) encourages collaboration and international solidarity.

(E) aspires to greatness but knows that he will never achieve it.

GO ON TO THE NEXT PAGE

Questions 29–41. Read the following passage carefully before you choose your answers.

To a professional critic (I have been one myself) theatre-going is the curse of Adam. The play is the evil he is paid to endure in the sweat of his brow; and the sooner it is over, the
(5) better. This would place him in irreconcilable opposition to the paying playgoer, from whose point of view the longer the play, the more entertainment he gets for his money. It does in fact so place him, especially in the provinces,
(10) where the playgoer goes to the theatre for the sake of the play solely, and insists so effectively on a certain number of hours' entertainment that touring managers are sometimes seriously embarrassed by the brevity of the London plays
(15) they have to deal in.

For in London the critics are reinforced by a considerable body of persons who go to the theatre as many others go to church, to display their best clothes and compare them
(20) with other people's; to be in the fashion, and to have something to talk about at dinner parties; to adore a pet performer; to pass the evening anywhere rather than home: in short, for any or every reason except interest in
(25) dramatic art as such. In fashionable centres the number of irreligious people who go to church, of unmusical people who go to concerts and operas, and of undramatic people who go to the theatre is so prodigious
(30) that sermons have been cut down to ten minutes and plays to two hours; and, even at that, congregations sit longing for the benediction and audiences for the final curtain, so that they may get away to the
(35) lunch or supper they really crave for, after arriving as late as (or later than) the hour of beginning can possibly be made for them.

Thus from the stalls and in the Press an atmosphere of hypocrisy spreads. Nobody says

(40) straight out that genuine drama is a tedious nuisance, and that to ask people to endure more than two hours of it (with two long intervals of relief) is an intolerable imposition. Nobody says "I hate classical tragedy and
(45) comedy as I hate sermons and symphonies; but I like police news and divorce news and any kind of dancing or decoration that has an aphrodisiac effect on me or on my wife or husband. And whatever superior people
(50) may pretend, I cannot associate pleasure with any sort of intellectual activity; and I don't believe anyone else can either." Such things are not said; yet nine-tenths of what is offered as criticism of the drama in the metropolitan
(55) Press of Europe and America is nothing but a muddled paraphrase of it. If it does not mean that, it means nothing.

I do not complain of this, though it complains very unreasonably of me. But I can
(60) take no more notice of it than Einstein of the people who are incapable of mathematics. I write in the classical manner for those who pay for admission to a theatre because they like classical comedy or tragedy for its own sake,
(65) and like it so much when it is good of its kind and well done that they tear themselves away from it with reluctance to catch the very latest train or omnibus that will take them home. Far from arriving late from an eight or half-past
(70) eight o'clock dinner so as to escape at least the first half-hour of the performance, they stand in queues outside the theatre doors for hours beforehand in bitingly cold weather to secure a seat. In countries where a play lasts a week,
(75) they bring baskets of provisions and sit it out. These are the patrons on whom I depend for my bread. I do not give them performances twelve hours long, because circumstances do not at present make such entertainments feasible; but
(80) an all-night sitting in a theatre would be at least

GO ON TO THE NEXT PAGE ⟶

as enjoyable as an all-night sitting in the House of Commons, and much more useful.

(85) Still I am sorry for the pseudo-critics and the fashionable people whose playgoing is a hypocrisy. They forget, however, that all men are not as they are. I cannot for their sakes undo my work and help the people who hate the theatre to drive out the people who love it, yet I may point out to them that they have several remedies in

(90) their own hands. They can escape the first part of the play by their usual practice of arriving late. They can escape the epilogue by not waiting for it. And if the irreducible minimum thus attained is still too painful, they can stay away altogether.

(95) But I deprecate this extreme course, because it is good neither for my pocket nor for their own soul. Already a few of them, noticing that what matters is not the absolute length of time occupied by a play, but the speed with which

(100) that time passes, are discovering that the theatre, though purgatorial in its Aristotelian moments, is not necessarily always the dull place they have so often found it. What do its discomforts matter when the play makes us forget them?

(105) George Bernard Shaw: "To the Critics, Lest They Should Feel Ignored" from *Saint Joan* (1924)

29. The writer's primary purpose in this passage is to

(A) explain why shorter plays need to be performed.

(B) criticize the provincial playgoers' dramatic demands.

(C) chastise the London public for their shallow-minded hypocrisy.

(D) explain why his plays are so long.

(E) berate the theater critics for their superficial reviews.

30. The tone of this passage can best be described as

(A) complex and formal.

(B) ambiguous and chastising.

(C) direct and uncomplicated.

(D) abstract and pedantic.

(E) scathing and libelous.

31. The dominant stylistic device used by the writer in paragraph 2 is

(A) antithesis.

(B) oxymoron.

(C) metaphor.

(D) analogy.

(E) metonymy.

32. The focus of paragraph 3 is

(A) people's preferences of classical tragedy.

(B) the public's preferences for entertainment.

(C) the lack of originality in theater audiences.

(D) society's general dislike of sermons and symphonies.

(E) the hypocrisy of the Press and the public for not stating what they feel.

GO ON TO THE NEXT PAGE

33. Paragraph 2 is best summarized by which of the following?

    (A) People often do the right thing for the wrong reason.

    (B) In a busy world, churches and theaters have to accommodate the busy lifestyles of potential audiences.

    (C) People will do just about anything to avoid returning home.

    (D) Churches and theaters are experiencing a dramatic increase in their attendance.

    (E) It is far more fashionable to attend a play than it is to attend church.

34. Lines 58–61 can best be understood as meaning which of the following?

    (A) The author won't complain about things he cannot fix, just as Einstein is unable to solve all problems.

    (B) The author cannot worry about the London public's view of theater any more than Einstein can worry about the math-challenged people of the world.

    (C) Einstein is more capable of helping people who dislike math than he is of helping people who dislike theater.

    (D) Theater people and math people rarely belong to the same social circles.

    (E) The author feels he has been unjustly criticized, just as Einstein has been unjustly misunderstood.

35. The main conclusion that one can draw from paragraph 4 (lines 58–82) is that

    (A) the long lines (queues) of ticket buyers at some theaters have become a problem.

    (B) standing in long theater lines can be an unpleasant experience, especially in the winter cold.

    (C) 12-hour-long performances are not unheard of.

    (D) week-long performances require theatergoers to bring their own food.

    (E) dedicated theater patrons are what make the author's efforts seem worthwhile.

36. The repetition of infinitive phrases used in paragraph 2 is an example of the stylistic device

    (A) anaphora.

    (B) apostrophe.

    (C) assonance.

    (D) ambiguity.

    (E) asyndeton.

37. The author's reference to the House of Commons is most likely used to

    (A) add credibility to the passage.

    (B) show that the author is politically correct.

    (C) indicate the author's probable disdain for the government.

    (D) demonstrate the author's intelligence.

    (E) provide an analogy to the point he is making.

GO ON TO THE NEXT PAGE

38. The phrase "irreducible minimum" (line 93) is a reference to

    (A) the fewest number of plays the public needs to attend to be considered appropriately sociable.

    (B) the shortest time left after the beginning and end of an event have been eliminated.

    (C) the sum total of entertainment possibilities people have at their disposal.

    (D) that which remains after all the pseudo-critics have been eliminated.

    (E) the smallest price theaters can charge and still pay the playwright and make a profit.

39. When the author says in lines 96–97 that people avoiding the theater altogether is "good neither for [his] pocket nor for their own soul," he most likely means

    (A) like church, the theater can be a religious experience.

    (B) hypocrisy is a sin, so people should avoid being guilty of it.

    (C) going to the theater will make audiences feel better.

    (D) inadvertently, people may actually learn something and possibly even come to appreciate the art of theater.

    (E) if people don't attend, they will be reducing the profits of the theaters and losing the opportunity to view plays.

40. In lines 100–103, ". . .[They] are discovering that the theatre, though purgatorial in its Aristotelian moments, is not necessarily always the dull place they have so often found it," the author utilizes a rhetorical device known as

    (A) ethical appeal.

    (B) historical reference.

    (C) analogy.

    (D) hyperbole.

    (E) allusion.

41. Overall, the conclusion of this passage is that

    (A) theater is boring and just an excuse to see and be seen.

    (B) if given a chance, theater has more to offer than simply providing a social opportunity for Londoners.

    (C) theater and church are closely aligned in their purpose and their audiences.

    (D) shallow people are incapable of understanding the true artistic benefits of theater.

    (E) attending a play is about as beneficial as attending a session of Parliament.

GO ON TO THE NEXT PAGE

Questions 42–54. Read the following passage carefully before you choose your answers.

It is now many years ago, my children, when I was quite a young woman, and your father, Freddy, was less than you are at present, that
Line
(5) we lived in a village more than a hundred miles from here. It was a very pretty village, situated on the bank of a broad, beautiful stream, which added much to the fertility and loveliness of the whole country through which it passed. We had not always dwelt in so pretty a place; but your
(10) grandfather, thinking it would be better for his business, concluded to take up his abode there. About the time we removed, another family took a steerage passage in a vessel bound from Ireland to this country. There were seven of
(15) them altogether—the father, mother, and five children. Their home had hitherto been a cabin, with a mud floor. A Bible, an iron pot, and a few wooden stools constituted their furniture; while their fare consisted of the scanty supply of milk
(20) afforded by one ill-fed cow, with a few potatoes. Willing to labor, yet finding wages humbled so low that they were often obliged to go both weary and hungry to bed, they concluded, after many struggles, to leave kindred and friends and
(25) come to America. How often, when speaking of this unhappy country, is the sentence 'Why don't they emigrate?' uttered with the greatest indifference. But to a warm Irish heart, this is often a severe trial. They are taxed, we might
(30) almost say, for the very air they breathe; yet how fondly they still cling to the soil of that island home, where nature must smile in spite of oppression; where the dust of their kindred repose; where are more loving hearts and words
(35) of warmer greeting than are to be met with elsewhere. No wonder the Irishman loves his country, crushed, trampled upon as she is. Her soil is among the most fertile, her sons among the noblest, and the language of even her rudest
(40) children the most poetical of any on earth. Oh, Ireland, fair Ireland, would we might yet live to see thee take thy proper place among the nations, to see the period approach when thy children will not be forced to seek in other countries the
(45) bare sustenance denied them at home. The Nevilles, after many struggles to obtain means sufficient to defray the expenses of a passage, and after borrowing from several neighbors small sums, which they promised to repay with
(50) interest, found themselves in the steerage of a vessel on their way to this land of promise. I will pass over the first few weeks of their arrival—strangers on a strange soil. Suffice it to say, that some one directed them to our village
(55) as a place where they could likely find steady employment. And here, one evening in early spring, cold, hungry, and penniless, they arrived. My husband, contrary to his usual custom, chanced to be abroad on that evening; and, as he
(60) was a devout believer in that blessed word which teaches that we may sometimes entertain angels unawares, on hearing the landlord refuse to keep them on account of their inability to pay, he brought them all home with him. I confess, I
(65) was taken a good deal by surprise at this unusual act; but, as it was his pleasure, I bade them welcome; and the heartfelt blessing which the poor strangers asked over the meal we prepared for them went far towards prepossessing me in
(70) their favor. The man, his wife, and the two little girls we accommodated in the house, while the three boys found lodgings among the fragrant hay in the well-stored mow. These people, my children, were not particularly attractive
(75) as far as appearance was concerned; they all appeared healthy and good-humored, and the little ones seemed uncommonly well-mannered for children in their rank of life; but still I was in some way unaccountably interested in

GO ON TO THE NEXT PAGE ⟶

(80) them; and I have since thought God permitted this feeling in order that I might bestir myself in behalf of those who were undoubtedly his followers. At any rate, we were willing to accommodate them a few days until something

(85) could be done for them; and, at the expiration of that time, a quiet-looking little cottage, with a willow tree before the door, standing just across the brook, was procured for them. I parted with several articles of furniture I could spare,

(90) in order to assist them in fitting out their new home; and my efforts among my neighbors procured them many other gifts of the same description. And now how happy was Mrs. Neville. Her husband had steady employment

(95) given him on a farm near by; her two eldest boys, of the ages of twelve and thirteen, both obtained good places; while the youngest boy, with the little girls, aged ten, eight, and six, were kept at home, where they were generally as busy

(100) as bees, for their mother held idleness to be the parent of all evil. I have often, on going in, been struck with the picture of neatness and humbled contentment their small kitchen presented.

The furniture was of the coarsest and most

(105) common description, yet scrupulously neat and clean. Here the family were generally found, pursuing their evening avocations, seated before the quiet blaze of their own fireside; and truly, where its comforts are properly appreciated,

(110) there is nothing gives the heart a finer or more touching idea of enjoyment than this same calm, domestic light. Evening, too, is the period of time which may truly be called the poor man's season of enjoyment; the implements of

(115) daily labor are laid aside, and it is then he may rest his wearied limbs and enjoy the prattle and playful wiles of his children, whose caresses sometimes lead him to forget the bitterness of his lot. The Nevilles were poor, very poor;

(120) the money they had borrowed from friends

in Ireland, they had obligated themselves to return, and they were straining every nerve to accomplish this. It was ten months before they were able, by their united labor, with practicing

(125) the most rigid self-denial, to realize this amount. At length, however, the sum was raised; and a benevolent gentleman inclosed and forwarded it in such a manner as it would be sure to reach its destination. They had, however, barely felt

(130) their minds relieved in this particular, when Mr. Neville was laid upon a bed of sickness. He had, perhaps, overworked himself and taken cold. His disease was inflammatory rheumatism. He lingered for a month, oftentimes suffering

(135) greatly; and then, after commending his wife and little ones to the care of that God who is the protector of the widow and the fatherless, strong in the hope of a blissful immortality, he died. As I told you before, my children, the Nevilles

(140) were pious people; and I could not but notice, in their mode of expression, a degree of intellectual refinement peculiar to those who make the Holy Scriptures an habitual study.

"You will observe, my children," said

(145) Mrs. Bruce, as she came to this portion of their discourse, "the unwavering faith which this poor woman possessed. She was a stranger in a strange land; there was no one upon whom she had any claim; yet I never heard

(150) her utter one repining word, or wonder how she was to get along without the assistance of her husband, there was so little selfishness in her grief. And although tears must flow at these sad sunderings of beloved ties, yet, when

(155) she did indulge in this outward exhibition of distress, she would almost immediately dry them, and give utterance to something which would discover how entire and unchanging was her trust in God. I was a great deal with

(160) her, and, I must say, after the last sad duties were performed, I was astonished to see how

GO ON TO THE NEXT PAGE →

energetically she set to work in order to support herself and her children. Her husband had often told me that all the fortune his wife had brought

(165) him was her religion, her energy, and her steady habits of industry, and that these had proved the blessing of his life. Now, too, she found ample exercise for these estimable qualities, and it was surprising how she could turn her hand

(170) to anything that offered; and, indeed, with the assistance the children were able to afford her, they managed to live very comfortably."

There, amid the far-stretching forests, on a farm which in Europe might be called a

(175) principality, a wife and mother, she is spending her days in the enjoyment of all that heart can desire. I have now done with the history of this family; yet I would have you observe how fearlessly Christian parents may repose upon

(180) the strength of the promises of Him who holds the hearts of all men in his hand. The skeptic may laugh and the worldling may sneer, but an appeal may confidently be made to those who have noted the dealings of Providence as

(185) to whether any who have trusted in him have been confounded.

From *Godey's Lady's Book* (1850)

42. In the lament expressed about Ireland and its people in lines 28–45, the narrator utilizes all of the following stylistic devices EXCEPT

(A) apostrophe.

(B) paradox.

(C) anaphora.

(D) personification.

(E) litote.

43. According to this passage, the Irish can best be described as

(A) people who are anxious to leave their unpleasant living conditions.

(B) rude people whose children do not have any manners.

(C) indifferent folks whose apathy makes it easy for them to be tolerant.

(D) oppressed people who regret having to leave the land that they love.

(E) complacent folks who have learned to embrace their situation with understanding.

44. Lines 1–37 utilize all of the following types of sentences EXCEPT

(A) compound-complex.

(B) imperative.

(C) rhetorical question.

(D) loose.

(E) periodic.

GO ON TO THE NEXT PAGE

45. Initially the Neville family can be characterized as

(A) penurious and devout.

(B) weak and hopeless.

(C) fortunate but ungrateful.

(D) indifferent and idle.

(E) self-sufficient and apathetic.

46. The narrator's attitude toward the Nevilles can be summed up as

(A) taken aback by their forwardness.

(B) fascinated by their intrepid spirit.

(C) prepossessed in their favor.

(D) distraught by their presence in her house.

(E) apathetic toward their situation.

47. Lines 94–101 encompass a long sentence with many independent clauses, without the aid of conjunctions. This is a syntactical device known as

(A) periodic.

(B) an apostrophe.

(C) rhetorical question.

(D) a run-on.

(E) asyndeton.

48. When the narrator states, "They [the Irish] are taxed, we might almost say, for the very air they breathe" (lines 29–30), she is using a rhetorical exaggeration known as

(A) juxtaposition.

(B) hyperbole.

(C) metonymy.

(D) parenthetical interruption.

(E) imperative declamation.

49. The phrase "uncommonly well-mannered for children in their rank of life" (lines 77–78) can be interpreted as meaning which of the following?

(A) It is uncommon for children of rank to have manners.

(B) Good manners were not commonly practiced during that historical time.

(C) Poor people were not uncommon at that time, nor were their children.

(D) Children of the poor were often less well mannered than those born to the more economically successful.

(E) For their age, the children's manners can be well ranked compared to other children's manners.

50. The verb "to realize" in line 125 can be best defined as meaning

(A) to amass.

(B) to recognize.

(C) to beg for.

(D) to squander.

(E) to return.

51. The sentence beginning "And although tears must flow . . . " (lines 153–159) can best be interpreted as meaning

(A) Mrs. Neville's love of God increases her sadness at her husband's death.

(B) Mrs. Neville's ties are reinforced by her beloved's tears and sundering.

(C) although Mrs. Neville inevitably cries due to her loss, she finds strength in her faith.

(D) although Mrs. Neville's trust in God is unchanging, her life is not.

(E) tears come and they go just as beloved people come and go in our own lives.

GO ON TO THE NEXT PAGE →

52. After the loss of her husband, Mrs. Neville can best be characterized as

    (A) irretrievably lost in grief.
    (B) so remorseful that she was unable to go on.
    (C) resourceful and plucky in her movement forward.
    (D) caught up in her need to exercise her energy amply in order to live comfortably.
    (E) so caught up in her own endeavors that she quickly forgot her grief.

53. The word "repining," line 150, means

    (A) resting.
    (B) depositing.
    (C) distrustful.
    (D) lamenting.
    (E) complaining.

54. The most significant message in this ladies' story is best summarized by which of the following?

    (A) Hard work and a good marriage are what bring you a successful life.
    (B) Sometimes we must leave our beloved home country in order to live comfortably and prosper.
    (C) No matter what difficulties one might encounter, a strong faith in Providence will help you through life.
    (D) A hard-working woman is always the center of a happy family.
    (E) Friendship and generosity are attributes worth having; they will bring you new and good-hearted friends.

STOP

Section II

Reading Period—15 minutes
Total Time—2 hours and 15 minutes
Number of questions—3
Percent of total grade—55%

Directions: This section contains three essay questions. For 15 minutes, you may read the essay questions and take notes on the question sheets. After this initial 15-minute reading period, you may begin writing your essay. You may not start writing on the lined paper until after the 15-minute reading period has ended. When you start writing on the three questions, budget your time carefully. Each essay counts as one-third of your total essay score.

QUESTION ONE

(Suggested reading time—15 minutes)
(Suggested writing time—40 minutes)

Directions: The following prompt is based on the accompanying six sources.

This question requires you to synthesize a variety of sources into a coherent, well-written essay. *Refer to the sources to support your position; avoid mere paraphrase or summary. Your argument should be central; the sources should support this argument.*

Remember to attribute both direct and indirect citations.

Introduction: The question of Political Correctness has been a hot-button topic on college campuses and in cultural circles for nearly two decades. To what extent are we more aware of the words we choose to use and the labels that we give to different ethnic, religious, and other groups? Likewise, to what degree has the backlash against all things "PC" contributed to a perceived rift in our country?

Assignment: Read the following sources (including any introductory information) carefully. **Then, in an essay that synthesizes at least three of the sources for support, take a position that defends, challenges, or qualifies the claim that the campaign to promote the usage of nonoffensive language and politically correct terminology has been a successful agent for positive change and increased sensitivity.**

You may refer to the sources by their titles (Source A, Source B, etc.) or by the descriptions in parentheses.

Source A (Wallace)

Source B (Hayakawa)

Source C (Mairs)

Source D (Random House)

Source E (The First Amendment Center)

Source F (Ravitch)

GO ON TO THE NEXT PAGE

Source A

Wallace, David Foster. "Tense Present: Democracy, English, and the Wars over Usage." *Harper's Magazine*, April 2001.

The following passage is excerpted from a monthly journal of literature, politics, culture, and the arts.

I refer here to Politically Correct English (PCE), under whose conventions failing students become "high-potential" students and poor people "economically disadvantaged" and people in wheelchairs "differently abled" and a sentence like "White English and Black English are different and you better learn White English if you don't want to flunk," is not blunt but "insensitive." Although it's common to make jokes about PCE (referring to ugly people as "aesthetically challenged" and so on), be advised that Politically Correct English's various pre- and proscriptions are taken very seriously indeed by colleges and corporations and government agencies, whose own institutional dialects now evolve under the beady scrutiny of a whole new kind of Language Police.

. . . Usage is always political, of course, but it's complexly political. With respect, for instance, to political change, usage conventions can function in two ways: On the one hand they can be a reflection of political change, and on the other they can be an instrument of political change. These two functions are different and have to be kept straight. Confusing them—in particular, mistaking for political efficacy what is really just a language's political symbolism—enables the bizarre conviction that America ceases to be elitist or unfair simply because Americans stop using certain vocabulary that is historically associated with elitism. This is PCE's central fallacy—that a society's mode of expression is productive of its attitudes rather than a product of those attitudes. . . .

GO ON TO THE NEXT PAGE

Source B

Hayakawa, S. I. *Language in Thought and Action* (Fifth Edition). New York: Harcourt Brace & Company, 1991.

The following passage is excerpted from a book that examines language and its essentially cooperative function necessary to survival in society.

Names that are "loaded" tend to influence behavior toward those to whom they are applied. Currently, the shop doorways and freeway underpasses of American cities are sheltering tens of thousands of people who have no work and no homes. These people used to be referred to as "bums"—a word that suggests not only a lack of employment but a lack of desire to work, people who are lazy, satisfied with little, and who have no desire to enter the mainstream of the American middle class or subscribe to its values. Thus, to think of these people as "bums" is to think that they are only getting what they deserve. With the search for new names for such people—"street people," "homeless," "displaced persons"—we may find new ways of helping deal with it.

. . . One other curious fact needs to be recorded about the words we apply to such hotly debated issues as race, religion, political heresy, and economic dissent. Every reader is acquainted with people who, according to their own flattering descriptions of themselves, "believe in being frank" and like to "tell it like it is." By "telling it like it is," such people usually mean calling anything or anyone by the term which has the strongest and most disagreeable affective connotations. Why people should pin medals on themselves for "candor" for performing this nasty feat has often puzzled me. Sometimes it is necessary to violate verbal taboos as an aid to clearer thinking, but, more often, to insist upon "telling it like it is" is to provide our minds with a greased runway down which we may slide back into unexamined and reactive patterns of evaluation and behavior.

GO ON TO THE NEXT PAGE

Source C

Mairs, Nancy. "On Being a Cripple" in *Plaintext*. Tucson: University of Arizona Press, 1986.

The following passage is excerpted from a personal essay.

. . . I am a cripple. I choose this word to name me. I choose from among several possibilities, the most common of which are "handicapped" and "disabled." I made the choice a number of years ago, without thinking, unaware of my motives for doing so. People—crippled or not—wince at the word "cripple," as they do not at "handicapped" or "disabled." Perhaps I want them to wince. I want them to see me as a tough customer, one to whom the fates/gods/viruses have not been kind, but who can face the brutal truth of her existence squarely.

But, to be fair to myself, a certain amount of honesty underlies my choice. "Cripple" seems to me a clean word, straightforward and precise. "Disabled," by contrast, suggests any incapacity, physical or mental. And I certainly don't like "handicapped," which implies that I have deliberately been put at a disadvantage. . . . These words seem to me to be moving away from my condition, to be widening the gap between word and reality.

Whatever you call me, I remain crippled. But I don't care what you call me, so long as it isn't "differently abled," which strikes me as pure verbal garbage designed, by its ability to describe anyone, to describe no one. And I refuse to participate in the degeneration of language to the extent that I deny that I have lost anything in the course of this calamitous disease . . . that the only differences between you and me are the various ordinary ones that distinguish any one person from another. But call me "disabled" or "handicapped" if you like. Society is no readier to accept crippledness than to accept death, war, sex, sweat, or wrinkles. I would never refer to another person as a cripple. It is the word I use to name myself.

GO ON TO THE NEXT PAGE ➡

Source D

"Avoiding Insensitive and Offensive Language." *Words@Random*. Available at *www.randomhouse.com/words/language/avoid_essay.html*

The following passage is excerpted from an explanatory essay on the inclusion of offensive terms in the dictionary and a guide on avoiding such usage.

Certain words are labeled in Random House *Webster's College Dictionary* as vulgar, offensive, or disparaging. Words in these categories, which include those referring to sexual or excretory functions and racial, ethnic, or social groups, are usually inappropriate and should be treated with caution. While there are some circumstances where these words are accepted, there are many others where their use can be hurtful and upsetting.

Other factors complicate the question. A group may disagree within itself as to what is acceptable and what is not. Many seemingly inoffensive terms develop negative connotations over time and become dated or go out of style as awareness changes. A "within the group" rule often applies, which allows a member of a group to use terms freely that would be considered offensive if used by a nonmember of the group.

What is considered acceptable shifts constantly as people become more aware of language and its power. The rapid changes of the last few decades have left many people puzzled and afraid of unintentionally insulting someone. At the same time, these changes have angered others, who decry what they see as extremes of "political correctness" in rules and locutions that alter language to the point of obscuring, even destroying, its meaning. The abandonment of traditional usages has also upset many people. But while it is true that some of the more extreme attempts to avoid offending language have resulted in ludicrous obfuscation (is "animal companion" necessary as a replacement for "pet"?), it is also true that heightened sensitivity in language is a statement of respect, indicates precision of thought, and is a positive move toward rectifying the unequal social status between one group and another.

GO ON TO THE NEXT PAGE ⟶

Source E

The First Amendment Center. 2005. STATE OF THE FIRST AMENDMENT 2005 [computer file]. Nashville, TN: First Amendment Center [producer and distributor].

The following chart comes from an online digital archive devoted to cultural policy studies.

American Attitudes Toward Freedom of Expression—2005

Should the following types of potentially offensive speech be allowed?

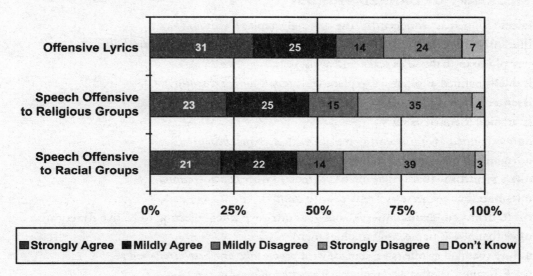

Source: State of the First Amendment Survey, 2005
© Princeton University 2005 | www.cpanda.org

GO ON TO THE NEXT PAGE

Source F

Ravitch, Diane. *The Language Police: How Pressure Groups Restrict What Students Learn*. New York: Knopf, 2003.

The following list was collected from more than 20 sets of guidelines produced by state departments of education, textbook publishers, test developers, educational research organizations, and other interest groups.

A GLOSSARY OF BANNED WORDS

Dialect (banned as ethnocentric, use sparingly, replace with *language*)

Differently abled (banned as offensive, replace with *person who has a disability*)

Dirty old man (banned as sexist and ageist)

Disabled (banned as offensive, replace with *people with a disability*)

Dissenter (ethnocentric, use with caution)

Distaff side (banned as sexist)

Dogma (banned as ethnocentric, replace with *doctrine, belief*)

Doorman (banned as sexist, replace with *door attendant*)

Down's syndrome (banned as offensive, replace with *Down syndrome*)

Draftsman (banned as sexist, replace with *drafter*)

Drunk, drunken, drunkenness (banned as offensive when referring to Native Americans)

Duffer (banned as demeaning to older men)

Dummy (banned as offensive, replace with *people who are speech impaired*)

Dwarf (banned as offensive, replace with *person of short stature*)

Heretic (use with caution when comparing religions)

Heroine (banned as sexist, replace with *hero*)

Hispanic American (use with caution as some groups object to the term's suggestion of a shared European cultural heritage, replace with specific nationality)

Homosexual (banned, replace with *person, child*)

Hordes (banned as reference to immigrant groups)

Horseman, horsewoman (banned as sexist, replace with *equestrian*)

Horsemanship (banned as sexist, replace with *riding skill*)

Hottentot (banned as a relic of colonialism, replace with *Khoi-khoi*)

Houseman, housemaid (banned as sexist, replace with *servant, housekeeper*)

Housewife (banned as sexist, replace with *homemaker, head of the household*)

Hussy (banned as sexist)

Huts (banned as ethnocentric, replace with *small houses*)

STOP

QUESTION TWO

(Suggested time—40 minutes)

Read the following selection by Annie Dillard carefully and consider the attitude of the narrator in the passage. Then, in a well-organized essay, identify this author's attitude and how her choice of diction, syntax, tone, and rhetorical devices helps demonstrate this attitude within the passage.

Here, on the obstetrical ward, is a double sink in a little room—a chrome faucet, two basins and drains, just like any kitchen sink. There is a counter on the left, and a counter on the right. Overhead, a long heat lamp lights and warms the two counters and the sink.

Line   This is where they wash the newborns like dishes. A nurse, one or another, spends most
(5)   of an eight-hour shift standing here at the sink.

Different nurses bring in newborns, one after another, and line them down the counter to the sink's left. The newborns wear flannel blankets. Knit hats the size of teacups keep sliding up their wet heads. Their faces run the spectrum from lavender through purple and red to pink and beige.

(10)   Nurse Pat Eisberg wears her curly blond hair short in back; her thin neck bends out of a blue collarless scrub as she leans left for the next bundle. The newborn's face is red.

"Now you," she says to it in a warm voice, unsmiling. She slides it along the counter toward her, plucks off its cap, unwraps its body and leaves the blanket underneath. This baby is red all over. His tadpole belly is red; his scrotum, the size of a plum, is fiercely

(15)   red, and looks as if it might explode. The top of his head looks like a dunce cap; he is a conehead. He gazes up attentively from the nurse's arms. The bright heat lamp does not seem to bother his eyes, nor do the silver nitrate eyedrops, which prevent gonorrhea. His plastic ID bracelet, an inch wide, covers a full third of his forearm. Someone has taped his blue umbilical cord—the inch or so left of it—upward on his belly. A black clamp grips

(20)   the cord's end, so it looks like a jumper cable.

The nurse washes this boy; she dips a thin washcloth again and again in warm water. She cleans his head and face, careful to wash every fold of his ears. She wipes white lines of crumbled vernix from folds in his groin and under his arms. She holds one wormy arm and one wormy leg to turn him over; then she cleans his dorsal side, and ends with his

(25)   anus. She has washed and rinsed every bit of his red skin. The heat lamp has dried him already. The Qur'an says Allah created man from a clot. The red baby is a ball of blood Allah wetted and into which he blew. So does a clown inflate a few thin balloons and twist them lickety-split into a rabbit, a dog, a giraffe.

Nurse Pat Eisberg drains the sink. She drops the newborn's old blanket and hat into

(30)   an open hamper, peels a new blanket and hat from the pile on the right and sticks the red baby on the right-hand counter. She diapers him. She swaddles him: she folds the right corner of the blanket over him and rolls him back to tuck it under him; she brings up the bottom blanket corner over his chest: she wraps the left corner around and around, and his weight holds it tight as he lies on his back. Now he is tidy and compact, the size of a

GO ON TO THE NEXT PAGE

(35) one-quart Thermos. She caps his conehead, and gives the bundle a push to slide it down the counter to the end of the line with the others she has just washed.

The red newborn looks up and studies his surroundings, alert, seemingly pleased, and preternaturally calm, as if enchanted. Every few minutes another nurse comes in to pick up whichever washed baby has reached the head of the line. The nurse returns the parcel

(40) to its mother. When the red boy's number is up, I follow.

The mother is propped on a clean hospital bed, and she looks a bit wan. The mother is white as the sheets, in her thirties, puffy, pretty, and completely stunned. She looks like the cartoon Road Runner who has just had a steamroller drive over it.

The nurse has put the baby on his back in a basinet cart. Americans place infants on

(45) their backs now—never on their stomachs, lest they smother in their sleep and die. Ten years ago, Americans placed infants on their stomachs—never on their backs, lest they choke in their sleep and die.

A nurse unwraps him. He does not like it; he hates being unwrapped. He is still red. His fingernail slivers are red, as if someone had painted nail polish on them. His toenails are

(50) red. The nurse shows the father how to swaddle him.

"... and then you wrap the last corner tight around the whole works," the nurse says. As she finishes binding him into his proper Thermos shape, the baby closes his mouth, opens his eyes, and peers about like a sibyl. He looks into our faces. When he meets our eyes in turn, his father and I each say "Hi," involuntarily. In the nurses, this impulse has perhaps

(55) worn out.

STOP

QUESTION THREE

(Suggested time—40 minutes)

In his description of springtime at Walden Pond, Henry David Thoreau shares his ideas about nature with us. After reading the passage closely, discuss Thoreau's attitudes toward nature and its importance to us. Be sure to discuss his uses of the resources of language to convey his feelings to the reader.

On the 29th of April, as I was fishing from the bank of the river near the Nine-Acre-Corner bridge, standing on the quaking grass and willow roots, where the muskrats lurk, I heard a singular rattling sound, somewhat like that of the sticks which *Line* boys play with their fingers, when, looking up, I observed a very slight and graceful hawk, (5) like a nighthawk, alternately soaring like a ripple and tumbling a rod or two over and over, showing the under side of its wings, which gleamed like a satin ribbon in the sun, or like the pearly inside of a shell. This sight reminded me of falconry and what nobleness and poetry are associated with that sport. The Merlin it seemed to me it might be called: but I care not for its name. It was the most ethereal flight I had ever witnessed. It did not simply (10) flutter like a butterfly, nor soar like the larger hawks, but it sported with proud reliance in the fields of air; mounting again and again with its strange chuckle, it repeated its free and beautiful fall, turning over and over like a kite, and then recovering from its lofty tumbling, as if it had never set its foot on *terra firma.* It appeared to have no companion in the universe—sporting there alone—and to need none but the morning and the ether (15) with which it played. It was not lonely, but made all the earth lonely beneath it. Where was the parent, which hatched it, its kindred, and its father in the heavens? The tenant of the air, it seemed related to the earth but by an egg hatched some time in the crevice of a crag;—or was its native nest made in the angle of a cloud, woven of the rainbow's trimmings and the sunset sky, and lined with some soft midsummer haze caught up from (20) earth? Its eyry[1] now some cliffy cloud.

Beside this I got a rare mess of golden and silver and bright cupreous fishes, which looked like a string of jewels. Ah! I have penetrated to those meadows on the morning of many a first spring day, jumping from hummock to hummock[2], from willow root to willow root, when the wild river valley and the woods were bathed in so pure and bright a (25) light as would have waked the dead, if they had been slumbering in their graves, as some suppose. There needs no stronger proof of immortality. All things must live in such a light. O Death, where was thy sting? O Grave, where was thy victory, then?

Our village life would stagnate if it were not for the unexplored forests and meadows which surround it. We need the tonic of wildness—to wade sometimes in marshes where (30) the bittern and the meadow-hen lurk, and hear the booming of the snipe; to smell the whispering sedge where only some wilder and more solitary fowl builds her nest, and the mink crawls with its belly close to the ground. At the same time that we are earnest to explore and learn all things, we require that all things be mysterious and unexplorable,

1. *eyry*—home for birds
2. *hummock*—a hill or a rise in the land

GO ON TO THE NEXT PAGE ⟶

(35) that land and sea be infinitely wild, unsurveyed and unfathomed by us because unfathomable. We can never have enough of nature. We must be refreshed by the sight of inexhaustible vigor, vast and titanic features, the sea-coast with its wrecks, the wilderness with its living and its decaying trees, the thunder-cloud, and the rain which lasts three weeks and produces freshets. We need to witness our own limits transgressed, and some life pasturing freely where we never wander. We are cheered when we observe the vulture

(40) feeding on the carrion which disgusts and disheartens us, and deriving health and strength from the repast. There was a dead horse in the hollow by the path to my house, which compelled me sometimes to go out of my way, especially in the night when the air was heavy, but the assurance it gave me of the strong appetite and inviolable health of Nature was my compensation for this. I love to see that Nature is so rife with life that myriads can

(45) be afforded to be sacrificed and suffered to prey on one another; that tender organizations can be so serenely squashed out of existence like pulp—tadpoles which herons gobble up, and tortoises and toads run over in the road; and that sometimes it has rained flesh and blood! With the liability to accident, we must see how little account is to be made of it. The impression made on a wise man is that of universal innocence. Poison is not

(50) poisonous after all, nor are any wounds fatal. Compassion is a very untenable ground. It must be expeditious. Its pleadings will not bear to be stereotyped.

STOP

DIAGNOSTIC TEST: ANSWER KEY

Passage 1	**Passage 2**	**Passage 3**	**Passage 4**
1. B	15. B	29. C	42. E
2. D	16. E	30. B	43. D
3. B	17. C	31. D	44. B
4. E	18. D	32. E	45. A
5. B	19. A	33. A	46. B
6. C	20. C	34. B	47. E
7. B	21. E	35. E	48. B
8. A	22. A	36. A	49. D
9. C	23. D	37. C	50. A
10. C	24. D	38. B	51. C
11. D	25. E	39. E	52. C
12. E	26. A	40. E	53. E
13. A	27. D	41. B	54. C
14. B	28. D		

ANSWERS AND EXPLANATIONS

QUESTIONS 1–14

Although my early life tended to encourage my flirting propensities it did not make me the real heartless coquette, I afterwards became. The flirtations of school life were

Line
(5)   harmless, for there was no real love between myself and the parties concerned. When I left school I was just seventeen. Young, gay, rich, happy and thoughtless, without a wish ungratified. I had been accustomed

(10) to admiration all my life, and now I really deserved it. I was rather stylish in my personal appearance, so every one said. Every advantage, that money could give, had been given me, and I do not flatter myself, when I

(15) say I improved my talents. I rode well, danced well, played and sang well, conversed well, and in truth everything I attempted I did well.

Among the first satellites that moved around my sphere, were two young gentlemen,

(20) both handsome, but very unlike in personal appearance and disposition. One was dark as a Spaniard, with eyes and hair as dark as night when the moon and stars have hid their beams under a canopy of cloud. He was very

(25) handsome and talented, yet I could not love the man, for I feared him. Still it amused me to lead him on, intending to tell him every time we met, that his love was vain; but I continued putting it off.

(30) The other—God knows I loved him, if woman is capable of loving. He was fair, very fair, with dark eyes and light hair. His mouth was beautiful, but deceit lurked in each exquisite curve of his lips. An Adonis

(35) was not more perfect in form: and he knew it. He was young in years, yet old in sin. I now sometimes think that he, like Bulwer's Zanoni, had found the true secret of perpetual youth, and that he had lived for centuries, so well was

(40) he versed in the ways of the world, and in each phase of human nature. He often boasted of the many conquests he had made, and said that no woman he chose to captivate could escape loving him. I did not like this speech; but I

(45) loved him. He had certainly many rare traits of character. His generosity was proverbial; he was a warm friend and had the most perfect control over his very high temper. It was not long before we became engaged. He said that

(50) he loved me at first sight; and God knows that his love was more than returned. He called to see me each day, and every night escorted me to some place of amusement. He was very jealous, but I liked that. He was my sun during

(55) the day, and my moon at night. There was a cloud over all my happiness when he failed to come. He was young, ardent, fiery and passionate, and I—I was a fool! The passionate devotion of my heart was lavished upon a

(60) worthless object. I knew nothing of his former conduct or character, as he had come to Macon but recently. Knowing how particular my father was about such things, I employed a friend to visit the town he was from, and

(65) enquire into his past history. Now, friends, bear with pity my sad trial, and paint to your own imaginations how you would feel in such a case.

Within two weeks of marriage, with a man

(70) that you loved with your whole heart and soul, a perfect man, as you thought, imagine how you would feel to hear that he had (Oh God! how can I relate truth as I heard it! but I must or you will never hear with charity my

(75) flirtations) that he had been compelled to leave the town in which he lived, on account of his base seduction of a most beautiful, but poor girl, under solemn promise of marriage. He lived as a husband with her for a few

(80) months, and then deserted her, leaving her to

die alone, in ignominy, and the most abject
poverty. On her death-bed she divulged her
secret to her brother, who traced the seducer
to the city and wounded him in a duel, and
(85) was fatally shot himself. A seducer and a
double murderer, the man I thought free from
guile as an angel in heaven! It was enough to
drive one mad, and I am sure I was crazed for
years.

(90)   He came to see me that night! How my
hand trembles! I can scarcely write to describe
our meeting. I was sitting alone, for I had
refused to receive visitors that night, when he
entered the room.

(95)   'Ah! darling,' said he, kissing me. 'Alone I
see. I am very glad too, for I wanted to see you
with no one near.' How handsome he looked,
with his flushed cheeks, red from his ride in
the wintry wind. 'What's the matter with my
(100) bird to-night? her voice is as sweet as ever, but
it is too sad for me.' 'Ella do let me urge you
to appoint our wedding day a week sooner,
for you are so pretty and sweet, you will tempt
me to'—he did not finish the sentence, but
(105) I understood his meaning but too well. It
was the first time he had ever acted in such
a singular manner, and I saw he was excited
highly by spirituous liquors.

'Indeed sir,' I answered, 'If I have heard
(110) the truth I am not the first woman who
proved too sweet and pretty for you, and in
whose presence you could not control your
passions.'

'Who told you that Ella?' he exclaimed,
(115) starting from his seat! 'By all that is sacred if I
find out, he shall not live an hour!'

'You shall never know,' said I. 'Two
murders are quite enough to doom your
blackened soul, Dudley Earle!'

(120)   How pale he looked, but not with
penitence, it was anger only toward the
person who had divulged his secret. He

remained an hour trying to persuade me
to revoke my decision, and then left me a
(125) heart-broken sad woman, without an object
in life. And then and there I bent my knee,
before the throne of God. (I know now it
was blasphemy) but I was crazy then! and
vowed to revenge myself upon the whole sex,
(130) for the misery one, I then supposed the type
of the species, had wrought in my soul; and
faithfully I kept that vow.

The Devil aids his own, and he surely
helped me. Even unsought, men would
(135) lay their love at my feet, and their foibles,
rendered harmless by my own self-control,
became my playthings. Often, very often
have I acted in such a way, that I knew would
inflame an even unimpressable man, and
(140) then would send his love back ungratified, to
corrode his very heart. Was that just or right?
No indeed, it was not. It was dangerous to me,
and outrageous to others. But dear reader in
pity for my anguish, and for the long years of
(145) intense mental suffering, forgive me. Never!
believe me, would I divulge this passage of my
life to any one, did I not think that perhaps it
may be a warning to the young, of both sexes.

Let the young gentlemen always think
(150) and know, that no matter how secret an evil
act may be committed, it will always come
to light, and at the very time you may wish it
to be kept concealed. To the girls: No matter
my dears, how handsome or fascinating a
(155) gentleman may appear, never allow your
affections to become fixed on any human
being, until you know that being worthy.
Often times the veriest serpent wears a
shining coat, most beautiful to look upon,
(160) but the poison of whose fangs will corrupt a
young heart and mar its peace a whole life time.

From *Confessions of a Flirt* by Mrs. Edward
Leigh (1859)

1. B
This first question is identifying the mode of discourse of the passage. The young lady is telling us about her own story. Although there is some justification of behavior going on (cause and effect), the dominant mode of discourse is a simple personal narrative, making (B) the correct response.

2. D
It is not unusual for the AP exam to ask you to make a judgment about the probable attitude or characteristics of the narrator. In this case, we have a young woman who is definitely out for revenge. However, she is so up-front and likeable that (D) is the best response to this question.

3. B
Basically, paragraph 2 is a foreshadowing of the young lady's later behavior. She talks about how she dallied with suitors and mercilessly kept stringing one man along. This early behavior is a precursor to her later vindication against men. Therefore, (B) is the correct response.

4. E
Paragraph 3 uses a couple of *allusions*, including a reference to mythology. In addition, lines 22–24 show *simile*; exaggeration, *hyperbole*, is evident in several places, in particular in her lavish description of the young gentleman; the narrator also presents a series of clauses, almost every one of them connected by conjunctions, *polysyndeton*. Nowhere, however, is there a repetition of wording in a series of phrases or clauses, making (E), *anaphora*, the correct answer.

5. B
In conjunction with the previous question, paragraph 3 has numerous independent clauses (connected by appropriate conjunctions). The syntactical structure of this paragraph is primarily compound sentences, (B).

6. C
Remember, you are being asked for the *best* description of the young man. Although several of

the responses describe his character, the *best* response is (C)—he is smooth and a man with a history.

7. B
"A seducer and a double murderer, the man I thought free from guile as an angel in heaven! It was enough to drive one mad, and I am sure I was crazed for years." These lines definitely display *irony*, contrast between the expected and the actual, as well as *hyperbole*, exaggeration. Response (B) is the correct answer to this question.

8. A
"It was the first time he had ever acted in such a singular manner. . . ." The narrator is surprised and taken aback by this young man's unusual behavior. Although several of the responses readily describe this young man, (A), *remarkable*, is the most accurate synonym in this case for singular.

9. C
This question is actually one of basic grammar. It asks you to identify the antecedent (word being replaced by the pronoun). Although all of the responses are present somewhere in the passage, the antecedent of *that* is the despicable gentleman, (C).

10. C
This question actually is a bit of a confession on the part of the narrator. She admits she is part devil, and therefore it apparently takes a devil to know and aid a fellow devil. Her successful revenge on all men was aided by the devil, (C).

11. D
Paragraph 11 (lines 133–148) demonstrates several rhetorical devices: although not abundant, *alliteration*, the repetition of initial consonant sounds, is present; *assonance*, the repetition of similar internal vowel sounds, is also present. In addition, a *rhetorical question* is asked in line 141; *exclamation* is used in line 145. Nowhere is *zeugma* present, that is, grammatically correct linkage of one subject with two or more verbs or a verb with two or more objects. Therefore, (D) is the correct response.

12.   E

The last paragraph is very moralistic and almost preachy. Given the response choices, *didactic*, (E), is the best.

13.   A

The *best* meaning for "veriest serpent wears a shining coat," is that even the lowliest snake can pass itself off as something glamorous. This makes (A) the best cliché to echo the meaning of this phrase.

14.   B

Overall, the story is a lesson to young women everywhere to beware of men who seem more than they are. This can best be stated by the cliché in (B), not to judge a book by its cover.

QUESTIONS 15–28

The only purpose of being in politics is to strive for the values and ideals we believe in: freedom, justice, what we Europeans *Line* call solidarity but you might call respect for (5) and help for others. These are the decent democratic values we all avow. But alongside the values we know we need a hard-headed pragmatism—a *realpolitik*—required to give us any chance of translating those values into (10) the practical world we live in.

The same tension exists in the two views of international affairs. One is utilitarian: each nation maximizes its own self-interest. The other is utopian: we try to create a (15) better world. Today I want to suggest that more than ever before those two views are merging.

I advocate an enlightened self-interest that puts fighting for our values right at the (20) heart of the policies necessary to protect our nations. Engagement in the world on the basis of these values, not isolationism from it, is the hard-headed pragmatism for the 21st century.

(25)   Why? In part it is because the countries and people of the world today are more interdependent than ever. In truth, it is very rare today that trouble in one part of the globe remains limited in its effect. Not just in (30) security, but in trade and finance—witness the crisis of 1998 which began in Thailand and ended in Brazil—the world is interlocked.

This is heightened by mass communications and technology. In Queen Victoria's time, (35) reports of battles came back weeks or months after they were won or lost. Today we see them enacted live on the BBC, Sky or CNN. Their very visibility, immediate and in technicolour, inflames feelings that can spread worldwide (40) across different ethnic, religious and cultural communities.

So today, more than ever, "their" problem becomes "our" problem. Instability is contagious and, again today, more than ever, (45) nations, at least most of them, crave stability. That's for a simple reason. Our people want it, because without it, they can't do business and prosper. What brings nations together—what brought them together (50) post–September 11—is the international recognition that the world needs order. Disorder is the enemy of progress.

The struggle is for stability, for the security within which progress can be (55) made. Of course, countries want to protect their territorial integrity but few are into empire-building. This is especially true of democracies whose people vote for higher living standards and punish governments who (60) don't deliver them. For 2,000 years Europe fought over territory.

Today boundaries are virtually fixed. Governments and people know that any territorial ambition threatens stability, and (65) instability threatens prosperity.

And of course the surest way to stability is through the very values of freedom, democracy and justice. Where these are strong, the people push for moderation and (70) order. Where they are absent, regimes act unchecked by popular accountability and pose a threat; and the threat spreads.

So the promotion of these values becomes not just right in itself but part of our (75) long-term security and prosperity. We can't intervene in every case. Not all the wrongs of the world can be put right, but where disorder threatens us all, we should act.

Like it or not, whether you are a utilitarian (80) or a utopian, the world is interdependent. One consequence of this is that foreign and domestic policy are ever more closely interwoven.

It was September 11 that brought these (85) thoughts into sharper focus. Watching the horror unfold, imagining the almost unimaginable suffering of the thousands of innocent victims of the terror and carnage, the dominant emotion after the obvious (90) feelings of revulsion, sympathy and anger was determination.

The guts and spirit of the people of New York and America in the aftermath of that terrible day were not just admirable, they (95) were awesome. They were the best riposte to the terrorists that humanity could give and you should be very proud of that. I want you to know too that the British people were with you from the first moment, and we will always (100) be with you at times like those. We are not half-hearted friends and we never will be. But the determination must be not just to pursue those responsible and bring them to justice but to learn from September 11. There is a (105) real danger we forget the lessons of September 11. Human beings recover from tragedy and the memory becomes less fraught. That is a

healthy part of living. But we should learn from our experience.

(110) The most obvious lesson is indeed our interdependence. For a time our world stood still. Quite apart from our security, the shock impacted on economic confidence, on business, on trade and it is only now with the (115) terrorist network on the run, that confidence is really returning. Every nation in the world felt the reverberation of that fateful day. And that has been well illustrated by the role which the United Nations—under Kofi Annan's (120) excellent leadership—has played since September 11.

So if we didn't know it before, we know now: these events and our response to them shape the fate not of one nation but of one (125) world.

For America, it has laid bare the reality. American power affects the world fundamentally. It is there. It is real. It is never irrelevant. It can affect the world for good, or (130) for bad. Stand aside or engage; it never fails to affect.

You know I want it engaged. Under President Bush, I am confident it will be and for good. But if that's what I and many others (135) want, it comes at a price for us too. It means we don't shirk our responsibility. It means that when America is fighting for those values, then, however tough, we fight with her. No grandstanding, no offering implausible but (140) impractical advice from the comfort of the touchline, no wishing away the hard not the easy choices, but working together, side by side.

Prime Minister Tony Blair to the American (145) citizens following 9/11

15.   B
The best way for the speaker to get his audience on his side and listening to him is to appeal to those ideas with which the majority of the audience will

agree. This is exactly what Tony Blair has done in this speech. Therefore, (B) is the correct response.

16. E

To answer this question correctly, you must go through a process of elimination. Although almost every choice has some validity, the focus of Prime Minister Blair's speech is that we can no longer be independent nations, that as John Donne reminded us many years ago, "No man is an island." Blair extends this sentiment by implying that each "island" is a part of the whole, making (E) the correct response to this question.

17. C

Common sense and your composition skills should lead you to the correct response, (C). Each time a short one-sentence paragraph is injected into Blair's speech, it indicates a transition to the next point he intends to make.

18. D

Lines 79–80 assure us that utilitarian and utopian are not necessarily contrasting ideas but philosophies that can coexist. Choice (D) is correct.

19. A

Although you might be tempted to respond with one of the other answers to this question, the inclusion of "guts" and "awesome" are examples of informal diction—an unusual inclusion in a British politician's vocabulary, (A).

20. C

When the main, independent clause follows a series of introductory phrases and clauses, the syntactical structure is known as (C), periodic sentence.

21. E

In paragraph 14, *parenthetical statement* (A) is found between the dashes. *Hyperbole*, exaggeration for effect, (B), is present throughout the paragraph. *Metonymy*—figure of speech that uses the name of one thing to name or designate something else—is present in the reference to "terrorist network" and United Nations. *Personification* is present in that nations, per se, cannot really "feel" reverberations, a human feeling. Therefore, the correct response is (E), *conceit*. There is no extended metaphor in this speech.

22. A

Because of Blair's well-crafted appeal to the majority of his audience, embracing of the United States in times of trauma and its consequential girding of strength, repetition of key points, all manipulated by the syntactical structure of short and long sentences as well as short, terse paragraphs, (A), *pointedly powerful*, best describes the major effect of his speech.

23. D

In the finale of this speech, Prime Minister Blair returns to his appeal to the audience. He shifts to the pronoun *you* and intones the camaraderie between Britain and the United States. He appeals to the audience directly, making (D) the correct response.

24. D

"They were the best riposte to the terrorists that humanity could give" indicates a response, or in this case a retort (strong response), making (D) the correct response.

25. E

A *zeugma*, (E), is when two or more parts of a sentence utilize another part that is only stated once. In other words, these lines really say, "It can affect the world for good, *or it can affect the world* for bad." In other words, the phrase "it can affect the world" is assumed but not stated. None of the other devices are present in this paragraph.

26. A

It is difficult to tell exactly how Blair feels about what he says in these lines. Although we might think it is just a statement, the word *inflame* indicates a possible negative inference, but this is not clear. Therefore, (A), *ambiguous*, is correct.

27. D

This question is basically just a grammar question. The job of pronouns is to replace or rename a noun somewhere else in the sentence. In this case, the antecedent for the pronoun *it* is American power, (D).

28. D

Prime Minister Blair focuses heavily in his speech on interdependence. He advocates that we can no longer be independent nations, but instead need a united engagement of democratic values with other countries. This makes (D) the correct answer.

QUESTIONS 29–41

To a professional critic (I have been one myself) theatre-going is the curse of Adam. The play is the evil he is paid to endure in the sweat of his brow; and the sooner it is over, the
Line
(5) better. This would place him in irreconcilable opposition to the paying playgoer, from whose point of view the longer the play, the more entertainment he gets for his money. It does in fact so place him, especially in the provinces,
(10) where the playgoer goes to the theatre for the sake of the play solely, and insists so effectively on a certain number of hours' entertainment that touring managers are sometimes seriously embarrassed by the brevity of the London plays
(15) they have to deal in.

For in London the critics are reinforced by a considerable body of persons who go to the theatre as many others go to church, to display their best clothes and compare them
(20) with other people's; to be in the fashion, and to have something to talk about at dinner parties; to adore a pet performer; to pass the evening anywhere rather than home: in short, for any or every reason except interest in
(25) dramatic art as such. In fashionable centres the number of irreligious people who go to church, of unmusical people who go to concerts and operas, and of undramatic people who go to the theatre is so prodigious
(30) that sermons have been cut down to ten minutes and plays to two hours; and, even at that, congregations sit longing for the benediction and audiences for the final curtain, so that they may get away to the
(35) lunch or supper they really crave for, after arriving as late as (or later than) the hour of beginning can possibly be made for them.

Thus from the stalls and in the Press an atmosphere of hypocrisy spreads. Nobody says

(40) straight out that genuine drama is a tedious nuisance, and that to ask people to endure more than two hours of it (with two long intervals of relief) is an intolerable imposition. Nobody says "I hate classical tragedy and
(45) comedy as I hate sermons and symphonies; but I like police news and divorce news and any kind of dancing or decoration that has an aphrodisiac effect on me or on my wife or husband. And whatever superior people
(50) may pretend, I cannot associate pleasure with any sort of intellectual activity; and I don't believe anyone else can either." Such things are not said; yet nine-tenths of what is offered as criticism of the drama in the metropolitan
(55) Press of Europe and America is nothing but a muddled paraphrase of it. If it does not mean that, it means nothing.

I do not complain of this, though it complains very unreasonably of me. But I can
(60) take no more notice of it than Einstein of the people who are incapable of mathematics. I write in the classical manner for those who pay for admission to a theatre because they like classical comedy or tragedy for its own sake,
(65) and like it so much when it is good of its kind and well done that they tear themselves away from it with reluctance to catch the very latest train or omnibus that will take them home. Far from arriving late from an eight or half-past
(70) eight o'clock dinner so as to escape at least the first half-hour of the performance, they stand in queues outside the theatre doors for hours beforehand in bitingly cold weather to secure a seat. In countries where a play lasts a week,
(75) they bring baskets of provisions and sit it out. These are the patrons on whom I depend for my bread. I do not give them performances twelve hours long, because circumstances do not at present make such entertainments feasible; but
(80) an all-night sitting in a theatre would be at least

as enjoyable as an all-night sitting in the House of Commons, and much more useful.

(85) Still I am sorry for the pseudo-critics and the fashionable people whose playgoing is a hypocrisy. They forget, however, that all men are not as they are. I cannot for their sakes undo my work and help the people who hate the theatre to drive out the people who love it, yet I may point out to them that they have several remedies in (90) their own hands. They can escape the first part of the play by their usual practice of arriving late. They can escape the epilogue by not waiting for it. And if the irreducible minimum thus attained is still too painful, they can stay away altogether.

(95) But I deprecate this extreme course, because it is good neither for my pocket nor for their own soul. Already a few of them, noticing that what matters is not the absolute length of time occupied by a play, but the speed with which (100) that time passes, are discovering that the theatre, though purgatorial in its Aristotelian moments, is not necessarily always the dull place they have so often found it. What do its discomforts matter when the play makes us forget them?

(105) George Bernard Shaw: "To the Critics, Lest They Should Feel Ignored" from *Saint Joan* (1924)

29. C

Although all of the answers are mentioned in the passage, the *overall* message comes across as (C), a chastisement of the London public for their lack of imagination or artistic appreciation.

30. B

Shaw's tone is not always clear. Often he chastises, but overall his messages are mixed, making them somewhat ambiguous, (B).

31. D

Antithesis is contradiction—although there is a bit of that, it does not dominate paragraph 2. There are no examples of oxymoron, metaphor, or metonymy

in this paragraph. However, the comparison between dramatic presentation and church services, particularly the sermon, is definitely an *analogy*, (D).

32. E

Reading paragraph 3, you can find several of the responses present; however, the focus of the paragraph is Shaw's criticism of the public audiences "from the stalls" and the Press for not coming out and saying what they really feel. This is the point of the topic sentence and is supported within the paragraph, making (E) the correct choice.

33. A

Shaw seems to be most concerned with the idea that the public comes to the theater in droves only so they can see and be seen. In reality, the public is bored by theater and finds it tedious; nevertheless, they continue to attend so they can be seen in public. This fact makes (A) the correct answer for this question.

34. B

These lines are "I do not complain of this, though it complains very unreasonably of me. But I can take no more notice of it than Einstein of the people who are incapable of mathematics." The best interpretation of these sentences is that Shaw cannot do anything about the attitude of the public and their ignorance any more than Einstein can worry that math-challenged people will be unable to grasp the depth of his theories, (B).

35. E

Paragraph 4 basically says that despite all the fools who come to the theater, there are still a few theatergoers who make Shaw's work worth doing. This makes choice (E) the best response for this question.

36. A

Anaphora (A) is the correct answer—it is a series of phrases or clauses that begin with parallel openings. *Apostrophe* is an address to an inanimate object; *assonance* is the repetition of vowel sounds, usually in close proximity. *Ambiguity* has the ideas of multiple interpretations, and *asyndeton* is a series of phrases or clauses in succession without being connected by conjunctions.

37. C

Shaw says that sitting all night in the theater cannot be worse than sitting all night in the House of Commons. This indicates that Shaw does not have much admiration or affection toward the government and its institutions. That makes (C) correct.

38. B

Shaw's use of the phrase "irreducible minimum" is preceded by "They can appreciate the first part of the play by their usual practice of arriving late. They can escape the epilogue by not waiting for it." In other words, audiences need only spend the shortest time possible while attending a play. This makes (B) the best choice.

39. E

If people avoid the theater altogether, Shaw will lose money, and the audience will lose the opportunity to view plays. The other answers may be true but the specific lines do not convey those points. Therefore, (E) is the *best* response for the question.

40. E

References to *purgatory* and *Aristotle* are references to religion and to ancient philosophy. References to history, mythology, religion, etc. are all *allusions*. Therefore, (E) is correct.

41. B

Considering the passage as a whole, what Shaw is trying to say is that those who shun the theater, or those who attend it just for the social interaction, are missing something special. If given the opportunity, they might find theater worthwhile and actually rewarding. This makes (B) the correct response.

QUESTIONS 42–54

It is now many years ago, my children, when I was quite a young woman, and your father, Freddy, was less than you are at present, that

Line
(5) we lived in a village more than a hundred miles from here. It was a very pretty village, situated on the bank of a broad, beautiful stream, which added much to the fertility and loveliness of the whole country through which it passed. We had not always dwelt in so pretty a place; but your

(10) grandfather, thinking it would be better for his business, concluded to take up his abode there. About the time we removed, another family took a steerage passage in a vessel bound from Ireland to this country. There were seven of

(15) them altogether—the father, mother, and five children. Their home had hitherto been a cabin, with a mud floor. A Bible, an iron pot, and a few wooden stools constituted their furniture; while their fare consisted of the scanty supply of milk

(20) afforded by one ill-fed cow, with a few potatoes. Willing to labor, yet finding wages humbled so low that they were often obliged to go both weary and hungry to bed, they concluded, after many struggles, to leave kindred and friends and

(25) come to America. How often, when speaking of this unhappy country, is the sentence 'Why don't they emigrate?' uttered with the greatest indifference. But to a warm Irish heart, this is often a severe trial. They are taxed, we might

(30) almost say, for the very air they breathe; yet how fondly they still cling to the soil of that island home, where nature must smile in spite of oppression; where the dust of their kindred repose; where are more loving hearts and words

(35) of warmer greeting than are to be met with elsewhere. No wonder the Irishman loves his country, crushed, trampled upon as she is. Her soil is among the most fertile, her sons among

the noblest, and the language of even her rudest

(40) children the most poetical of any on earth. Oh, Ireland, fair Ireland, would we might yet live to see thee take thy proper place among the nations, to see the period approach when thy children will not be forced to seek in other countries the

(45) bare sustenance denied them at home. The Nevilles, after many struggles to obtain means sufficient to defray the expenses of a passage, and after borrowing from several neighbors small sums, which they promised to repay with

(50) interest, found themselves in the steerage of a vessel on their way to this land of promise. I will pass over the first few weeks of their arrival—strangers on a strange soil. Suffice it to say, that some one directed them to our village

(55) as a place where they could likely find steady employment. And here, one evening in early spring, cold, hungry, and penniless, they arrived. My husband, contrary to his usual custom, chanced to be abroad on that evening; and, as he

(60) was a devout believer in that blessed word which teaches that we may sometimes entertain angels unawares, on hearing the landlord refuse to keep them on account of their inability to pay, he brought them all home with him. I confess, I

(65) was taken a good deal by surprise at this unusual act; but, as it was his pleasure, I bade them welcome; and the heartfelt blessing which the poor strangers asked over the meal we prepared for them went far towards prepossessing me in

(70) their favor. The man, his wife, and the two little girls we accommodated in the house, while the three boys found lodgings among the fragrant hay in the well-stored mow. These people, my children, were not particularly attractive

(75) as far as appearance was concerned; they all appeared healthy and good-humored, and the little ones seemed uncommonly well-mannered for children in their rank of life; but still I was in some way unaccountably interested in

(80) them; and I have since thought God permitted this feeling in order that I might bestir myself in behalf of those who were undoubtedly his followers. At any rate, we were willing to accommodate them a few days until something

(85) could be done for them; and, at the expiration of that time, a quiet-looking little cottage, with a willow tree before the door, standing just across the brook, was procured for them. I parted with several articles of furniture I could spare,

(90) in order to assist them in fitting out their new home; and my efforts among my neighbors procured them many other gifts of the same description. And now how happy was Mrs. Neville. Her husband had steady employment

(95) given him on a farm near by; her two eldest boys, of the ages of twelve and thirteen, both obtained good places; while the youngest boy, with the little girls, aged ten, eight, and six, were kept at home, where they were generally as busy

(100) as bees, for their mother held idleness to be the parent of all evil. I have often, on going in, been struck with the picture of neatness and humbled contentment their small kitchen presented.

The furniture was of the coarsest and most

(105) common description, yet scrupulously neat and clean. Here the family were generally found, pursuing their evening avocations, seated before the quiet blaze of their own fireside; and truly, where its comforts are properly appreciated,

(110) there is nothing gives the heart a finer or more touching idea of enjoyment than this same calm, domestic light. Evening, too, is the period of time which may truly be called the poor man's season of enjoyment; the implements of

(115) daily labor are laid aside, and it is then he may rest his wearied limbs and enjoy the prattle and playful wiles of his children, whose caresses sometimes lead him to forget the bitterness of his lot. The Nevilles were poor, very poor;

(120) the money they had borrowed from friends in

Ireland, they had obligated themselves to
return, and they were straining every nerve to
accomplish this. It was ten months before they
were able, by their united labor, with practicing
(125) the most rigid self-denial, to realize this amount.
At length, however, the sum was raised; and a
benevolent gentleman inclosed and forwarded
it in such a manner as it would be sure to reach
its destination. They had, however, barely felt
(130) their minds relieved in this particular, when
Mr. Neville was laid upon a bed of sickness. He
had, perhaps, overworked himself and taken
cold. His disease was inflammatory rheumatism.
He lingered for a month, oftentimes suffering
(135) greatly; and then, after commending his wife
and little ones to the care of that God who is the
protector of the widow and the fatherless, strong
in the hope of a blissful immortality, he died.
As I told you before, my children, the Nevilles
(140) were pious people; and I could not but notice, in
their mode of expression, a degree of intellectual
refinement peculiar to those who make the Holy
Scriptures an habitual study.

   "You will observe, my children," said
(145) Mrs. Bruce, as she came to this portion of their
discourse, "the unwavering faith which this
poor woman possessed. She was a stranger
in a strange land; there was no one upon
whom she had any claim; yet I never heard
(150) her utter one repining word, or wonder how
she was to get along without the assistance
of her husband, there was so little selfishness
in her grief. And although tears must flow at
these sad sunderings of beloved ties, yet, when
(155) she did indulge in this outward exhibition of
distress, she would almost immediately dry
them, and give utterance to something which
would discover how entire and unchanging
was her trust in God. I was a great deal with
(160) her, and, I must say, after the last sad duties

were performed, I was astonished to see how
energetically she set to work in order to support
herself and her children. Her husband had often
told me that all the fortune his wife had brought
(165) him was her religion, her energy, and her steady
habits of industry, and that these had proved
the blessing of his life. Now, too, she found
ample exercise for these estimable qualities, and
it was surprising how she could turn her hand
(170) to anything that offered; and, indeed, with the
assistance the children were able to afford her,
they managed to live very comfortably."

   There, amid the far-stretching forests,
on a farm which in Europe might be called a
(175) principality, a wife and mother, she is spending
her days in the enjoyment of all that heart can
desire. I have now done with the history of
this family; yet I would have you observe how
fearlessly Christian parents may repose upon
(180) the strength of the promises of Him who holds
the hearts of all men in his hand. The skeptic
may laugh and the worldling may sneer, but
an appeal may confidently be made to those
who have noted the dealings of Providence as
(185) to whether any who have trusted in him have
been confounded.
   From *Godey's Lady's Book* (1850)

42.   E

If you look at these lines, you will find that they
include an address to Ireland, an *apostrophe*; a
paradox, or contradiction, in that people who
love their land still have to leave it; an *anaphora*,
repetition of opening phrases or clauses; and
personification of the home country. Therefore,
litote, (E), understatement, is the correct answer.

43.   D

Because the passage talks about how the Irish are so
torn about leaving the land they love and the land
that has brought them heartache, (D), is the correct
response to this question.

44. B

The first part of this passage contains all of the different kinds of sentences except the imperative—that is, a command or a directive, (B). Nowhere is there such a sentence within these lines.

45. A

The important word here is *initially*. You are to consider the very first impressions of the Neville family. No doubt they are devout in their religion/faith. In addition, after reading the description of their situation, it is easy to see they are penurious, that is, destitute. This makes (A) the correct response to this question.

46. B

The Nevilles are easy to understand. The narrator finds them fascinating, and despite her initial surprise at their presence in her house, she is impressed by their strong character. This makes (B) the correct response.

47. E

Phrases and clauses in a series that do not use any conjunctions are *asyndeton*, that is, without "syn" (together) conjunctions. These lines do not present any of the other choices, so (E) is the correct response to this question.

48. B

Air is yet to be taxed by any country. Therefore, this is an exaggeration. *Hyperbole*, (B), is an exaggeration used for stylistic effect. None of the other choices is appropriate for this question.

49. D

Rank in this situation has to do with socioeconomic level. Therefore, (D), the children of the poor, were expected to be less well mannered than those of more economically successful parents.

50. A

"To realize" comes from the sentence before that talks about how poor the Nevilles were; nevertheless, straining and practicing self-denial, they were able to *realize* the amount that the family owed back home.

Therefore, (A), *to amass* (collect/save), is the correct response.

51. C

The key to this entire section has to do with the word *although*. Basically, Mrs. Neville is saddened by her husband's death, but her faith in Providence keeps her strong. This makes (C) the correct choice for this question.

52. C

Mrs. Neville is easily characterized as being able to pick up and move forward. This makes (C) the best response for this question.

53. E

Repining in this case means to comment in a negative way. Therefore, (E) is the correct response for this question.

54. C

The reader is likely to be aware of the concept of a "ladies' book" written in the mid-1800s. Most of you will realize that this was an era in which piety and morals were highly valued. Although (D) may seem correct, the passage does not indicate that all families with hard-working matriarchs are happy. The author continually points to Mrs. Neville's unwavering faith in God despite hardships; therefore, (C) is the correct response.

ESSAY QUESTION ONE: POLITICAL CORRECTNESS

ANALYSIS OF QUESTION ONE

Students have a number of options available in what they may take from the source material provided and the direction they may wish to take in addressing the question itself. Given the fact that most teenagers have grown up in the age of political correctness, most students writing on this prompt will find it accessible, and most teenagers will definitely have an opinion.

As one looks at the sources, some more salient ideas bubble to the surface—the David Foster Wallace piece (Source A) makes a keen distinction that the dictates of politically correct speech conventions do not translate to politically correct attitudes. S. I. Hayakawa (Source B) offers the idea that usage and connotations of words like "bums" contribute to our attitude toward the groups identified. The excerpt from Nancy Mairs (Source C) is a startling rebuff of politically correct terminology in praise of claiming one's own "crippled" identity and condition. Insightful readers will draw from Mairs's referencing of George Orwell's "The Politics of the English Language." Source D offers the reference book rules on avoiding offensive language but is also careful to note the "ludicrous obfuscations" that may sometimes appear ("Snow White and the Seven Persons of Short Stature," for example). Essays that respond to this aspect of political correctness will have much to go on with the "Glossary of Banned Words" provided by Diane Ravitch (Source F). Source E, as the nontextual source, provides some concrete numbers that students could use for either argument—a slim majority of respondents seem to favor restrictions on offensive speech toward religious and ethnic groups. When it comes to offensive lyrics, however, a slim majority believe that this "politically incorrect" expression is allowable as a First Amendment right.

The important aspect of this sort of argument synthesis prompt is that you choose a position on the issue and use evidence that only supports your case. The Mairs piece (Source C), for example, would not be useful (and would have been egregiously misread) if a student held Mairs up as someone who used offensive terminology because she was politically incorrect and insensitive. Obviously, she's not ("I would never refer to another person as a cripple").

SCORING GUIDE FOR QUESTION ONE

9 Essays earning a score of 9 meet the criteria for essays that are scored an 8 and, in addition, are especially sophisticated in their argument and synthesis* of cited sources or impressive in their control of language.

8 Effective

Essays earning a score of 8 effectively take a position that defends, challenges, or qualifies the claim that the campaign to promote the usage of nonoffensive language and politically correct terminology has been a successful agent for positive change and increased sensitivity. They successfully support their position by capably synthesizing and citing at least three sources. The writer's argument is convincing, and the cited sources support the writer's position. The prose demonstrates an ability to control a wide range of the elements of effective writing but is not flawless.

7 Essays earning a score of 7 fit the description of essays that are scored a 6 but are distinguished by more complete or more purposeful argumentation and synthesis of cited sources or a more mature prose style.

6 Adequate

Essays earning a score of 6 adequately take a position that defends, challenges, or qualifies the claim that the campaign to promote the usage of nonoffensive language and politically correct terminology has been a successful agent for positive change and increased sensitivity. They adequately synthesize and cite at least three sources. The writer's argument is generally convincing, and the cited sources generally support the writer's position, but the argument is less developed or less cogent than in the essays earning higher scores. Though the language may contain lapses in diction or syntax, generally the prose is clear.

5 Essays earning a score of 5 take a position that defends, challenges, or qualifies the claim that the campaign to promote the usage of nonoffensive language and politically correct terminology has been a successful agent for positive change and increased sensitivity. They support their position by synthesizing at least three sources, but their arguments and their use of cited sources are somewhat limited, inconsistent, or uneven. The writer's argument is generally clear, and the sources generally support the writer's position, but the links between the sources and the argument may be strained. The writing may contain lapses in diction or syntax, but it usually conveys the writer's ideas adequately.

4 Inadequate

Essays earning a score of 4 inadequately take a position that defends, challenges, or qualifies the claim that the campaign to promote the usage of nonoffensive language and politically correct terminology has been a successful agent for positive change and increased sensitivity. They attempt to present an argument and support their position by synthesizing and citing at least two sources but may misunderstand, misrepresent, or oversimplify either their own argument or the cited sources they include. The link between the argument and the cited sources is weak. The prose of 4 essays may suggest immature control of writing.

3 Essays earning a score of 3 meet the criteria for the score of 4 but demonstrate less understanding of the cited sources, less success in developing their own position, or less control of writing.

2 Little Success

Essays earning a score of 2 demonstrate little success in taking a position that defends, challenges, or qualifies the claim that the campaign to promote the usage of nonoffensive language and politically correct terminology has been a successful agent for positive change and increased sensitivity. They may merely allude to knowledge gained from reading the sources rather than citing the sources themselves. These essays may misread the sources, fail to present an argument, or substitute a simpler task by merely responding to the question tangentially or by summarizing the sources. The prose of essays scored a 2 often demonstrates consistent weaknesses in writing, such as a lack of development or organization, grammatical problems, or a lack of control.

1   Essays earning a score of 1 meet the criteria for the score of 2 but are especially simplistic or weak in their control of writing or do not cite even one source.

0   Essays earning a score of zero (0) are on-topic responses that receive no credit, such as those that merely repeat the prompt.

–   Essays earning a dash (–) are blank responses or responses that are completely off topic.

*For the purposes of scoring, *synthesis* refers to combining the sources and the writer's position to form a cohesive, supported argument and accurately citing all sources.

STUDENT A'S RESPONSE TO QUESTION ONE

"The doorman, who spoke slowly and courteously in a Southern dialect, was especially deft in assisting differently abled residents to their taxis."

You wouldn't realize it by an initial glance, but the sentence above would be considered offensive according to a list compiled by Diane Ravitch. Words such as "doorman," "dialect," "differently abled" in the first sentence should not be used. Instead a more gender-neutral term such as "door attendant" is more appropriate. The less ethnocentric "language" (Southern language?) is more appropriate. The less offensive "person with a disability" is more appropriate. How do we know what language to use and when? How do we know for sure if we are offending others? How do we know if what we've always been taught to say is or is not the "correct terminology"?

In the above example, it is difficult to know sometimes what the current correct term is for a group or a person. But more often than not, we encounter situations where we do know what the acceptable term is. With all the concern for politically correct language, we should know the difference, and I think for the most part we do. But there are certain exceptions to any trend. Not everyone is on board. Not everyone thinks that thinking before speaking is such a big deal.

For the most part, there is quite a large amount of evidence that shows that people are much more careful in their speech patterns—especially when it comes to naming different cultural and ethnic groups. I know when we had a unit on Native American literature, my teacher Ms. Zimmerman actually stopped herself a number of times when she said "Indians" and corrected herself—"I mean, Native Americans." My question would be, was that really what she meant? Why doesn't she always say "Native Americans" the first time? What Ms. Zimmerman means to say and what she actually says may be two different things. She means not to be offensive, but as it turns out, sometimes she "slips" and says "Indian"—considered offensive by some. Ms. Zimmerman is a great example of someone who carefully considers her language. Her awareness and "heightened sensitivity in language is a statement of respect . . . and is a positive statement of rectifying the unequal social status between one group and another" (Source D). Native Americans have had a rough go of it since the Europeans landed, the least we can do is not give them an Asian misnomer.

On the other hand, people make the news when they use language that is largely considered inappropriate. In Chicago, former White Sox Manager Ozzie Guillen came under fire back in 2006 for comments directed at *Sun-Times* columnist Jay Mariotti. When the story broke, most news sources reported that Guillen, in one of his tirades, called Mariotti "an offensive term for homosexuals." For the entire week more editorials were written concerning Ozzie's insensitivity and apologies were demanded from gay and lesbian groups, and people were generally intolerant of a public figure such as Ozzie Guillen using an offensive term freely. This turned out to be a bigger story than the White Sox winning nine straight games at that time. This is certainly evidence that our overall level of tolerance of offensive terminology has changed, but still there is an offensive thought present here. Guillen used the term he did to strike at Mariotti's manliness. To call someone such a term is to emasculate him in print. The offensive connection is still there. No matter how many sensitivity training classes Guillen may take, he thinks that homosexuality is bad.

David Foster Wallace warns us that we should not confuse the functions of politically correct language—"usage conventions can function in two ways: On one hand they can be a reflection of political change, and on the other they can be an instrument of political change." In Guillen's case, his use of an offensive term reflected his political insensitivity. And what if Guillen ceases to use the offensive term because he is told to by Major League Baseball? Could such a mandate be the instrument of change? Wallace continues to say that the central fallacy of politically correct speech is the assumption that "a society's mode of expression is productive of its attitudes rather than a product of those attitudes." Politically correct language, it seems, may only mask real attitudes toward things. Perhaps it is better that we know where people really stand on issues of race, gender identity, and sexism rather than campaigning for labels.

As much as we may encourage politically correct speech, tolerance and acceptance and changing attitudes must precede terminology and language policing.

STUDENT B'S RESPONSE TO QUESTION ONE

In today's society, there is a lot more concern about the way we talk to each other. Because we try to use more inoffensive language, we definitely have become more sensitive to other groups.

"Usage is political, of course, but it's complexly political" (Source A). One should always remember that when using political language. When you see someone walking down the street and you're not sure what to call that person, you should just ask. Sometimes people might want to be called something you don't expect. Someone in a wheelchair might not want you to call them handicapped or disabled. "I am a cripple. I choose this word to name me" (Source C). In cases like this, it is often best to go with what they want, because it is what they want. You see, it's all political.

One thing many people understand about being careful with language is that some language is only allowed to be used by certain groups at certain times. "A 'within the group' rule often applies, which allows a member of the group to use terms freely that would be considered offensive if used by a nonmember of the group" (Source D). In my school we were talking about the use of the n-word in the book Huck Finn. But in the "Born to Trouble" video we watched, we saw comedians like Chris Rock and Bill Cosby use the term to get laughs. I would never use the term because I know how offensive it is.

There is also survey proof that people are much more concerned about the political correctness of the language they use. Over one-half (53%) of those responding to a survey said that speech offensive to racial groups should not be allowed (Source E). Half of those surveyed also said speech offensive to religious groups should not be allowed (Source E). So you see there is definitely a positive change happening.

So in using politically correct language, it's always important to call people what they want to be called, to understand that some language should only be used by certain groups, and that most people do try to say and do the right thing when it comes to political correctness.

COMMENTARY ON STUDENT RESPONSE A

This essay would score at least an 8. Student A's strength comes from her adept use of a personal example (Ms. Zimmerman) as well as an example that was in the news (Ozzie Guillen) to support her overall qualification of the claim that the campaign to promote politically correct speech has been a successful agent for positive change and increased sensitivity.

Student A opens with a unique strategy—using a seemingly benign sentence that is actually loaded with terms that would be considered politically incorrect. She raises the issue about how we sometimes don't know we're being offensive and then turns her focus toward times when we do. The use of the Diane Ravitch source is most important here—all the offensive terms she used were lifted right from the glossary of offensive terminology. Note also the nice repetition of "is more appropriate" as a kind of politically correct refrain.

Moving toward her two key examples, the student develops one situation with Ms. Zimmerman, who is very aware and careful of her speech—enough to correct herself when she thinks she "slips."

Student A also develops an example where a speaker uses an offensive term with offensive intent. Here is where the analysis gets more complex—with the help of David Foster Wallace's assertion. She synthesizes the Random House quote to show how Ms. Zimmerman is the careful language user. Guillen, in contrast, is the "loose cannon" using language indiscrim-inately but with incriminating consequences.

One key aspect of Student A's essay is that she chose to use the minimum three sources.

There may have been opportunity to use other sources in the course of this response, but she opted for quality of development rather than quantity of sources. Because of the sophistication of her argument, Student A may even earn a 9.

COMMENTARY ON STUDENT RESPONSE B

Compared to Student A's response, Student B's is rather simplistic and inadequate. He attempts to do all that is asked of the prompt—he even uses more sources than Student A—but there is insufficient development and a lack of control in Student B's prose. His essay would rate no higher than a 4 by an AP reader.

Fatal mistakes in Student B's prose begin with the worn-out "In today's society" opening (which reads like fingernails on a chalkboard). He also falters by beginning his first body paragraph by abruptly jumping right into a quote without providing any context. The student has difficulty seamlessly integrating quotes from other sources—most seem plopped down and forced into the conversation.

Student B is never able, it seems, to develop his ideas thoroughly in a cogent manner. The ideas are definitely there, but he limits himself to examples, not elaborating to convince a reader fully of his position. He seems limited to a simplified five-paragraph essay format—he fails to provide transitional elements between paragraphs, which makes for abrupt shifts.

The conclusion is an obvious rehashing of what has already been said. No "signature stamp" is given to defend or assert his position. Student B finishes with the same old same old.

ESSAY QUESTION TWO: OBSTETRICS

ANALYSIS OF QUESTION TWO

This is a very interesting and challenging passage from *For the Time Being* by Annie Dillard. It is intriguing because Dillard's description and reactions to the obstetrics ward seem almost blasphemous to the reader. The passage offers stimulating imagery and interesting word choice. If you are faced with a passage such as this, just take it for what is in front of you. Do not get upset or critical of the narrator's stance. You have been asked to deal with what is on the page—no more.

Student response to this passage is always interesting and varied. You will see that the two student samples, albeit overlapping in a couple of ideas, are also quite different.

SCORING GUIDE FOR QUESTION TWO

9 Essays meet all of the criteria for 8 papers and, in addition, are especially full or apt in their analysis or demonstrate particularly impressive composition skills.

8 Essays successfully analyze the rhetorical and stylistic strategies Annie Dillard employs to convey her attitude about newborns and the obstetrics ward. They refer to the passage directly or indirectly and explain convincingly how specific strategies, such as imagery, tone, and figurative language, contribute to an understanding of the writer's attitude. Their prose controls a wide range of effective writing but is not flawless.

7 Essays fit the description of 6 essays but employ more complete analysis or demonstrate a more mature prose style.

6 Essays adequately analyze how the stylistic devices Dillard employs in this passage reveal her attitude about the obstetrics ward and the newborns. They refer to the passage directly or indirectly, and they recognize the narrator's attitude and how she conveys it by utilizing strategies such as choice of detail, tone, or figurative language. A few lapses in diction or syntax may be present, but generally the prose of 6 essays is clear.

5 Essays analyze Dillard's rhetorical techniques, but the development of those techniques and how they reveal Dillard's attitude is limited or too simplistic. These essays may treat techniques superficially or develop ideas about the narrator's attitude inconsistently. A few lapses in diction or syntax may appear, but the prose in these essays usually conveys the writers' ideas adequately.

4 Essays inadequately respond to the task of the prompt. They may misrepresent Dillard's attitude or analyze rhetorical strategies inaccurately or with little understanding of how strategies reveal her attitude. Sometimes these writers will paraphrase and/or summarize more than analyze. Often the prose of these essays suggests immature control over organization, diction, or syntax.

3 Essays meet the same criteria as essays with a score of 4 but are less perceptive about how rhetorical strategies convey attitude or are less consistent in controlling the elements of writing.

2 Essays are unsuccessful in analyzing how stylistic strategies convey Dillard's attitude about the obstetrics ward and the newborns. These essays tend to pay little or cursory attention to the specific features, and they may generalize or simplify about attitude and tone. They may simply paraphrase or comment on the passage without analyzing technique. The prose of 2 papers often reveals consistent weaknesses in writing, such as a lack of development or organization, grammatical problems, or a lack of control.

1 Essays meet the criteria for the score of 2 but are especially simplistic in their discussion or weak in controlling elements of language.

STUDENT A'S RESPONSE TO QUESTION TWO

Childbirth and newborns have always been perceived as the miracle of life and a joy and privilege to every parent. Annie Dillard uses nurse Pat Eisberg and her job to show how all the joy of such a wonderful event is vanishing. Dillard uses a deliberate word choice to develop her tone to relate how childbirth and the immediate events following have become so efficient as to become an assembly line. Her attitude is one of regret. She laments our society's loss of wonder for the phenomenon of bringing new life into the world.

At the very beginning of the passage she sets the tone by comparing the babies to dishes. By saying that a nurse spends most of the eight-hour shift at the sink, she involves images of a factory worker mindlessly working at the cleaning station of an assembly line. In all that nurse Eisberg does, she demonstrates no emotion. Only a comment in a warm voice, "Now you" expresses her reaction to what she is doing. If anything it expresses the boredom and monotony of one who is stuck doing the same thing hour after hour, day after day. Dillard likens the boy's limbs to worms, implying that there is no tenderness or joy in this job. The nurse grabs one arm and deliberately turns him over. Again, no tenderness. The chosen method of turning him over is similar to the description one might use to describe handling a small dog or a large baby doll, or a newly caught fish with a dorsal fin.

In the sixth paragraph, she changes tactics a bit. She mentions Allah and the Qur'an. Here she mentions the creation of man from near nothing. The spiritual wonder of such a feat is soon canceled in the following sentence when she introduces the image of a clown twisting a few skinny balloons into a dog, a giraffe (or a child?). This seems to be Dillard's main tactic in this passage: just when she suggests the "miracle" she cancels it with an antithesis of the clown. By mentioning the clown and his balloons she belittles the creation—Allah's sacred breath becomes "lickety-split." Nothing is sacred on this obstetrics ward. It's just another job in another type of factory. After Eisberg finishes washing the babies, they are left on the counter until someone comes to collect them, one at a time. The coldness of this assembly line process reminds me of the clinical, matter-of fact tone of *Brave New World*.

Even in wrapping the babies there is standardization. Do it correctly and the child is restrained and kept warm. Throughout the piece, the wrapped child is compared to a Thermos. The comparison emphasizes the idea of mass production of an object, with most feelings gone. Even with the parents, their reaction seems automatic, not heartfelt. They "involuntarily" say "hi!" It seems an impulse, not an act of love.

Throughout the piece, Annie Dillard's use of diction and the nurse Pat Eisberg's (iceberg's?) actions show that the production of children and their subsequent care have lost the tenderness, and possibly the love, we would expect in exchange for the cold, mass-produced assembly line. The magic of the process has been replaced by the tedium of the job.

STUDENT B's RESPONSE TO QUESTION TWO

In this passage, Annie Dillard conveys a slightly disturbed attitude towards her experience in an obstetrical ward. She sees the process of cleaning the newly-born children as almost industrial, and uses diction, antithesis and imagery to effectively convey her opinions.

When describing the process of washing the infant, Dillard opts for cold, scientific words regarding the baby's anatomy. Words such as dorsal and anus are most certainly not what one would expect to describe the fragility and innocence of infants. Dillard also compares the child's newly severed umbilical cord to a jumper cable. This in addition to her previously mentioned word choices, creates a factory-like atmosphere. This creation of a "birthing factory" very clearly conveys Dillard's view of American obstetrics as cold and uncaring.

Dillard's view of Americans is also conveyed in the ninth paragraph through her use of antithesis. She states, "Americans place infants on their backs now. . . lest they choke and die." Dillard, throughout the passage, seems to view the events as not only an observer, but an outsider. Through this statement we can infer that some of her sense of isolation may come from the fact that she is possibly a foreigner. Through her use of antithesis, one can examine her confusion over American practices and their swiftly changing nature.

Much of the mood in this passage is set up by the visuals Dillard creates. In the first sentence of the first paragraph, a sterile metal sink is described as the common kitchen variety. These cold images are carried throughout the passage. Examples include the reference to the jumper cable in paragraph 4 and the "wormy" limbs in paragraph 5. Even the reference to Allah and humankind's divine origins is quickly demeaned by something as trite as a clown's balloon animals. The final image in the passage, one of a blasé nurse, brings about the realization that the sterility seen in the sinks and equipment has transcended to the people who work with the infants.

Dillard's view of this event as an outsider definitely increased her awareness of the situation, and through this she effectively conveys her views through her word choice, rhetorical devices, and imagery.

COMMENTARY ON STUDENT RESPONSE A

Without a doubt, this student has successfully understood the prompt, read and understood the passage, and written a strong composition. This writer has a good vocabulary and uses it well. In addition, the examples from the passage he has chosen to include are ample and apt.

The focus of this response is actually the antithesis of Allah and the clown. This is the crux of the problem, as this student rightly sees it. Birth is no longer something special. It's just another day of work in the obstetrics factory—wormy limbs, dorsal fins, clowns, and all.

The student has identified the iceberg nurse accurately, and it is her attitude that seems to pervade the entire nursery. The reference to *Brave New World* is apt, and with more time, this might have been an interesting analogy to pursue.

This is a very well-written essay. Errors are minimal. Yes, it is five paragraphs, but nowhere do you have the feeling of an essay written on an assembly line. The ideas flow between the paragraphs, and excellent composition skills are demonstrated.

No doubt this response will receive many 8s from readers. Perhaps some may think it needs a bit more bulk and give it a 7. However, given the limited time and the tightness of the essay, this is a very successful response to a challenging question.

COMMENTARY ON STUDENT RESPONSE B

This is an adequate analysis of Annie Dillard's passage. This student cites many different aspects of the essay in support of what she says. However, it is not as successful as Student Response A, and this is a good pair for you to look at.

Response B includes many of the same concepts mentioned in A, such as the lack of emotion, factory-like nature, mechanical handling of the newborns, and others. However, it is easy to see that the first response is better written; there is a tightness to it.

You would not necessarily be graded down because of the misconception of Annie Dillard's being an outsider or perhaps a foreigner. The misunderstanding of the comments about whether babies should be placed on their backs or on their stomachs is included mostly to remind us how the "rules" that govern child rearing are constantly changing. This student is not too sure about the meaning of this. Notice, however, Response A doesn't mention it at all. Such a minor misunderstanding won't gravely affect one's grade, but to have made such a point of this paragraph, and then do so incorrectly, is going to affect the score somewhat.

Overall, this is an acceptable response to the Annie Dillard question. It would be scored a 6. A few readers might be disturbed enough about the multiple inaccuracies found in paragraph 3 that they might award this response a 5.

No doubt, however, this student understands the task of the prompt and most of the passage and has responded with an adequate composition.

ESSAY QUESTION THREE: THOREAU

ANALYSIS OF QUESTION THREE

This passage is, of course, from Thoreau's *Walden*. It is readily accessible, although some find it less than exciting to read and "get into." However, those who give it a chance will find that Thoreau's wonderful language and rich imagery offer an easy passage to respond to.

SCORING GUIDE FOR QUESTION THREE

9   Essays meet all of the criteria for 8 papers and, in addition, are especially full or apt in their analysis or demonstrate particularly impressive composition skills.

8   Essays successfully analyze the rhetorical and stylistic strategies Thoreau employs to convey his attitude about nature and the onset of spring. They refer to the passage directly or indirectly and explain convincingly how specific strategies, such as imagery, tone, and figurative language, contribute to an understanding of the writer's attitude. Their prose controls a wide range of effective writing but is not flawless.

7   Essays fit the description of 6 essays but employ more complete analysis or demonstrate a more mature prose style.

6   Essays adequately analyze how the stylistic devices Thoreau employs in his passage reveal his attitude about nature and springtime. They refer to the passage directly or indirectly, and they recognize the narrator's attitude and how he conveys it by utilizing strategies such as choice of detail, tone, or figurative language. A few lapses in diction or syntax may be present, but generally the prose of 6 essays is clear.

5   Essays analyze Thoreau's rhetorical techniques, but the development of those techniques and of the understanding of Thoreau's attitude is limited or too simplistic. These essays may treat techniques superficially or develop ideas about the narrator's attitude inconsistently. A few lapses in diction or syntax may appear, but the prose in these essays usually conveys the writers' ideas adequately.

4   Essays inadequately respond to the task of the prompt. They may misrepresent Thoreau's attitude or analyze rhetorical strategies inaccurately or with little understanding of how strategies reveal his attitude. Often the prose of these essays suggests immature control over organization, diction, or syntax.

3   Essays meet the criteria for the score of 4 but are less perceptive about how rhetorical strategies convey attitude or are less consistent in controlling the elements of writing.

2   Essays are unsuccessful in analyzing how stylistic strategies convey Thoreau's attitude about spring. These essays tend to pay little or cursory attention to the specific features, and they may generalize or simplify about attitude and tone. They may simply paraphrase or comment on the passage without analyzing technique. The prose of 2 papers often reveals

consistent weaknesses in writing, such as a lack of development or organization, grammatical problems, or a lack of control.

1 Essays meet the criteria for the score of 2 but are especially simplistic in their discussion or weak in controlling elements of language.

STUDENT A's RESPONSE TO QUESTION THREE

Thoreau uses devices such as imagery, diction, and anaphora to convey his awe of nature and his happy and contented attitude.

The speaker in this passage is euphoric at the dawn of springtime. He sees a "graceful" and "beautiful" hawk soar through the air and he feels that everything in the world is connected. He asks, "or was its native nest made in the angle of a cloud . . . from the earth?" (lines 18–20). All at once the speaker feels like Nature's kindred spirit and he begins to feel, see, and understand the true beauty of nature. He sees "a rare mess of golden and silver and bright cupreous fishes" (line 21). He notices that Nature is life and death, and in that way all things are immortal. He realizes that "Poison is not poisonous after all, nor are any wounds fatal" (lines 49–50). Suddenly it all falls into place for the narrator: Nature is important to us because it is us, and we are nature.

Thoreau expresses his journey to this realization with a succession of images. He uses similes and metaphors to help the reader see what he sees. The hawk "sported" in the "fields of air," "turning over and over like a kite." The reader has a clear image of this playful hawk, as well as the fishes "which looked like a strand of jewels." Likewise, the reader can see "tadpoles which herons gobble up, and tortoises and toads run over in the road, and [it seems] that sometimes it has rained flesh and blood." But the death is as much a part of nature as the beautiful life. All is one, and the narrator challenges: "death where is thy victory now?"

The reader is able to feel these effects through the pace of the passage as well. As the speaker becomes more engrossed in the actions of the hawk, his tone becomes more animated and the narrator starts to use words in pairs, as if to emphasize the glory he sees and the excitement he feels. The hawk mounts the air "again and again" and turns "over and over." At the climax of the passage, the speaker jumps "from hummock to hummock, from willow root to willow root," and the author feels the energy and the warmth of the bright sunlight. The pace slows when the speaker contemplates death's role in nature. However, this is not because of sadness or regret but to emphasize to us that because we are one with nature, we have nothing to fear.

The author successfully conveys his blissful tone and opinions of nature to the reader through vivid imagery, very connotative diction, and other stylistic devices. He "refreshes" the reader with his account of the "inexhaustible vigor" of nature.

STUDENT B'S RESPONSE TO QUESTION THREE

Thoreau uses various methods to express his awe with nature. His tone is somewhat poetic in the middle of the passage. He describes the Merlin's (hawk's) wings as "satin ribbons in the sun" and "the pearly inside of a shell." He also states that he does not care about the name of the animal. He is so awestruck by simply how it looks and flies through the air that nothing else matters. He even describes how, though the bird is alone, it is not lonely, but the world is lonely beneath it. He implies that the hawk is so divine that without its presence the earth is incomplete.

In the second paragraph Thoreau begins by describing a school of fish in a river. When he sees the meadow beyond the river, he tells of how the sunlight on it "would have waked the dead." He says that anything in such a light has to be immortal, and he challenges death with a hypothetical question: "Oh Death where was thy sting? O grave, where was thy victory then?" He is completely enveloped in the greatness of nature and describes it again (like the bird in paragraph one) as if it is completely above his world. In nature's cycle things constantly die and are reborn, so in reality there is no death.

In the final paragraph the author brings forth the point that people need nature to be beyond their realm of thinking. Finally completing his description, he describes it as though nature were not as it is, the world would cease to spin on its axis! People need to see the beauty of nature in order to live.

Thoreau brings the passage to a close by telling about the beauty of the cycle of the environment. He is overjoyed to see that the carcasses of dead animals still fuel the whole of nature and sustain life, which sets the readers up for his ending statement: "Poison is not Poison after all. . . ." He is completely fulfilled to see that the death of great beasts is never a waste in such an environment.

COMMENTARY ON STUDENT RESPONSE A

This essay is very well executed. Not only does it demonstrate all the characteristics of a strong writer, it also demonstrates an excellent understanding of both the task of the prompt and the passage being analyzed.

The introduction is brief and to the point. It shows no special insight, but nevertheless it permits the writer to move right to her points. In fact, the first body paragraph is the controlling point of the entire passage: the epiphany of the narrator understanding that man and nature are one and that there is hope to be had in this—although not everything is alive and vibrant, even death is a part of the vibrancy.

In her next paragraph, she explores the animated imagery of the passage. The essay provides numerous examples of these images, explaining them where necessary. The following paragraph discusses the syntax of the passage. The writer has cleverly connected the syntax with the nearly effervescent tone of the passage. There is no doubt that Thoreau is deliriously excited by the coming of spring; this student has captured the essence of this with her mention of specific details and pace, and she brings good examples in for support.

Finally, the conclusion ties it all together. If the introduction had been longer, the conclusion may have seemed like only an echo of the beginning. Here, however, the writer has managed to pull together all the ideas developed in the passage. Readers no doubt would award this essay a score of 8.

COMMENTARY ON STUDENT RESPONSE B

This student has some great ideas and insights. Although many of the comments are very accurate, this writer does not go into detail about any of the specific stylistic devices that the writer uses.

Many of the references to style are implied; however, the specific examples are quite apt and numerous. The student no doubt has a good grasp on the significance of the passage and the task of the prompt. This is one of those responses that needs a rewrite. Unfortunately, however, there are no such opportunities on this AP exam.

Too much is told without being shown directly through examples.

This student clearly has a handle on the task at hand. Unfortunately, he was unable to pull enough together to earn an upper-half score. This response is on target for the understanding of the passage but less than successful with the presentation. Because of the limited development of specific ideas and scarcity of examples, this essay would most likely earn the score of 5.

HOW TO MAKE THIS BOOK WORK FOR YOU BASED ON THE RESULTS OF YOUR DIAGNOSTIC

Your score on the Diagnostic will go a long way toward helping you perform well by helping you identify areas in which you need further study. The answer explanations for questions you got wrong can steer you to specific chapters of this book on which you should focus or to specific areas of literature in which you show weakness. To score well on the AP exam, you'll need to do your homework. Don't just skim over what you read; try to apply it to other contexts and to connect it to what you already know.

Part Three

THE AP ENGLISH LANGUAGE AND COMPOSITION EXAM

CHAPTER 3: KEY TERMINOLOGY

IF YOU LEARN ONLY TWO THINGS IN THIS CHAPTER . . .

1. Learn the key terminology and use it in your free-response essays.

2. The more familiar you are with the terms on this list, the better prepared you will be on Test Day.

INTRODUCTION

Every academic subject has a vocabulary that describes and identifies its inherent substance. You will be expected to apply that vocabulary to any piece of writing presented in the AP English Language and Composition exam.

On the following pages are the most common terms you have to face on the AP English Language and Composition exam. You should be able to use some of this terminology—correctly of course!—as you describe the writing within the passages that you must read and write about on the essay questions.

KEY TERMS

Review unfamiliar terms. Notice how many language terms are also used to describe aspects of literature. That's because they have to do with an author's writing style. In addition, the AP English Language and Composition exam has terminology that is specific to rhetoric and argument.

As you begin to see some of these terms appear, especially in multiple-choice questions, do not hesitate to refer to this list for clarification. The more you use it, the more familiar the terms will become. Many examples are given within the definitions to help you commit the terms to memory.

USING KEY TERMINOLOGY

Know how to apply these terms appropriately in your essay writing. Just presenting a bunch of terms without relating them appropriately is never successful.

Allegory—a narrative in which the characters, behavior, and even the setting demonstrate multiple levels of meaning and significance. Often allegory is a universal symbol or personified abstraction, such as Cupid portrayed as a chubby angel with a bow and arrows.

Alliteration—the sequential repetition of a similar initial sound, usually applied to consonants, usually in closely proximate stressed syllables. For instance, "She sells seashells by the seashore."

Allusion—a literary, historical, religious, or mythological reference. For example, one might contrast the life and tribulations of Frederick Douglass to the trials of Job.

Anaphora—the regular repetition of the same words or phrases at the beginning of successive phrases or clauses. The following is an example: "To raise a happy, healthful, and hopeful child, it takes a family; it takes teachers; it takes clergy; it takes businesspeople; it takes community leaders; it takes those who protect our health and safety; it takes all of us." (Hillary Clinton, Democratic National Convention Address, 1996)

Antithesis—the juxtaposition of sharply contrasting ideas in balanced or parallel words, phrases, grammatical structure, or ideas. For example, Alexander Pope reminds us that "to err is human, to forgive divine."

Aphorism—a concise statement designed to make a point or illustrate a commonly held belief. For example, "Spare the rod and spoil the child" is an aphorism.

Apostrophe—the act of addressing some inanimate abstraction or person that is not physically present: It often helps the speaker to be able to express his or her thoughts aloud. For instance, King Lear intones, "Ingratitude! Thou marble-hearted fiend, more hideous when thou show'st thee in a child than the sea-monster." In this example, ingratitude is a personified concept; by addressing the abstract, Lear commands a significant rhetorical power.

Appeals to . . . authority, emotion, or logic—rhetorical arguments in which the speaker claims to be an authority or expert in a field, attempts to play upon the emotions, or appeals to the use of reason. Classically trained rhetoricians identify these appeals with their Greek names: *ethos* is authority, *pathos* is emotion, and *logos* is logic.

Assonance—the repetition of identical or similar vowel sounds, usually in successive or proximate words. The alliteration example also demonstrates assonance: "She sells seashells by the seashore."

Asyndeton—a syntactical structure in which conjunctions are omitted in a series, usually producing more rapid prose. For example: "*Veni, vidi, vici*" (I came, I saw, I conquered), supposedly said by Julius Caesar.

Attitude—the sense expressed by the tone of voice or the mood of a piece of writing; the author's feelings toward his or her subject, characters, events, or theme. It might even be his or her feelings for the reader. AP English exam essay prompts often require students to respond to some aspect of the attitude of the writer, speaker, or narrator.

Begging the question—an argumentative ploy where the arguer sidesteps the question or the conflict, evading or ignoring the real question.

Canon—that which has been accepted as authentic, such as in canon law, or the "Canon According to the Theories of Einstein."

Chiasmus—a figure of speech and generally a syntactical structure wherein the order of the terms in the first half of a parallel clause is reversed in the second. For example, "He thinks I am but a fool. A fool, perhaps I am."

Claim—in argumentation, an assertion of something as fact.

Colloquial—a term identifying the diction of the common, ordinary folks, especially in a specific region or area. For instance, most people expect Southerners to use the colloquial expression "y'all" to engage the attention of a group of people. In some parts of the United States, a Coke® is a product of the Coca-Cola Company, while in other parts of the country, "coke" means any type of carbonated beverage. Other people refer to such beverages as "pop" or "soda pop." These are all colloquial terms for the drink.

Comparison and contrast—a mode of discourse in which two or more things are compared, contrasted, or both. On one English Language exam, students were asked to contrast two marriage proposals taken from literature, analyzing them for the use the narrators made of rhetorical devices and their argumentative success.

Conceit—a comparison of two unlikely things that is drawn out within a piece of literature, in particular an extended metaphor within a poem. However, conceits can also be used in non-fiction and prose. For instance, Richard Selzer's passage "The Knife" compares the preparation and actions of surgery to preparing for and conducting a religious service or a sacred ritual.

Connotation—the implied, suggested, or underlying meaning of a word or phrase. It is the opposite of denotation, which is the "dictionary definition" of the word.

Consonance—the repetition of two or more consonants with a change in the intervening vowels, such as in pitter-patter, splish-splash, and click-clack. Consonance is not be confused with alliteration, the repeated consonant sound at the beginning of a word.

Convention—an accepted manner, model, or tradition; for instance, Aristotle's conventions of tragedy.

Critique—an assessment or analysis of something, such as a passage of writing, for the purpose of determining what it is, what its limitations are, and how it conforms to the standard of the genre.

Deductive reasoning (deduction)—the method of argument in which specific statements and conclusions are drawn from general principles; movement from the general to the specific, in contrast to inductive reasoning (induction).

Dialect—the language and speech idiosyncrasies of a specific area, region, or group. For example, Minnesotans say "you betcha" when they agree with you. Southerners refer to the gathering of folks as "y'all." Although dialect is most often found in fiction, sometimes it is evident in speeches from a different era or from a different culture.

Diction—the specific word choice an author uses to persuade or convey tone, purpose, or effect. A past English Language exam included Adlai Stevenson's famous "Cat Bill" veto addressed to the Illinois State Senate. Cats roaming without leashes constituted "feline delinquency," and irritated citizen reactions were referred to as "small game hunts by zealous citizens." On the AP exam, you must relate how a writer's diction, combined with syntax, figurative language, literary devices, etc., all come together to become the author's style.

Didactic—(from the Greek, meaning "good teaching") writing or speech is didactic when it has an instructive purpose or a lesson. It is often associated with a dry, pompous presentation, regardless of its innate value to the reader/listener. Some of Aesop's fables are didactic in that they contain an underlying moral or social message.

Elegy—a poem or prose work that laments, or meditates upon the death of, a person or persons. Sometimes an elegy will end with words of consolation. Many public elegies were presented in the aftermath of Hurricane Katrina.

Epistrophe—in rhetoric, the repetition of a phrase at the end of successive sentences. For example: "If women are healthy and educated, their families will flourish. If women are free from violence, their families will flourish. If women have a chance to work . . . their families will flourish" (Hillary Clinton, October 1, 1995).

Epitaph—writing in praise of a dead person, most often inscribed upon a headstone.

Ethos—in rhetoric, the appeal of a text to the credibility and character of the speaker, writer, or narrator. (Who is this person saying so, and what makes him able to say so?)

Eulogy—a speech or written passage in praise of a person; an oration in honor of a deceased person. Elegy laments; eulogy praises. Many eulogies are spoken in honor of the brave firefighters who heroically risk their lives while saving the lives of others.

Euphemism—an indirect, kinder, or less harsh or hurtful way of expressing unpleasant information. For instance, it is much nicer for a person who has just been given a pink slip to hear that she has been made redundant rather than she has hereby been terminated.

Exposition—writing that explains its own meaning or purpose.

Extended metaphor—a series of comparisons within a piece of writing. If they consistently involve one concept, this is also known as a conceit.

Figurative language/figure of speech—figurative (in contrast to literal) language has levels of meaning expressed through figures of speech such as personification, metaphor, hyperbole, irony, oxymoron, litote, and others.

Flashback—(also known as retrospection) an earlier event is inserted into the normal chronology of the narration.

Genre—a type or class of literature, such as epic, narrative, poetry, biography, history.

Homily—a sermon, but more contemporary uses include any serious talk, speech, or lecture involving moral or spiritual life. John Donne was known for his homilies, among other things.

Hyperbole—overstatement characterized by exaggerated language, usually to make a point or draw attention. If you are hungry and say, "I'm starving," that is hyperbole.

Imagery—broadly defined, any sensory detail or evocation in a work; more narrowly, the use of figurative language to evoke a feeling, to call to mind an idea, or to describe an object. Basically, imagery involves any or all of the five senses. A writer generally uses imagery in conjunction with other figures of speech, such as simile and metaphor. "Her cheeks were rosy and so was my love—bursting with fragrance and softness." Here metaphor is used with the images of rosy cheeks (the visual color) and the smell and feel of roses.

Imperative sentence: A type of sentence that gives instructions, advice, or commands.

Inductive reasoning (induction)—the method of reasoning or argument in which general statements and conclusions are drawn from specific principles; movement from the specific to the general. In other words, a general supposition is made after investigating specific instances, a common logic used in scientific study. See deductive reasoning.

Inference—a conclusion or proposition arrived at by considering facts, observations, or some other specific data. It is through inference—looking at the clues, learning the facts—that Sherlock Holmes was able to solve the crimes.

Irony (ironic)—the contrast between what is stated explicitly and what is really meant. The intended meaning is often the opposite of what is stated, often suggesting light sarcasm. The most famous classical ironist is Jonathan Swift, who wrote "A Modest Proposal." Irony is used for many reasons, often to create poignancy or humor. There are three major types of irony:

Verbal irony—what the author/narrator says is actually the opposite of what is meant.

Situational irony—when events end up the opposite of what is expected.

Dramatic irony—in drama and fiction, facts or situations are known to the reader or audience but not to the characters.

Isocolon—parallel structure in which the parallel elements are similar not only in grammatical structure but also in length. For example, the Biblical admonition "Many are called, but few are chosen" is an isocolon.

Jargon—specialized or technical language of a trade, profession, or similar group. The computer industry, for example, has introduced much jargon into our vocabulary, such as *geek, crash, down, interface, delete, virus,* and *bug.*

Juxtaposition—the location of one thing adjacent to or juxtaposed with another to create an effect, reveal an attitude, or accomplish some other purpose.

Litote—a figure of speech that emphasizes its subject by conscious understatement; for instance, the understated "not bad" as a comment about something especially well done. George Orwell wrote, "Last week I saw a woman flayed and you would hardly believe how much it altered her person for the worse."

Loose sentence—(a term from syntax) a long sentence that starts with its main clause, which is followed by several dependent clauses and modifying phrases; for example, "The child ran, frenzied and ignoring all hazards, as if being chased by demons."

Metaphor—one thing pictured as if it were something else, suggesting a likeness or analogy. Metaphor is an implicit comparison or identification of one thing with another, without the use of a verbal signal such as *like* or *as,* which is a simile. Shakespeare's Romeo says, "It is the east and Juliet is the sun," directly comparing Juliet to the sun. Sometimes the term *metaphor* is used as a general term for any figure of speech.

Metonymy—a figure of speech in which an attribute or commonly associated feature is used to name or designate something, as in "Buckingham Palace announced today . . ."

Mode of discourse—the way in which information is presented in written or spoken form. The Greeks believed there were only four modes of discourse: narration, description, exposition, and argumentation. Contemporary thought often includes other modes, such as personal observation and narrative reflection.

Mood—a feeling or ambience resulting from the tone of a piece as well as the writer/narrator's attitude and point of view. It is a "feeling" that establishes the atmosphere in a work of literature or other discourse.

Narrative—a mode of discourse that tells a story of some sort. It is based on sequences of connected events, usually presented in a straightforward, chronological framework.

Onomatopoeia—a word capturing or approximating the sound of what it describes; *buzz* is a good example. The purpose of these words is to make a passage more effective for the reader or listener; for example, "Becca *whacked* the ball over the fence and took her time walking the bases."

Oxymoron—a figure of speech that combines two apparently contradictory elements, as in "wise fool," "baggy tights," or "deafening silence."

Paradox—a statement that seems contradictory but is probably true. A popular paradox from the 1960s was that war protesters would "fight for peace."

Parallel structure—the use of similar forms in writing for nouns, verbs, phrases, or thoughts; for example, "Jane enjoys read*ing*, writ*ing*, and ski*ing*." In prose, this is the parallel, recurrent syntactical similarity where several parts of a sentence or several sentences are expressed alike to show that their ideas are equal in importance. *A Tale of Two Cities* opens with "It was the best of times, it was the worst of times, it was the age of wisdom, it was the age of foolishness. . . ."

Pathos—that element in literature that stimulates pity or sorrow. In argument or persuasion, it tends to be the evocation of pity from the reader/listener. Think of it as the "poor starving children" approach to convincing you.

Periodic sentence—a long sentence in which the main clause is not completed until the end; for example, "Looking as if she were being chased by demons, ignoring all hazards, the child ran," or "The child, who looked as if she were being chased by demons, frenzied and ignoring all hazards, ran."

Personification—treating an abstraction or nonhuman object as if it were a person by endowing it with human features or qualities. William Wordsworth speaks of the stars "tossing their heads in sprightly dance." An example from a prose speech is: "Once again the heart of America is heavy. The spirit of America weeps for a tragedy that denies the very meaning of our land" (Lyndon B. Johnson).

Point of view—the relation in which a narrator/author stands to a subject of discourse. Determining point of view in nonfiction requires the reader to establish the historical perspective of what is being said.

Prose—the ordinary form of written language without metrical structure, in contrast to verse and poetry.

Realism—attempting to describe nature and life without idealization and with attention to detail. Mark Twain is an author of this school. Thoreau, with his romantic outlook toward nature, is not.

Rebuttal/refutation—an argument technique wherein opposing arguments are anticipated and countered.

Rhetoric—the art of using words to persuade in writing or speaking. All types of writing may seek to persuade, and rhetoricians study writing for its persuasive qualities.

Rhetorical question—a question that is asked simply for the sake of stylistic effect and is not expected to be answered.

Sarcasm—a form of verbal irony in which apparent praise is actually critical. Sarcasm can be light and gently poke fun at something, or it can be harsh, caustic, and mean.

Satire—a literary work that holds up human failings to ridicule and censure. Jonathan Swift and George Orwell were masters of satire. Several years ago, the AP English Language and Composition exam included a satirical piece by columnist Ellen Goodman, "The Company Man," a satire attacking the struggle for corporate survival by the little man. Arthur Miller exposes the same subject in his tragic play *Death of a Salesman*.

Simile—a direct, explicit comparison of one thing to another, usually using the words *like* or *as* to draw the connection. For instance, Charles Dickens wrote: "There was a steamy mist in all the hollows, and it had roared in its forlornness up the hill *like* an evil spirit."

Style—the manner in which a writer combines and arranges words, shapes ideas, and utilizes syntax and structure. It is the distinctive manner of expression that represents that author's typical writing style. This is often queried on the AP English Language and Composition exam. In particular, when two passages on the same topic are presented, you must pay the most attention to comparing their styles.

Symbolism—use of a person, place, thing, event, or pattern that figuratively represents or "stands for" something else. Often the thing or idea represented is more abstract or general than the symbol, which is concrete. Everyone recognizes the symbol of the golden arches representing McDonald's™ restaurants.

Synecdoche—a figure of speech in which a part signifies the whole, such as "50 *masts*" representing 50 ships, or "100 *head* [of steer] had to be moved to their grazing land."

Syntax—the way words are put together to form phrases, clauses, and sentences. Syntax is sentence structure and how it influences the way the reader receives a particular piece of writing. It is important in establishing the tone of a piece and the attitude of the author/narrator. See loose sentence, parallel structure, and periodic sentence.

Theme—the central or dominant idea or focus of a work; the statement a passage makes about its subject.

Tone—the attitude the narrator/writer takes toward a subject and theme; the tenor of a piece of writing based on particular stylistic devices employed by the writer. Tone reflects the narrator/author's attitude.

Voice—the acknowledged or unacknowledged source of the words of the story; the speaker's or narrator's particular "take" on an idea based on a particular passage and how all the elements of the style of the piece come together to express his or her feelings.

Zeugma—a grammatically correct construction in which a word, usually a verb or adjective, is applied to two or more nouns without being repeated. Often used to comic effect ("the thief *took my wallet* and the Fifth Avenue *bus*").

APPLYING KEY TERMINOLOGY

The following passage is followed by several questions not unlike those in the multiple-choice section of the AP English Language and Composition exam.

The following passage was written (on the last night of 1849) by Florence Nightingale. She was not only a pioneer in the profession of nursing but also one of the first European women to travel into Egypt (1849–50) and keep a detailed journal of her letters and reflections of her journey.

My Dear People,

Yes, I think your imagination has hardly followed me through the place where I have been spending the last night of the old year. Did you listen to it passing away and think of me? Where do you think I heard it sigh out its soul? In the dim unearthly colonnades of

Line
(5) Karnak, which stood and watched it, motionless, silent, and awful, as they had done for thousands of years, to whom, no doubt, thousands of years seem but as a day. Would that I could call up Karnak before your eyes for one moment, but it "is beyond expression."

No one could trust themselves with their imagination alone there. Gigantic shadows spring upon every side; "the dead are stirred up for thee to meet thee at thy coming, even

(10) the chief ones of the earth," and they look out from among the columns, and you feel as terror-stricken to be there, miserable intruder, among these mighty dead, as if you had awakened the angel of the Last Day. Imagine six columns on either side, of which the last is almost out of sight, though they stand very near each other, while you look up to the stars from between them, as you would from a deep narrow gorge in the Alps, and then,

(15) passing through 160 of these, ranged in eight aisles on either side, the end choked up with heaps of rubbish, this rubbish consisting of stones twenty and thirty feet long, so that it looks like a mountain fallen to ruin, not a temple. How art thou fallen from heaven, oh Lucifer, son of the morning! He did exalt his throne above the stars of God; for I looked through a colonnade, and under the roof saw the deep blue sky and star shining brightly;

(20) and as you look upon these mighty ruins, a voice seems continually saying to you, And seekest thou good things for thyself? Seek them not, for is there ought like this ruin? One wonders that people come back from Egypt and live lives as they did before.

Yet Karnak by starlight is not to me painful: we had seen Luxor in the sunshine. I had expected the temples of Thebes to be solemn, but Luxor was fearful. Rows of painted

(25) columns, propylae, colossi, and—built up in the Holy Place—mud [not even huts, but] unroofed enclosures chalked out, or rather mudded out, for families, with their one oven and broken earthen vessel; and, squatting on the ground among the painted hieroglyphs, creatures with large nose-rings, the children's eyes streaming with matter, on which the mothers let the flies rest, because "it is good for them," without an attempt to drive them off;

(30) tattooed men on the ground, with camels feeding out of their laps, and nothing but a few doura stalks strewed for their beds;—I cannot describe the impression it makes: it is as if one were steering towards the sun, the glorious Eastern sun, arrayed in its golden clouds, and

were to find, on nearing it, that it were full—instead of glorified beings as one expected—of a race of dwarf cannibals, stained with blood and dressed in bones. The contrast could not
(35) be more terrible than the savages of the Present in the temples of the Past at Luxor.

But Karnak by starlight is peace; not peace and joy, but peace—solemn peace. You feel like spirits revisiting your former world, strange and fallen to ruins; but it has done its work, and there is nothing agonizing about it. Egypt should have no sun and no day, no human beings. It should always be seen in solitude and by night; one eternal night it should have,
(40) like Job's, and let the stars of the twilight be its lamps; neither let it see the dawning of the day.

1. The mode of discourse that best describes this passage is

    (A) exposition.
    (B) description.
    (C) argumentation.
    (D) comparison/contrast.
    (E) personal reflection and narration.

Answer (B)

Although there are certain elements of exposition and personal reflection, the predominant mode of discourse of this passage is that of description. Nightingale is telling her readers, the recipients of her letter, what she has seen and felt.

2. Because this is a letter sent to faraway recipients, the questions posed in paragraph 1 can be described as

    (A) useless.
    (B) imperative.
    (C) interrogative.
    (D) rhetorical.
    (E) redundant.

Answer (D)

Rhetorical questions are those asked by a speaker or writer strictly for stylistic purposes—often bringing focus or emphasis to a particular idea. The writer/speaker does not expect such questions to be answered.

3. This passage relies upon the writer's appeal to the reader's reaction to

    (A) logic.
    (B) authority.
    (C) emotion.
    (D) humor.
    (E) sarcasm.

Answer (C)
Florence Nightingale is appealing to her readers to react emotionally to her vivid descriptions.

4. In paragraph 2, references to the angel of the Last Day, line 12, and to
    Lucifer, line 18, are a stylistic device known as

    (A) oxymoron.
    (B) onomatopoeia.
    (C) metaphor.
    (D) exaggeration.
    (E) allusion.

Answer (E)
An allusion is a reference to a literary, historical, religious, or mythological reference. In this case, the reference is to Judgment Day and to the fallen archangel Lucifer.

5. The six columns on either side mentioned by the writer are described using
    a comparison that is known as

    (A) contrast.
    (B) simile.
    (C) metaphor.
    (D) antithesis.
    (E) juxtaposition.

Answer (B)
The columns are compared to the Alps, and the phrase "as you would from . . ." indicates that this is a simile, a comparison using *like* or *as*.

6. The writer describes Karnak awaiting the dawning of a new year by using
    the stylistic device of

    (A) metaphor.
    (B) simile.
    (C) personification.
    (D) imagery.
    (E) diction.

Answer (C)
Although you might argue that metaphor and imagery would work for this response, the AP exam is always looking for the most exact response. Consequently, (C), personification, is the most accurate response. Karnak seems to come alive as it stands motionless and silent, waiting for the advent of a new year.

7. The fact that the writer is more comfortable "seeing" Karnak in the dark is
   an example of

   (A) situational irony.

   (B) verbal irony.

   (C) dramatic irony.

   (D) juxtaposition.

   (E) antithesis.

Answer (A)

Situational irony is a contrast between what is expected and what really happens. In this case, it is truly ironic that the writer is most comfortable "seeing" a place in the dark in contrast to the bright light of day.

8. ". . . ranged in eight aisles on either side, the end choked up with heaps of
   rubbish," lines 15–16, utilizes the stylistic device known as

   (A) allusion.

   (B) onomatopoeia.

   (C) anaphora.

   (D) alliteration.

   (E) assonance.

Answer (E)

Assonance is the repetition of identical or similar vowel sounds, usually in successive or proximate words. You can hear the assonance: "r*a*nged in *ei*ght" and "*ai*sles on *ei*ther s*i*de"

9. Paragraph 2 (lines 8–22) contains all of the following stylistic devices
   EXCEPT

   (A) simile.

   (B) apostrophe.

   (C) allusion.

   (D) rhetorical question.

   (E) hyperbole.

Answer (B)

This paragraph contains a couple of similes, comparisons using *like* or *as*. It has an allusion to the Old Testament with the mention of Lucifer, and it uses a couple of questions for stylistic effect. Finally, although the ruins are gargantuan, it is an exaggeration to compare them to a fallen mountain.

10. Nightingale contrasts her reaction to the beauties of Karnak with the horrors of

    (A) London streets at night.
    (B) the alleys of Cairo at midnight.
    (C) Luxor in the daylight.
    (D) Egypt by moonlight.
    (E) the Last Day of judgment.

Answer (C)
Lines 23–35 describe the horrors that Nightingale had experienced during an earlier daytime trip to Luxor.

Multiple-choice sections that accompany reading passages rarely have this many questions asking about specific key terminology. Nevertheless, this should give you an idea of the types of questions you might be asked among the 50–55 questions on your AP exam.

CHAPTER 4: READING FOR UNDERSTANDING

IF YOU LEARN ONLY THREE THINGS IN THIS CHAPTER . . .

1. Learn to read critically. This will prepare you to analyze your writing.

2. Apply the How-What approach to the passage you are reading.

3. Annotate as you go so that you have an idea of the things you need to be seeing and thinking about as you go along.

INTRODUCTION

Much of your exam score—for both the multiple-choice passages and the free-response (essay) passages—will be earned through your ability as a reader. You will find information specific to reading passages for multiple-choice questions and for essays later in this book. This chapter is an overview of reading for understanding.

You will see later how the multiple-choice questions and essay prompts not only expect you to understand what is being said in a passage, but also require you to understand the author's purpose, tone, attitude, style, use of structure, and many other things.

DON'T FORGET

Successful reading on the AP English Language and Composition exam requires you to decode everything that goes into a piece of writing and subsequently synthesize it as required for an essay.

READING CRITICALLY

Careful, close reading of a text is the first stage in writing an essay that responds to or builds upon the ideas in the original source. Sometimes, this process referred to as "reader response" writing. This reading goes beyond merely extracting facts from the original text. It prepares you to analyze it critically through your own writing.

Such a close reading process involves the following steps:

1. ANNOTATE AS YOU READ.

With a pencil or pen in hand, read through the text quickly but do not just skim it. Highlight key words, phrases, or ideas that strike you as unusual or important. Note how the writer goes about providing details and significant information.

2. READ FOR TOPIC, SCOPE, PURPOSE, AND MAIN IDEA.

After reading the text, consider the author's position. What do you interpret as the main points of the passage, and how does the author arrive at a conclusion? If the passage is an argument, follow the logic to ensure that you are correctly interpreting what the author is saying, and be sure that the passage is indeed logical.

3. EVALUATE THE AUTHOR'S EFFECTIVENESS.

Having deciphered the author's meaning, do you agree or disagree? What questions do you still have? Go back to the passage and see if the answers are still there to be discovered. What about the passage is convincing or not convincing? Have you begun to establish an internal dialogue about the passage as you engage the text more closely?

4. ORGANIZE.

Now that you have examined the text and extracted what you can from it, you should be ready to organize and present your interpretation and/or evaluation of it. Go to your notes and any annotations you have made. Review the information and details that you found particularly engaging. If you agree with the author's argument, how can you extend it and, perhaps, relate it to more global issues? If you disagree, be sure you have sound reasons and details to support your position. You might even consider how the author could have improved his or her stance within the passage. Double-check to make sure you are not misrepresenting the author's intention or manipulating information to fit your interpretation. Remember, you are responding to, not summarizing, the original text.

5. SELECT.

Unless you have unlimited time, you probably have to pick and choose things to write about. Under timed conditions, it is rare to cover everything. Be discerning and ready to synthesize ideas and do not be afraid to think outside the box.

Needless to say, mastering this level of reading does not come easily to most people. It is a painstaking process that needs to start slowly and long before the day of the AP English Language and Composition exam. Remember that nothing in a well-written passage happens by accident.

THE HOW-WHAT APPROACH

When reading a passage to which you must quickly respond, in particular with a written response of your own, a good strategy is the How-What approach.

How does the author or narrator indicate his or her attitude, purpose, and intent? Is there a slant or a bias you can discover? Are things obvious or implied? Is this passage meant to purely entertain, or inform, or persuade?

What is the main idea? Can you summarize it in a couple of sentences? Can you identify an underlying thesis or purpose of the passage? When you aren't pressed for time, it is helpful to actually write down this purpose or focus in a couple of sentences.

What underlying structure does this passage rely on? What is presented first or last? Might this be significant? Does the passage use repetition or other stylistic or rhetorical devices that are a part of the underlying structure of the piece?

How does the author or narrator create an effect on the reader? Is there a difference between the intended effect and the actual effect? Is this disparity important to the passage?

What are the author's qualifications on the topic of the passage? Is this important to the passage or not?

How can you best recognize/identify the necessary information?

The first thing you generally do when you read a passage is to consider the opening. How does the author, or how does the opening, catch your attention or direct you to read further? Can you make a judgment from the opening about the tone or attitude of the writer/narrator? What major points are you immediately aware of from reading the opening?

You should be aware of any particular stylistic devices the author has employed to make a point. Is the passage rife with images, for instance, or does it offer a cold, clinical presentation? These are all things you must become aware of as you read the multiple-choice or essay passages on the AP English Language and Composition exam.

DON'T FORGET

When you read the body of a passage, pay particular attention to the connotations of words and nuances of the tone words the author has chosen and how they are presented. Is the author's/narrator's attitude detectable from the diction or tone?

KEY POINT

In addition to words, as you read, you also want to be aware of individual sentences, groups of sentences, and paragraphs. Just how is the passage put together? What makes it work (or not work, as the case may be)?

Finally, you must not overlook the conclusion of a passage. Sometimes most of what you need to know can be gleaned from the last paragraph or last several sentences of a passage. Successful writing tends to have a summarizing quality at the end of a passage. It is this quality that evokes satisfaction from the reader. However, rarely will a well-written passage merely reiterate what has already been said. Instead, a successful writer will give the reader a bit extra. That's what makes a piece meaningful. Often successful closings will not hold up out of context. They need the entire piece to provide them with significance.

Take a look at the following passage, a reproduction of Abraham Lincoln's "Second Inaugural Address," given one month before the end of the Civil War. It is the shortest presidential inaugural address ever given. This address appeared as a passage in one of the essays on a past AP English Language and Composition exam.

At this second appearing to take the oath of the Presidential office there is less occasion for an extended address than there was at the first. Then, a statement somewhat in detail of a course to be pursued seemed fitting and proper. Now, at the expiration of four years, during which public declarations have been constantly called forth on every point and phase of the great contest which still absorbs the attention and engrosses the energies of the nation, little that is new would be presented. The progress of our arms, upon which all else chiefly depends, is as well known to the public as to myself, and it is, I trust, reasonably satisfactory and encouraging to all. With high hope for the future, no prediction in regard to it is ventured.

On the occasion corresponding to this four years ago all thoughts were anxiously directed to an impending civil war. All dreaded it, all sought to avert it. While the inaugural address was being delivered from this place, devoted altogether to *saving* the Union without war, urgent agents were in the city seeking to *destroy* it without war—seeking to dissolve the Union and divide effects by negotiation. Both parties deprecated war, but one of them would *make* war rather than let the nation survive, and the other would *accept* war rather than let it perish, and the war came.

One-eighth of the whole population were colored slaves, not distributed generally over the Union, but localized in the southern part of it. These slaves constituted a peculiar and powerful interest. All knew that this interest was somehow the cause of the war. To strengthen, perpetuate, and extend this interest was the object for which the insurgents would rend the Union, even by war; while the Government claimed no right to do more than to restrict the territorial enlargement of it. Neither party expected for the war the magnitude or the duration which it has already attained. Neither anticipated that the *cause* of the conflict might cease with or even before the conflict itself should cease. Each looked for an easier triumph, and a result less fundamental and astounding. Both read the same Bible and pray to the same God, and each invokes His aid against the other. It may seem strange that any men should dare to ask a just God's assistance in wringing their bread from the sweat of other men's faces, but let us judge not, that we be not judged. The prayers of both could not be answered. That of neither has been answered fully. The Almighty has His own purposes. "Woe unto the world because of offenses; for it must needs be that offenses come, but woe to that man by whom offense cometh." If we shall suppose that American slavery is one of those offenses which, in the providence of God, must needs come, but which, having continued through His appointed time, He now wills to remove, and that He gives to both North and South this terrible war as the woe due to those by whom the offense came, shall we discern therein any departure from those divine attributes which the believers in a living God always ascribe to Him? Fondly do we hope, fervently do we pray, that this mighty scourge of war may speedily pass away. Yet, if God wills that it continue until all the wealth piled by the bondsman's two hundred and fifty years of unrequited toil shall be sunk, and until every drop of blood drawn with the lash shall be paid by another drawn with the sword, as was said three thousand years ago, so still it must be said "the judgments of the Lord are true and righteous altogether."

With malice toward none, with charity for all, with firmness in the right as God gives us to see the right, let us strive on to finish the work we are in, to bind up the nation's wounds, to care for him who shall have borne the battle and for his widow and his orphan, to do all which may achieve and cherish a just and lasting peace among ourselves and with all nations.

(March 4, 1865)

APPLYING THE HOW-WHAT APPROACH

Go through the questions methodically, and mark the passage to help you keep track of your answers.

WHAT IS LINCOLN'S MAIN IDEA?

They must bind up the nation's wounds and work together as a union to make amends and move forward with a minimum of recrimination from either side.

HOW DOES HE DO IT?

Lincoln appeals to the common decency of both sides. He assures them that neither shall be held at fault and that the nation cannot move forward without both.

WHAT IS THE UNDERLYING STRUCTURE?

He begins by recalling his inauguration of four years ago and the imminence of disaster that loomed. The North and the South, each believing it had justice on its side, consequently moved forward. Lincoln highlights a few things in the middle of his speech, including the subject of slavery, but notice how he always returns to the commonality of both sides—for instance, both sides reading the same Bible and believing in the same God, both suffering losses, both leaving loved ones behind. He builds up to his brilliant conclusion, his fervent appeal to all: "With malice toward none and charity for all."

HOW DOES THE NARRATOR CREATE AN EFFECT?

Lincoln mostly appeals to mankind's common feelings of doing the right thing and wanting the horror and waste to be over. Without dwelling on particular details, Lincoln refers to the horrors of the war and the damage—the numbers lost and the morale destroyed, both for those fighting and for the bereft back home. He reminds his audience that both sides read the same Bible and believed in what they were doing. He takes special pains to not point the finger of blame at anyone. All listeners would have felt cared about as a result of hearing this speech. Not only does it persuade listeners to go along with him, but it also lauds them for all that they have done or endured.

WHAT ARE HIS QUALIFICATIONS?

Not all answers are this easy. This was the onset of a second term for this president. Not only had he been deemed an outstanding leader, but he was also an intelligent person who had studied much and seemed to know about the basic psychology of the masses.

HOW CAN YOU BEST IDENTIFY THE MOST PERTINENT INFORMATION?

Luckily for us, Lincoln was a good statesman. He knew how to appeal to the people's better conscience by appealing to the common man in us all. He is straightforward with his words, and he pulls no punches. The challenge is to uncover within the simplicity of his lines and his words the great depth and richness of what he says.

SAMPLE ANNOTATIONS

Look at the following annotations; yours should look fairly similar. Critics and historians have spent decades studying every nuance of this speech. Some of the most obvious points have been noted here. Hopefully, you found these and others as well.

tells us it will be short

At this second appearing to take the oath of the Presidential office there is <u>less</u> occasion for an extended address than there was at the first. Then, a statement somewhat in detail of a course to be pursued seemed fitting and proper. Now, at the expiration of four years, during which public declarations have been constantly called forth on every point and phase of the <u>great contest</u> which still absorbs the attention and <u>engrosses the energies</u> of the nation, little that is new would be presented. The progress of our arms, upon which all else chiefly depends, is as well known to the public as to myself, and it is, I trust, reasonably satisfactory and encouraging to all. With high hope for the future, no prediction in regard to it is ventured.

That was then, this is now

euphemism/ understatement

nice phrase

inevitable end

1st inaugural

On <u>the occasion corresponding to this</u> four years ago all thoughts were anxiously directed to an impending civil war. <u>All dreaded it, all sought to avert it.</u> While the inaugural address was being delivered from this place, devoted altogether to *saving* the Union without war, urgent agents were in the city seeking to *destroy* it without war—seeking to dissolve the Union and divide effects by negotiation. Both parties deprecated war, but one of them would *make* war rather than let the nation survive, and the other would *accept* war rather than let it perish, and the war came.

parallelism

Everyone dreaded it; no one wanted it, but one side would make war

One-eighth of the whole population were colored slaves, not distributed generally over the Union, but localized in the southern part of it. <u>These slaves constituted a peculiar and powerful interest.</u> All knew that this interest was somehow the cause of the war. To strengthen, perpetuate, and extend this interest was the object for which the insurgents would rend the Union, even by war; while the Government claimed no right to do more than to restrict the territorial enlargement of it. (Neither) party expected for the war the magnitude or the duration which it has already attained. (Neither) anticipated that the *cause* of the conflict might cease with or even before the conflict itself should cease. (Each) looked for an easier triumph, and a result less fundamental and astounding. (Both) read the same Bible and pray to the same God, and each invokes His aid against the other. It may seem strange that any men should dare to ask a just God's assistance in wringing their bread from the sweat of other men's faces, but let us judge not, that we be not judged. <u>The prayers of both could not be</u>

clunky-sounding

separate

together

archaic language

answered. <u>That of neither has been answered fully.</u> The Almighty has His own purposes. "(Woe) unto the world because of offenses; for it must (needs be) that offenses come, but woe to that man by whom offense (cometh.)" If we shall suppose that American slavery is one of those offenses which, in the providence of God, must needs come, but which, having continued through His appointed time, He now wills to remove, and that He gives to both North and South this terrible war as the woe due to those by whom the offense came, shall we discern therein any departure from those divine attributes which the believers in a living God always ascribe to Him? Fondly do we hope, fervently do we pray, that this mighty scourge of war may speedily pass away. Yet, if God wills that it continue until all the wealth piled by the bondsman's two hundred and fifty years of unrequited toil shall be sunk, and until every drop of blood drawn with the lash shall be paid by another drawn with the sword, as was said three thousand years ago, so still it must be said "the <u>judgments of the Lord</u> are true and righteous altogether."

this will pass— nation move forward together

much use of religious reference; compare Obama's inaugural?

(With) malice toward none, (with) charity for all, (with) firmness in the right as God gives us to see the right, let us strive on to finish the work we are in, to bind up the nation's wounds, to care for him who shall have borne the battle and for his widow and his orphan, to do all which may <u>achieve and cherish</u> a just and lasting peace among ourselves and with all nations.

parallel—anaphc

similar sounds

(March 4, 1865)

While most of the notation has to do with the What of the passage, some of the marks and comments relate to the How.

Some quick conclusions are obvious: Lincoln used a lot of parallelism—yes, it makes good copy, but more importantly, he was trying to align two antagonistic parts of the country. How better than to use parallelism in his speech as well? A very strong religious sense pervades this speech. Perhaps today's audiences would object to such a thing, but Lincoln held strong religious beliefs in common with the vast majority of the nation's citizens. Of course, the United States at the time of the Civil War was a much different country from what it is today. Concepts of God and religion were strong influences on our forebearers and the shaping of the nation, and to understand what they were saying and doing, we have to be mindful of the context in which they spoke and acted.

This should give you an idea of the things you need to be seeing and thinking about as you read. What you see here is the beginning of a "dialogue" between you and the passage. As mentioned before, close reading skills are not developed overnight. This is something you must work on long before your AP English Language and Composition exam.

CHAPTER 5: THE MULTIPLE-CHOICE SECTION

IF YOU LEARN ONLY THREE THINGS IN THIS CHAPTER . . .

1. The multiple-choice section consists of four or five passages, each followed by a set of questions.

2. Remember Kaplan's multiple-choice question attack plan:
   - Read critically.
   - Know what the question asks.
   - Predict an answer.
   - Read every answer choice.
   - Find the best answer.

3. Know the different question categories in advance of the exam—it can boost your confidence and test-taking speed.

ABOUT THE MULTIPLE-CHOICE SECTION

The multiple-choice section of the AP English Language and Composition exam consists of four or five passages each, followed by a set of questions. On this exam, the passages will be prose of some sort—perhaps fiction but more likely from essays, letters, journals, diaries, biographies, speeches, or government documents. Several might be persuasive or argumentative.

You will not have time to do an in-depth analysis of a passage on the multiple-choice section. Remember, you have 12 to 15 minutes per passage and question set.

If you are unsure of an answer, mark your book and return to that question (if you have time) before you start reading the next passage. If you have no idea of the answer—you are totally clueless—guess and move on. Work with what you know and what you think you know. You are *not* expected to know all the answers.

DON'T FORGET

On the multiple-choice section of the test, you will have to read for meaning and use your close analysis and annotation habits, circling, underlining, and evaluating as you read. Then you will need to attack the questions, returning to the passage for the information you need to answer each one.

KEY STRATEGY

The best strategy for preparing for this section is to have a *specific reading plan* for the questions and passages and to familiarize yourself with the categories *and types of questions* you will face.

READING THE QUESTIONS

Earlier, you got a look at "Reading for Understanding." Now, let's apply that information specifically to test Section I, the multiple-choice questions.

QUESTIONS OR PASSAGE FIRST

Many debate the comparative wisdom of skimming the questions before reading the passage or quickly reading the passage first and then tackling the questions. That is something that you will have to decide for yourself.

If you are a slow reader, you may not have enough time to look at the questions first. You may have to eliminate that step. On the other hand, some students find that skimming the questions helps them to focus better when they read, so their reading time is actually shorter. While you practice the multiple-choice section in this book, try it both ways and decide what works best for you.

READ CRITICALLY

Whether you read the passage first or second, read actively and critically; that is, mark key words and ideas.

READ CRITICALLY

Whether you read the passage first or second, read actively and critically; that is, mark key words and ideas.

KNOW WHAT THE QUESTION ASKS

Read the question stem carefully. Sometimes it helps to mark that as well, to help you to decide just what it is you are being asked.

PREDICT AN ANSWER

Try to formulate the answer in your mind before you look at the choices given.

READ EVERY ANSWER CHOICE

Next, read every answer choice, even if the correct response jumps out at you right away. It is not unusual to have more than one acceptable answer but only one *best* answer.

DON'T WASTE TIME ON HARD QUESTIONS

If you have no clue about a question, guess and move on to the next one. If you just need a bit of time to "work it out," mark it in the book and move on. Return questions to any you have marked proceeding on to the next passage. If you are pushing the time limit (an average of 12 minutes per passage for five passages, 15 minutes per passage for four passages), go on to the next passage and return at the end of the multiple-choice section.

READ THE EXPLANATIONS AND LOOK FOR PATTERNS

On practice sets, review your performance. Can you detect a pattern to your errors? If so, what do you need to do? What types of questions are you missing? Try to refurbish those shaky areas.

IMPORTANT

Think like the test maker. One very valuable activity you can do in preparation for the AP English Language and Composition exam is to create your own multiple-choice questions based on passages you find in your textbook or other sources. You might even want to work with a partner, swapping questions with each other to test your skills.

THE TYPES OF QUESTIONS

AP English Language and Composition exam multiple-choice questions are surprisingly predictable. They fall into only a few categories, with a variety of approaches within each category. Once you are familiar with the basic types of questions, you will find your confidence growing and your response speed increasing. Because the multiple-choice section of the exam makes up 45 percent of your AP English Language and Composition exam score, conquering multiple-choice questions is essential for your success.

QUESTION CATEGORIES

The categories are as follows:

- The main idea/theme/attitude
- The author's meaning and purpose (Why did the writer. . . ?)
- The language of rhetoric (syntax, diction, figurative language, tone, etc.)
- The speaker or narrator
- The attitude (of the narrator or of the author)
- Word choice and selection of details (connotation)
- Sentence structure (syntax)
- Rhetorical reasoning
- Inferences
- General conclusions
- Organization and structure (Is there contrast, deduction, spatial description, etc.?)
- Rhetorical modes (narration, description, argumentation, etc.)
- Documentation and citation

MAIN IDEA

Questions about the passage's main idea are very common on the exam. Often, the first or last questions of a series have to do with the main idea. What is the author saying? Can you restate it? That's what you need to do, at least in your mind. You might have to make a few marginal notes, or you may find the main idea stated in one or two lines that you can underline. You will want to mark this somehow. Work on developing an annotation code that works for you.

TESTING THE MAIN IDEA

The main idea is tested by a variety of question stems:

The author would most likely agree with which of the following?

The narrator's/writer's/author's/speaker's attitude can be best described as . . .

The author would most/least likely agree that . . .

The writer has presented all of the following ideas EXCEPT . . .

We can infer that the author values the quality of . . .

The attitude of the narrator helps the writer create a mood of . . .

In context, lines _____ most likely refer to . . .

RHETORIC

Questions about rhetoric dominate the AP English Language and Composition exam. How does the language work in a passage? What is the point of view or the syntax and diction? How does the author express his or her tone? What is the narrator's attitude? These are not words to be thrown around recklessly. You need to understand how all of the elements synthesize to make the entire passage. How does each "rhetorical device" affect the whole?

SPOTTING RHETORIC QUESTIONS

Rhetoric questions appear in a variety of different forms:

A shift in point of view is demonstrated by . . .

The repetitive syntax of lines _____ serves to . . .

"_____" can best be said to represent . . .

The second sentence is unified by the writer's use of which rhetorical device?

The word "___" is the antecedent for . . .

The style of the passage can best be characterized as . . .

The author employs _____ sentence structure to establish . . .

The tone of the passage changes when the writer . . .

MEANING AND PURPOSE

Multiple-choice questions often ask about meaning and purpose. What is the purpose of the passage? How does it fit a meaning? Why was it written? Because so many of the passages on the English Language and Composition exam are taken from nonfiction speeches, letters, autobiographies, and essays, the author typically had a very strong reason for writing the passage. Usually, you can discover meaning by looking at the connotations of the author's words.

You will have to determine how or why the specific word choice demonstrates the author's thematic intention(s).

SPOTTING MEANING AND PURPOSE QUESTIONS

These questions also take a variety of forms:

"_____" can best be defined as . . .

The purpose of lines _____ can best be interpreted as . . .

The writer clarifies "_____" by . . .

The writer emphasizes "_____" in order to . . .

By saying "_____," the author intends for us to understand that . . .

By "_____," the author most likely means . . .

The purpose of the sentence/paragraph/passage can best be summarized as . . .

The passage can be interpreted as meaning all of the following EXCEPT . . .

STRUCTURE AND ORGANIZATION

How has the author organized the passage? Is there a consistency or a planned inconsistency that should be noted? Is this an argument? If so, is it deductive or inductive? Is this a personal observation? How is the information presented? Although not many structure and organization questions appear in the multiple-choice section of the exam, you need to know what to expect when you are faced with one.

SPOTTING STRUCTURE AND ORGANIZATION QUESTIONS

Some sample forms for structure and organization questions are:

The shift from "___" to "____" is seen by the author's use of . . .

In presenting the author's point, the passage utilizes all of the following EXCEPT . . .

The speaker has included "____" in her argument in order to . . .

The type of argument employed by the author is most similar to which of the following?

The passage can be said to move from "___" to "____."

The "___" paragraph can be said to be ___ in relation to "___."

The structure of this passage is primarily one of . . .

RHETORICAL MODES

Only a few questions about modes are on the test. A mode (rhetorical mode, mode of discourse) simply means what type of writing the author has used. Is it description, narration, argumentation, comparison and contrast, etc.? Sometimes understanding the author's choice of mode helps us to understand the author's purpose in writing.

SPOTTING RHETORICAL MODE QUESTIONS

These questions may appear in the following forms:

All of the following modes can be found within the passage EXCEPT . . .

The rhetorical mode that best describes this passage is . . .

The author uses cause and effect in order to . . .

Which of the following best describes the author's method of presenting the information?

The author combines retrospection with which other rhetorical mode within this passage?

DOCUMENTATION AND CITATION

At least one reading passage in the multiple-choice section of the AP English Language and Composition exam will be excerpted from a scholarly journal article, magazine article, or book that has used extensive documentation and citation of sources.

You will be expected to understand what is learned from reading and tracing these in-text citations. Because the English Language and Composition exam is increasingly trying to simulate the types of reading and writing you will do in college, the developers of the exam (which include freshman writing program directors) see great value in students' ability to understand the function and purpose of finding, synthesizing, and citing appropriate sources, as well as formal bibliography.

You can breathe a sigh of relief because the exam will not require you to memorize any of the various styles of documentation (APA, MLA, Chicago, etc.). However, you *are* expected to be able to read and interpret the footnotes and/or bibliographic entries that are present.

SPOTTING DOCUMENTATION AND CITATION QUESTIONS

Documentation and citation questions will take a number of different forms:

Which of the following is an accurate reading of footnote ___?

The purpose of footnote ___ is to inform the reader that the quotation in line ___ . . .

Taken as a whole, the footnotes suggest that . . .

From reading footnote ___, the reader can infer that . . .

MISCELLANEOUS

The question types listed in this chapter do not constitute a complete list. You will most likely encounter questions that don't seem to fit into a category. It is important, however, to become familiar with the more common types of questions you will encounter. Just don't be so set on every question fitting into a particular category that you get flustered when faced with one that does not.

DON'T FORGET

One thing you can always count on is that just when you think you have an AP test completely figured out, the test makers will surprise you with something you never anticipated.

APPLYING THE STRATEGIES

You must practice applying the strategies as you work to make them second nature by Test Day.

Read the following passages and answer the questions that follow. Each represents a category or type of multiple-choice question that corresponds to those typically found in the multiple-choice section of the AP English Language and Composition exam. Don't forget to practice the methods and strategies discussed in this chapter for reading the multiple-choice questions.

Directions: The following excerpt is from the *Narrative of the Life of Frederick Douglass, an American Slave*. After reading the passage, answer the questions that follow.

His mistress had been severely reprimanded by her husband for helping Frederick Douglass learn to read. After all, the husband admonished, giving a slave the knowledge to
Line
(5) *read was like giving the slave access to thinking he or she was human. If you give the slaves an inch, they will take the ell.*

My mistress was, as I have said, a kind and tender-hearted woman; and in the simplicity
(10) of her soul she commenced, when I first went to live with her, to treat me as she supposed one human being ought to treat another. In entertaining upon the duties of a slaveholder, she did not seem to perceive that I sustained
(15) to her the relation of a mere chattel, and that for her to treat me as a human being was not only wrong, but dangerously so. Slavery proved as injurious to her as it did to me. When I went there, she was a pious, warm, and
(20) tender-hearted woman. There was no sorrow or suffering for which she had not a tear. She had bread for the hungry, clothes for the naked, and comfort for every mourner that came within her reach. Slavery soon proved its
(25) ability to divest her of these heavenly qualities. Under its influence, the tender heart became stone, and the lamblike disposition gave way to one of tiger-like fierceness. The first step in her downward course was in her ceasing to
(30) instruct me. She now commenced to practice her husband's precepts. She finally became even more violent in her opposition [to my learning to read] than her husband himself. She was not satisfied with simply doing as well
(35) as he had commanded; she seemed anxious to do better. Nothing seemed to make her more angry than to see me with a newspaper. She seemed to think that here lay the danger. I have had her rush at me with a face made all up of
(40) fury, and snatch from me a newspaper, in a manner that fully revealed her apprehension. She was an apt woman; and a little experience soon demonstrated, to her satisfaction, that education and slavery were incompatible with
(45) each other.

From this time I was most narrowly watched. If I was in a separate room any considerable length of time, I was sure to be suspected of having a book, and was at once
(50) called to give an account of myself. All this, however, was too late. The first step had been taken. Mistress, in teaching me the alphabet, had given me the inch, and no precaution could prevent me from taking the *ell.*

(55) The plan which I adopted, and the one by which I was most successful, was that of making friends of all the little white boys whom I met in the street. As many of these as I could, I converted into teachers. With
(60) their kindly aid, obtained at different times and in different places, I finally succeeded in learning to read. When I was sent on errands, I always took my book with me, and by going one part of my errand quickly, I found time
(65) to get a lesson before my return. I used also to carry bread with me, enough of which was always in the house, and to which I was always welcome, for I was much better off in this regard than many of the poor white children in
(70) our neighborhood. This bread I used to bestow upon the hungry little urchins, who, in return, would give me that more valuable bread of knowledge. I am strongly tempted to give the names of two or three of those little boys, as
(75) a testimonial of the gratitude and affection I bear them; but prudence forbids;—not that it

would injure me, but it might embarrass them; for it is almost a unpardonable offence to teach slaves to read in this Christian country. I used (80) to talk this matter of slavery over with them. I would sometimes say to them, I wished I could be as free as they would be when they got to be men. This used to trouble them; they would express for me the liveliest sympathy, (85) and console me with the hope that something would occur by which I might be free.

1. The narrator's attitude toward his mistress can best be described as

   (A) compassion and understanding.
   (B) hatred and vengeance.
   (C) ridicule and dismissal.
   (D) disgust and disappointment.
   (E) regret and thankfulness.

Answer (E)

The narrator regrets that his mistress turned against him so vehemently, but he nevertheless is thankful that she gave him the rudiments of reading and awakened in him the desire to learn as much as he could. This question would fit under the *main idea* category of questions. When you are presented with descriptors in pairs or in threes, remember that all must apply correctly to the question.

2. The narrator would most likely adhere to the concept that

   (A) all's well that ends well.
   (B) some people's piety is only skin deep.
   (C) one must take advantage of that which is close at hand.
   (D) sometimes things don't work out the way you want them to.
   (E) white people are not to be trusted.

Answer (C)

This narrator is going places; he will take any advantage he can in pursuing his goals. This is also a *main idea* question. Although Frederick Douglass might agree with one or two of the other choices, (C) is certainly the most accurate.

3. The short paragraph 3 concludes with the author's clever use of

   (A) a sentence.
   (B) a version of an aphorism.
   (C) an alliteration.
   (D) a trite expression.
   (E) a metaphor.

Answer (B)

"Give an inch and take an ell (mile)" is what is known as an *aphorism*. Ben Franklin was full of such aphorisms, about early birds getting worms and mending something before the tear gets worse. If you know what an aphorism is, then this was an easy question for you. If not, at least you do now. Sayings, aphorisms, allusions to things past—these are all a part of *rhetoric*.

4. The repetition of the opening word "She" in the sentences starting in lines 22, 30, 31, 34, 37, and 42 is an example of the specific rhetorical device known as

   (A) repetition.
   (B) alliteration.
   (C) rhetorical statement.
   (D) anaphora.
   (E) allusion.

Answer (D)

If you look in the key terminology section of this book, you will see that *anaphora* is a repetition that occurs in opening words of phrases or clauses in a series. This is a *rhetoric* question—that is, it asked about a term of rhetorical language. You will possibly find a number of these questions in the multiple-choice section of the AP English Language and Composition exam.

5. In line 79, the words "Christian country" are most specifically chosen to

    (A) express an irony.
    (B) demonstrate alliteration.
    (C) show the religious element of the passage.
    (D) express the spiritual feelings of the writer.
    (E) present an allusion.

Answer (A)
This response shows that you recognize that Frederick Douglass did indeed have a bit of an attitude when he wrote this passage. The juxtaposition of the treatment of slaves and the phrase "Christian country" demonstrates Douglass's deeper understanding of the vagaries of humankind and the double standard by which many white people lived at this time. None of the alternative responses make sense as an answer. This question tests whether you understand the *meaning and purpose* of this passage.

6. The purpose of this passage can be interpreted as all of the following EXCEPT

    (A) to relate a Negro slave's struggle to learn to read.
    (B) to explain the impetus of a slave to seek freedom.
    (C) to expose the hypocrisy of Christian slave owners.
    (D) to reveal the determination of one man to seek freedom.
    (E) to show the changing attitude of the slave's mistress.

Answer (B)
You might say that several of the answer choices might work. However, only one truly responds to

the question asked. This is another *meaning/purpose* question.

7. Paragraph 3, in contrast to paragraphs 1 and 2, can best be described as

    (A) the narrator's shift from being passive to proactive.
    (B) the difference in what went on inside versus outside the house.
    (C) a discussion of children's behavior versus adult behavior.
    (D) a movement from the metaphoric to the concrete.
    (E) a solution to a problem.

Answer (A)
This question requires you to take a look at the *structure* of the passage. However, not only do you need to recognize structure, but you need to understand shifts or changes in attitude or point of view of the narrator.

8. The author uses all of the following elements to tell his story EXCEPT

    (A) retrospective storytelling.
    (B) personal perspective.
    (C) movement from the personal to the general.
    (D) movement from the narrator's childhood to his adulthood.
    (E) reference from specific people to a more general population.

Answer (D)
Here's another *structure/organization* question. This question expects you to get a "feel" for the narrator's perspective. What you need to realize is that the earlier part of this essay has nothing to do with the narrator's childhood. This narrator is an adult—older when he writes, but still a young adult when he recalls himself learning to read.

9. The rhetorical mode that best describes the characteristics of this passage is one of

   (A) comparison and contrast.

   (B) argumentation.

   (C) personal reflection.

   (D) description.

   (E) cause and effect.

Answer (C)
This is a question having to do with *rhetorical mode* or mode of discourse. Actually, there is only one response—this is a reminiscence piece. In other words, this is a personal reflection.

10. One could characterize the narrator of this passage as

   (A) an angry young man.

   (B) a despairing slave.

   (C) one who had it better than most of his peers.

   (D) a frustrated author who knew he could write.

   (E) a young man determined to succeed.

Answer (E)
In this case, the narrator is a young man determined to succeed. This is a *miscellaneous* type of question. It doesn't quite fit any of the other categories, but it is not unlike other multiple-choice questions you might face.

PRACTICE SETS

PRACTICE SET 1

A child was standing on a street corner. He leaned with one shoulder against a high board-fence and swayed the other to and fro, the while kicking carelessly at the gravel.

(5) Sunshine beat upon the cobbles, and the lazy summer wind raised yellow dust which trailed in clouds down the avenue. Clattering trucks moved with indistinctness through it. The child stood dreamily gazing.

(10) After a time, a little dark-brown dog came trotting with an intent air down the sidewalk. A short rope was dragging from his neck. Occasionally he trod upon the end of it and stumbled.

(15) He stopped opposite the child, and the two regarded each other. The dog hesitated for a moment, but presently he made some little advances with his tail. The child put out his hand and called him. In an apologetic manner

(20) the dog came close, and the two had an interchange of friendly pattings and waggles. The dog became more enthusiastic with each moment of the interview, until with his gleeful caperings he threatened to overturn

(25) the child. Whereupon the child lifted his hand and struck the dog a blow upon the head.

This thing seemed to overpower and astonish the little dark-brown dog, and wounded him to the heart. He sank down

(30) in despair at the child's feet. When the blow was repeated, together with an admonition in childish sentences, he turned over upon his back, and held his paws in a peculiar manner. At the same time with his ears and his eyes he

(35) offered a small prayer to the child.

He looked so comical on his back, and holding his paws peculiarly, that the child was greatly amused and gave him little taps repeatedly, to keep him so. But the little

(40) dark-brown dog took this chastisement in the most serious way, and no doubt considered that he had committed some grave crime, for he wriggled contritely and showed his repentance in every way that was in his power.

(45) He pleaded with the child and petitioned him, and offered more prayers.

At last the child grew weary of this amusement and turned toward home. The dog was praying at the time. He lay on his

(50) back and turned his eyes upon the retreating form.

Presently he struggled to his feet and stared after the child. The latter wandered in a perfunctory way toward his home, stopping

(55) at times to investigate various matters. During one of these pauses he discovered the little dark-brown dog who was following him with the air of a footpad.

The child beat his pursuer with a small

(60) stick he had found. The dog lay down and prayed until the child had finished, and resumed his journey. Then he scrambled erect and took up the pursuit again.

On the way to his home the child turned

(65) many times and beat the dog, proclaiming with childish gestures that he held him in contempt as an unimportant dog, with no value save for a moment. For being this quality of animal the dog apologized and

(70) eloquently expressed regret, but he continued stealthily to follow the child. His manner grew so very guilty that he slunk like an assassin.

When the child reached his door step, the dog was industriously ambling a few yards in

(75) the rear. He became so agitated with shame when he again confronted the child that he forgot the dragging rope. He tripped upon it and fell forward.

The child sat down on the step and the (80) two had another interview. During it the dog greatly exerted himself to please the child. He performed a few gambols with such abandon that the child suddenly saw him to be a valuable thing. He made a swift, avaricious (85) charge and seized the rope.

He dragged his captive into a hall and up many long stairways in a dark tenement. The dog made willing efforts, but he could not hobble very skillfully up the stairs because he (90) was very small and soft, and the last pace of the engrossed child grew so energetic that the dog became panic-stricken. In his mind he was being dragged toward a grim unknown. His eyes grew wild with the terror of it. He (95) began to wiggle his head frantically and to brace his legs.

The child redoubled his exertions. They had a battle on the stairs. The child was victorious because he was completely (100) absorbed in his purpose, and because the dog was very small. He dragged his acquirement to the door of his home, and finally with triumph across the threshold.

No one was in. The child sat down on the (105) floor and made overtures to the dog. These the dog instantly accepted. He beamed with affection upon his new friend. In a short time they were firm and abiding comrades.

When the child's family appeared, they (110) made a great row. The dog was examined and commented upon and called names. Scorn was leveled at him from all eyes, so that he became much embarrassed and drooped like a scorched plant. But the child went sturdily (115) to the center of the floor, and, at the top of his voice, championed the dog. It happened that

he was roaring protestations, with his arms clasped about the dog's neck, when the father of the family came in from work.

(120) The parent demanded to know what the blazes they were making the kid howl for. It was explained in many words that the infernal kid wanted to introduce a disreputable dog into the family.

(125) A family council was held. On this depended the dog's fate, but he in no way heeded, being busily engaged in chewing the end of the child's shoe.

The affair was quickly ended. The father (130) of the family, it appears, was in a particularly savage temper that evening, and when he perceived that it would amaze and anger everybody if such a dog were allowed to remain, he decided that it should be so. The (135) child, crying softly, took his friend off to a retired part of the room to hobnob with him, while the father quelled a fierce rebellion of his wife. So it came to pass that the dog was a member of the household.

(140) From "A Dark Brown Dog" by Stephen Crane (published 1901)

1. The rhetorical mode that best describes this passage is

   (A) description.
   (B) cause and effect.
   (C) personal observation.
   (D) process.
   (E) narration.

2. The dominant structural characteristic of this passage is the use of

   (A) a preponderance of compound sentences.
   (B) rhetorical questions.
   (C) an abundance of short paragraphs.
   (D) a variety of parallel structure.
   (E) numerous complex sentences.

3. Which of the following best describes the author's method of presenting the information?

   (A) The use of much flashback and foreshadowing

   (B) A sequential, naturally evolving manner

   (C) A deductive manner in which the answer appears near the end

   (D) A series of sad reminiscences

   (E) The liberal employment of humor

4. Lines 25–26 are most significant because they

   (A) indicate an abrupt mood shift in the passage.

   (B) demonstrate a positive action on the part of the main character.

   (C) display the submissive attitude of the dog.

   (D) exhibit a change in the action.

   (E) show the pettiness of the main character.

5. The writer has presented all of the following ideas EXCEPT

   (A) children can be cruel.

   (B) animals are often more human than humans.

   (C) a strong bond is easily established between boy and dog.

   (D) mothers always make the decision on whether or not a stray can become a pet.

   (E) boys often display an innate, unexplainable cruelty.

6. Paragraphs 2–4, lines 5–26, contain all of the following stylistic devices EXCEPT

   (A) personification.

   (B) onomatopoeia.

   (C) synecdoche.

   (D) imagery.

   (E) oxymoron.

7. The word "row" in line 110 most likely means

   (A) a line of people in the family standing at the door.

   (B) a commotion.

   (C) an objection to the dog.

   (D) a criticism of the poor pooch.

   (E) a reaction of praise and admiration for the fine animal.

8. Lines 30–46 can best be compared to

   (A) a supplicant at the feet of his master.

   (B) a silly animal playing tricks.

   (C) a stray dog who is demonstrating an unusual behavior.

   (D) a common animal who seems to have a religious leaning.

   (E) a human being trying to get his own way with someone who disagrees with him.

9. In line 105, the term "overtures" most likely means

   (A) symphonic movements.

   (B) extensions beyond the norm.

   (C) gambit toward conciliation.

   (D) hyperbolic exaggeration.

   (E) a movement leading to the next step.

10. The irony that concludes this passage can best be summed up as

   (A) the little boy hurts the dog that wants to be his friend.

   (B) the dog is too stupid to realize he is not wanted.

   (C) the family thinks the dog is beneath them.

   (D) the little boy really does not want the dog.

   (E) the father's ill-humor is what establishes the dog as a part of the family.

PRACTICE SET 2

I thought the matter over, and concluded I could do it. So I went down and bought a barrel of Pond's Extract and a bicycle.
Line The Expert came home with me to instruct
(5) me. We chose the back yard, for the sake of privacy, and went to work.

Mine was not a full-grown bicycle, but only a colt—a fifty-inch, with pedals shortened up to forty-eight—and skittish,
(10) like any other colt. The Expert explained the thing's points briefly, then he got on its back and rode around a little, to show me how easy it was to do. He said that the dismounting was perhaps the hardest thing to learn, and so
(15) we would leave that to the last. But he was in error there. He found, to his surprise and joy, that all that he needed to do was to get me on to the machine and stand out of the way; I could get off, myself. Although I was wholly
(20) inexperienced, I dismounted in the best time on record. He was on that side, shoving up the machine; we all came down with a crash, he at the bottom, I next, and the machine on top.

(25) We examined the machine, but it was not in the least injured. This was hardly believable. Yet the Expert assured me that it was true; in fact, the examination proved it. I was partly to realize, then, how admirably
(30) these things are constructed. We applied some Pond's Extract, and resumed. The Expert got on the other side to shove up this time, but I dismounted on that side; so the result was as before.

(35) The machine was not hurt. We oiled ourselves up again, and resumed. This time the Expert took up a sheltered position behind, but somehow or other we landed on him again.

He was full of surprised admiration; said it
(40) was abnormal. She was all right, not a scratch on her, not a timber started anywhere. I said it was wonderful, while we were greasing up, but he said that when I came to know these steel spider-webs I would realize that nothing
(45) but dynamite could cripple them. Then he limped out to position, and we resumed once more. This time the Expert took up the position of a short-stop, and got a man to shove up behind. We got up a handsome
(50) speed, and presently traversed a brick, and I went out over the top of the tiller and landed, head down, on the instructor's back, and saw the machine fluttering in the air between me and the sun. It was well it came down on us,
(55) for that broke the fall, and it was not injured.

Five days later I got out and was carried down to the hospital, and found the Expert doing pretty fairly. In a few more days I was quite sound. I attribute this to my prudence
(60) in always dismounting on something soft. Some recommend a feather bed, but I think an Expert is better.

The Expert got out at last, brought four assistants with him. It was a good idea. These
(65) four held the graceful cobweb upright while I climbed into the saddle; then they formed in column and marched on either side of me while the Expert pushed behind; all hands assisted at the dismount.

(70) The bicycle had what is called the "wabbles," and had them very badly. In order to keep my position, a good many things were required of me, and in every instance the thing required was against nature. Against nature, but not against
(75) the laws of nature. That is to say, that whatever the needed thing might be, my nature, habit,

and breeding moved me to attempt it in one way, while some immutable and unsuspected law of physics required that it be done in just (80) the other way. I perceived by this how radically and grotesquely wrong had been the life-long education of my body and members. They were steeped in ignorance; they know nothing— nothing which it could profit them to know. For (85) instance, if I found myself falling to the right, I put the tiller hard down the other way, by a quite natural impulse, and so violated a law, and kept on going down. The law required the opposite thing—the big wheel must be turned (90) in the direction in which you are falling. It is hard to believe this, when you are told it. And not merely hard to believe it, but impossible; it is opposed to all your notions. And it is just as hard to do it, after you do come to believe it. (95) Believing it, and knowing by the most convincing proof that it is true, does not help it; you can't any more do it than you could before; you can neither force nor persuade yourself to do it at first. The intellect has to come to the (100) front, now. It has to teach the limbs to discard their old education and adopt the new.

When you have reached the point in bicycling where you can balance the machine tolerably fairly and propel it and steer it, then (105) comes your next task—how to mount it. You do it in this way: you hop along behind it on your right foot, resting the other on the mounting-peg, and grasping the tiller with your hands. At the word, you rise on the peg, stiffen (110) your left leg, hang your other one around in the air in a general and indefinite way, lean your stomach against the rear of the saddle, and then fall off, maybe on one side, maybe on the other; but you fall off. You get up and do it again; and (115) once more; and then several times.

By this time you have learned to keep your balance; and also to steer without wrenching the tiller out by the roots (I say tiller because it is a tiller; "handle-bar" is a lamely descriptive (120) phrase). So you steer along, straight ahead, a little while, then you rise forward, and with a steady strain, bringing your right leg, and then your body into the saddle, catch your breath, fetch a violent hitch this way and then that, (125) and down you go again.

But you have ceased to mind the going down by this time; you are getting to light on one foot or the other with considerable certainty. Six or seven more attempts and six more falls make (130) you perfect. You land in the saddle comfortable, next time, and stay there—that is, if you can be content to let your legs dangle, and leave the pedals alone awhile; but if you grab at once for the pedals, you are gone again. You soon learn (135) to wait a little and perfect your balance before reaching for the pedals; then the mounting art is acquired, is complete, and a little practice will make it simple and easy to you, though spectators ought to keep off a rod or two to one (140) side, along at first, if you have nothing against them.

And now you come to the voluntary dismount; you learned the other kind first of all. It is quite easy to tell one how to do (145) the voluntary dismount; the words are few, the requirements simple, and apparently undifficult; let your left pedal go down till your left leg is nearly straight, turn your wheel to the left, and get off as you would from a horse. It (150) certainly does sound exceedingly easy; but it isn't. I don't know why it isn't, but it isn't. Try as you may, you don't get down as you would from a horse, you get down as you would from a house afire. You make a spectacle of yourself (155) every time.

From "Taming the Bicycle" by Mark Twain (1886)

1. The mode of discourse of this passage can be best described as

   (A) narration and description.
   (B) cause and effect.
   (C) classification and division.
   (D) exposition and description.
   (E) process analysis and narration.

2. The central idea of this passage can best be described as

   (A) a demonstration of the narrator's determination and stamina.
   (B) a treatise on the early bicycle.
   (C) an example of one man's stupidity.
   (D) a pathetic endeavor by the narrator to amuse his audience.
   (E) a description of a funny experience.

3. The word "Expert" is most likely capitalized because

   (A) Twain admired the man who helped him with the bicycle.
   (B) that is what name he uses.
   (C) Twain was being ironic.
   (D) Twain respected this man's expertise.
   (E) Twain did not care for this person at all.

4. In this passage, Twain refers to the bicycle by all of the following terms EXCEPT

   (A) steel spider webs.
   (B) graceful cobweb.
   (C) infernal beast.
   (D) the machine.
   (E) a colt.

5. Paragraph 8, lines 70–101 contains all of the following rhetorical devices EXCEPT

   (A) oxymoron.
   (B) personification.
   (C) antithesis.
   (D) irony.
   (E) alliteration.

6. The narrator likens the handlebars of the bicycle to

   (A) chest depressors.
   (B) unreliable motion directors.
   (C) recalcitrant rudders.
   (D) a tiller.
   (E) the sail on a boat.

7. In lines 109–115, the verbs that go with the subject "you" include

   (A) stiffen.
   (B) lean.
   (C) hang.
   (D) fall off.
   (E) All of the above

8. The main point established in lines 126–141 is

   (A) the term "handle-bar" does not do that part of the bicycle justice.
   (B) Twain is totally discouraged by his lack of progress.
   (C) Twain's continued description of falling down.
   (D) Twain's quiet triumph in having mastered the mount.
   (E) the mortification that he underwent as he tried to get on the bicycle.

9. The author/narrator would most likely agree that

(A) things are rarely as simple as they seem.

(B) the bicycle is a ridiculous machine.

(C) public humiliation is good for the soul.

(D) triumph comes at a high price.

(E) one can become used to falling from grace.

10. In paragraph 12, lines 142–155, the author utilizes all of the following rhetorical devices EXCEPT

(A) personification.

(B) litote.

(C) metaphor.

(D) hyperbole.

(E) asyndeton.

ANSWERS AND EXPLANATIONS

SET 1

1. E

This is a rhetorical *mode* question. This passage is actually a story by Stephen Crane, author of the novel *The Red Badge of Courage*. A narrative is basically a story, and this passage is a story. None of the other choices fit this passage.

2. C

Questions about *structure* can cover a number of things. In this case, a quick glance at the passage reveals that it contains a lot of very short paragraphs. The passage contains no rhetorical questions, very few compound sentences, no parallelism, and a small number of complex sentences.

3. B

Presentation of information actually falls under the category of *structure*. In this case, the passage begins with the first meeting of child and dog and ends with the dog as a pet. Therefore, (B)—sequential and naturally evolving—is the best response to this question.

4. A

These lines demonstrate a change in the behavior of the young boy. "Whereupon the child lifted his hand and struck the dog a blow upon the head" is definitely a shift in the direction of this passage. Until now, the child seems to be entranced by the dog and really likes it.

5. D

This is a *main idea* question. In this case, four of the choices are possible, but choice (D) is an exception. The mother's part in the establishment of this dog into the family seems to have no bearing. The young boy brings the dog home, and the father seems to have a perverse streak that causes him to okay the dog's presence in their family.

6. E

Oxymoron is the one rhetorical term that cannot be found in these lines. *Personification* is present in the phrase "Sunshine beat against the cobbles." *Onomatopoeia* can be found in the words "pattings and waggles." The expression about the dog "making advances with his tail" is *synecdoche. Imagery*, appeals to the senses, is strong within these lines.

7. B

This question is simply clarifying the *definition of a word* based upon the context in which it is used. We generally think of the word *row* as something in a straight line or that which you do with a small boat or dinghy. In this case, however, the word is used to mean a commotion.

8. A

These lines have to do with an *image*. In this case, it is the image of the little dark-brown dog on his back, with his paws together and his ears splayed out. This is the picture of a pooch in prayer mode. He wants the boy to stop hitting him, but more importantly, he is importuning the boy to take pity on him and take him home.

9. C

This question falls under the *miscellaneous* category. Although it is not especially common on the English AP exams for vocabulary to appear, that is what we have here. Some of this you can gather from the connotation of the sentence. The rest requires you to know the definitions of *gambit* and *conciliation*. A *gambit* is a movement forward (a term often used in the game of chess). *Conciliation* means becoming friends. The dark-brown dog is trying to forge a relationship with the narrator.

10. E

Irony is a turn of affairs unlike what is expected. Based on the child's seeming cruelty toward the stray dog as well as his family's overwhelming criticism of the creature, the reader could easily expect a bad ending to this narrative. Instead, the boy's father returns home from a seemingly bad day at work in the middle of the chaos of his family and the nonacceptance of the stray dog. By this time, the young boy/narrator wants to keep the animal, if only to contradict the wishes of his siblings and mother. In a perverse action, the father sees the dog's remaining as contradictory to most of his family. Therefore, he decrees the dog will stay. Therein lies the irony.

SET 2

1.   E

Obviously, this question is asking you to identify what *mode of discourse* has been utilized in presenting this passage. Twain is recalling an incident, supposedly from his life. That makes the passage *narration*. In addition, he gives us how-to instructions, albeit very dated, which also makes it *process*.

2.   A

This question is asking for your evaluation of the overall *meaning* or significance of the passage. Although several of the responses might be argued, choice (A) is the most accurate. Above all else, Twain shows us his diligence and definitely his stamina in this passage.

3.   C

Expert becomes the instructor's name. However, the more we read, the more we realize that bicycle riding is something that one has to learn for oneself and no Expert can really do it for us. Therefore, there is an ironic twist to his use of the capital *E* in Expert.

4.   C

Although Twain surely thought that the bicycle was an "infernal beast," his words only mention the other choices.

5.   A

This is a question having to do with *rhetorical/stylistic terminology*. You must decide what specific devices Twain does (and does not) employ in this passage. All of the others are present except for oxymoron, a contradiction in terms, such as jumbo shrimp. Although an antithesis is present, natural instinct versus reality, oxymoron is not present.

6.   D

The narrator has a lot to say about the bicycle and the handlebars, among other things, such as falling off the machine at an alarming rate. If you peruse the passage, however, he refers to the handlebars as the "tiller." Apparently "handlebars" just does not do this part of the bicycle justice. And it is true: the handlebars do steer the bike as a tiller steers a boat.

7.   E

Rarely does the AP exam include a question like this. However, you must be ready for anything. Actually, you do need to look at these lines and note how the subject pronoun *you* has a stream of verbs attached to it. You—rise, stiffen, hang, lean, fall off.

8.   D

These lines direct us to a very significant part of this passage, the entire second-to-last paragraph. The answer, however, is not blatant. What we have to pick up on is the subtle tone of pride that Twain, though trying to hide it, seems to have developed. He *has* conquered the dismount, at least most of the time.

9. A

This is an *overview* question. Sometimes these are placed at the beginning of a question sequence; sometimes near the end. You are actually being asked to put yourself in Twain's shoes (or head) for a time. What *is* the point/purpose of all that he has told us? Based on the choices given, the only logical response is (A)—he is admitting that what he thought would be a lark has turned into a turkey.

10. B

The last paragraph is full. Twain's finale utilizes a number of *stylistic (rhetorical) devices* in this paragraph. However, *litote*, understatement for stylistic effect, is not among them and, therefore, the correct response.

CHAPTER 6: WRITING THE ESSAYS

IF YOU LEARN ONLY FOUR THINGS IN THIS CHAPTER . . .

1. Understand how the essay portion of the exam is scored and what graders are looking for as you plan for Test Day.

2. Know the keys to successful essay writing:
   - Appropriate use of wide-ranging vocabulary
   - Proper use of varied sentence structure
   - Logical organization
   - Balanced use of details
   - Effective use of rhetoric

3. Know the types of essay prompts you're likely to see on Test Day:
   - Prose analysis
   - Argumentation/persuasion
   - Comparison/contrast
   - Synthesis

4. Consider using Kaplan's 3-D approach to essays for Test Day success.

A BRIEF REVIEW

Before we start, let's recall the highlights of the earlier discussion on How to Approach the Essay Questions:

- Be sure you understand what the question (the prompt) is asking.
- Read the prompt; read the passage; read the prompt again.
- Choose the easiest question (for you) to start with.

- Read critically and mark the text as you read.

- Organize your essay before you start to write.

- Quote from the passage judiciously. Discuss and explain; don't retell or list.

- Make your response long enough to get the job done.

- Use suitable outside references.

- Be sure your writing is legible.

Now let's take a closer look at the Section II essay questions.

First and foremost (excuse the trite expression), you need to go to the AP Students website, *apstudent.collegeboard.org/home*, where you will find past essay questions, as well as some student responses and scoring guides used to assess these responses. It is imperative that you check these out. The prompts on the AP English Language and Composition exam are more involved and complex than those on other writing tests you may have taken. Before you begin to practice writing responses to the essay questions, spend time analyzing the prompts themselves. Analyze the accompanying passage in light of the task in the prompt.

THE SCORING GUIDE

When you view past AP English Language and Composition essays on the AP Students website, and when you look at the samples found in the following pages, pay particular attention to the scores given to the student responses *as well as* to the scoring guides. The scoring guides (sometimes referred to as *rubrics*) are extremely important to understanding the assessment of the AP English Langauge and Composition essay responses.

8—6—4—2 SCORING GUIDE

If you break the scoring system down to the even scores, 8—6—4—2, you find the following:

- An 8 is a *successful* response to the prompt.

- A 6 is an *adequate* response to the prompt.

- A 4 is an *inadequate* response to the prompt.

- A 2 is an *inadequate* response and barely addresses the prompt.

Although every question has a scoring guide that is unique to the prompt, overall the scoring guides have some basic norms to which they adhere. The scoring guide is a nine-point rubric (which we'll examine in more detail in connection with the types of essay prompts).

If you keep this in mind, you can better understand the idea of upper-half and lower-half essays. What you want to write is an upper-half essay: a 6–9 assessment. What you want to avoid is a lower-half essay, a 4–1 assessment.

Now you are wondering whatever happened to number 5. It is still there. Usually it distinguishes those responses that are erratic and/or inconsistent. You are better off aiming for a 6 or above. As you read the student responses to some of the essay prompts, you may want to take notes on what you see as the successful and unsuccessful parts of the essay. Then read any commentary that might be available and pay special attention to the scoring guide.

In particular, note what the successful responses (scores of 7, 8, or 9) have in common, as well as what is lacking in the unsuccessful responses (scores of 3, 2, or 1). After that, study the less-successful-to-middle score responses (4, 5, or 6). What are their characteristics? How could you improve upon these responses? Establish a mantra for yourself: "6 and higher; 6 and higher; 6 and higher."

SUCCESSFUL WRITING

The College Board's *AP Course Description in English* makes an excellent statement about writing successfully. The following skills are expected of a successful AP English student:

- A wide-ranging vocabulary used appropriately and effectively

- A variety of sentence structures, including appropriate use of subordination and coordination

- A logical organization, enhanced by specific techniques to increase coherence, such as judicious repetition, strong transitions, and appropriate emphasis

- A balance of generalization and specific illustrative detail

- An effective use of rhetoric, including controlling tone, establishing and maintaining voice, and achieving appropriate emphasis through diction and sentence structure

THE TYPES OF PROMPTS

At this time, the AP English Language and Composition exam consists of three types of essay prompts.

1. PROSE ANALYSIS

In this essay prompt, students are asked to identify the central idea of a passage or consider the attitude of the writer toward the subject and how rhetorical devices were used to express this attitude. In some cases, the attitude is identified for the students, such as "Discuss the writer's conflicted attitudes toward nature." Often, however, students must figure out the attitude for themselves. In the past, sometimes a so-called "laundry list" of rhetorical or stylistic devices would be mentioned in the prompt. In other cases, students had to identify which devices were the best to discuss based on the passage.

The AP English Language and Composition exam tests your skills at reading and analyzing prose—some fiction, but mostly nonfiction. Some of the recent prose analysis questions have included passages by George Eliot, Annie Dillard, Jamaica Kincaid, Richard Rodriguez, Mary Oliver, Joan Didion, Frederick Douglass, Meena Alexander, Charles Lamb, and Abraham Lincoln. Recently, selections have been nonfiction prose, although college composition textbooks include fiction for the study of rhetoric. The same questions asked about a narrative from an autobiography can be asked about a short story.

Whatever the case, you will need to be tuned into stylistic devices such as diction; images; details; and nuances of connotation, tone, mood, and attitude.

Usually the passages of the essay questions are not too lengthy because the test's Development Committee realizes that you have only two hours in which to read, synthesize, and respond to the essays. The committee takes all these things into consideration as they choose the passages and prompts that best go together on each exam. Nevertheless, a passage might be as lengthy as a page. Only occasionally are passages longer. If a passage is longer, then the other two question passages are predictably shorter.

SPOTTING PROSE ANALYSIS QUESTIONS

Prose analysis prompts might be similar to any of the following:

- Carefully read the following passage by _____. Then, paying particular attention to the changing tone within the passage, write an essay in which you analyze the techniques the author has used to express his attitude toward _____.

- The passage below is from _____ by ____. Read the entire passage carefully. Then, write an essay analyzing the rhetorical strategies the author employs to convey her attitude toward_____.

- Read the following two passages about _____ carefully. Then, write an essay in which you analyze how the distinctive style of each passage reveals the purpose of its writer.

- Read the passage carefully. Then, write an essay in which you define the attitude toward_____ that the author would like his readers to adopt, and analyze the rhetorical strategies the author employs to promote that attitude.

- The following paragraphs are from the essay _____ by _____. Read them carefully. Then, write an essay in which you characterize the author's view of _____ and analyze how the author conveys this view. Your analysis might consider such stylistic elements as diction, imagery, syntax, structure, tone, and selection of detail.

- In the following excerpt from the memoirs of _____, the author reflects upon ____. Read the passage carefully. Then, write an essay in which you analyze how the author uses language to convey the significance of these moments from her past (or . . . to convey the significance of these past moments on the development of the author's _____ today).

2. ARGUMENTATION/PERSUASION

Argument questions require you to have a basic understanding of rhetorical argument and presentation of *pro* and *con* information to support your response. Some of the issues may be contemporary—such as the question about entertainment leading to our ruination. Others may be more universal—such as the notion that the rich can get away with things that the poor cannot, or that some things in life are private and should remain that way.

SPOTTING ARGUMENTATION PERSUASION QUESTIONS

This essay can assume a number of guises:

- You might be given a controversial quotation and asked to defend, challenge, or qualify what has been stated.

- You may be presented with an argument and asked to analyze it. In this case, you are expected to look at the logic of the argument but not necessarily to offer your own opinion on the subject.

- You may be presented with two different views on an idea or belief and then asked to explain each side of the argument and develop your own opinion.

The common argumentation question is a short passage or quotation by someone with the prompt asking the student to read it carefully; consider the topic discussed; and then write an essay to defend, challenge, or qualify the writer's position. Over the years, some of the controversial topics have included the following:

- Discussion about the relationship between the artist and society

- That your language and how you speak is your "key to identity"

- Neil Postman's view that the ideas in Huxley's *Brave New World* are more relevant than those found in Orwell's *1984*

- John Ruskin's claim that precedence should be given to the soldier over the merchant or manufacturer

- Lewis Lapham's observations about the attitudes of Americans toward wealth

- Sophocles's declaration that man's only crime is his pride

- King Lear's comments on the relationship between justice and wealth

- Neal Gabler's statment that entertainment will be our ruin

These are just a few examples from many years of argument topics. Argument passages have included writings by Neil Postman, George Orwell, William Shakespeare, James Baldwin, Milan Kundera, Neil Gabler, Susan Sontag, and many others.

VARIATIONS AND RECENT EVOLUTION

Although not very common, occasionally the prose analysis of two passages also has an underlying persuasive message. In 1984, for instance, two short pieces—one by Percy Shelley and one by John Milton—both defined freedom. The prompt asked that the student discuss the concept as it was presented in each passage and draw some conclusions. This prompt had only the suggestion of persuasion.

In 1993, the two passages were two marriage proposals: one from *Pride and Prejudice* and the other from a novel by Charles Dickens. Students were asked to compare rhetorical strategies in each and the possible effect each might have on the listener. Again, this wasn't strong argumentation, but since the subject of each was supposedly a persuasive speech by a man asking a woman to marry him, an element of persuasion was certainly present.

This pattern has changed a bit in recent years. Students have been asked to explain both sides of an issue and then formulate their own persuasive response supporting one side or the other, supplemented with the students' own background, reading, and observations.

In 2005, the AP English Language and Composition exam actually had two argument prompts:

1. The first question asked students to read a passage from "Training for Statesmanship," an article by George F. Kennan. Students were then asked to select what they thought were Kennan's most compelling observations and write an essay that discussed the extent to which these observations held true for the United States or any other country.

2. The second argument essay was based on a quotation by Peter Singer, who suggested that whatever money one spends above the necessity level should be given away. Students were asked to evaluate the pros and cons of Singer's argument and, using appropriate evidence and support, to develop an essay based on whichever position they found more persuasive.

As you can see, the test is evolving. Students are being asked to consider more than one point of view before they respond. This is probably realistic, given what students have to consider in their college classes.

One other argumentative essay might be an analysis of an argument already written. This is a challenging essay to write. One such question appeared in 2000, about a persuasive essay in which George Orwell criticized Gandhi for believing in such strict adherence to his beliefs that he would let his own family die rather than feed them life-sustaining chicken broth. If you are confronted with such a challenge, follow the directives of the prompt. If you are *not* invited to partake in the subject of the argument, but only told to analyze the argument according to_____, then do *only* that. Only if you are asked for your opinion should you offer it.

A similar question appeared in 1981 concerning the veto of a bill by the one-time governor of Illinois, Adlai Stevenson. This argument question asked students to analyze the strategies or rhetorical devices that made the argument effective for the audience. Over the years, this has affectionately been called the "Cat Bill" question because the governor effectively and humorously stopped all attempts to pass leash laws for cats. Nevertheless, students were not asked their opinion of the topic. They were only to analyze the passage as an argument and substantiate their responses with specific examples from the text.

This third type of argumentative essay is less common, but not to be overlooked. The key to the entire effort is *read the prompt*. Decipher the task it asks you to perform. Do that well; don't get involved in arguing when you haven't been asked to do so.

3. COMPARISON/CONTRAST

For these questions, you will be given two shorter passages on a similar topic by different writers. You will be asked to analyze the essays for certain specified aspects or qualities.

Usually, the essays are two different interpretations of the same topic, and you might be expected to compare tone, diction, structure, language, style, or other rhetorical or stylistic devices. In recent years, comparison/contrast prompts have dealt with descriptions of the Galapagos Islands (by Melville and Darwin), two marriage proposals (by Charles Dickens and Jane Austen), and descriptions of the Okefenokee Swamp in Florida (from a chamber of commerce pamphlet and an encyclopedia). Often, one comparison/contrast passage is a romanticized, imagistic passage, and the other is factual—even tediously detailed.

Prose analysis and compare-and-contrast prompts are really more alike than different. The main thing to remember when you are given two passages to consider is that you will do a prose analysis of each passage, including their similarities and differences.

You can either analyze one and then the other or, better yet, analyze both of them as you develop the focus points of your essay.

4. SYNTHESIS

What does the synthesis essay question require? What does it look like?

The question is broken down into four essential parts:

1. **Directions:** They will tell you that the prompt is based on the following six sources. You will be required to synthesize a variety of sources into a coherent, well-written essay, citing a minimum of three of the sources provided. The directions will tell you to refer to the sources to support your position or explanation and to avoid mere paraphrase or summary. They will tell you (and this is important) that *your* argument should be central and that the sources should be used to support *your* argument.

2. **Introduction:** Just as advertised, this is a lead-in to the actual question/assignment you are to write on. Some background material might be provided, but nothing that necessarily needs to be used in your written piece. The introduction contextualizes and sets the tone for the upcoming question.

3. **Assignment:** This part of the question will either take the form of a claim you will be defending, qualifying, or refuting, or it will be a question demanding that you examine different facets of a problem or situation. *For the synthesis essay response, it is important that*

SPOTTING COMPARISON/CONTRAST QUESTIONS

Here are examples of double passage prompts from AP English Language and Composition exams over the last dozen years or so:

- Read the following two passages carefully. Then write an essay in which you analyze how the distinctive style of each passage reveals the purpose of its writer.

- The two passages that follow begin essays dealing with the same historical event. The writers approach their subject and audiences very differently. Write an essay in which you analyze the specific stylistic and rhetorical differences between these introductory passages.

- In the following passages, two Native American writers describe similar landscapes. Read the passages carefully. Then, in a well-organized essay, explain how the passages reveal the differences in the authors' purposes. Consider such features as diction, syntax, imagery, and tone.

- Both passages that follow, written in the nineteenth century, describe the same place. Read the passages carefully. Then, in a well-organized essay, analyze the specific stylistic and rhetorical differences between the two descriptions.

- Each of the two passages that follow offers a definition of freedom. In a well-written essay, describe the concept of freedom embodied in each and discuss the differences between the two.

- The excerpts that follow represent early and later drafts of prose passages that record the writer's thoughts on how the experience of war affected his attitude toward language. Write a well-organized essay in which you discuss the probable reasons for the writer's additions and deletions and the ways in which those revisions change the effect of the paragraph.

you take a position and make that position clear from the start. For an explanatory synthesis essay response, you should make it clear which aspects of the problem/situation you are going to address. The assignment section also very clearly states that *you must synthesize at least three of the sources for support.*

4. **Sources:** The six sources you are given will vary in voice, time, and form. You may get some textbook material, a news article, an editorial, a glossary excerpt, or any number of textual sources. One thing is certain—of the six sources provided, you will get *at least* one nontextual source. The nontextual or visual source may be a chart or graph. It could be a political cartoon. It could be a photograph. It could be a piece of art. It could be a design on a T-shirt. Whatever it is, the nontextual element could be used to support an argument or clarify an explanation.

Concerning the number of sources used, it is important to note the following:

The synthesis essay question requires that you use at least three sources in your synthesis. That means that if you use only two, according to the scoring guide, you can earn no higher than a score of 4. You will not be rewarded for using more than three sources. Even if you manage to work all six sources into your response, your feat will only earn points in your own mind. The AP readers will be counting only as high as three. Understand that even though all sources should be valuable for the question, not all sources will be useful for your argument or explanation. You are not required to use any particular sources; just use at least three that work well to support your own argument or explanation.

Concerning citation of sources, you absolutely must give a citation of the source—either parenthetically, such as (Source A), (Holland), or (Jones and McGee), or with a mention or internal citation. You might write something like this:

> Joseph Holland notes that "even the severest of penalties fails to deter drivers from going over posted speed limits."

IMPORTANT

*Every time you use one of the sources, you **must** cite it.* Failure to do so will result in a score no higher than a 2. Scoring commentaries published by the College Board see this as plagiarism and treat it as severely as they would if it were a college essay.

Concerning the types of sources: The nontextual source has created quite a buzz among teachers of the course. How do we interpret numbers? How do we interpret images? The developers of the exam have made a leap here, and a bold one at that. You are not required to use this nontextual source, but it might prove to be useful. Also, expect the textual sources to be nonfiction and originally written in English. It would be very unusual to see poetry or fiction used as one of the sources for the synthesis question.

As in the open argument question, it is very useful for students to bring in their own examples and outside knowledge to answer the question. Since the prompt states, "Your argument should be central," your choices for examples to develop should be your own as well. Just make sure that your use of outside sources and information is synthesized with the source materials you are given. And remember, you must use a minimum of three of the sources provided!

KEY POINT

You do not need to consider the reliability or authority of the source material given. Take each source at face value as something that could be used reliably to support your argument or explanation.

So what will work to earn a high score? Enter into a conversation with the sources you have chosen to use. Use the sources as springboards or buttresses to your own argument; don't let the sources themselves overwhelm or dictate your development of ideas. Attribute all the sources you do use. Conclude forcefully by leaving the reader with something to think about.

THE SCORING GUIDE AND THE PROMPTS

We've discussed the scoring rubric generally; now consider how it is affected by the type of prompt you are given.

9-POINT SCORING GUIDE FOR PROSE ANALYSIS AND COMPARE AND CONTRAST

9   Essays meet all of the criteria for 8 essays and, in addition, are especially full or apt in their analysis or demonstrate particularly impressive composition skills.

8   Essays successfully analyze the rhetorical and stylistic strategies the writer employs to convey her attitude. They refer to the passage directly or indirectly and convincingly explain how specific strategies, such as imagery, tone, and figurative language, contribute to an understanding of the writer's attitude. Their prose controls a wide range of effective writing but is not flawless.

7   Essays fit the description of 6 essays but employ more complete analysis or demonstrate a more mature prose style.

6   Essays adequately analyze how the stylistic devices that the author employs in the passage reveal his attitude. They refer to the passage directly or indirectly, and they recognize the narrator's attitude and how he conveys it by utilizing strategies such as choice of detail, tone, or figurative language. A few lapses in diction or syntax may be present, but generally the prose of 6 essays is clear.

5   Essays analyze the author's rhetorical techniques, but the development of those techniques and how they reveal the writer's attitude is limited or too simplistic. These essays may treat techniques superficially or develop ideas about the narrator's attitude inconsistently. A few lapses in diction or syntax may appear, but the prose in these essays usually conveys the writers' ideas adequately.

4   Essays inadequately respond to the task of the prompt. They may misrepresent the author's attitude or analyze rhetorical strategies inaccurately or with little understanding of how strategies reveal the author's attitude. Sometimes these writers will paraphrase and/or summarize more than analyze. Often the prose of these essays suggests immature control over organization, diction, or syntax.

3   Essays meet the same criteria as essays with a score of 4 but are less perceptive of how rhetorical strategies convey attitude or are less consistent in controlling the elements of writing.

2   Essays are unsuccessful in analyzing how stylistic strategies convey the writer's attitude. These essays tend to pay little or cursory attention to the specific features, and they may generalize or simplify attitude and tone. They may simply paraphrase or comment on the passage without analyzing technique. The prose of 2 papers often reveals consistent weaknesses in writing, such as a lack of development or organization, grammatical problems, or a lack of control.

1   Essays meet the criteria for the score of 2 but are especially simplistic in their discussion or weak in controlling elements of language.

9-POINT SCORING GUIDE FOR ARGUMENT QUESTIONS

9 Essays meet all of the criteria for 8 essays and, in addition, are especially full or apt in their analysis or demonstrate particularly impressive composition skills.

8 Essays successfully analyze the various ideas presented. These essays discuss the significance and effect of these ideas. They refer to the quotations directly or indirectly and convincingly explain how specific quotations support their arguments. Their prose controls a wide range of effective writing but is not flawless.

7 Essays fit the description of 6 essays but employ more complete analysis or demonstrate a more mature prose style.

6 Essays adequately analyze the ideas presented. They refer to the passage directly or indirectly, and they talk about the significance and effect of those ideas. A few lapses in diction or syntax may be present, but generally the prose of 6 essays is clear.

5 Essays analyze the ideas, but the development of this analysis is limited or too simplistic. These essays may treat some of the ideas superficially or develop ideas for their argument inconsistently. A few lapses in diction or syntax may appear, but the prose in these essays usually conveys the writers' ideas adequately.

4 Essays inadequately respond to the task of the prompt. They may misrepresent the ideas presented by the quotations or generalize the concepts therein. Sometimes these essays use the quotations in lieu of original synthesis and development. The arguments of these essays are often trite, and/or the prose of these essays suggests immature control over organization, diction, or syntax.

3 Essays meet the same criteria as essays with a score of 4 but are less perceptive about the ideas presented and/or less successful in developing an original argument, or they are less consistent in controlling the elements of writing.

2 Essays are unsuccessful in analyzing concepts conveyed in the prompt. These essays tend to pay little or cursory attention to the specific quotes, and their arguments may be very general, trite, and/or oversimplified. The prose of 2 essays often reveals consistent weaknesses in writing, such as a lack of development or organization, grammatical problems, or a lack of control.

1 Essays meet the criteria for the score of 2 but are especially simplistic in their discussion or weak in controlling elements of language.

9-POINT SCORING GUIDE FOR SYNTHESIS QUESTIONS

Note that the scoring guide for the synthesis prompt is very similar to the scoring guide for the argument prompt. The synthesis prompt requires that you take a position on the claim given in the assignment and utilize the sources available to you to build your argument. In order to score in the upper half, you must synthesize and correctly cite at least three sources.

9   Essays earning a score of 9 meet the criteria for essays that are scored an 8 and, in addition, are especially sophisticated in their argument and synthesis* of cited sources or are impressive in their control of language.

8   Effective
Essays earning a score of 8 effectively take a position that defends, challenges, or qualifies the claim. They effectively support their position by capably synthesizing and citing at least three sources. The writer's argument is convincing, and the cited sources successfully support the writer's position. The prose demonstrates an ability to control a wide range of the elements of effective writing but is not flawless.

7   Essays earning a score of 7 fit the description of essays that are scored a 6 but are distinguished by more complete or more purposeful argumentation and synthesis of cited sources or a more mature prose style.

6   Adequate
Essays earning a score of 6 adequately take a position that defends, challenges, or qualifies the claim. They adequately synthesize and cite at least three sources. The writer's argument is generally convincing, and the cited sources generally support the writer's position, but the argument is less developed or less cogent than in the essays earning higher scores. Though the language may contain lapses in diction or syntax, generally the prose is clear.

5   Essays earning a score of 5 take a position that defends, challenges, or qualifies the claim. They support their position by synthesizing at least three sources, but their arguments and their use of cited sources are somewhat limited, inconsistent, or uneven. The writer's argument is generally clear, and the sources generally support the writer's position, but the links between the sources and the argument may be strained. The writing may contain lapses in diction or syntax, but it usually conveys the writer's ideas adequately.

4   Inadequate
Essays earning a score of 4 inadequately take a position that defends, challenges, or qualifies the claim. They attempt to present an argument and support their position by synthesizing and citing at least two sources but may misunderstand,

9-POINT SCORING GUIDE FOR SYNTHESIS QUESTIONS

misrepresent, or oversimplify either their own argument or the cited sources they include. The link between the argument and the cited sources is weak. The prose of essays scored 4 may suggest immature control of writing.

3 Essays earning a score of 3 meet the criteria for the score of 4 but *demonstrate less understanding of the cited sources*, less success in developing their own position, or less control of writing.

2 Little Success

Essays earning a score of 2 demonstrate little success in taking a position that defends, challenges, or qualifies the claim. They may merely allude to knowledge gained from reading the sources rather than citing the sources themselves. These essays may misread the sources, fail to present an argument, or substitute a simpler task by merely responding to the question tangentially or by summarizing the sources. The prose of essays scored a 2 often demonstrates consistent weaknesses in writing, such as a lack of development or organization, grammatical problems, or a lack of control.

1 Essays earning a score of 1 meet the criteria for the score of 2 but are especially simplistic or weak in their control of writing *or do not cite even one source*.

0 Essays earning a score of 0 are on-topic responses that receive no credit, such as those that merely repeat the prompt.

– Essays earning a dash (–) are blank responses or responses that are completely off topic.

* For the purposes of scoring, synthesis refers to combining the sources and the writer's position to form a cohesive, supported argument and accurately citing all sources.

THE 3-D APPROACH

Not all suggestions work for all students. However, some find that the 3-D approach to the essay passages is helpful: **Discover, Define, and Develop.**

Discover meaning as directed by the focus of the prompt: attitude, purpose, effect, assertion, challenge.

Discover what rhetorical devices are used by the author to create meaning: diction, imagery, tone, allusion, syntax, selection of detail, syntax and structure, pacing, contrast, repetition, figurative language.

Discover broader implications in meaning through reading, rereading, and thinking.

Define how the language used by the author reveals more subtle meaning, such as through connotation, shifts in tone, conflicted attitudes, or patterns of ideas.

Develop a connection throughout the essay by beginning with a thesis (focus) statement and maintaining this controlling idea throughout each paragraph to the conclusion. Add information if it is relevant and supportive.

Discover new ideas and insights as you develop your response.

Develop the conclusion based on all the evidence. The final product must be a coherent explanation of the writer's multiple insights into the text-based prompt.

Discover errors and polish the essay into its final form. Cross-outs are all right and will not detract from the quality of the essay. Always keep your eye on the time.

APPLYING THE 3-D APPROACH

Let's look at how this would work with the following speech by Helen Keller at Mount Airy, a school for the hearing- and sight-disabled.

In the following speech, Helen Keller, deaf and blind since soon after her birth, tells her audience about the joy of speaking. Read the speech carefully, then write an essay in which you analyze how Ms. Keller presents herself in this speech. In addition to what she says about her struggle, consider the attitude she conveys concerning her limitations. You should consider such rhetorical features as tone, word choice, and rhetorical structure.

> If you knew all the joy I feel in being able to speak to you to-day, I think you would have some idea of the value of speech to the deaf, and you would understand why I want every little deaf child in all this great world to have an opportunity to learn to speak. I know that much has been said and written on this subject, and that there is a wide difference of opinion among teachers of the deaf in regard to oral instruction. It seems very strange to me that there should be this difference of opinion; I cannot understand how any one interested in our education can fail to appreciate the satisfaction we feel in being able to express our thoughts in living words. Why I use speech constantly, and I cannot begin to tell you how much pleasure it gives me to do so. Of course I know that it is not always easy for strangers to understand me, but it will be by and by; and in the meantime I have the unspeakable happiness of knowing that my family and friends rejoice in my ability to speak. My little sister and baby brother

love to have me tell them stories in the long summer evenings when I am at home; and my mother and teacher often ask me to read to them from my favourite books. I also discuss the political situation with my dear father, and we decide the most perplexing questions quite as satisfactorily to ourselves as if I could see and hear. So you see what a blessing speech is to me. It brings me into closer and tenderer relationship with those I love, and makes it possible for me to enjoy the sweet companionship of a great many persons from whom I should be entirely cut off if I could not talk.

I can remember the time before I learned to speak, and how I used to struggle to express my thoughts by means of the manual alphabet—how my thoughts used to beat against my finger tips like little birds striving to gain their freedom, until one day Miss Fuller opened wide the prison-door and let them escape. I wonder if she remembers how eagerly and gladly they spread their wings and flew away. Of course, it was not easy at first to fly. The speech-wings were weak and broken, and had lost all the grace and beauty that had once been theirs; indeed, nothing was left save the impulse to fly, but that was something. One can never consent to creep when one feels an impulse to soar. But, nevertheless, it seemed to me sometimes that I could never use my speech wings as God intended I should use them; there were so many difficulties in the way, so many discouragements; but I kept on trying, knowing that patience and perseverance would win in the end. And while I worked, I built the most beautiful air-castles, and dreamed dreams, the pleasantest of which was of the time when I should talk like other people; and the thought of the pleasure it would give my mother to hear my voice once more, sweetened every effort and made every failure an incentive to try harder the next time. So I want to say to those who are trying to learn to speak and those who are teaching them: Be of good cheer. Do not think of to-day's failures, but of the success that may come to-morrow. You have set yourselves a difficult task, but you will succeed if you persevere; and you will find a joy in overcoming obstacles— a delight in climbing rugged paths, which you would perhaps never know if you did not sometime slip backward—if the road was always smooth and pleasant. Remember, no effort that we make to attain something beautiful is ever lost. Sometime, somewhere, somehow we shall find that which we seek. We shall speak, yes, and sing, too, as God intended we should speak and sing.

Helen Keller speaking at Mount Airy

All right—so now you have read a passage and prompt not unlike what you might face on the AP English Language and Composition exam. Read the prompt one more time. Now let's look at the passage again with some editorial comments to the side, which should simulate the thoughts and ideas you might consider as you read the passage.

She questions the experts on the controversy re: teaching deaf to speak—her great satisfaction

If you knew all the joy I feel in being able to speak to you to-day, I think you would have some idea of the value of speech to the deaf, and you would understand why I want every little deaf child in all this great world to have an opportunity to learn to speak. I know that much has been said and written on this subject, and that there is a wide difference of opinion among teachers of the deaf in regard to oral instruction. It seems very strange to me that there should be this difference of opinion; I cannot understand how any one interested in our education can fail to appreciate the satisfaction we feel in being able to express our thoughts in living words. Why I use speech constantly, and I cannot begin to tell you how much pleasure it gives me to do so. Of course I know that it is not always easy for strangers to understand me, but it will be by and by; and in the meantime I have the unspeakable happiness of knowing that my family and friends rejoice in my ability to speak. My little sister and baby brother love to have me tell them stories in the long summer evenings when I am at home; and my mother and teacher often ask me to read to them from my favourite books. I also discuss the political situation with my dear father, and we decide the most perplexing questions quite as satisfactorily to ourselves as if I could see and hear. So you see what a blessing speech is to me. It brings me into closer and tenderer relationship with those I love, and makes it possible for me to enjoy the sweet companionship of a great many persons from whom I should be entirely cut off if I could not talk.

Appeal to the audience, pathos

Admits she is hard t[o] understand—how does she know this?

Talking, reading, discussing—make her more complete

Irony/antithesis— loves to speak but has unspeakable happiness

Blessing, closeness to others, companionship from those she might never have known

What it was befo[re]

I can remember the time before I learned to speak, and how I used to struggle to express my thoughts by means of the manual alphabet—how my thoughts used to beat against my finger tips like little birds striving to gain their freedom, until one day Miss Fuller opened wide the prison-door and let them escape. I wonder if she remembers how eagerly and gladly they spread their wings and flew away. Of course, it was not easy at first to fly. The speech-wings were weak and broken, and had lost all the grace and beauty that had once been theirs; indeed, nothing was left save the impulse to fly, but that was something. One can never consent to creep when one feels an impulse to soar. But, nevertheless, it seemed to me sometimes that I could never use my speech wings as God intended I should use them; there were so many difficulties in the way, so many discouragements; but I kept on trying, knowing that patience and perseverance would win in the end. And while I worked, I built the most

Metaphor— manual alphabet=birds

Metaphor—prison door (silence)

Speech=impulse to fly

Can't creep/must soar

Incredible perseverance

Air-castles= dreams of speaking

beautiful air-castles, and dreamed dreams, the pleasantest of which was of the time when I should talk like other people; and the thought of the pleasure it would give my mother to hear my voice once more, sweetened every effort and made every failure an incentive to try harder the next time. So I want to say to those who are trying to learn to speak and those who are teaching them: Be of good cheer. Do not think of to-day's failures, but of the success that may come to-morrow. You have set yourselves a difficult task, but you will succeed if you persevere; and you will find a joy in overcoming obstacles—a delight in climbing rugged paths, which you would perhaps never know if you did not sometime slip backward—if the road was always smooth and pleasant. Remember, no effort that we make to attain something beautiful is ever lost. Sometime, somewhere, somehow we shall find that which we seek. We shall speak, yes, and sing, too, as God intended we should speak and sing.

Incredible optimism

Recurring sentiments= pleasure in the power of speech, feeling blessed and optimistic

Helen Keller speaking at Mount Airy

DISCUSSION

With this in mind, let us consider Helen Keller's speech at Mount Airy. One assumption is that the AP English Language and Composition reader would be at least vaguely familiar with who Helen Keller was. Helen was born in the late 1800s to a family in northern Alabama. When she was 19 months old, she suffered a life-threatening illness, identified at that time as "brain fever," which left her both deaf and blind. Through the remarkable perseverance of her teacher, Anne Sullivan, Helen learned the meaning of language. By using a hand spelling technique, Helen was able to understand that the "spellings" in her hand actually represented words that stood for different things. It was not until some time later that she was able to speak. Her speech always remained difficult for all but those closest to her to understand. Nevertheless, she did learn to speak, and in her address at Mount Airy, she shares her feelings about this conquest.

Are you expected to know all of this about Helen Keller? No, not all of it, but it would be expected that anyone taking an AP class and/or the exam would have at least some knowledge of who Helen Keller was and why she is significant.

RHETORIC

Rhetoric can be defined as the art of using words to persuade in writing or speaking. *All* modes of discourse—nonfiction, fiction, drama, and poetry—can be persuasive. It is up to the reader or listener—us as novice rhetoricians—to study language for its persuasive qualities. For the AP English Language and Composition exam, rhetoric is how speakers and writers use language and how listeners and readers process this language.

Generally speaking, rhetoric has three basic components: (1) the *speaker* or *writer*, (2) the *audience*, and (3) the *subject*. In reality, however, these three components rely very heavily on three other factors: (1) *context*, (2) *purpose or intention*, and (3) *genre*, that is, the type of text that is used to deliver the message. Without getting too philosophical, just think about this: It is not possible to grasp and analyze any passage of writing or speech without considering the problem or the need that prompted the piece to be written or spoken. And depending upon the writer's or speaker's goal, one method of delivery may be preferable to another. Ask yourself why and how a particular passage was written or spoken to its audience.

The first three components of rhetoric are these:

speaker	= Helen Keller
audience	= Those at Mount Airy listening to the speech (presumably school officials and others connected with the world of educating the deaf)
subject	= Helen's feelings about learning to speak

Of the next components, we have these:

context	= Helen has triumphed; she cannot stress enough how important speech is to her and should be for other deaf people, even if this is contradictory to some opposing philosophies.
purpose/intention	= This seems to be threefold—first, to celebrate her joy in learning to speak; then, to urge others to give deaf people a similar experience, despite some contrary beliefs; and finally, a motivational testament to optimism and perseverance.

All of these pieces come together to form the rhetoric of this speech.

The prompt gives us a bit of background about Helen Keller. Then the prompt gives you some tasks: analyze how Ms. Keller presents herself during her struggle to learn; consider the attitude she conveys concerning her limitations.

It doesn't sound too bad, does it? In fact, if you think about the tasks given in the prompt in light of the passage, fulfilling one task should lead you to the next. The prompt also reminds you to consider rhetorical features—*tone* (Can you hear her speaking? How do you think she is coming across?); *diction* (Pay attention to connotation of words—are any words used more consistently than others?); *attitude* (How does she feel? How do you, the audience/reader feel? Is there a difference, and is that significant? How can she get away with such an I-centered speech? How is it that we find her inspiring rather than a braggart?). Consider the *structure* (starts with her joy, reflects on her struggles, returns in triumph); consider *imagery* (spelling out words with her fingers in the manual alphabet, her fingers are struggling, caged birds, beating to soar loose, to be not "silent" any more).

You are probably wondering how you can possibly take this much time with three different questions and write three decent essays in two hours. You can't. That's why you need to take some time to work through this thinking while you have the time. Then later, when the clock is ticking, much of this thinking process will be subconscious; you'll be able to do much of it in just one quick reading. Let us look at some student responses to this AP English Language and Composition question.

STUDENT SAMPLE A

Helen Keller expresses her love of speaking in her speech about the joys in overcoming the tribulations when initially learning to speak. She describes this joy by metaphorically comparing speech to freedom, and by empathizing with those who are struggling to learn how to speak.

Keller's attitude toward speech is conveyed in the very beginning of the passage. "If you knew all the joy I feel in being able to speak to you to-day. . .," describes this theme of excitement and triumph she has in conquering the struggles of learning to speak. Although she is deaf and blind, Keller never expects pity for her condition or dwells on the immense limitations she was born with. She describes the struggle, by comparing her thoughts to "little birds striving to gain their freedom." The whole process is described by Ms. Keller as an extended metaphor for young birds learning to fly and experiencing freedom. Throughout the entire piece, she is positive, evident in her choice of words. Although she reflects on the difficulties, the positive words emphasize the persistence and determination that she talks about, ". . .but I kept on trying, knowing that patience and perseverance would win in the end."

Not only does Keller talk about her initial experience of learning to speak, but she also reaches out to those with similar difficulties. She states, "You have set yourselves a difficult task, but you will succeed if you persevere." Besides the fact that she wishes to help others, this phrase further demonstrates Ms. Keller's unflagging resolve to conquer speech. Keller is a woman of conviction, ready to make the best of the situation that has been handed to her. She shares her images of "beautiful air-castles, and dreams" to those who are trying to follow her footsteps. Her attitude is one of sheer joy of being able to live, speak loud and reach out to others. Her message is simple: "Be of good cheer."

Unlike some who might blame God for their handicapped condition, Helen Keller accepts what has been dealt her. She does not see herself as not as good as others, but she embraces her differences. Overcoming obstacles becomes a part of who she is. In her final statement, she reaches the height of her message, "We shall speak, yes, and sing, too, as God intended we should speak and sing."

Think of the scoring guide:

9 Essays meet all of the criteria for 8 essays and, in addition, are especially full or apt in their analysis or demonstrate particularly impressive composition skills.

8 Essays successfully analyze the rhetorical and stylistic strategies the writer employs to convey her attitude. They refer to the passage directly or indirectly and convincingly explain how specific strategies, such as imagery, tone, and figurative language, contribute to an understanding of the writer's attitude. Their prose controls a wide range of effective writing but is not flawless.

7 Essays fit the description of 6 essays but employ more complete analysis or demonstrate a more mature prose style.

6 Essays adequately analyze how the stylistic devices that the author employs in the passage reveal her attitude. They refer to the passage directly or indirectly, and they recognize the narrator's attitude and how she conveys it by utilizing strategies such as choice of detail, tone, and figurative language. A few lapses in diction or syntax may be present, but generally the prose of 6 essays is clear.

5 Essays analyze the author's rhetorical techniques, but the development of those techniques and how they reveal the writer's attitude is limited or too simplistic. These essays may treat techniques superficially or develop ideas about the narrator's attitude inconsistently. A few lapses in diction or syntax may appear, but the prose in these essays usually conveys the writers' ideas adequately.

4 Essays inadequately respond to the task of the prompt. They may misrepresent the author's attitude or analyze rhetorical strategies inaccurately or with little understanding of how strategies reveal the author's attitude. Sometimes these writers will paraphrase and/or summarize more than analyze. Often the prose of these essays suggests immature control over organization, diction, or syntax.

3 Essays meet the same criteria as essays with a score of 4 but are less perceptive of how rhetorical strategies convey attitude or are less consistent in controlling the elements of writing.

2 Essays are unsuccessful in analyzing how stylistic strategies convey the writer's attitude. These essays tend to pay little or cursory attention to specific features, and they may generalize or simplify attitude and tone. They may simply paraphrase or comment on the passage without analyzing technique. The prose of 2 essays often reveals consistent weaknesses in writing, such as a lack of development or organization, grammatical problems, or a lack of control.

1 Essays meet the criteria for the score of 2 but are especially simplistic in their discussion or weak in controlling elements of language.

COMMENTS ON STUDENT SAMPLE A

This response seems good on the surface. The student has made no egregious errors and seems to understand Keller's twofold purpose—to sing praise of being able to speak and to encourage others to persevere.

However, that is just about all this response does. It does not take any one thing far enough. If you look at the description of a 5 response on the scoring guide, it says that essays earning a score of 5 "analyze the author's rhetorical techniques, but the development of those techniques and how they reveal the writer's attitude is limited or too simplistic. These essays may treat techniques superficially or develop ideas about the narrator's attitude inconsistently."

Student Sample A is more superficial than inconsistent. She gives little space to discussion of rhetorical techniques. In fact, only the "fingers as frustrated birds" are mentioned. She does, however, recognize Keller's unflagging optimism: nowhere is pity sought, only admiration. As this young writer says, Keller embraced her differences and conquering her limitations had made her what she was.

This is not a bad response and could easily be considered a high 5 by some readers. This writer has good language control. She uses apt transitions that give coherence and unity to the response. The essay does, however, lack the depth and breadth that is required of an upper-half response.

STUDENT SAMPLE B

Can anyone really imagine what living as a deaf and blind person would be like? One can try, but the full extent of the isolations would be impossible to imagine. Helen Keller does not attempt to describe what being deaf and blind is like, but instead she expounds upon the beauty of speech, the ability that "opened wide the prison-door" and allowed her to communicate with the world.

Keller begins her speech by expressing the joy that being able to speak gives her. She knows that able people cannot fully comprehend the "value of speech to the deaf," but she expresses much happiness and wishes that "every little deaf child in all this great world" be given the opportunity to learn to speak. Keller's optimism even in the face of the many obstacles in her life shines through in her choice of words. While "great" can be interpreted to mean "large" as well as "wonderful," Keller's love for the word and its many meanings in relationship to her ability to speak are evident.

Moreover, Keller disagrees with the idea that some teachers do not think the deaf should be given a chance to learn to speak. That makes little sense. The "satisfaction" and "unspeakable happiness" she finds in being able to use "living words" emphasizes her point that speech is a blessing. I wonder what she would think about the debate over the surgical implants for deaf people? As a hearing person, I find that difficult to understand. Why wouldn't a deaf person want to hear and, like Helen Keller, to speak as well?

Besides the obvious irony in her choice of the term "unspeakable" as a descriptor of her joy, Keller infuses the passage with an even more intense feeling of awe and gratitude at being able to speak when she describes spoken words as "living," as if her unspoken words—manual spelling, the written word or unspoken thoughts—were dead, useless in a world of speech. The unexpressed contrast between the spoken living words and unspoken dead words makes Keller appear to be all the more optimistic, despite her plight. Now she, too, has mastered the living word.

Further in her speech, Keller talks about the shared joy her family finds in being able to communicate with her, how speech makes the relationship between disabled Helen and the rest of the family "closer and tenderer." Speech also allows Keller the pleasure of the "sweet companionship" of many people with whom she would never have been able to communicate due to her inability to speak. To emphasize that she is exceedingly happy to be speaking, Keller describes her ability to discuss issues "as if [she] could see and hear." She feels that her life has definitely improved and become more pleasant and complete because of speaking.

Following her declarations of happy contentment, Keller describes the struggle she had gone through in attempting to communicate with the manual alphabet. She creates a metaphor of how her thoughts, transmitted through her clumsy fingers, were like birds prisoned in a cage. She expands this comparison when she compares learning to speak to [the birds=her thoughts] escaping to freedom. Now the birds and her thoughts can fly and soar. This creative metaphor reveals the struggle Keller experienced in first learning to speak, how her "speech-wings" were "weak and broken," and they needed to be trained and nursed back to health. Many times she felt discouraged, but she "kept on trying," because she knew that "patience and perseverance should win in the end," and any world is better when one is not isolated.

Keller ends her speech with an encouragement. First she describes the motivating thoughts at the joy her family would have in hearing her voice, then addresses "those who are trying to learn to speak and those who are teaching them" with a reassurance that optimism is rewarded. As a further emphasis of the positive attitude Ms. Keller has demonstrated throughout this speech, she says: "When one does not think of present failures but only of the future successes." Speech is beautiful, Keller states, despite not having actually seen anything, and therefore being unable to know what a traditionally beautiful thing is. Nevertheless, her use of the word is effective and quite appropriate, when one considers the overwhelming joy a deaf person must feel in being able to communicate with other people.

Finally, her optimism reveals itself again as she finishes her speech with the emotionally-loaded statement, "We shall speak, yes, and sing, too, as God intended we should speak and sing." To Helen Keller, her disabilities are not great inconveniences, but only obstacles in her experience of the world, obstacles that she has overcome, and thus obstacles that have made her who she is.

COMMENTS ON STUDENT SAMPLE B

Of course, the most obvious difference between these two responses is length. This student response is eight rather well-developed paragraphs versus Sample A's four paragraphs. Does length guarantee a higher score? Absolutely not! Many AP English Language and Composition readers will roll their eyes and tell you about four-page responses that merited only a 3 or 4 based on the scoring guide. On the other hand, use your common sense: a longer paper does give a writer more opportunity to develop ideas. That is the case here. Student B has written not only a longer response, but also a very good and complete response. It would most likely garner a score of 8 or 9 from a reader.

Looking at the guide and considering this response, it is apparent that this student has successfully analyzed the strategies the author used to convey her attitude. In addition, in response to the prompt, this student has a good understanding of just how Helen Keller presents herself—totally optimistic. Specific strategies are discussed and analyzed. This student also speculates about Keller's probable response to present-day controversies concerning the deaf in light of her dismissal of those "experts" of her time who thought it was not judicious to teach the deaf to speak. This comment makes it clear that the student has a good handle on the character of Helen Keller.

Finally, in addition to demonstrating a wide range of composition skills, this response successfully discusses the irony of Keller's choice of the words, "unspeakable happiness." Many less successful essays mention this particular phrase, but they fail to go anywhere with the concept. This essay, however, insightfully continues the discussion of irony with the phrase "living words" as ironic as well.

Review the prompt and the essay. Then look at the scoring guide and these two sample papers. You should be able to see the differences, as well as understand the justification for their scores.

PRACTICE SET

Practice on your own with the following argument prompt, which asks you to consider several angles of an issue before drawing your own conclusions about the topic.

Consider the ideas presented in the following quotations. In a well-organized essay, discuss the concept of whether or not clothes reflect who we are or whether we are influenced by what we wear. How significant is our clothing, aside from keeping us covered? Incorporate at least three of the quotations that follow, as well as your experiences, observations, or reading to support your argument.

"Those who make their dress a principal part of themselves, will, in general, become of no more value than their dress." (William Hazlitt, 1810)

"Nothing that belongs to me is any measure of me. Certainly clothes don't express me, and heaven forbid they should!" (Henry James, 1881)

"There's no way I set out to be a certain kind of symbol—the way I dress is the way I am, the way I live my life." (Pamela Anderson, contemporary)

"Know first, who you are; and then adorn yourself accordingly." (Epictetus, 100 AD)

"Costly thy habit as thy purse can buy, but not expressed in fancy; rich not gaudy; for the apparel oft proclaims the man." (Shakespeare, 1600)

"Our clothes are too much a part of us for most of us ever to be entirely indifferent to their condition: it is as though the fabric were indeed a natural extension of the body, or even of the soul." (Quentin Bell, 1950)

"The first purpose of clothes . . . was not warmth or decency, but ornamental. . . . Among wild people, we find tattooing and painting even prior to clothes. The first spiritual want of a barbarous man is decoration; as indeed we still see among the barbarous classes in civilized countries." (Thomas Carlyle, 1795–1881)

ANALYSIS

You may wonder at the number of quotations that are in this prompt. However, the students are asked to only use three in their response.

Students have a variety of resources to consider and from which to draw their own argument and conclusions. The topic, clothing, is one that most every student will have some thoughts about.

Consider this 9-point scoring guide for this question:

9 Essays meet all of the criteria for 8 essays and, in addition, are especially full or apt in their analysis or demonstrate particularly impressive composition skills.

8 Essays successfully analyze the various ideas presented by the quotations on clothing. These essays discuss the significance of clothing and its effect on our character. They refer to the quotations directly or indirectly and explain convincingly how specific quotations support their arguments. Their prose controls a wide range of effective writing but is not flawless.

7 Essays fit the description of 6 essays but employ more complete analysis or demonstrate a more mature prose style.

6 Essays adequately analyze the ideas presented by the quotations on clothing. They refer to the quotations directly or indirectly, and talk about the significance of clothing and its effect on our character. A few lapses in diction or syntax may be present, but generally, the prose of 6 essays is clear.

5 Essays analyze the ideas about clothing, but the development of this analysis is limited or too simplistic. These essays may treat some of the ideas superficially or develop their argument inconsistently. A few lapses in diction or syntax may appear, but the prose in these essays usually conveys the writers' ideas adequately.

4 Essays inadequately respond to the task of the prompt. They may misrepresent the ideas presented by the quotations or generalize the concepts therein. Sometimes these essays use the quotations in lieu of original synthesis and development. The arguments of these papers are often trite, and/or the prose of these essays suggests immature control over organization, diction, or syntax.

3 Essays meet the same criteria as essays with a score of 4 but are less perceptive about the ideas presented in the quotations and/or less successful in developing an original argument, or they are less consistent in controlling the elements of writing.

2 Essays are unsuccessful in analyzing concepts conveyed by the quotations. These essays tend to pay little or cursory attention to the specific quotes, and their arguments may be very general, trite, and/or oversimplified. The prose of 2 essays often reveals consistent weaknesses in writing, such as a lack of development or organization, grammatical problems, or a lack of control.

1 Essays meet the criteria for the score of 2 but are especially simplistic in their discussion or weak in controlling elements of language.

STUDENT SAMPLE A

The debate over whether or not the "clothes make the man" is one with a long history. The majority of the given statements seem to have the belief that clothes may not decide who you are, but they are used to express the individual. Even Adam and Eve made a statement both with and without their clothes on.

Shakespeare said, "The apparel oft proclaims the man." In this he is correct. Walk into just about any high school in the nation and the various cliques and groups become evident very quickly. The goth/punk kids hang around in dark colors, typically black with chains or collars and piercings. The skaters wear a certain kind of shoes and jeans with a certain degree of bagginess. You can usually find a knit cap in their back pack. The jocks typically wear t-shirts with torn sleeves and jeans that aren't quite so baggy. In colder weather, they usually wear sweatshirts naming their sport or a particular event, and some still wear the traditional letter jacket. Also, the new kid in school is judged or tried by his dress. If he is dressed well in designer clothes it is a safe bet that he used to be one of the popular, preppy kids in his old school.

Epictetus said, "Know first, who you are; then adorn yourself accordingly." In high school or even sometimes in colleges, the casual observer can get to know a little about someone by what they wear. Generally, an observer can tell if a person has a lot of money or what school a person has attended or a relative might have attended by the t-shirt and sweatshirt logos he or she wears. In high school, it is easy to see who has been in what sport or activity. It is easy because the person has a shirt or sweatshirt proclaiming to the world, "Yes, I was in soccer or tennis or baseball, and I'm proud of it."

Thomas Carlyle states that "the first purpose of clothes. . .was not warmth or decency, but ornamental." In the inner city especially, but also elsewhere, this is obvious. People wear shirts that cost $50 or $60 just because of the brand or designer. No offense to those who are deprived, but in the poorest areas of the city one can see many people, barely able to pay rent, walking around in clothes that cost hundreds of dollars. They adorn themselves with clothes from Tommy or Billabong, and expect people to be impressed at their greatness or wealth of this man. In this, Quentin Bell is right when he said, "It is as though the fabric were indeed a natural extension of . . . the soul." Christianity says that while the soul is desired by God, it is a selfish thing born into sin and wrongdoing. People's desire to have attention focused on them, while being a natural and understandable desire, is a selfish desire. People's pride and longing to be someone who is rich and important drive them to purchase outrageously priced clothes to put forward an important or rich front to the rest of the world. What they should be concentrating on is their inner self. What sort of person are they? That's what they should be worried about.

To sum up, clothes do not make the man but simply express him and his desire for attention and respect.

COMMENTS ON STUDENT SAMPLE A

This essay would probably earn a score of 6. The introduction and second paragraph are good. Paragraph 2, in particular, offers some good examples to support what the writer is saying. Paragraph 3 is all right, but somewhat repetitious of the second paragraph. Although, Paragraph 4 has some really good insights, it seems to be somewhat disconnected from the other two body paragraphs. The final, very brief statement is actually the main point that the entire essay is making.

The essay is adequate, no more. It doesn't flow really well because it seems not to have a central idea. A thesis is implied, but the reader has to work too hard to find it. The examples and support for statements are well chosen and easily identifiable. Although some of the references may seem a bit trite, this writer has developed his ideas enough that one is not bored.

This is one of those papers that could be an 8 or a 9 with a little bit of rewrite work. However, that is a luxury the AP English Language and Composition exam doesn't allow time for. Some might wonder why it is not a 5, but the strength of the writing and the fullness of the examples make this a bit better than a 5. It may not be the strongest 6 ever written, but it is truly an adequate response to the prompt.

STUDENT SAMPLE B

Clothes are something we all wear and we are all familiar with them. Some people see clothes as a way of staying covered; others look further and say it reflects who we are. Personally, I think that others identify us by our clothes, but clothes do not accurately describe how a person is. Our personality may cause us to wear a certain style of clothing, but it does not identify who we are. Overall, I think that who we are is reflected in what we wear.

"Nothing that belongs to me is any measure of me. Certainly clothes do not express me, and heaven forbid they should!" (Henry James) This quotation shows that clothes do not express a person. An example of this is that a poor person could have about the same personality of a rich person, but the poor person's clothes are a lot frumpier, and usually made of a cheaper fabric than those of the rich. Clothes do not identify us—what we do and how we react to things is what identifies us. What belongs to us does not measure who we are, rather it shows others how fortunate we are. Usually a rich man's things are a lot more costly than those of a poor man even if they both have the same kind of personality.

"Those who make their dress a principal part of themselves, will, in general, become of no more value than their dress." (Hazlitt) This quote explains how clothes are just material possessions. If we allow ourselves to become obsessive in the way we dress, we will be worth no more than the value of the clothes themselves. This is very true in our society. The rich and popular worry about their clothes and spend hundreds of dollars on one outfit, and they are seen as materialistic. They do not look past these clothes because they make their clothes more salient than their own personalities. Therefore, they are seen as materialistic or superficial as the clothes they wear.

"There is no way I set out to be a certain kind of symbol—the way I dress is the way I am, the way I live my life." (Pamela Anderson) People do not want to be seen as symbols. They want to be looked at more deeply—past their clothes and into their personality. "... The way I dress is the way I am. . ." I do not fully agree with this part of the quote because the way anyone dresses does not, or at least should not, truly represent that person. We can all look elegant at a fancy restaurant and we can all look frumpy when cleaning the house. We should not identify ourselves with some material possessions; instead we should judge and be judged by the way we carry ourselves—by our manners, actions, and personality characteristics.

"Know first, who you are; and then adorn yourself accordingly." (Epictetus) We should worry about ourselves before we worry about the way we dress. If we have strong personalities and are confident in ourselves, we do not need clothes to identify us. We should not hide behind material things. Clothes are not significant, and we should not make them significant. We should dress properly for each event in our lives, but other than that, we should not use clothes as a means of identification. People do judge others on the way they dress, but they shouldn't. We must get to know people before judging them. Finally, we all need to understand what kind of person we are, and then worry about what to wear. We must not let clothes identify us; we must identify the clothes.

COMMENTS ON STUDENT SAMPLE B

This student response would garner a score of 8. This student has let the quotations guide each paragraph she develops and creates the rhythm of her essay through this development. She has successfully responded to the prompt and very aptly included relevant quotations.

Paragraph 3 is the essay's weak spot. Although it is clear what the student is trying to say, she fumbles a bit with the ideas. Otherwise, each paragraph progressively builds on her ideas; each paragraph grows out of one of the quotations. The introduction presents the controlling idea: clothing is a reflection of who we are; it does not and should not identify who we are. Although there is no separate concluding paragraph, it is not necessary, because the last paragraph brings everything to a nice conclusion.

If you look at the description of an 8 essay from the Scoring Guide, this essay successfully analyzes the various ideas presented by the selected quotations. This essay discusses the significance of clothing and its effect on our character or, in the case of this essay, how the significance of our character affects our clothing. The writer convincingly explains how specific quotations support her argument aptly.

STUDENT SAMPLE C

I think what we wear depends on our moods. The exception to this is people with professions.

For example, high school students, administrators, teachers, custodians and coworkers all dress differently. Students can wear whatever they want; they are not expected to dress professionally. But administrators have to wear suits because they are expected to dress that way, and they want to dress that way to get people's respect for them. I'm sure when they are not in school they will wear more comfy clothing. Teachers are different because some teachers want respect, while others want to be friends with the student and they will dress the new age. Like mentioned before, people will wear clothes depending upon their profession.

On the other hand, custodians have a dress policy, like a uniform. They all have a blue shirt. That way we can tell who they are. That doesn't influence who they are, it's just part of their job.

For me, my mood definitely affects what I wear. During some days of the month, my body just doesn't want to dress up. I just wear sweatpants or something comfortable. Other days I feel more preppy, and I find myself reaching for my Dockers in the morning. One time I missed my old home, India, and I wore my Sari to school that day.

Overall, different types of people have different ways of dressing. People with professions are expected to have standards, so they will wear what will make them look the best. Others, without real professions, will wear whatever they want and that makes them look good—not. Certainly clothes do reflect who we are, and who we are influence what we wear.

COMMENTS ON STUDENT SAMPLE C

This student has made a major error. She has failed to respond to the tasks of the essay prompt. Yes, she does create a rather shallow argument about clothing being a result of one's mood, with the exception of those who must wear a certain type of clothing because of their profession. There is nothing wrong with her ideas, but she doesn't go very far with her discussion.

However, this essay fails to include any mention of the quotations. Of course, reference to them is implied. Nevertheless, implication is not enough. Because of this, this essay is a lower-half response—somewhere between a 3 and a 4. The lack of quotations keeps it in the 3 range, although her decent development of ideas within the paragraphs would probably push it into the 4 range. Obviously, this student has a good grasp of composition skills. However, the essay falls short of its potential because it fails to include any reference to the quotations.

PRACTICE TESTS

HOW TO TAKE THE PRACTICE TESTS

This section of the book contains two Practice Tests. Taking a practice AP English Language and Composition exam under test-like conditions will give you an idea of what it's like to sit through a full AP English Language and Composition exam. You'll find out which areas you're strong in and where additional review may be required. Any mistakes you make now are ones you won't make on the actual exam, as long as you take the time to learn where you went wrong.

The two tests are full-length; allow a total of three hours and 15 minutes to complete one test.

Each test includes 54 multiple-choice questions in Section I and three essay questions in Section II. You will have one hour to read the passages in Section I and answer the multiple-choice questions. There will be either four or five reading selections; review the entire section and pace yourself accordingly. If there are four passages, plan to spend about 15 minutes on each; if there are five, plan to spend about 12 minutes on each.

Section II, the essay section, begins with a *mandatory* 15-minute reading period during which you may read the documents in that section and make notes in your exam booklet. When the 15 minutes are over, you will have two hours to answer the three essay questions in Section II; plan to spend about 40 minutes on each essay question. Use blank paper for your practice essays. You will receive a 16-page booklet for the real thing. Time yourself and make use of all the time allowed for each section.

Before taking a Practice Test, find a quiet place and a time when you can work uninterrupted for three hours. Time yourself according to the time limit at the beginning of each section. It's okay to take a short break between sections, but for the most accurate results you should approximate real test conditions as much as possible.

Pace yourself. Note the different types of questions and what strategies seem to work for you. After taking a practice exam, be sure to read the detailed answer explanations that follow. These will help you identify areas in which you could use additional review. Even when you've answered a question correctly, you can learn additional information by looking at the answer explanation.

Finally, it's important to approach the test with the right attitude. You're going to get a great score because you've reviewed the material and learned the strategies in this book.

Good luck!

COMPUTING YOUR SCORE

Remember not to take on the Practice Test too literally. There is no way to determine precisely what your AP grade will be because:

- the conditions under which you take the Practice Test will not exactly mirror real test conditions.
- while the multiple-choice questions are scored by computer, the free-response questions are graded manually by faculty consultants. You will not be able to grade your own essays accurately.

SECTION I: MULTIPLE-CHOICE

Number Correct ☐ × 1.298 = ☐ = Multiple-Choice Raw Score

SECTION II: FREE-RESPONSE (DO NOT ROUND)

Question 1: (out of 9 points possible) ☐ × 3.0556 = ☐

Question 2: (out of 9 points possible) ☐ × 3.0556 = ☐

Question 3: (out of 9 points possible) ☐ × 3.0556 = ☐

Total Questions 1, 2, and 3 = ☐ = Free-Response Raw Score

COMPOSITE SCORE

Section I Multiple-Choice Score ☐ + Section II Free-Response Score ☐ = ☐ = Composite Score (round to the nearest whole number)

CONVERSION CHART

Composite Score Range	AP Grade
112–150	5
98–111	4
80–97	3
55–79	2
0–54	1

Practice Test 1 Answer Grid

Before taking this Practice Test, find a quiet place where you can work uninterrupted for about three hours. Make sure you have a comfortable desk, several No. 2 pencils, and a few ballpoint pens.

The Practice Test includes a multiple-choice section and a free-response question. Use the answer grid to record your multiple-choice answers. Write the essays on the pages provided; use additional sheets if needed.

Once you start the test, don't stop until you've finished, except for a 10-minute break between the multiple-choice and essay sections. The answer key and explanations follow the test.

Good luck!

1. Ⓐ Ⓑ Ⓒ Ⓓ Ⓔ   15. Ⓐ Ⓑ Ⓒ Ⓓ Ⓔ   29. Ⓐ Ⓑ Ⓒ Ⓓ Ⓔ   43. Ⓐ Ⓑ Ⓒ Ⓓ Ⓔ
2. Ⓐ Ⓑ Ⓒ Ⓓ Ⓔ   16. Ⓐ Ⓑ Ⓒ Ⓓ Ⓔ   30. Ⓐ Ⓑ Ⓒ Ⓓ Ⓔ   44. Ⓐ Ⓑ Ⓒ Ⓓ Ⓔ
3. Ⓐ Ⓑ Ⓒ Ⓓ Ⓔ   17. Ⓐ Ⓑ Ⓒ Ⓓ Ⓔ   31. Ⓐ Ⓑ Ⓒ Ⓓ Ⓔ   45. Ⓐ Ⓑ Ⓒ Ⓓ Ⓔ
4. Ⓐ Ⓑ Ⓒ Ⓓ Ⓔ   18. Ⓐ Ⓑ Ⓒ Ⓓ Ⓔ   32. Ⓐ Ⓑ Ⓒ Ⓓ Ⓔ   46. Ⓐ Ⓑ Ⓒ Ⓓ Ⓔ
5. Ⓐ Ⓑ Ⓒ Ⓓ Ⓔ   19. Ⓐ Ⓑ Ⓒ Ⓓ Ⓔ   33. Ⓐ Ⓑ Ⓒ Ⓓ Ⓔ   47. Ⓐ Ⓑ Ⓒ Ⓓ Ⓔ
6. Ⓐ Ⓑ Ⓒ Ⓓ Ⓔ   20. Ⓐ Ⓑ Ⓒ Ⓓ Ⓔ   34. Ⓐ Ⓑ Ⓒ Ⓓ Ⓔ   48. Ⓐ Ⓑ Ⓒ Ⓓ Ⓔ
7. Ⓐ Ⓑ Ⓒ Ⓓ Ⓔ   21. Ⓐ Ⓑ Ⓒ Ⓓ Ⓔ   35. Ⓐ Ⓑ Ⓒ Ⓓ Ⓔ   49. Ⓐ Ⓑ Ⓒ Ⓓ Ⓔ
8. Ⓐ Ⓑ Ⓒ Ⓓ Ⓔ   22. Ⓐ Ⓑ Ⓒ Ⓓ Ⓔ   36. Ⓐ Ⓑ Ⓒ Ⓓ Ⓔ   50. Ⓐ Ⓑ Ⓒ Ⓓ Ⓔ
9. Ⓐ Ⓑ Ⓒ Ⓓ Ⓔ   23. Ⓐ Ⓑ Ⓒ Ⓓ Ⓔ   37. Ⓐ Ⓑ Ⓒ Ⓓ Ⓔ   51. Ⓐ Ⓑ Ⓒ Ⓓ Ⓔ
10. Ⓐ Ⓑ Ⓒ Ⓓ Ⓔ   24. Ⓐ Ⓑ Ⓒ Ⓓ Ⓔ   38. Ⓐ Ⓑ Ⓒ Ⓓ Ⓔ   52. Ⓐ Ⓑ Ⓒ Ⓓ Ⓔ
11. Ⓐ Ⓑ Ⓒ Ⓓ Ⓔ   25. Ⓐ Ⓑ Ⓒ Ⓓ Ⓔ   39. Ⓐ Ⓑ Ⓒ Ⓓ Ⓔ   53. Ⓐ Ⓑ Ⓒ Ⓓ Ⓔ
12. Ⓐ Ⓑ Ⓒ Ⓓ Ⓔ   26. Ⓐ Ⓑ Ⓒ Ⓓ Ⓔ   40. Ⓐ Ⓑ Ⓒ Ⓓ Ⓔ   54. Ⓐ Ⓑ Ⓒ Ⓓ Ⓔ
13. Ⓐ Ⓑ Ⓒ Ⓓ Ⓔ   27. Ⓐ Ⓑ Ⓒ Ⓓ Ⓔ   41. Ⓐ Ⓑ Ⓒ Ⓓ Ⓔ
14. Ⓐ Ⓑ Ⓒ Ⓓ Ⓔ   28. Ⓐ Ⓑ Ⓒ Ⓓ Ⓔ   42. Ⓐ Ⓑ Ⓒ Ⓓ Ⓔ

PRACTICE TEST 1

Section I: Multiple-Choice Questions

Time—1 hour
Number of questions—54
Percent of total grade—45%

Directions: This section contains selections from prose works with questions on their content, style, form, structure, and purpose. Read each selection. Then read each question, choosing the best of the five responses that follow. Fill in each oval with the correct answer, checking to be sure the number of the question corresponds to the number on the answer sheet.

Questions 1–13. Read the following essay carefully before responding to the questions.

We stand here in the name of freedom.

At the heart of that Western freedom and democracy is the belief that the individual man, the child of God, is the touchstone of
Line
(5) value, and all society, groups, the state, exist for his benefit. Therefore the enlargement of liberty for individual human beings must be the supreme goal and the abiding practice of any Western society.

(10) The first element of this individual liberty is the freedom of speech.

The right to express and communicate ideas, to set oneself apart from the dumb beasts of field and forest; to recall governments to
(15) their duties and obligations; above all, the right to affirm one's membership and allegiance to the body politic—to society—to the men with whom we share our land, our heritage and our children's future.

(20) Hand in hand with freedom of speech goes the power to be heard—to share the decisions of government which shape men's lives. Everything that makes life worthwhile— family, work, education, a place to rear one's
(25) children and a place to rest one's head—all this rests on decisions of government; all can be swept away by a government which does not heed the demands of its people. Therefore, the essential humanity of men
(30) can be protected and preserved only where government must answer—not just to those of a particular religion, or a particular race; but to all its people.

And even government by the consent of the
(35) governed, as in our own Constitution, must be limited in its power to act against its people: so that there may be no interference with the right to worship, or with the security of the home; no arbitrary imposition of pains or penalties

(40) by officials high or low; no restrictions on the freedom of men to seek education or work or opportunity of any kind so that each man may become all he is capable of becoming.

These are the sacred rights of Western
(45) society. These are the essential differences between us and Nazi Germany, as they were between Athens and Persia.

They are the essence of our difference with Communism today. I am inalterably
(50) opposed to Communism because it exalts the state over the individual and the family, and because of the lack of freedom of speech, of protest, of religion and of the press, which is characteristic of totalitarian states.

(55) The way of opposition to Communism is not to imitate its dictatorship, but to enlarge individual human freedom—in our own countries and all over the globe. There are those in every land who would label as "Communist"
(60) every threat to their privilege. But as I have seen on my travels in all sections of the world, reform is not Communism. And the denial of freedom, in whatever name, only strengthens the very Communism it claims to oppose.

(65) For two centuries, my own country has struggled to overcome the self-imposed handicap of prejudice and discrimination based on nationality, social class or race— discrimination profoundly repugnant to the
(70) theory and command of our Constitution. Even as my father grew up in Boston, signs told him that "No Irish need apply."

Two generations later President Kennedy became the first Catholic to head the nation;
(75) but how many men of ability had, before 1961, been denied the opportunity to contribute to the nation's progress because they were Catholic, or of Irish extraction.

GO ON TO THE NEXT PAGE →

(80) In the last five years, the winds of change have blown as fiercely in the United States as anywhere in the world. But they will not—they cannot—abate.

For there are millions of Negroes untrained for the simplest jobs, and thousands every (85) day denied their full equal rights under the law; and the violence of the disinherited, the insulated, the injured, looms over the streets of Harlem and Watts and South Chicago.

But a Negro American trains as an (90) astronaut, one of mankind's first explorers into outer space; another is the chief barrister of the United States Government, and dozens sit on the benches of court; and another, Dr. Martin Luther King, is the second man of (95) African descent to win the Nobel Peace Prize for his nonviolent efforts for social justice between the races.

We must recognize the full human equality of all our people before God, before the law, and (100) in the councils of government. We must do this not because it is economically advantageous, although it is; not because the laws of God and man command it, although they do command it; not because people in other lands wish it so. (105) We must do it for the single and fundamental reason that it is the right thing to do.

And this must be our commitment outside our borders as well as within.

It is your job, the task of the young people (110) of this world, to strip the last remnants of that ancient, cruel belief from the civilization of man.

Each nation has different obstacles and different goals, shadowed by the vagaries of (115) history and experience. Yet as I talk to young people around the world I am impressed not by the diversity but by the closeness of their goals, their desires and concerns and hopes for the future. There is discrimination in New York, apartheid (120) in South Africa and serfdom in the mountains of Peru. People stagnate in the streets of India; intellectuals go to jail in Russia; thousands are slaughtered in Indonesia; wealth is lavished on armaments everywhere. These are differing (125) evils. But they are common works of man.

And therefore they call upon common qualities of conscience and of indignation, a shared determination to wipe away the unnecessary sufferings of our fellow human (130) beings at home and particularly around the world.

In the world we would like to build, South Africa could play an outstanding role, and a role of leadership in that effort. This country (135) is without question a preeminent repository of the wealth and the knowledge and the skill of the continent. Here are the greater part of Africa's research scientists and steel production, most of its reservoirs of coal and of electric (140) power. Many South Africans have made major contributions to African technical development and world science; the names of some are known wherever men seek to eliminate the ravages of tropical disease and of pestilence. In (145) your faculties and councils, here in this very audience, are hundreds and thousands of men and women who could transform the lives of millions for all time to come.

So we part, I to my country and you to (150) remain. We are—if a man of forty can claim the privilege—fellow members of the world's largest younger generation. Each of us has our own work to do. I know at times you must feel very alone with your problems and (155) with your difficulties. But I want to say how impressed I am with what you stand for and for the effort you are making; and I say this not just for myself, but men and women all over the world. And I hope you will often (160) take heart from the knowledge that you are

GO ON TO THE NEXT PAGE ⟶

joined with your fellow young people in every land, they struggling with their problems and you with yours, but all joined in a common purpose; that, like the young people of my (165) own country and of every country that I have visited, you are all in many ways more closely united to the brothers of your time than to the older generation in any of these nations; and that you are determined to build a better (170) future.

From Robert F. Kennedy's address to the National Union of South African Students' Day of Affirmation, 6 June 1966

1. Which of the following best states the main idea of this address?

   (A) It is the job of everyone to recognize the laws of God and of our land.

   (B) Undemocratic governments can destroy one's family, one's work, one's education, and the place to rear one's children.

   (C) Even government by the consent of the governed must be limited in its power against its people.

   (D) Freedom of speech is the most important freedom if one is to have true individual liberty.

   (E) The enlargement of liberty for all must be the supreme goal and abiding practice of any Western society.

2. All of the following characteristics are present in paragraph 4 (lines 12–19) EXCEPT

   (A) compound-complex sentence structure.

   (B) asyndeton.

   (C) parenthetical appositive.

   (D) anaphora.

   (E) items in a series.

3. The main focus of paragraph 5 (lines 20–33) is the

   (A) freedom of speech.

   (B) power to be heard.

   (C) liberty to raise one's children.

   (D) decisions of the government.

   (E) essential humanity of man.

4. Kennedy most strongly emphasizes that a government by the consent of the governed must be limited in its power to act against its people so that man

   (A) can worship wherever he wishes.

   (B) can attain an education of his choice.

   (C) can become all that he is capable of.

   (D) feels secure within his home.

   (E) is able to pursue the work of his choice.

5. Kennedy refers to the admonition "No Irish need apply" in order to

   (A) show a personal cultural bias.

   (B) imply that the business is owned by the British.

   (C) emphasize the weakness of the American Constitution.

   (D) exemplify historical discrimination in the United States.

   (E) win over his audience by reminding them of his heritage.

GO ON TO THE NEXT PAGE

6. The sentence "But they will not—they cannot—abate" (lines 81–82) demonstrates all of the following EXCEPT

   (A) parenthetical emphasis.

   (B) pronoun reference to "winds of change."

   (C) a type of anaphora.

   (D) imperative tone.

   (E) a sentence fragment.

7. Kennedy maintains that Communism is

   (A) exalting the state over the individual.

   (B) about to be extinguished from the globe.

   (C) a threat to personal privilege.

   (D) any sort of major reform.

   (E) all denials of freedom.

8. Paragraph 6 strings together a series of alternatives, several connected by the conjunction "or." This is a syntactical structure known as

   (A) polyparallelism.

   (B) polysyndeton.

   (C) hyperbole.

   (D) onomatopoeia.

   (E) zeugma.

9. The end of this passage is most directly addressed to

   (A) people of the world.

   (B) citizens of South Africa.

   (C) the youth in the audience.

   (D) people in the many countries Kennedy had visited.

   (E) the blacks of South Africa as well as those in America.

10. Within the context of this address, "moral courage" can best be described as

    (A) a rare commodity.

    (B) bravery in battle.

    (C) great intelligence.

    (D) changing one's beliefs for the general good.

    (E) maintaining one's ideals and goals in life.

11. As Kennedy closes the speech, he makes a special effort to

    (A) drive home the poignancy of his argument.

    (B) appeal to the older generation that has suffered so much.

    (C) ingratiate himself with the people of South Africa.

    (D) identify himself as one of the world's largest younger generations.

    (E) embrace the Chinese as well by quoting a Chinese proverb.

12. At the time this speech was given in 1966, we can infer that South Africa was not known as a great repository of

    (A) wealth and knowledge.

    (B) steel production.

    (C) scientific research.

    (D) power sources.

    (E) unique racial tolerance.

13. Robert Kennedy would most likely agree that the hope for the world's future relies upon its

    (A) wisdom.

    (B) toleration.

    (C) determination.

    (D) youth.

    (E) moral conscience.

GO ON TO THE NEXT PAGE →

Questions 14–26. Read the following essay carefully before responding to the questions.

On a winter day some years ago, coming out of Pittsburgh on one of the expresses of the Pennsylvania Railroad, I rolled eastward for an hour through the coal and steel towns
Line
(5) of Westmoreland county. It was familiar ground; boy and man, I had been through it often before. But somehow I had never quite sensed its appalling desolation. Here was the very heart of industrial America, the center of
(10) its most lucrative and characteristic activity, the boast and pride of the richest and grandest nation ever seen on earth—and here was a scene so dreadfully hideous, so intolerably bleak and forlorn that it reduced the whole
(15) aspiration of man to a macabre and depressing joke. Here was wealth beyond computation, almost beyond imagination—and here were human habitations so abominable that they would have disgraced a race of alley cats.

(20) I am not speaking of mere filth. One expects steel towns to be dirty. What I allude to is the unbroken and agonizing ugliness, the sheer revolting monstrousness, of every house in sight. From East Liberty to
(25) Greensburg, a distance of twenty-five miles, there was not one in sight from the train that did not insult and lacerate the eye. Some were so bad, and they were among the most pretentious—churches, stores, warehouses,
(30) and the like—that they were downright startling; one blinked before them as one blinks before a man with his face shot away. A few linger in memory, horrible even there: a crazy little church just west of Jeannette, set
(35) like a dormer-window on the side of a bare, leprous hill; the headquarters of the Veterans of Foreign Wars at another forlorn town, a steel stadium like a huge rat-trap somewhere further down the line. But most of all I recall

(40) the general effect—of hideousness without a break. There was not a single decent house within eye range from the Pittsburgh suburbs to the Greensburg yards. There was not one that was not misshapen, and there was not
(45) one that was not shabby.

The country itself is not uncomely, despite the grime of the endless mills. It is, in form, a narrow river valley, with deep gullies running up into the hills. It is thickly settled, but not
(50) noticeably overcrowded. There is still plenty of room for building, even in the larger towns, and there are very few solid blocks. Nearly every house, big and little, has space on all four sides. Obviously, if there were architects of
(55) any professional sense or dignity in the region, they would have perfected a chalet to hug the hillsides—a chalet with a high-pitched roof to throw off the heavy winter snows, but still essentially a low and clinging building, wider
(60) than it was tall. But what have they done? They have taken as their model a brick set on end. This they have converted into a thing of dingy clapboards, with a narrow, low-pitched roof. And the whole they have set upon thin,
(65) preposterous brick piers. By the hundreds and thousands these abominable houses cover the bare hillsides, like gravestones in some gigantic and decaying cemetery on their deep sides they are three, four and even five stories high; on
(70) their low sides they bury themselves swinishly in the mud. Not a fifth of them are perpendicular. They lean this way and that, hanging on to their bases precariously. And one and all they are streaked in grime, with dead and eczematous
(75) patches of paint peeping through the streaks.

Now and then there is a house of brick. But what brick! When it is new it is the color of a fried egg. When it has taken on the patina

GO ON TO THE NEXT PAGE

of the mills it is the color of an egg long past
(80) all hope or caring. Was it necessary to adopt
that shocking color? No more than it was
necessary to set all of the houses on end. Red
brick, even in a steel town, ages with some
dignity. Let it become downright black, and
(85) it is still sightly, especially if its trimmings
are of white stone, with soot in the depths
and the high spots washed by the rain. But in
Westmoreland they prefer that uremic yellow,
and so they have the most loathsome towns
(90) and villages ever seen by mortal eye.

I award this championship only after
laborious research and incessant prayer. I
have seen, I believe, all of the most unlovely
towns of the world; they are all to be found
(95) in the United States. I have seen the mill
towns of decomposing New England and the
desert towns of Utah, Arizona and Texas. I
am familiar with the back streets of Newark,
Brooklyn and Chicago, and have made
(100) scientific explorations to Camden, N.J. and
Newport News, Va. Safe in a Pullman, I have
whirled through the gloomy, God-forsaken
villages of Iowa and Kansas, and the malarious
tide-water hamlets of Georgia. I have been to
(105) Bridgeport, Conn., and to Los Angeles. But
nowhere on this earth, at home or abroad,
have I seen anything to compare to the villages
that huddle along the line of the Pennsylvania
from the Pittsburgh yards to Greensburg.
(110) They are incomparable in color, and they are
incomparable in design. It is as if some titanic
and aberrant genius, uncompromisingly
inimical to man, had devoted all the ingenuity
of Hell to the making of them. They show
(115) grotesqueries of ugliness that, in retrospect,
become almost diabolical. One cannot imagine
mere human beings concocting such dreadful
things, and one can scarcely imagine human
beings bearing life in them.

(120) Are they so frightful because the valley is
full of foreigners—dull, insensate brutes, with
no love of beauty in them? Then why didn't
these foreigners set up similar abominations
in the countries that they came from? You
(125) will, in fact, find nothing of the sort in Europe
save perhaps in the more putrid parts of
England. There is scarcely an ugly village on
the whole Continent. The peasants, however
poor, somehow manage to make themselves
(130) graceful and charming habitations, even in
Spain. But in the American village and small
town the pull is always toward ugliness, and in
that Westmoreland valley it has been yielded
to with an eagerness bordering upon passion. It
(135) is incredible that mere ignorance should have
achieved such masterpieces of horror.

On certain levels of the American race,
indeed, there seems to be a positive libido
for the ugly, as on other and less Christian
(140) levels there is a libido for the beautiful. It is
impossible to put down the wallpaper that
defaces the average American home of the
lower middle class to mere inadvertence, or to
the obscene humor of the manufacturers.
(145) Such ghastly designs, it must be obvious, give a
genuine delight to a certain type of mind. They
meet, in some unfathomable way, its obscure
and unintelligible demands. They caress it as
"The Palms" caresses it, or the art of the movie,
(150) or jazz. The taste for them is as enigmatical
and yet as common as the taste for dogmatic
theology and the poetry of Edgar A. Guest.

Thus I suspect (though confessedly without
knowing) that the vast majority of the honest
(155) folk of Westmoreland county, and especially
the 100% Americans among them, actually
admire the houses they live in, and are proud
of them. For the same money they could get
vastly better ones, but they prefer what they
(160) have got. Certainly there was no pressure

GO ON TO THE NEXT PAGE ⇨

upon the Veterans of Foreign Wars to choose
the dreadful edifice that bears their banner,
for there are plenty of vacant buildings
along the track-side, and some of them are
(165) appreciably better. They might, indeed, have
built a better one of their own. But they chose
that clapboarded horror with their eyes open,
and having chosen it, they let it mellow into
its present shocking depravity. They like it
(170) as it is: beside it, the Parthenon would no
doubt offend them. In precisely the same
way the authors of the rattrap stadium that
I have mentioned made a deliberate choice.
After painfully designing and erecting it, they
(175) made it perfect in their own sight by putting
a completely impossible pent-house, painted
a staring yellow, on top of it. The effect is that
of a fat woman with a black eye. It is that of a
Presbyterian grinning. But they like it.
(180)   Here is something that the psychologists
have so far neglected: the love of ugliness for its
own sake, the lust to make the world intolerable.
Its habitat is the United States. Out of the
melting pot emerges a race which hates beauty
(185) as it hates truth. The etiology of this madness
deserves a great deal more study than it has got.
There must be causes behind it; it arises and
flourishes in obedience to biological laws, and
not as a mere act of God. What, precisely, are
(190) the terms of those laws? And why do they run
stronger in America than elsewhere? Let some
honest *Privat Dozent* in pathological sociology
apply himself to the problem.
        From "The Libido for the Ugly" by H. L.
(195) Mencken in *Prejudices: Sixth Series* (1927)

14. The primary focus of this passage is

(A) a portrayal of ugliness found in parts of
Pennsylvania.

(B) a discussion of idiosyncrasies common to
immigrants.

(C) a commentary on America's lust to make
the world intolerant.

(D) to explore how some people can hate
both truth and beauty.

(E) to discuss architectural preferences in a
particular area of Pennsylvania.

15. In describing the unusual characteristics of the
houses he sees, the writer does NOT utilize the
analogy of

(A) a brick set upright on its small end.

(B) diabolic ingenuity of an aberrant genius.

(C) a steel trap like one for used for a rat.

(D) swine buried in the mud.

(E) an egg long past all hope or caring.

16. Which of the following best describes the
rhetorical development of the passage as a
whole?

(A) Expansion from definition to description

(B) Development from description to
argumentation

(C) Transition from personal narrative to
description

(D) Movement from description to
psychological reflection

(E) Progress from description to definition

GO ON TO THE NEXT PAGE

17. Paragraph 3 shows irony when the narrator wonders

   (A) how beauty can live among such squalor.

   (B) how such a decent countryside can spawn such ugliness.

   (C) how foreigners coming from beautiful homelands can settle for ugliness.

   (D) why the houses are taller than they are wide.

   (E) why houses seem to lean precariously on the hillside.

18. As emphasized in paragraph 2, the narrator disdains the ugliness he sees by utilizing all of the following stylistic devices EXCEPT

   (A) harsh-sounding words in succession.

   (B) strong image-evoking adjectives.

   (C) whimsical speculation as to possible reasons for the ugliness.

   (D) harsh verbs that enhance the power of the ugliness.

   (E) specific identification of the geographical location.

19. It can be inferred from the sentence "I award this championship . . . prayer" (lines 91–92) that the narrator

   (A) has seen his share of ugly places.

   (B) is in charge of an ugly location contest.

   (C) possesses an unwarranted sense of superiority.

   (D) is an architectural critic.

   (E) is basically a snob.

20. In paragraph 4, the descriptive term "uremic yellow" (line 88) emphasizes

   (A) a reference to a biological hue.

   (B) the writer's dislike for the color of the brick houses.

   (C) a critical analysis of the array of colors available to architects.

   (D) a metaphor relating to physiological functions.

   (E) a color alternative for traditional red brick.

21. The writer has utilized what stylistic device within the sentence "The peasants . . . in Spain" (lines 128–131)?

   (A) Hyperbole

   (B) Metaphor

   (C) Alliteration

   (D) Rhetorical question

   (E) Direct address

22. The author refers to the Parthenon in line 170 in order to

   (A) demonstrate his advanced education.

   (B) provide an anachronism.

   (C) make an historic allusion.

   (D) contrast contemporary preferences for ugliness with traditional desire for beauty.

   (E) show that the clapboard horrors are the preference of the inhabitants who own them.

GO ON TO THE NEXT PAGE

23. The narrator facetiously criticizes psychologists for not studying all of the following EXCEPT

   (A) a race that hates beauty.

   (B) a race that hates truth.

   (C) etiology of the madness for ugliness.

   (D) the lust to make the world intolerably ugly.

   (E) why America runs strongly toward pathological sociology.

24. It can be inferred that "*Privat Dozent*" (line 192) is a reference to

   (A) a dozen experts.

   (B) a field of higher education.

   (C) the reason for preferring ugliness.

   (D) a sociological condition.

   (E) an expert of some sort, usually academic.

25. The author of this passage would most likely agree that

   (A) some houses are unavoidably ugly.

   (B) architecture isn't what it used to be.

   (C) there's no accounting for taste.

   (D) Europe also has its ugly areas.

   (E) there's no explanation for pride of ownership.

26. When the author says, "Here was wealth beyond computation, almost beyond imagination—and here were human habitations so abominable that they would have disgraced a race of alley cats" (lines 16–19), he establishes his tone as one of

   (A) harsh disparagement.

   (B) strong satire.

   (C) critical technology.

   (D) sociological exploration.

   (E) unbelievable integrity.

GO ON TO THE NEXT PAGE

Questions 27–39. Read the following essay carefully before responding to the questions.

The struggle between Liberty and Authority is the most conspicuous feature in the portions of history with which we are familiar. By liberty, was meant protection against the tyranny of
(5) the political rulers. The rulers were conceived (except in some of the popular governments of Greece) as in a necessarily antagonistic position to the people whom they ruled. They consisted of a governing One, or a governing tribe or caste,
(10) who derived their authority from inheritance or conquest, who, at all events, did not hold it at the pleasure of the governed, and whose supremacy men did not venture, perhaps did not desire, to contest, whatever precautions might be taken
(15) against its oppressive exercise. Their power was regarded as necessary, but also as highly dangerous; as a weapon which they would attempt to use against their subjects, no less than against external enemies. To prevent the weaker
(20) members of the community from being preyed on by innumerable vultures, it was needful that there should be an animal of prey stronger than the rest, commissioned to keep them down. But as the king of the vultures would be no less bent
(25) upon preying upon the flock than of the minor harpies, it was indispensable to be in a perpetual attitude of defence against his beak and claws. The aim, therefore, of patriots was to set limits to the power which the ruler should be suffered to
(30) exercise over the community; and this limitation was what they meant by liberty. It was attempted in two ways. First, by obtaining a recognition of certain immunities, called political liberties or rights, which it was to be regarded as a
(35) breach of duty in the ruler to infringe, and which, if he did infringe, specific resistance, or general rebellion, was held to be justifiable. A second, and generally a later expedient, was the establishment of constitutional checks, by

(40) which the consent of the community, or a body of some sort, supposed to represent its interests, was made a necessary condition to some of the more important acts of the governing power.
A time came, in the progress of human
(45) affairs, when men ceased to think it a necessity of nature that their governors should be an independent power, opposed in interest to themselves. The notion, that the people have no need to limit their power over themselves, might
(50) seem axiomatic, when popular government was a thing only dreamed about, or read of as having existed at some distant period of the past. In time, however, a democratic republic came to occupy a large portion of the earth's surface,
(55) and made itself felt as one of the most powerful members of the community of nations; and elective and responsible government became subject to the observations and criticisms which wait upon a great existing fact. It was
(60) now perceived that such phrases as "self-government," and "the power of the people over themselves," do not express the true state of the case. The "people" who exercise the power are not always the same people with those over
(65) whom it is exercised; and the "self-government" spoken of is not the government of each by himself, but of each by all the rest. The will of the people, moreover, practically means the will of the most numerous or the most active *part* of
(70) the people; the majority, or those who succeed in making themselves accepted as the majority; the people, consequently, *may* desire to oppress a part of their number; and precautions are as much needed against this as against any other
(75) abuse of power. The limitation, therefore, of the power of government over individuals loses none of its importance when the holders of power are regularly accountable to the

GO ON TO THE NEXT PAGE ⟶

community, that is, to the strongest party
(80) therein. This view of things, recommending
itself equally to the intelligence of thinkers and
to the inclination of those important classes in
European society to whose real or supposed
interests democracy is adverse, has had no
(85) difficulty in establishing itself; and in political
speculations "the tyranny of the majority" is now
generally included among the evils against which
society requires to be on its guard.

    Like other tyrannies, the tyranny of the
(90) majority was at first, and is still vulgarly, held
in dread, chiefly as operating through the acts
of the public authorities. But reflecting persons
perceived that when society is itself the tyrant—
society collectively, over the separate individuals
(95) who compose it—its means of tyrannizing are
not restricted to the acts which it may do by the
hands of its political functionaries. Society can
and does execute its own mandates: and if it
issues wrong mandates instead of right, or any
(100) mandates at all in things with which it ought
not to meddle, it practices a social tyranny
more formidable than many kinds of political
oppression, since, though not usually upheld by
such extreme penalties, it leaves fewer means of
(105) escape, penetrating much more deeply into the
details of life, and enslaving itself. Protection,
therefore, against the tyranny of the magistrate
is not enough: there needs to be protection also
against the tyranny of the prevailing opinion
(110) and feelings; against the tendency of society to
impose, by other means than civil penalties,
its own ideas and practices as rules of conduct
on those whose dissent from them; to fetter
development, and, if possible, prevent the
(115) formation, of any individuality not in harmony
with its ways, and compel all characters to
fashion themselves upon the model of its own.

    From Chapter 1 of *On Liberty* by John
Stuart Mill (1859)

27. In the parenthetical phrase (lines 6–7) the
word "popular" can best be defined as

(A) most congenial.

(B) very famous.

(C) publicly elected.

(D) most notable.

(E) unusually well known.

28. The stylistic mode of discourse the writer has
used in this essay can best be described as

(A) exposition.

(B) narration.

(C) argumentation.

(D) compare/contrast.

(E) cause and effect.

29. In the first paragraph, outside foes to the
community are referred to in all of the
following ways EXCEPT

(A) innumerable vultures.

(B) marauding hordes.

(C) beak and claws.

(D) animals of prey.

(E) external enemies.

30. The author of this passage defines "liberty"
(line 31) as

(A) freedom to govern oneself.

(B) supremacy of the populace.

(C) freedom of the flock.

(D) protection against tyranny of the
governing One.

(E) safety from enemy vultures.

GO ON TO THE NEXT PAGE →

31. The term "axiomatic" (line 50) can best be defined as

    (A) noncommittal.

    (B) extrasensory.

    (C) vaguely confusing.

    (D) reliably consistent.

    (E) self-evident.

32. The irony expressed by the writer regarding governing by the people is best expressed by which of the following?

    (A) The people are the ones who ought to be responsible for governing themselves.

    (B) The people who are really in charge of governing are not always the same people who are being governed.

    (C) Government by the people is really government by the powers who are in control.

    (D) Power by the few cannot overrule power by the many.

    (E) Power by the majority is not really power at all.

33. A significant conflict within this passage can be identified as

    (A) freedom versus tyranny.

    (B) the immune versus the tainted.

    (C) governing versus the governed.

    (D) resistance versus compliance.

    (E) elected versus inherited.

34. In paragraph 1, the author's use of the term "minor harpies" is a stylistic reference known as

    (A) metaphor.

    (B) personification.

    (C) allusion.

    (D) anachronism.

    (E) hyperbole.

35. Italics in paragraph 2 are used in order to

    (A) make sure the reader pays attention to what is being said.

    (B) give some stylistic flair to this rather long paragraph.

    (C) show the author is not sure of the veracity of what he is saying.

    (D) provide a syntactical detail not found in the other paragraphs.

    (E) emphasize the critical nuances of these words in relation to what is being said.

36. In the sentence beginning "Society can . . . " (lines 97–106) the pronoun "it" refers to the noun

    (A) mandates.

    (B) social tyranny.

    (C) extreme penalties.

    (D) society.

    (E) political oppression.

GO ON TO THE NEXT PAGE

37. Paragraph 2 focuses on one of the main concerns of this passage. This can be identified as control by

(A) tyranny.

(B) the governing One.

(C) selection of the majority.

(D) those accepted as the majority.

(E) those who abuse the power.

38. In this passage, the narrator seems most concerned about the fact that

(A) society executes its own mandates.

(B) society imposes civil penalties for rules that are disregarded.

(C) social tyranny is to be avoided at all costs.

(D) tyranny of the majority no longer exists.

(E) majority rule can result in abuses of power.

39. The somewhat antithetical conclusion to this passage can be interpreted as

(A) the governors often need to be governed.

(B) societies that rule themselves are always better.

(C) individual tyranny of the majority guarantees harmony.

(D) practices of social tyranny can often be more formidable than political oppression.

(E) some people were better off when they were oppressed than after they were liberated.

GO ON TO THE NEXT PAGE

Questions 40–54. Read the following essay carefully before responding to the questions.

Moths that fly by day are not properly to be called moths; they do not excite that pleasant sense of dark autumn nights and ivy-blossom *Line* which the commonest yellow-underwing asleep
(5) in the shadow of the curtain never fails to rouse in us. They are hybrid creatures, neither gay like butterflies nor sombre like their own species. Nevertheless the present specimen, with his narrow hay-coloured wings, fringed with a
(10) tassel of the same colour, seemed to be content with life. It was a pleasant morning, mid-September, mild, benignant, yet with a keener breath than that of the summer months. The plough was already scoring the field opposite
(15) the window, and where the share had been, the earth was pressed flat and gleamed with moisture. Such vigour came rolling in from the fields and the down beyond that it was difficult to keep the eyes strictly turned upon the book.
(20) The rooks too were keeping one of their annual festivities; soaring round the tree tops until it looked as if a vast net with thousands of black knots in it had been cast up into the air; which, after a few moments sank slowly down upon
(25) the trees until every twig seemed to have a knot at the end of it. Then, suddenly, the net would be thrown into the air again in a wider circle this time, with the utmost clamour and vociferation, as though to be thrown into the
(30) air and settle slowly down upon the tree tops were a tremendously exciting experience.

The same energy which inspired the rooks, the ploughmen, the horses, and even, it seemed, the lean bare-backed downs, sent the
(35) moth fluttering from side to side of his square of the window-pane. One could not help watching him. One was, indeed, conscious of a queer feeling of pity for him. The possibilities of pleasure seemed that morning so enormous

(40) and so various that to have only a moth's part in life, and a day moth's at that, appeared a hard fate, and his zest in enjoying his meagre opportunities to the full, pathetic. He flew vigorously to one corner of his compartment,
(45) and, after waiting there a second, flew across to the other. What remained for him but to fly to a third corner and then to a fourth? That was all he could do, in spite of the size of the downs, the width of the sky, the far-off smoke
(50) of houses, and the romantic voice, now and then, of a steamer out at sea. What he could do he did. Watching him, it seemed as if a fibre, very thin but pure, of the enormous energy of the world had been thrust into his frail and
(55) diminutive body. As often as he crossed the pane, I could fancy that a thread of vital light became visible. He was little or nothing but life.

Yet, because he was so small, and so simple a form of the energy that was rolling in at the open
(60) window and driving its way through so many narrow and intricate corridors in my own brain and in those of other human beings, there was something marvellous as well as pathetic about him. It was as if someone had taken a tiny bead
(65) of pure life and decking it as lightly as possible with down and feathers, had set it dancing and zigzagging to show us the true nature of life. Thus displayed one could not get over the strangeness of it. One is apt to forget all about
(70) life, seeing it humped and bossed and garnished and cumbered so that it has to move with the greatest circumspection and dignity. Again, the thought of all that life might have been had he been born in any other shape caused one to view
(75) his simple activities with a kind of pity.

After a time, tired by his dancing apparently, he settled on the window ledge in the sun, and, the queer spectacle being at an

GO ON TO THE NEXT PAGE

end, I forgot about him. Then, looking up,
(80) my eye was caught by him. He was trying to
resume his dancing, but seemed either so stiff
or so awkward that he could only flutter to the
bottom of the window-pane; and when he tried
to fly across it he failed. Being intent on other
(85) matters I watched these futile attempts for a
time without thinking, unconsciously waiting
for him to resume his flight, as one waits for
a machine, that has stopped momentarily, to
start again without considering the reason of
(90) its failure. After perhaps a seventh attempt
he slipped from the wooden ledge and fell,
fluttering his wings, on to his back on the
window sill. The helplessness of his attitude
roused me. It flashed upon me that he was in
(95) difficulties; he could no longer raise himself;
his legs struggled vainly. But, as I stretched
out a pencil, meaning to help him to right
himself, it came over me that the failure and
awkwardness were the approach of death. I laid
(100) the pencil down again.

The legs agitated themselves once more. I
looked as if for the enemy against which
he struggled. I looked out of doors. What
had happened there? Presumably it was
(105) midday, and work in the fields had stopped.
Stillness and quiet had replaced the previous
animation. The birds had taken themselves off
to feed in the brooks. The horses stood still.
Yet the power was there all the same, massed
(110) outside indifferent, impersonal, not attending
to anything in particular. Somehow it was
opposed to the little hay-coloured moth. It was
useless to try to do anything. One could only
watch the extraordinary efforts made by those
(115) tiny legs against an oncoming doom which
could, had it chosen, have submerged an entire
city, not merely a city, but masses of human
beings; nothing, I knew, had any chance against
death. Nevertheless after a pause of exhaustion

(120) the legs fluttered again. It was superb this last
protest, and so frantic that he succeeded at
last in righting himself. One's sympathies, of
course, were all on the side of life. Also, when
there was nobody to care or to know, this
(125) gigantic effort on the part of an insignificant
little moth, against a power of such magnitude,
to retain what no one else valued or desired to
keep, moved one strangely. Again, somehow,
one saw life, a pure bead. I lifted the pencil
(130) again, useless though I knew it to be. But even
as I did so, the unmistakable tokens of death
showed themselves. The body relaxed, and
instantly grew stiff. The struggle was over. The
insignificant little creature now knew death. As
(135) I looked at the dead moth, this minute wayside
triumph of so great a force over so mean an
antagonist filled me with wonder. Just as life
had been strange a few minutes before, so
death was now as strange. The moth having
(140) righted himself now lay most decently and
uncomplainingly composed. O yes, he seemed
to say, death is stronger than I am.

"The Death of the Moth" by Virginia Woolf
(published 1942)

40. This passage opens with a contradiction that
states

(A) moths are not as beautiful as butterflies.

(B) moths only fly around at night.

(C) butterflies cannot be seen at night.

(D) moths that fly in the daytime are not
proper moths.

(E) moths can be more beautiful than
butterflies.

GO ON TO THE NEXT PAGE

41. The narrator calls daytime moths "hybrid" (line 6) because they

 (A) are present in the daylight.

 (B) are not as beautiful as butterflies but not as drab as moths.

 (C) are active not only at night but in the daytime too.

 (D) are in competition with butterflies.

 (E) don't know whether they should be coming or going.

42. This passage can best be described as

 (A) rhetorical argument.

 (B) personal reflection.

 (C) definition.

 (D) pure description.

 (E) technical writing.

43. Identification of the season of the year is accomplished by all of the following EXCEPT

 (A) keener breath.

 (B) rook activity.

 (C) scored fields.

 (D) ripe pumpkins.

 (E) moth's activity.

44. In lines 52–68, "Watching him . . . show us the true nature of life," the narrator identifies the moth as

 (A) a pathetic creature.

 (B) a diminuitive body.

 (C) the embodiment of life itself.

 (D) energy gone amok.

 (E) a dancing, zigagging insect.

45. The description of the rooks as a vast, stylistic net rising and falling employs the stylistic device of

 (A) anaphora.

 (B) alliteration.

 (C) analogy.

 (D) aphorism.

 (E) apostrophe.

46. Lines 37–46 utilize sounds that make these lines both

 (A) hyperbolic and stressful.

 (B) parallel and consonant.

 (C) tedious and boring.

 (D) consonant and onomatopoeic.

 (E) assonant and alliterative.

47. In lines 64–68, the narrator acknowledges the moth as

 (A) an apathetic creature.

 (B) demonstrating the true nature of life.

 (C) made of feathers and down.

 (D) a dignified creature.

 (E) something strange and awesome.

48. "It flashed . . . vainly" (lines 94–96) is a sentence of several clauses connected with no conjunctions, demonstrating the syntactical structure known as

 (A) a run-on sentence.

 (B) a periodical sentence.

 (C) asyndeton.

 (D) anaphora.

 (E) parallelism.

GO ON TO THE NEXT PAGE

49. In paragraph 4, the narrator most likely lays down her pencil because

    (A) she is tired of studying.

    (B) her hand is cramped from writing.

    (C) she used it to flick the moth away.

    (D) she recognizes that the moth cannot be revived.

    (E) the moth has died and she is sad.

50. The tone of the last paragraph of this passage can best be identified as

    (A) overwhelming and sad.

    (B) resignedly fatalistic.

    (C) spitefully satisfied.

    (D) humanly superior.

    (E) regretful and awed.

51. In line 141, "composed" refers to which of the following?

    I. The end of the moth's endeavors

    II. The creation of something artistic

    III. The production of many parts

    (A) I only

    (B) II only

    (C) I and II only

    (D) II and III only

    (E) I, II, and III

52. The narrator of this passage would most likely agree with all EXCEPT which of the following comments?

    (A) Despite a creature's most valiant efforts, death is inevitable.

    (B) In nature, the moth is but an insignificant creature.

    (C) The moth is to be admired for its valiant, albeit futile struggle.

    (D) Death is stronger than any opponent.

    (E) Even in death the moth displayed a courageous dignity.

53. The author's tone in the passage as a whole is best described as

    (A) unsympathetic and raucous.

    (B) conversational and analytical.

    (C) contemplative and obsequious.

    (D) superficial and capricious.

    (E) passionate and optimistic.

54. Within the context of the entire passage, the narrator's feelings can best be described as

    (A) empowered by her sense of strength.

    (B) energized by the beauty of the fall morning.

    (C) entranced by the moth's plight.

    (D) sadness regarding the onset of a new season.

    (E) unexplainable pity for the creature's limitations.

STOP

Section II

Reading Period—15 minutes
Total Time—2 hours and 15 minutes
Number of questions—3
Percent of total grade—55%

Directions: This section contains three essay questions. For 15 minutes, you may read the essay questions and take notes on the question sheets. After this initial 15-minute reading period, you may begin writing your essay on the paper provided. You may not start writing on the lined paper until after the 15-minute reading period has ended. When you start writing on the three questions, budget your time carefully. Each essay counts as one-third of your total essay score.

GO ON TO THE NEXT PAGE

QUESTION ONE
(Suggested reading time—15 minutes)
(Suggested writing time—40 minutes)

Directions: The following prompt is based on the accompanying six sources.

This question requires you to integrate a variety of sources into a coherent, well-written essay. *Refer to the sources to support your position; avoid mere paraphrase or summary. Your analysis should be central; the sources cited should support your explanation.*

Remember to credit both direct and indirect citations.

Introduction: There is no question that skateboarding has developed into one of the fastest-growing activities for youth. Along with this increase in popularity, a definite skateboarding culture has literally taken to the streets, meeting resistance in communities across the country. It has been difficult in many areas to strike a balance between the desires of skateboarders honing their skills and park districts scrambling to build adequate facilities. How would you handle the task?

Assignment: Read the following sources (including any introductory information) carefully. **Then, in an essay that synthesizes at least three of the sources for support, analyze and explain some of the complex community issues involved in addressing the needs of growing numbers of skateboarders.**

You may refer to the sources by their titles (Source A, Source B, etc.) or by the descriptions in parentheses.

Source A (Aperio)
Source B (Csaszar)
Source C (Yamhill)
Source D (Smith)
Source E (Taylor)
Source F (Umminger)

GO ON TO THE NEXT PAGE

Source A

Aperio Consulting (Ellie Fiore, Sarah Heinicke, Beth Ragel, Laura Weigel). *The Urban Grind.*
Available online at *www.portlandonline.com/shared/cfm/image.cfm?id=106307*

The following passage is an excerpt from a spring 2005 project summary by four Portland State graduate students designed for park planners and community members.

Skateboarding is the fastest growing sport in the United States. It appeals to children, teens, and adults and provides recreation, entertainment, and exercise. The number of skateboarders across the country has gone up 128 percent over the past ten years. There are currently 11 million skateboarders in the U.S., which equates to almost 4 percent of the U.S. population.

Despite the fact that skateboarding has become so popular, there is a lack of allocated parks space for the sport. There is far less parks space dedicated to skateboarding than other sports such as baseball. For example, in Portland there are approximately five million square feet dedicated to sports fields and only 8,500 square feet dedicated to existing skateparks.

In the past, as baseball became more popular, parks departments responded by building more baseball fields. Parks and recreation departments across the country are currently struggling to provide the same opportunity for skaters.

Because of a lack of publicly provided skateparks, skaters continue to use public and private parking lots, business plazas, streets, and sidewalks for their sport—none of which are intended or designed for skateboarding. Skateboarding on public streets is still illegal in most places in America. Many cities have responded by enlisting law enforcement to regulate skateboarding. The criminalization of this sport means that tickets and the possibility of arrest are common for skaters.

Skaters often occupy transitional spaces that are neither exclusively public nor private, generating hostility on the part of property and business owners. "Skaters have encountered a politics of space similar to the experiences of the homeless. Like the homeless, skaters occupy urban space without engaging in economic activity. . . ." Responses to these tensions include adding spikes or bumps to handrails or ledges or placing chains across ditches and steps to render them unusable for skating.

GO ON TO THE NEXT PAGE

Source B

Csaszar, Lawrence. "Arrest Me, I Skate, Pt. 1." *Rampway Online.*

Csaszar, Lawrence. "Arrest Me, I Skate, Pt. 2." *Rampway Online.*

The following passage is excerpted from a two-part article in the student-run online magazine of Georgia State University (now offline).

. . . I love skateboarding: I feel a sense of euphoria every time I step on my board and cruise down a gently sloped hill. I also hate skateboarding: Whenever I fall, get hurt, or break a board due to a bad landing, I feel a sense of rage that cannot be easily nullified. But for the most part, I really do enjoy skateboarding. It has been with me since the day my parents bought me my first "Nash" skateboard in 1991. To me, skateboarding is just as much of a sport as baseball or football, except that it does not require more than one person.

For a long time, skateboarding was viewed as something that only punks and vagrants of society did. But with the commercialization of extreme sports, skateboarding has become a widely accepted and practiced sport. So why then are there still laws in place that deny enthusiasts the opportunity to pursue this widely accepted sport? The most common answer to this is that skateboarding is a liability issue that most property owners (parks, schools, etc.) would rather not face. But then why do we allow people to ride bicycles, roller blades, and scooters? There is no justice in this discrimination.

. . . To me, it's almost funny that someone who has no intentions at all to be a deviant can be harassed, fined, and even arrested for just wanting to skateboard. I'm sorry if I scratch your pretty marble ledges. I'm sorry if I fall and my board hits a pedestrian. But I'm especially sorry to see a society act so hypocritically and treat athletes as criminals. Although all of this sounds like whining, there is a valid concern behind my complaints. If we as a society continue to send a mixed message to our youth—commercialize and glorify extreme sports athletes (the video game "Tony Hawk's Pro Skater" is a perfect example) and then turn around and condemn anyone who tries to do it in their street—then an escalating rift between them and the law will grow.

I don't think of myself as a criminal when I go out to skate, but the minute I see a police cruiser drive up, I know that I'm being treated as one. This is just something that I have come to accept, with the insight that police and authority, in general, should be avoided when I'm skateboarding. So there it is. I admit to being a criminal who runs and hides in the shadows whenever the red and blue lights start to shine. And to think, all this because I fell in love with a piece of wood on wheels.

GO ON TO THE NEXT PAGE ⟶

Source C

City of Yamhill's Active Municipal Code. Available online at *www.cityofyamhill.com/amc/0628.htm.*

The following is an excerpt from the Yamhill, Oregon, Municipal Code, Traffic Section.

6.28.010 Definition. Skateboard means a board of any material (natural or synthetic) with wheels affixed to the underside, designed to be ridden by a person.

6.28.020 Prohibited Riding Areas. A skateboard shall not be ridden on a sidewalk in the following areas:

> (A) On Maple Street between Second and Azalea Streets.
> (B) On E. Main Street between N. Larch and Maple Streets.
> (C) All other areas specifically posted to prohibit the use of skateboards.

6.28.030 Duty to Yield. A person riding a skateboard shall yield the right-of-way to pedestrians, and shall yield the right-of-way to motor vehicles when approaching or crossing a driveway.

6.28.040 Duty to Obey Traffic Control Devices. A person riding a skateboard upon a public street shall obey all traffic control devices.

6.28.050 Seizure of Skateboards. At such time as a citation is issued to a skateboard rider who is in violation of this Chapter, the police may seize the skateboard upon which the violator was riding.

> (A) A skateboard may be recovered from the Yamhill Police Department during the office hours of City Hall by an adult rider 24 hours after being seized.
> (B) A skateboard may be recovered from the Yamhill Police Department during the office hours of City Hall by a juvenile offender 24 hours after being seized. A board shall only be released to a juvenile offender when accompanied by a parent or guardian.

6.28.060 Procedure. A citation to appear in the Yamhill Municipal Court for violation of this Chapter shall be issued to the alleged violator stating the date, time, and place to appear and the date and place of the alleged offense.

6.28.070 Penalty. The penalty for violation of any provisions of this Chapter shall be a fine not less than $5, and not more than $100.

GO ON TO THE NEXT PAGE

Source D

Smith, Grady W. "Warning Bells for Skateboard Park." *Mountain Xpress*, February 23, 2000.

The following letter is excerpted from the "Letters to the Editor" section of an Asheville, North Carolina, independent news and entertainment weekly.

It seems everyone has heard about the new and glorious skateboard park that is going to be constructed. . . . What some people don't know are the problems . . . that merchants in the area of the "temporary" skateboard park . . . have encountered.

Since the temporary skateboard park was installed . . . graffiti has increased dramatically. . . . We, the merchants, try to keep up with the removal of the marks, but the constant painting and repainting is beginning to get old.

It has also been drawn to my attention that [Asheville] Parks and Recreation Department has given the skateboarders permission to paint and mark their temporary park. It does not take a child psychologist—just a parent—to know that you don't take a child and sit him in front of a wall and tell him that this is the only place [he] can draw.

. . . At the north end of the parking garage is a stairwell with glass/wire-mesh windows. [A couple of weeks ago] the three windows that had been broken were finally replaced. Debris has been tossed from the upper parking deck onto cars parked at the north end of the parking deck.

. . . I witnessed five juvenile males climbing the elevator shaft from the skateboard deck. . . . What they were smoking and passing [around] was not a cigarette. I understand this happens frequently.

. . . I spoke with Parks and Recreation Director Irby Brinson in regards to the safety and security of the area. I told him what I had witnessed and my concerns about it being safe. . . . I was told by Mr. Brinson, "That is your opinion."

This has nothing to do with opinion—it is fact!

If the city officials and . . . the Parks and Recreation director were to get up from behind their desks and bother to come to the area, they would clearly see the problems that exist.

GO ON TO THE NEXT PAGE >

Source E

Taylor, Scott. "Bob—switch flip." *Skateboarder Magazine* (online edition).
Photo available at *http://skateboardermag.com/skateboarder-photos-videos/photos/gumdem/index5.html*.

This image is from a series of captioned pictures on the Skateboarder Magazine *website.*

GO ON TO THE NEXT PAGE

Source F

Umminger, April. "New Plaza Puts Street Skating in the Park." *USA Today*, April 15, 2004.

The following passage is excerpted from a major national daily paper.

Rob Dyrdek knows what it's like to suffer for your sport.

Dyrdek, a professional street skateboarder, has been 'cuffed and ticketed, arrested more times than he can remember, stripped down, and put in jail.

"I make six figures a year and I have to run from the cops when I'm trying to do my job," he says.

But now, animosity toward skaters could be on the way out, when Dyrdek, his hometown of Kettering, Ohio, and D.C. Shoe open Kettering Skate Plaza, a first-of-its-kind street-skating park.

. . . To the untrained eye . . . street skating looks like kids running amok on private, state, and civic property.

But Dyrdek champions the anti-organized sport as one that is mentally more creative and freeing than "ones where you start and score, then win or lose."

More than 70 percent of skateboarders consider themselves street skaters, a style defined by sliding or "grinding" down handrails, flipping the board onto ledges or jumping down a flight of stairs.

This style is different from transition skating . . . made mainstream by Tony Hawk.

To date, street skaters have had to improvise their own parks. They skate in the streets, at apartment complexes and shopping centers, not down ramps found in more than 2,000 public parks across the nation.

"It's a vicious cycle," says Dyrdek, "because the bigger the sport gets, you end up building transition skate parks that are badly constructed, and the authorities get frustrated because nobody's using them."

But come summer, street skaters will have a plaza to call their own and, potentially, new status in the community.

"Skateboarding really does address kids that we don't typically reach with our traditional programs," says Mary Beth Thaman, Kettering's parks, recreation and cultural arts director. "It shows that you don't have to play baseball to be an athlete."

STOP

QUESTION TWO
(Suggested time—40 minutes)

Directions: Read the following two passages about human skin carefully. Then write an essay in which you analyze how the distinctive stylistic and rhetorical differences between the passages reveal the purposes of their writers.

Passage 1

I sing of skin, layered fine as baklava,
whose colors shame the dawn, at once
the scabbard upon which we are thrilled,
Line protected and kept constant in our natural
(5) place. Here is each man bagged and trussed in
perfect amiability. See how it upholsters the
bone and muscle underneath, now accenting
the point of an elbow, now rolling over the
pectorals to hollow the grotto of an armpit.
(10) Nippled and umbilicated, and perforated by
the most diverse and marvelous openings, each
with its singular rim and curtain.

What is it, then, this seamless body-
stocking some two yards square, this our
(15) casing, our façade, that flushes, pales, and
pains us all our days, at once keeper of the
organs within and sensitive probe, adventurer
to the world outside?

Two layers compose the skin—the
(20) superficial epidermis and, deeper, the dermis.
Between is a plan of pure energy where the
life force is in full gallop. Identical cells spring
full-grown here, each as tall and columnar as
its brother, to form an unbroken line over the
(25) body. No sooner are these cells formed than
they move toward the surface, whether drawn
to the open air by some proto-plasmic hunger
or pushed outward by the birth of still newer
cells behind. In migration the skin cells flatten,
(30) first to cubes, then plates. Twenty-six days
later the plates are no more than attenuated
wisps of keratin meshed together to guard

against forces that would damage the skin by
shearing or compression. Here they lie, having
(35) lost all semblance of living cellularity, until
they are shed from the body in a continuous
dismal rain. Thus into the valley of death this
number marches in well-stepped soldiery,
gallant, summoned to a sacrifice beyond its
(40) ken. But . . . let the skin be cut or burned, and
the brigade breaks into a charge, fanning out
laterally across the wound, racing to seal off
the defect. The margins are shored up; healing
earthworks are raised, and guerilla squads of
(45) invading bacteria are isolated and mopped up.
The reserves too are called to the colors and
the rate of mitosis increases throughout the
injured area. Hurrah for stratified squamous
epithelium!
(50) Beneath the epidermis lies the dermis, a
resilient pad of elastic tissue in which glands,
hair follicles, nerves and blood vessels are
arranged in an infinitely variable mosaic. The
three million sweat glands are helpmates
(55) to the kidney as they labor to keep the body
cleansed and comfortable.

Passage 2

Human skin is the body's largest organ.
An adult's skin comprises between 15
and 20 percent of the total body weight.
Line Each square centimeter has 6 million cells,
(5) 5,000 sensory points, 100 sweat glands and
15 sebaceous glands. The outer layer, the
epidermis, consists of rows of cells about

GO ON TO THE NEXT PAGE

12 to 15 deep, and is between .07 and
.12 millimeters thick (the thickness of a piece
(10) of paper). This top layer is mainly composed
of dead cells, and these are constantly being
replaced by newer cells. One square inch of
skin contains up to 4.5 m of blood vessels
which have as one of their functions the
(15) regulation of body temperature. The skin
varies in thickness from .5 mm on the eyelids
to 4 mm or more on the palms and the soles.

The skin forms a protective barrier against
the action of physical, chemical, and bacterial
(20) agents on the deeper tissues and contains the
special nerve organs for the various sensations
commonly grouped as the sense of touch.
The body replaces its skin every month, and
because the skin constitutes the first line
(25) of defense against dehydration, infection, injuries
and temperature, the skin detoxifies harmful
substances with many of the same enzymatic
processes the liver uses.

Skin is constantly being regenerated. A cell
(30) is born in the lower layer of the skin called the
dermis, which is supplied with blood vessels
and nerve endings. For the next two weeks
the cell migrates upward until it reaches the
bottom portion epidermis, which is the outer
(35) most skin layer. The cell then flattens out and
continues moving toward the surface until it
dies and is shed.

The most important property of the skin
is that it contains our sense of touch. All other
(40) senses have a definite key organ which can
be studied, but the skin is spread over the
entire body and cannot be as easily studied.
Receptors located at the ends of nerve fibers
are used to detect stimuli and convert them
(45) into neural impulses to be sent to the brain
through the peripheral and central nervous
systems. The sense of touch is actually

recorded in the dermis (skin) and passed on to
the central nervous system.

(50) The most important job of the skin is that
it protects the inside of the body; it acts like
a "shock absorber." If a body falls, the skin
protects all of the internal organs. When the
skin is broken, it has its own defense system
(55) that immediately goes into repair mode. It
also acts as a thermostat to balance body
temperature.

STOP

QUESTION THREE
(Suggested time—40 minutes)

Directions: The following letter was written by Sandy Kempner to his family while he was fighting in Vietnam. Read the letter carefully, analyzing the particular stylistic and rhetorical techniques Sandy uses to convey his attitude toward war. Be sure to consider whether or not this letter is a successful example of antiwar sentiment.

2 September 1966

Dear Mom, Dad, Shrub, the Egg and Peach:

Sorry to be so long in writing, but I have just come back from an abortion called *Line* Operation Jackson. I spent a three-day "walk in the sun" (and paddies and fields and
(5) mountains and impenetrable jungle and saw grass and ants, and screwed-up radios and no word, and deaf radio operators, and no chow, and too many C-rations, and blisters and torn trousers and jungle rot, and wet socks and sprained ankles and no heels, and, and, and) for a battalion that walked on roads and dikes the whole way and a regiment that didn't even know where the battalion was, finished off by a 14,000-meter forced
(10) march on a hard road.

My God the epic poems I could write to that ambrosia of Marine Corps cuisine—peanut butter and/or hot coffee after three days of that! The only person in the whole battalion to see a VC was, of course, me. I was walking along a trail doing a village sweep all alone, and here comes Charlie, rifle in hand, with not a care in the world until
(15) he sees me, and then it's a race to see if he can get off the road before I can draw my .45 and get off an accurate shot (he won). Of course there was an incident when four snipers took on the battalion, which promptly, more to release the weight of all that unexpended ammunition than anything else, threw everything at them but the Missouri, and that would have been there too, except it could not get up the Sang Tra Bong [River]. So goes
(20) about $50,000 worth of ammo. They probably played it up as a second Iwo Jima at home, but it wasn't.

Then, two days after we got back, we played Indian Scout, and my platoon splashed its way through a rice paddy at 3:30 in the morning in a rainstorm to surround a hamlet which we managed to do somehow without alerting everyone in the district, which is
(25) surprising as we made enough noise to wake up a Marine sentry. It was "very successful" since we managed to kill a few probably innocent civilians, found a few caves and burned a few houses, all in a driving rainstorm. There's nothing more, I'm afraid.

Love,

Sandy

(30) *On 11 November 1966, Marion Lee (Sandy) Kempner was killed by shrapnel from a mine explosion. He was 24 years old.*

STOP

PRACTICE TEST 1: ANSWER KEY

PASSAGE 1		PASSAGE 2		PASSAGE 3		PASSAGE 4	
1.	E	14.	A	27.	C	40.	D
2.	A	15.	C	28.	A	41.	B
3.	B	16.	D	29.	B	42.	B
4.	C	17.	B	30.	D	43.	D
5.	E	18.	E	31.	E	44.	C
6.	E	19.	A	32.	B	45.	C
7.	A	20.	B	33.	C	46.	E
8.	B	21.	C	34.	C	47.	B
9.	C	22.	D	35.	E	48.	C
10.	E	23.	E	36.	D	49.	D
11.	D	24.	E	37.	D	50.	E
12.	E	25.	C	38.	E	51.	C
13.	D	26.	A	39.	A	52.	B
						53.	B
						54.	E

ANSWERS AND EXPLANATIONS

SECTION I: MULTIPLE CHOICE

We stand here in the name of freedom.

At the heart of that Western freedom and democracy is the belief that the individual
Line
(5) man, the child of God, is the touchstone of value, and all society, groups, the state, exist for his benefit. Therefore the enlargement of liberty for individual human beings must be the supreme goal and the abiding practice of any Western society.

(10) The first element of this individual liberty is the freedom of speech.

The right to express and communicate ideas, to set oneself apart from the dumb beasts of field and forest; to recall governments to
(15) their duties and obligations; above all, the right to affirm one's membership and allegiance to the body politic—to society—to the men with whom we share our land, our heritage and our children's future.

(20) Hand in hand with freedom of speech goes the power to be heard—to share the decisions of government which shape men's lives. Everything that makes life worthwhile— family, work, education, a place to rear one's
(25) children and a place to rest one's head—all this rests on decisions of government; all can be swept away by a government which does not heed the demands of its people. Therefore, the essential humanity of men
(30) can be protected and preserved only where government must answer—not just to those of a particular religion, or a particular race; but to all its people.

And even government by the consent of the
(35) governed, as in our own Constitution, must be limited in its power to act against its people: so that there may be no interference with the right to worship, or with the security of the home; no arbitrary imposition of pains or penalties

(40) by officials high or low; no restrictions on the freedom of men to seek education or work or opportunity of any kind so that each man may become all he is capable of becoming.

These are the sacred rights of Western
(45) society. These are the essential differences between us and Nazi Germany, as they were between Athens and Persia.

They are the essence of our difference with Communism today. I am inalterably
(50) opposed to Communism because it exalts the state over the individual and the family, and because of the lack of freedom of speech, of protest, of religion and of the press, which is characteristic of totalitarian states.

(55) The way of opposition to Communism is not to imitate its dictatorship, but to enlarge individual human freedom—in our own countries and all over the globe. There are those in every land who would label as "Communist"
(60) every threat to their privilege. But as I have seen on my travels in all sections of the world, reform is not Communism. And the denial of freedom, in whatever name, only strengthens the very Communism it claims to oppose.

(65) For two centuries, my own country has struggled to overcome the self-imposed handicap of prejudice and discrimination based on nationality, social class or race— discrimination profoundly repugnant to the
(70) theory and command of our Constitution. Even as my father grew up in Boston, signs told him that "No Irish need apply."

Two generations later President Kennedy became the first Catholic to head the nation;
(75) but how many men of ability had, before 1961, been denied the opportunity to contribute to the nation's progress because they were Catholic, or of Irish extraction.

In the last five years, the winds of change
(80) have blown as fiercely in the United States as anywhere in the world. But they will not— they cannot—abate.

For there are millions of Negroes untrained for the simplest jobs, and thousands every (85) day denied their full equal rights under the law; and the violence of the disinherited, the insulated the injured, looms over the streets of Harlem and Watts and South Chicago.

But a Negro American trains as an (90) astronaut, one of mankind's first explorers into outer space; another is the chief barrister of the United States Government, and dozens sit on the benches of court; and another, Dr. Martin Luther King, is the second man of (95) African descent to win the Nobel Peace Prize for his nonviolent efforts for social justice between the races.

We must recognize the full human equality of all our people before God, before the law, and (100) in the councils of government. We must do this not because it is economically advantageous, although it is; not because the laws of God and man command it, although they do command it; not because people in other lands wish it so. (105) We must do it for the single and fundamental reason that it is the right thing to do.

And this must be our commitment outside our borders as well as within.

It is your job, the task of the young people (110) of this world, to strip the last remnants of that ancient, cruel belief from the civilization of man.

Each nation has different obstacles and different goals, shadowed by the vagaries of (115) history and experience. Yet as I talk to young people around the world I am impressed not by the diversity but by the closeness of their goals, their desires and concerns and hopes for the future. There is discrimination in New York, apartheid (120) in South Africa and serfdom in the mountains of Peru. People stagnate in the streets of India; intellectuals go to jail in Russia; thousands are slaughtered in Indonesia; wealth is lavished on armaments everywhere. These are differing (125) evils. But they are common works of man.

And therefore they call upon common qualities of conscience and of indignation, a shared determination to wipe away the unnecessary sufferings of our fellow human (130) beings at home and particularly around the world.

In the world we would like to build, South Africa could play an outstanding role, and a role of leadership in that effort. This country (135) is without question a preeminent repository of the wealth and the knowledge and the skill of the continent. Here are the greater part of Africa's research scientists and steel production, most of its reservoirs of coal and of electric (140) power. Many South Africans have made major contributions to African technical development and world science; the names of some are known wherever men seek to eliminate the ravages of tropical disease and of pestilence. In (145) your faculties and councils, here in this very audience, are hundreds and thousands of men and women who could transform the lives of millions for all time to come.

So we part, I to my country and you to (150) remain. We are—if a man of forty can claim the privilege—fellow members of the world's largest younger generation. Each of us has our own work to do. I know at times you must feel very alone with your problems and (155) with your difficulties. But I want to say how impressed I am with what you stand for and for the effort you are making; and I say this not just for myself, but men and women all over the world. And I hope you will often (160) take heart from the knowledge that you are joined with your fellow young people in every land, they struggling with their problems and you with yours, but all joined in a common purpose; that, like the young people of my

(165) own country and of every country that I have
visited, you are all in many ways more closely
united to the brothers of your time than to
the older generation in any of these nations;
and that you are determined to build a better
(170) future.

From Robert F. Kennedy's address to the
National Union of South African Students'
Day of Affirmation, 6 June 1966

1.   E

This main idea is actually expressed in paragraph 2:
"Therefore the enlargement of liberty for individaul
human beings must be the supreme goal and the
abiding practice of any Western society." Robert
Kennedy then proceeds to elaborate on this point
throughout the remainder of his speech.

2.   A

It is not unusual for the multiple-choice questions to
move from an idea question, such as question 1, to a
stylistic question, such as this one. If you take a close
look at paragraph 4, you will find everything but
compound-complex sentence structure. Paragraph 4
is actually one very long fragment. It does, however,
have items in a series without conjunctions, (B);
a parenthetical appositive, (C), "to society," which
renames or defines what is meant by the "body
politic"; anaphora, (D), or phrases starting with the
same infinitive opening; and certainly many items in
a series, (E).

3.   B

It is common for the main idea of a paragraph to
appear in the topic sentence, and that is exactly what
we have here. A lot of other very important things
are mentioned in this paragraph as well, but they are
all supportive of the idea of "hearing" the common
voice of man.

4.   C

You can find the answer to this question at the end
of paragraph 6. The main point that Kennedy is
making is that governments must allow people to
have as much freedom as is reasonably possible.

Man has certain unalienable rights, and it is through
these rights that one can fulfill one's potential.

5.   E

Kennedy is attempting to establish common ground
with his audience. When he gave this speech in
South Africa, apartheid was rampant. He wants
his listeners to understand that they are not alone
in suffering discrimination. Of course, by his
generation, most of the anti-Irish sentiments in the
United States had dissipated.

6.   E

The sentence "But they will not—they cannot—
abate," demonstrates parenthetical emphasis, (A),
with the use of the dashes. The pronoun *they* is a
reference to "winds of change" in the first sentence
of the paragraph. The near repetition of the phrasing
"they will not" and "they cannot" is a loose form
of anaphora, (C). And there is no mistaking the
imperative, almost imperious tone of the sentence, (D).

7.   A

Kennedy makes several references to Communism,
but the main point he makes is that Communism
sacrifices the individual for the common good,
which is unacceptable.

8.   B

When a series of words or phrases is strung together
without the use of conjunctions, it is referred to as
asyndeton (without conjunctions). When a series
uses conjunctions between the parts of the series,
then it is polysyndeton (many conjunctions).

9.   C

Although Kennedy is addressing the entire audience
in South Africa, as well as knowing that he would
be heard and read by the people of the world,
the presentation was given at a Students' Day
Affirmation, and as he draws his speech to a close,
he particularly addresses the youth in his audience.

10.   E

Basically, Kennedy is expressing the need for people
around the world to stand up for what is right and

to have the courage of their convictions—to be like Martin Luther King and say and do what is right for all mankind, regardless of opposition or the ease in just accepting what is happening instead of becoming involved.

11. D

As Kennedy closes his speech, he attempts to do many things, but most of all, he appeals to the younger generation, identifying with them (in the last paragraph) in the burden that they must shoulder to make the world a better place in which all people may live.

12. E

Kennedy highlights the strengths that South Africa has. He commends South Africans for their advancements and hopes that they will participate more with the rest of the world. All of the responses are covered in this passage except racial tolerance, which, of course, South Africa was not known for.

13. D

This response makes the most sense because the speech was addressed to the National Union of South African Students' Day of Affirmation. As he concludes the speech, he calls upon the youth of South Africa to join with the youth from around the world in creating a better world for all of their futures.

On a winter day some years ago, coming out of Pittsburgh on one of the expresses of the Pennsylvania Railroad, I rolled eastward for an hour through the coal and steel towns
Line
(5) of Westmoreland county. It was familiar ground; boy and man, I had been through it often before. But somehow I had never quite sensed its appalling desolation. Here was the very heart of industrial America, the center of
(10) its most lucrative and characteristic activity, the boast and pride of the richest and grandest nation ever seen on earth—and here was a scene so dreadfully hideous, so intolerably bleak and forlorn that it reduced the whole
(15) aspiration of man to a macabre and depressing joke. Here was wealth beyond computation, almost beyond imagination—and here were human habitations so abominable that they would have disgraced a race of alley cats.

(20)   I am not speaking of mere filth. One expects steel towns to be dirty. What I allude to is the unbroken and agonizing ugliness, the sheer revolting monstrousness, of every house in sight. From East Liberty to
(25) Greensburg, a distance of twenty-five miles, there was not one in sight from the train that did not insult and lacerate the eye. Some were so bad, and they were among the most pretentious—churches, stores, warehouses,
(30) and the like—that they were downright startling; one blinked before them as one blinks before a man with his face shot away. A few linger in memory, horrible even there: a crazy little church just west of Jeannette, set
(35) like a dormer-window on the side of a bare, leprous hill; the headquarters of the Veterans of Foreign Wars at another forlorn town, a steel stadium like a huge rat-trap somewhere further down the line. But most of all I recall
(40) the general effect—of hideousness without a break. There was not a single decent house within eye range from the Pittsburgh suburbs to the Greensburg yards. There was not one that was not misshapen, and there was not
(45) one that was not shabby.

The country itself is not uncomely, despite the grime of the endless mills. It is, in form, a narrow river valley, with deep gullies running up into the hills. It is thickly settled, but not
(50) noticeably overcrowded. There is still plenty of room for building, even in the larger towns, and there are very few solid blocks. Nearly every house, big and little, has space on all four sides. Obviously, if there were architects of

(55) any professional sense or dignity in the region, they would have perfected a chalet to hug the hillsides—a chalet with a high-pitched roof to throw off the heavy winter snows, but still essentially a low and clinging building, wider

(60) than it was tall. But what have they done? They have taken as their model a brick set on end. This they have converted into a thing of dingy clapboards, with a narrow, low-pitched roof. And the whole they have set upon thin,

(65) preposterous brick piers. By the hundreds and thousands these abominable houses cover the bare hillsides, like gravestones in some gigantic and decaying cemetery on their deep sides they are three, four and even five stories high; on

(70) their low sides they bury themselves swinishly in the mud. Not a fifth of them are perpendicular. They lean this way and that, hanging on to their bases precariously. And one and all they are streaked in grime, with dead and eczematous

(75) patches of paint peeping through the streaks.

Now and then there is a house of brick. But what brick! When it is new it is the color of a fried egg. When it has taken on the patina of the mills it is the color of an egg long past

(80) all hope or caring. Was it necessary to adopt that shocking color? No more than it was necessary to set all of the houses on end. Red brick, even in a steel town, ages with some dignity. Let it become downright black, and

(85) it is still sightly, especially if its trimmings are of white stone, with soot in the depths and the high spots washed by the rain. But in Westmoreland they prefer that uremic yellow, and so they have the most loathsome towns

(90) and villages ever seen by mortal eye.

I award this championship only after laborious research and incessant prayer. I have seen, I believe, all of the most unlovely towns of the world; they are all to be found

(95) in the United States. I have seen the mill towns of decomposing New England and the desert towns of Utah, Arizona and Texas. I am familiar with the back streets of Newark, Brooklyn and Chicago, and have made

(100) scientific explorations to Camden, N.J. and Newport News, Va. Safe in a Pullman, I have whirled through the gloomy, God-forsaken villages of Iowa and Kansas, and the malarious tide-water hamlets of Georgia. I have been to

(105) Bridgeport, Conn., and to Los Angeles. But nowhere on this earth, at home or abroad, have I seen anything to compare to the villages that huddle along the line of the Pennsylvania from the Pittsburgh yards to Greensburg.

(110) They are incomparable in color, and they are incomparable in design. It is as if some titanic and aberrant genius, uncompromisingly inimical to man, had devoted all the ingenuity of Hell to the making of them. They show

(115) grotesqueries of ugliness that, in retrospect, become almost diabolical. One cannot imagine mere human beings concocting such dreadful things, and one can scarcely imagine human beings bearing life in them.

(120) Are they so frightful because the valley is full of foreigners—dull, insensate brutes, with no love of beauty in them? Then why didn't these foreigners set up similar abominations in the countries that they came from? You

(125) will, in fact, find nothing of the sort in Europe save perhaps in the more putrid parts of England. There is scarcely an ugly village on the whole Continent. The peasants, however poor, somehow manage to make themselves

(130) graceful and charming habitations, even in Spain. But in the American village and small town the pull is always toward ugliness, and in that Westmoreland valley it has been yielded to with an eagerness bordering upon passion. It

(135) is incredible that mere ignorance should have achieved such masterpieces of horror.

On certain levels of the American race, indeed, there seems to be a positive libido for the ugly, as on other and less Christian (140) levels there is a libido for the beautiful. It is impossible to put down the wallpaper that defaces the average American home of the lower middle class to mere inadvertence, or to the obscene humor of the manufacturers. (145) Such ghastly designs, it must be obvious, give a genuine delight to a certain type of mind. They meet, in some unfathomable way, its obscure and unintelligible demands. They caress it as "The Palms" caresses it, or the art of the movie, (150) or jazz. The taste for them is as enigmatical and yet as common as the taste for dogmatic theology and the poetry of Edgar A. Guest.

Thus I suspect (though confessedly without knowing) that the vast majority of the honest (155) folk of Westmoreland county, and especially the 100% Americans among them, actually admire the houses they live in, and are proud of them. For the same money they could get vastly better ones, but they prefer what they (160) have got. Certainly there was no pressure upon the Veterans of Foreign Wars to choose the dreadful edifice that bears their banner, for there are plenty of vacant buildings along the track-side, and some of them are (165) appreciably better. They might, indeed, have built a better one of their own. But they chose that clapboarded horror with their eyes open, and having chosen it, they let it mellow into its present shocking depravity. They like it (170) as it is: beside it, the Parthenon would no doubt offend them. In precisely the same way the authors of the rattrap stadium that I have mentioned made a deliberate choice. After painfully designing and erecting it, they (175) made it perfect in their own sight by putting a completely impossible pent-house, painted a staring yellow, on top of it. The effect is that of a fat woman with a black eye. It is that of a Presbyterian grinning. But they like it.

(180) Here is something that the psychologists have so far neglected: the love of ugliness for its own sake, the lust to make the world intolerable. Its habitat is the United States. Out of the melting pot emerges a race which hates beauty (185) as it hates truth. The etiology of this madness deserves a great deal more study than it has got. There must be causes behind it; it arises and flourishes in obedience to biological laws, and not as a mere act of God. What, precisely, are (190) the terms of those laws? And why do they run stronger in America than elsewhere? Let some honest *Privat Dozent* in pathological sociology apply himself to the problem.

From "The Libido for the Ugly" by H. L. Mencken in *Prejudices: Sixth Series* (1927)

14. A

The narrator of this passage has a mission, and that mission is to describe the extreme ugliness of this section of Pennsylvania. Although some of the other choices may be found within the passage, the primary focus is on ugliness.

15. C

All of the choices except this one are used to describe the houses. The reference to a rat trap is used to describe a steel stadium.

16. D

At first, the narrator describes what he sees and depicts its ugliness. As the passage continues, however, he begins musing over just why humanity would tolerate and even choose to surround itself with such incredible ugliness.

17. B

The narrator says in paragraph 3 that "the country itself is not uncomely, despite the grime of the endless mills. It is in form, a narrow river valley, with deep gullies running up into the hills. It is thickly settled, but not noticeably overcrowded," and so on. What he just cannot understand is how such ugliness could be built upon a landscape that seemingly deserves much better.

18. E
Paragraph 2 has much in it that demonstrates the author's disdain of the horrors he views. However, the specific identification of the geographical location is not one of those characteristics. Perhaps it could be, by connotation, for some, but it is not specifically a device used to express the ugliness.

19. A
The author's words make it sound like he is holding an ugliness contest. In order to have such a contest, it can be assumed that the narrator has seen several, perhaps many, other displeasing places that have offended his eye. Nevertheless, the one he talks about in this passage is the worst.

20. B
The descriptor "uremic yellow," a phrase that the writer seems to have coined, is simply more proof of his total disdain for the ugliness of the houses he is viewing.

21. C
The phrase "peasants however poor" is nicely alliterative, giving the sentence a stylistic ring.

22. D
In paragraph 8, the narrator says, "They like it [the ugliness of their houses] as it is: beside it, the Parthenon would no doubt offend them." Again the narrator is flabbergasted by the inhabitants' preference for the ugly. Their tastes are so skewed that the Parthenon—traditionally considered a building of great beauty—would be found offensive by these people who prefer ugliness.

23. E
The narrator thinks that the ugliness of the architecture and the people who seem to prefer it would all make great psychological studies. Nowhere, however, does he mention pathological sociology.

24. E
"*Privat Dozent*" actually refers to someone who is an expert. You would not be expected to know this term, but from context, you should be able to gather that this would be some kind of specialist who might want to study such aberrations of ugliness.

25. C
Responses (A), (B), and (E) might work as responses, but the author would be *most likely* to agree that sometimes there is just no explanation for bad taste.

26. A
Looking at this sentence, you should be able to pick up on how the narrator feels about the situation. In addition, you are being asked to strain your knowledge of vocabulary to do some elimination. The most accurate description of tone is that of harsh disparagement (disgust).

The struggle between Liberty and Authority is the most conspicuous feature in the portions of history with which we are familiar. By liberty, was meant protection against the tyranny of
Line
(5) the political rulers. The rulers were conceived (except in some of the popular governments of Greece) as in a necessarily antagonistic position to the people whom they ruled. They consisted of a governing One, or a governing tribe or caste,
(10) who derived their authority from inheritance or conquest, who, at all events, did not hold it at the pleasure of the governed, and whose supremacy men did not venture, perhaps did not desire, to contest, whatever precautions might be taken
(15) against its oppressive exercise. Their power was regarded as necessary, but also as highly dangerous; as a weapon which they would attempt to use against their subjects, no less than against external enemies. To prevent the weaker
(20) members of the community from being preyed on by innumerable vultures, it was needful that there should be an animal of prey stronger than

the rest, commissioned to keep them down. But as the king of the vultures would be no less bent
(25) upon preying upon the flock than of the minor harpies, it was indispensable to be in a perpetual attitude of defence against his beak and claws. The aim, therefore, of patriots was to set limits to the power which the ruler should be suffered to
(30) exercise over the community; and this limitation was what they meant by liberty. It was attempted in two ways. First, by obtaining a recognition of certain immunities, called political liberties or rights, which it was to be regarded as a
(35) breach of duty in the ruler to infringe, and which, if he did infringe, specific resistance, or general rebellion, was held to be justifiable. A second, and generally a later expedient, was the establishment of constitutional checks, by
(40) which the consent of the community, or a body of some sort, supposed to represent its interests, was made a necessary condition to some of the more important acts of the governing power.

A time came, in the progress of human
(45) affairs, when men ceased to think it a necessity of nature that their governors should be an independent power, opposed in interest to themselves. The notion, that the people have no need to limit their power over themselves, might
(50) seem axiomatic, when popular government was a thing only dreamed about, or read of as having existed at some distant period of the past. In time, however, a democratic republic came to occupy a large portion of the earth's surface,
(55) and made itself felt as one of the most powerful members of the community of nations; and elective and responsible government became subject to the observations and criticisms which wait upon a great existing fact. It was
(60) now perceived that such phrases as "self-government," and "the power of the people over themselves," do not express the true state of the case. The "people" who exercise the power

are not always the same people with those over
(65) whom it is exercised; and the "self-government" spoken of is not the government of each by himself, but of each by all the rest. The will of the people, moreover, practically means the will of the most numerous or the most active *part* of
(70) the people; the majority, or those who succeed in making themselves accepted as the majority; the people, consequently, *may* desire to oppress a part of their number; and precautions are as much needed against this as against any other
(75) abuse of power. The limitation, therefore, of the power of government over individuals loses none of its importance when the holders of power are regularly accountable to the community, that is, to the strongest party
(80) therein. This view of things, recommending itself equally to the intelligence of thinkers and to the inclination of those important classes in European society to whose real or supposed interests democracy is adverse, has had no
(85) difficulty in establishing itself; and in political speculations "the tyranny of the majority" is now generally included among the evils against which society requires to be on its guard.

Like other tyrannies, the tyranny of the
(90) majority was at first, and is still vulgarly, held in dread, chiefly as operating through the acts of the public authorities. But reflecting persons perceived that when society is itself the tyrant— society collectively, over the separate individuals
(95) who compose it—its means of tyrannizing are not restricted to the acts which it may do by the hands of its political functionaries. Society can and does execute its own mandates: and if it issues wrong mandates instead of right, or any
(100) mandates at all in things with which it ought not to meddle, it practices a social tyranny more formidable than many kinds of political oppression, since, though not usually upheld by such extreme penalties, it leaves fewer means of

(105) escape, penetrating much more deeply into the details of life, and enslaving itself. Protection, therefore, against the tyranny of the magistrate is not enough: there needs to be protection also against the tyranny of the prevailing opinion *(110)* and feelings; against the tendency of society to impose, by other means than civil penalties, its own ideas and practices as rules of conduct on those whose dissent from them; to fetter development, and, if possible, prevent the *(115)* formation, of any individuality not in harmony with its ways, and compel all characters to fashion themselves upon the model of its own.

From Chapter 1 of *On Liberty* by John Stuart Mill (1859)

27. C
In this question we are being asked to consider a word, *popular*, whose meaning has changed over the centuries. Popular vote is the vote of the people, similar to the idea conveyed by the word *populous*. It has nothing to do with having or not having a lot of friends, as the word often means today.

28. A
Occasionally, you have to identify just what mode or manner of writing the writer is using in a passage. Exposition generally means explanation. It is the best response for this question. (B), narration, is telling a story. This passage is not really an argument, (C); nor is it comparison and contrast, (D), or cause and effect, (E).

29. B
Paragraph 1 has numerous descriptions of the enemy as an animal, especially a predator. The author does not, however, refer to the enemy as the marauding hordes.

30. D
The author's fundamental belief is that the governing One cannot have total, unrestrained control over anyone. That would be tyranny. The author believes that liberty can be won only by

eliminating the tyranny of the One, as well as monitoring governance by the majority.

31. E
"Axiomatic" means that something is self-evident. You may have heard the term *axiom*—it is an idea or a belief that is evident, something that can be relied upon as universally true.

32. B
One irony that this author seems to want to stress is that government by the people may be misleading. Sometimes those who are in charge of governing manage to be outside the government that they establish. True government by the people would include everyone—the governed and the governors.

33. C
This entire passage has to do with the governed and the governing of the governed. The writer tries to explain how best to achieve a reasonable balance that will give people the most freedom without encroaching upon others' freedoms.

34. C
If you recall from Key Terminology, an allusion is a historic or mythological reference that is brought in for comparison purposes. Harpies are from mythology—they were a type of witch. In fact, the witches in Macbeth are referred to as three harpies.

35. E
The words *part* and *may* are italicized for emphasis. The writer wants you to pay attention to the distinction he is making. He is also being very critical about so-called self-government, and he is emphasizing that there is often a discrepancy within such a setup.

36. D
The antecedent for the pronoun *it* is the word *society*.

37. D
Go back to paragraph 2; you will see that it deals with the emergence of government by the populace and the inherent problems even such a long-dreamt-of government can hold. Control by

the majority must not be allowed without certain restrictions upon those who rule.

38. E

What the narrator seems most concerned about is the fact that even in a government by the people, those who exercise the power sometimes manage not to be those over whom the power is exercised. Sometimes these people in power can take unfair advantage of this situation.

39. A

In line with the last two questions, this narrator concludes that we must always be watchful. Even in the world of government by the people, checks and balances must be established, for the governors are also in need of being governed.

Moths that fly by day are not properly to be called moths; they do not excite that pleasant sense of dark autumn nights and ivy-blossom
Line which the commonest yellow-underwing asleep
(5) in the shadow of the curtain never fails to rouse in us. They are hybrid creatures, neither gay like butterflies nor sombre like their own species. Nevertheless the present specimen, with his narrow hay-coloured wings, fringed with a
(10) tassel of the same colour, seemed to be content with life. It was a pleasant morning, mid-September, mild, benignant, yet with a keener breath than that of the summer months. The plough was already scoring the field opposite
(15) the window, and where the share had been, the earth was pressed flat and gleamed with moisture. Such vigour came rolling in from the fields and the down beyond that it was difficult to keep the eyes strictly turned upon the book.
(20) The rooks too were keeping one of their annual festivities; soaring round the tree tops until it looked as if a vast net with thousands of black knots in it had been cast up into the air; which, after a few moments sank slowly down upon

(25) the trees until every twig seemed to have a knot at the end of it. Then, suddenly, the net would be thrown into the air again in a wider circle this time, with the utmost clamour and vociferation, as though to be thrown into the
(30) air and settle slowly down upon the tree tops were a tremendously exciting experience.

The same energy which inspired the rooks, the ploughmen, the horses, and even, it seemed, the lean bare-backed downs, sent the
(35) moth fluttering from side to side of his square of the window-pane. One could not help watching him. One was, indeed, conscious of a queer feeling of pity for him. The possibilities of pleasure seemed that morning so enormous
(40) and so various that to have only a moth's part in life, and a day moth's at that, appeared a hard fate, and his zest in enjoying his meagre opportunities to the full, pathetic. He flew vigorously to one corner of his compartment,
(45) and, after waiting there a second, flew across to the other. What remained for him but to fly to a third corner and then to a fourth? That was all he could do, in spite of the size of the downs, the width of the sky, the far-off smoke
(50) of houses, and the romantic voice, now and then, of a steamer out at sea. What he could do he did. Watching him, it seemed as if a fibre, very thin but pure, of the enormous energy of the world had been thrust into his frail and
(55) diminutive body. As often as he crossed the pane, I could fancy that a thread of vital light became visible. He was little or nothing but life.

Yet, because he was so small, and so simple a form of the energy that was rolling in at the open
(60) window and driving its way through so many narrow and intricate corridors in my own brain and in those of other human beings, there was something marvellous as well as pathetic about him. It was as if someone had taken a tiny bead
(65) of pure life and decking it as lightly as possible

with down and feathers, had set it dancing
and zigzagging to show us the true nature of
life. Thus displayed one could not get over the
strangeness of it. One is apt to forget all about
(70) life, seeing it humped and bossed and garnished
and cumbered so that it has to move with the
greatest circumspection and dignity. Again, the
thought of all that life might have been had he
been born in any other shape caused one to view
(75) his simple activities with a kind of pity.

After a time, tired by his dancing
apparently, he settled on the window ledge in
the sun, and, the queer spectacle being at an
end, I forgot about him. Then, looking up,
(80) my eye was caught by him. He was trying to
resume his dancing, but seemed either so stiff
or so awkward that he could only flutter to the
bottom of the window-pane; and when he tried
to fly across it he failed. Being intent on other
(85) matters I watched these futile attempts for a
time without thinking, unconsciously waiting
for him to resume his flight, as one waits for
a machine, that has stopped momentarily, to
start again without considering the reason of
(90) its failure. After perhaps a seventh attempt
he slipped from the wooden ledge and fell,
fluttering his wings, on to his back on the
window sill. The helplessness of his attitude
roused me. It flashed upon me that he was in
(95) difficulties; he could no longer raise himself;
his legs struggled vainly. But, as I stretched
out a pencil, meaning to help him to right
himself, it came over me that the failure and
awkwardness were the approach of death. I laid
(100) the pencil down again.

The legs agitated themselves once more. I
looked as if for the enemy against which
he struggled. I looked out of doors. What
had happened there? Presumably it was
(105) midday, and work in the fields had stopped.
Stillness and quiet had replaced the previous

animation. The birds had taken themselves off
to feed in the brooks. The horses stood still.
Yet the power was there all the same, massed
(110) outside indifferent, impersonal, not attending
to anything in particular. Somehow it was
opposed to the little hay-coloured moth. It was
useless to try to do anything. One could only
watch the extraordinary efforts made by those
(115) tiny legs against an oncoming doom which
could, had it chosen, have submerged an entire
city, not merely a city, but masses of human
beings; nothing, I knew, had any chance against
death. Nevertheless after a pause of exhaustion
(120) the legs fluttered again. It was superb this last
protest, and so frantic that he succeeded at
last in righting himself. One's sympathies, of
course, were all on the side of life. Also, when
there was nobody to care or to know, this
(125) gigantic effort on the part of an insignificant
little moth, against a power of such magnitude,
to retain what no one else valued or desired to
keep, moved one strangely. Again, somehow,
one saw life, a pure bead. I lifted the pencil
(130) again, useless though I knew it to be. But even
as I did so, the unmistakable tokens of death
showed themselves. The body relaxed, and
instantly grew stiff. The struggle was over. The
insignificant little creature now knew death. As
(135) I looked at the dead moth, this minute wayside
triumph of so great a force over so mean an
antagonist filled me with wonder. Just as life
had been strange a few minutes before, so
death was now as strange. The moth having
(140) righted himself now lay most decently and
uncomplainingly composed. O yes, he seemed
to say, death is stronger than I am.

"The Death of the Moth" by Virginia
Woolf (published 1942)

40. D

The first two sentences of this passage establish the fact that daytime moths are not like those who haunt the darkness, nor are they a part of the butterfly world of daylight.

41. B

In line with question 40, the narrator calls the daytime moths hybrid—having characteristics of the nighttime moth and the daytime butterfly but not belonging to either of these species.

42. B

Personal reflection, or personal observation, is the best descriptor for this passage. It is not an argument, (A), nor a definition, (C). It seems to be description, but there is also an element of the narrator's own musings in this passage, and that removes it from the mode of pure description, (D). This passage lacks any real scientific information about moths, just personal observations, so it cannot be classified as technical writing, (E).

43. D

Ripe pumpkins are not mentioned in this passage anywhere. Even though pumpkins in their prime connote the fall season, only the other characteristics of fall are included.

44. C

These lines reiterate the idea of life several times: "a thread of *vital* light became visible. He was little or nothing but *life* . . . as if someone had taken a tiny bead of pure *life* . . . to show us the true nature of *life*."

45. C

An analogy is a comparison of one thing to another for clarification, often used in enhancing a descriptive passage. Metaphors and similes are simple analogies. In this passage, however, the vision of the rooks to the net is extended as the rooks rise and fall as if lifted by the edge, raised and lowered once again into the trees.

46. E

These lines read: "One was, indeed, conscious of a queer feeling of pity for him. The possibilities of pleasure seemed that morning so enormous and so various that to have only a moth's part in life, and a day moth's at that, appeared a hard fate, and his zest in enjoying his meagre opportunities to the full, pathetic. He flew vigorously to one corner of his compartment, and, after waiting there a second, flew across to the other." It is easy to hear the alliteration (of *p, m, c*), and the open vowel sounds (*was, conscious, possibilities, morning,* etc.) repeat, giving the lines strong assonance as well.

47. B

This question takes us to the second sentence of paragraph 3: "It was as if someone had taken a tiny bead of pure life and decking it as lightly as possible with down and feathers, had set it dancing and zigzagging to show us the true nature of life."

48. C

If you check the Key Terminology words, you will find that asyndeton is a series of words or phrases connected without the use of conjunctions. It is neither a periodic sentence nor run-on, (A) and (B). Anaphora is the repetition of opening words of phrases or clauses in a series, (D). And there is no parallelism, (E).

49. D

Without referring to paragraph 4, it seems as if any one of these responses might be the possible correct answer. However, the paragraph concludes with these words: "As I stretched out a pencil, meaning to help him to right himself, it came over me that the failure and awkwardness were the approach of death. I laid the pencil down again."

50. E

Understanding tone is sometimes difficult to do. One must first get a feeling for the passage, a feeling for the message of the passage, and a feeling for the feelings of the narrator. In this case, the narrator is truly regretful for the brief heroic life of the little moth, and she has imbued this creature with a sense that it represents something far greater than what it seems at a glance, thus making (E) the correct response.

51. C

While the word *composed* illustrates the death of the moth, and thus an end to its struggles, the word is also a pun, intended to indicate that the moth is analogous to a musical or literary work of art. (C) is the correct answer.

52. B

Although the narrator calls the moth *insignificant* in line 125, she describes the pity and admiration she feels for it as it dies. The moth is clearly significant to the narrator; therefore, all of the answer choices EXCEPT (B) would be agreeable to the narrator.

53. B

The author's narrative describes the physical struggle of a dying moth and, simultaneously, the writer's own inner struggle. Throughout the passage, the tone remains conversational, as the narrator comes to terms with her own consciousness and creativity. The moth and author are connected: the cyclical nature of the moth's life and death is symbolic of the artistic process that illustrates the survival of a tragedy. This analysis also remains constant through the narration, making (B) correct.

54. E

These last questions are making you delve into the narrator's point of view. She feels regret that such a stalwart fighter has such a brief life; she is also impressed that this creature seems to have the courage to make the most of its brief hours.

ESSAY QUESTION ONE: SKATEBOARDING

ANALYSIS OF ESSAY QUESTION ONE

Most teenagers will be delighted to write on a topic with which they can closely identify. Skateboarding is an activity and a culture most associated with youth. There will be many entries into this conversation.

This prompt is an example of the expository prompt. Students are asked to write more of an expository synthesis essay rather than an argument. In this case, you are given a variety of sources ranging from first-person accounts of one college student's love of skateboarding, to complaint letters, to municipal codes. The writer needs to *explain* the "complex community issues involved." Not all of these issues are explicitly addressed in the prompt; many of the issues will need to be inferred from the source material. Herein lies the challenge.

So what are the "complex community issues" involved? Aperio Consulting (Source A) seems to give a sort of overview of the issue. Many writers will use this prompt as a safe starting point. Lawrence Csaszar (Source B) provides a source with some "attitude"—a passionate skateboarder himself, Csaszar is upset with how skateboarding is perceived and how it does not get the same respect as other sports or activities. The municipal code (Source C) shows how communities have responded to skateboarders gathering and practicing in certain areas (usually downtown) of cities. Source D is a letter to the editor that shows some real concerns about supervising youth at public skateboard parks. Source E, the nontextual source, shows a couple things of note: the undeniable athleticism of the skateboarder and the demand for more spaces to skate. Source F seems to build on what the photograph begins. There is some concern about the perception of skateboarders, but there is also a distinction made between the different styles of skating (old-school transitional/half-pipe versus new-school street). The last line in Source F, "It shows that you don't have to play baseball to be an athlete," will be a popular choice to use.

Obviously, those students who know something about skateboarding will have an advantage in drawing from outside knowledge on this question, but writers will have to be careful that they stick to the question asked—to explain the complex issues involved, not to take a position. Students who take on a voice like Csaszar's will score less than if they write a carefully developed essay that addresses the many sides of this issue.

SCORING GUIDE FOR QUESTION ONE

9 Essays earning a score of 9 meet the criteria for essays that are scored an 8 and, in addition, are especially sophisticated in their analysis and synthesis* of cited sources or impressive in their control of language.

8 Effective
Essays earning a score of 8 effectively analyze and explain the complex community issues involved in addressing the needs of growing numbers of skateboarders. They successfully

support their explanation by synthesizing and citing at least three sources. The writer's analysis is thorough, and the cited sources support the writer's conclusions. The prose demonstrates an ability to control a wide range of the elements of effective writing but is not flawless.

7   Essays earning a score of 7 fit the description of essays that are scored a 6 but are distinguished by more complete or more purposeful argumentation and synthesis of cited sources or a more mature prose style.

6   Adequate

Essays earning a score of 6 adequately analyze and explain some of the complex community issues involved in addressing the needs of growing numbers of skateboarders. They adequately synthesize and cite at least three sources. The writer's explanation is generally convincing, and the cited sources generally support the writer's analysis, but the essay is less developed or less cogent than the essays earning higher scores. Though the language may contain lapses in diction or syntax, generally the prose is clear.

5   Essays earning a score of 5 analyze and explain some of the complex community issues involved in addressing the needs of growing numbers of skateboarders. They support their position by synthesizing at least three sources, but their explanations and their use of cited sources are somewhat limited, inconsistent, or uneven. The writer's focus is generally clear, and the sources generally support the writer's position, but the links to the sources may be strained. The writing may contain lapses in diction or syntax, but it usually conveys the writer's ideas adequately.

4   Inadequate

Essays earning a score of 4 inadequately analyze and explain some of the complex community issues involved in addressing the needs of growing numbers of skateboarders. They attempt to present an argument and support their position by synthesizing and citing at least two sources but may misunderstand, misrepresent, or oversimplify either their own argument or the cited sources they include. The link between the argument and the cited sources is weak. The prose of essays scored 4 may suggest immature control of writing.

3   Essays earning a score of 3 meet the criteria for the score of 4 but demonstrate less understanding of the cited sources, less success in developing their own analysis, or less control of writing.

2   Little Success

Essays earning a score of 2 demonstrate little success in analyzing and explaining some of the complex community issues involved in addressing the needs of growing numbers of skateboarders. They may merely allude to knowledge gained from reading the sources rather than citing the sources themselves. These essays may misread the sources, fail to present an analysis or explanation, or substitute a simpler task by merely responding to the question tangentially or by summarizing the sources. The prose of essays scored a 2 often demonstrates consistent weaknesses in writing, such as a lack of development or organization, grammatical problems, or a lack of control.

1 Essays earning a score of 1 meet the criteria for the score of 2 but are especially simplistic or weak in their control of writing or do not cite even one source.

0 Essays earning a score of 0 are on-topic responses that receive no credit, such as those that merely repeat the prompt.

— Essays earning a dash (–) are blank responses or responses that are completely off topic.

*For the purposes of scoring, *synthesis* refers to combining the sources and the writer's position to form a cohesive, supported argument and accurately citing all sources.

STUDENT A'S RESPONSE TO QUESTION ONE

Skateboarding is a legitimate sport, but unfortunately it doesn't often get treated like one. Sure, there's the occasional X-Games hype or Mountain Dew commercial, but for the most part skateboarders are viewed, and treated, as outsiders bent on destruction and chaos. How did it get to be this way? Does it have to stay this way? Communities all across the United States are attempting to come to terms with ever-growing numbers of youth who love to skateboard. The complex issues involved deal with the use of public and private space, generational and cultural misunderstanding, as well as irresponsibility. As much as skateboarders may complain sometimes about being misunderstood, and by and large they are, in most communities they haven't really done much to help their own case by their actions.

In the popular media, skateboarding is a sport where Tony Hawk (he's the only skateboarder 90 percent of Americans can name) rolls back and forth on half-pipe ramps and catches "big air" while judges score and audiences cheer (Source F). But more and more skateboarders have taken to street skating, making the curbs and benches and stairways of concrete U.S.A. their skatepark when the curves and undulations of the local skatepark have grown tired. Note in Source E how the skater demonstrates a daring feat of intricate skill. This new form of art needs a canvas, but what is available? The streets. The downtowns. The plazas, which were seemingly made for old ladies to feed pigeons in. These places are all ripe for the taking. And they are taken. "Skaters often occupy transitional spaces that are neither exclusively public nor private, generating hostility on the part of property and business owners" (Source A). If not there, then where? The battleground for space has been drawn—if communities will not provide a place for skateboarders to play/skate, then skateboarders will find a place to skate.

Towns like Kettering, Ohio, have the right idea. They have built a new skate park with street skaters in mind (Source F). The story there was the same: Before, "street skaters had to improvise their own parks . . . in the streets, at apartment complexes, and shopping centers" (Source F). With a new street park, skaters have their place while they can better respect other public and private areas. Kettering is unfortunately the exception, not the rule.

Because of the "outlaw" perception that skateboarders have, authority figures such as police and city governments have the wrong idea about skateboarders in general. "For a long time, skateboarding was viewed as something that only punks and vagrants of society did" (Source B). Why would that be? Could it be because skateboarders cause thousands of dollars a year in damage to public property by "grinding" their trucks (Lawrence Csaszar says sarcastically, "I'm sorry if I scratch your pretty marble ledges")? Could it be because skateboarders have been known to be a danger to unwary passersby (Csaszar continues, "I'm sorry if I fall and my board hits a pedestrian")? Could it be because skateboarders have been known to "tag" parks and other areas with graffiti (Source D)? All of these reasons do not help the case of skateboarders—they need to sell the sport on its merits, not the hoodlum image that pervades many suburban communities.

There are great opportunities in skateboarding that many communities don't know about or overlook. Skateboarding is a sport "that is mentally more creative and freeing" than traditional sports (Source F). Communities need to realize "that you don't have to play baseball to be an athlete" (Source F). As soon as this happens, skaters will have a place to skate, park benches and railings will only be used for their intended use, and police looking to pass out tickets to skateboarders will have to go victimize more motorists driving 35 in a 25 zone.

The blame for misunderstanding doesn't all lie with city hall nor does it all lie with the skateboarders who abuse the city monuments. Both have been adversarial, but for the good of all parties, a win-win situation can only happen if both sides give up one thing to gain another.

STUDENT B'S RESPONSE TO QUESTION ONE

Skateboarding. Just saying the word brings images of high-flying, tattooed, punk rockers to mind. This is the X-Games image that is projected on TV. The real image of a skateboarder is a junior-high kid who just came home to an empty house and gets together with his friends at a local church to grind the outside bench edges until someone chases him off. That's the kid that is looking for something to do. His community isn't helping much.

Communities need to build newer and better skateparks. "There is far less space dedicated to skateboarding than other sports such as baseball" (Aperio). If more skateparks were built, then kids like the one grinding church benches would have a place to go. Everyone wants to have a place to go skate.

Also, communities need to abolish laws against skateboarders. In Yamhill, Oregon, you can get a $100 ticket for violating the municipal code on skateboarding. "A skateboard shall not be ridden on a sidewalk in the following areas: (A) On Maple Street between Second and Azalea Streets" (Source C). Why aren't there such strict rules about other things? ". . . Why do we allow people to ride bicycles, roller blades, and scooters? There is no justice in this discrimination" (Source B). No justice indeed.

One thing that communities have to understand is that graffiti is a part of skateboard culture. The lady in Source D didn't understand why there was graffiti: "It has also been drawn to my attention that [Asheville] Parks and Recreation Department has given the skateboarders permission to paint and mark their temporary park." Why is she so upset? Obviously someone in the park district understood how important graffiti and art is to skateboard culture. So they paint up some walls—it looks better that way anyway.

Lastly, communities need to recognize skateboarding for the awesome sport that it is. It takes balance and coordination to be able to do the kinds of tricks you might see. An Ollie is only the beginning. There's also the fakie and the axle grind. Unlike snowboards, skateboards are not stuck to your boots. Look at the picture in Source E—if he's not an athlete then I'm not writing this essay right now. Skateboarding combines the balance of gymnastics with the grace of dancing. When a rider lands a perfect trick, you just have to know how athletic it is.

All in all, skateboarding needs to be reconsidered in many different ways in communities. Until then, the struggle continues.

COMMENTARY ON STUDENT A'S RESPONSE

This essay scores at least an 8. This is an excellent synthesis that uses the source material effectively to forward the discussion on the complex issues that have developed a rift between the public and skateboarders. Student A maintains throughout that both sides are to blame and both sides need to see the problem from a different point of view before making progress. In the course of his essay, Student A manages to differentiate between the old style and new style of skating, prove that skateboarding is a legitimate athletic activity, chide skateboarders for having a "who cares" attitude, and propose solutions that could lead communities to reconsider their policies and planning.

Student A skillfully synthesizes almost all of the sources to present his explanation. In addition, his stylistic devices solidify his 8. A nice repetition ("Could it be that . . ."), an apt metaphor ("This new form of art needs a canvas"), and smooth integration of source material provide a pleasurable read that has a definite edge to it (note the comment on police—Student A must have gotten a ticket recently!).

COMMENTARY ON STUDENT B'S RESPONSE

Student B gets the job done, but she struggles to get there. The overall unevenness and strained attempts to integrate the source material rates this essay at a 4 or 5. The student does achieve the goals of the assignment but not at an adequate level.

Interestingly enough, Student B seems to have enough knowledge on the subject to develop her essay. It seems as if she structured her paragraphs in such a way that it was going to be one source to each paragraph. No more, no less. There is evidence of immaturity of voice in Student B's prose that keeps it from achieving a higher score. Almost all the quotes she uses are full sentences—none are fully integrated into her own prose.

Structurally, this essay doesn't flow well—each paragraph is almost a separate entity unto itself— the transitional "Also" or "Lastly" demonstrate a lack of sophistication and a formulaic approach.

ESSAY QUESTION TWO: SKIN

ANALYSIS OF ESSAY QUESTION TWO

Double passage questions are not unusual on the AP English Language and Composition exam. Many have been presented to students over the years. These have included two passages about the Oklahoma plains by Scott Momaday and D. Brown; two marriage proposals, one from Jane Austen, the other from Charles Dickens; two on the launching of the Sputnik satellite; two on the Galapagos Islands, one by Melville, the other by Darwin; and more recently, two descriptions of the Okeefenokee Swamp in Florida.

These questions require you to analyze the prose of each passage, paying particular attention to the techniques and stylistic devices each of the writers uses. In addition, you may be asked about the effect of each piece, the respective attitude of each author, the purpose of the pieces, etc.

The two passages on skin are similar to others that have appeared on the exam. The first passage, by Richard Selzer, a physician and writer, is poetic: he celebrates the skin he discusses. The second passage is more clinical and much more objective. Such passages are not difficult to understand or to analyze, but you must be able to answer the entire prompt—in this case, analyze stylistic differences as well as discuss the purpose of each passage. Balancing these is sometimes tricky, and it is the expression of these ideas that separate okay writing from very good writing.

SCORING GUIDE FOR QUESTION TWO

9 Essays meet all the criteria for 8 papers and, in addition, are especially full or apt in their analysis or demonstrate particularly impressive insight and/or stylistic control.

8 Essays effectively analyze how the differing styles of the two descriptions reveal each writer's purpose. They refer to the texts, directly or indirectly, assessing how selection and organization of detail, tone, point of view, syntax, and diction convey each writer's aim. Their prose demonstrates an ability to control a wide range of the elements of effective writing but need not be flawless.

7 Essays fit the description of 6 essays but provide more complex analysis or demonstrate a more mature prose style.

6 Essays clearly show the relationship between stylistic choice and purpose and adequately analyze that relationship. Referring to the texts, directly or indirectly, these essays compare the writers' use of specific stylistic elements in revealing purpose. A few lapses in diction or syntax may be present, but generally the prose of 6 essays demonstrates control of ideas and writing.

5 Essays analyze stylistic techniques, but their discussion of varying styles and purposes in the two passages is limited. They may treat techniques of style in a superficial way or develop ideas about purpose inconsistently. A few lapses in diction or syntax may be present, but usually the prose in 5 essays conveys the writers' ideas.

4 Essays inadequately respond to the question's tasks. They may misrepresent or merely touch on purpose, analyze stylistic elements inaccurately, or identify techniques without much development or understanding. The prose of 4 essays may convey the writers' ideas but may suggest immature control over organization, diction, or syntax.

3 Essays meet the same criteria as essays with a score of 4 but are less perceptive about how the techniques of style convey varying purposes or are less consistent in controlling elements of writing.

2 Essays demonstrate little success in analyzing the stylistic elements that convey varying purposes in the two passages. They may lack development or substitute simpler tasks by summarizing passages or simply listing stylistic elements. They may misunderstand or ignore purpose. The prose of 2 papers often reveals consistent weaknesses in writing, such as a lack of development or organization, grammatical problems, or a lack of control.

1 Essays meet the criteria for the score of 2 but, in addition, are especially simplistic in their ideas or weak in their control of language.

STUDENT A'S RESPONSE TO QUESTION TWO

The skin on our bodies is an incredible and complex organ that has inspired extensive research and esthetic admiration from a wide range of people. The writers of these two passages on skin were both impressed with this organ; however, their purposes in writing about human skin were quite different. By analyzing the literary devices that each writer employs, we can see that the writer of the first passage intended to entertain his or her audience and celebrate the skin's amazing capacity, while the author of the second passage meant to inform his audience in a straightforward manner.

The first line of Passage 1 reveals a great deal about the author's purpose in writing the selection. By using a simile, "layered fine as baklava" (comparing it to a delectable dessert), and a metaphor, "the scabbard upon which we are thrilled," in the introduction to the passage, the author indicated that the essay will be an ode to the skin, not an informative, scientific report.

The second paragraph of the first passage also provides evidence that the author's intent is to stir the reader's emotions. The entire paragraph is a rhetorical question, and it is filled with emotionally charged words such as "sensitive" and "flushes, pales and pains," that show the author's intense feelings for the skin. It is a reflection of who we are.

Although Passage I is chiefly a celebration of the skin, it is also informative. It does provide details about the skin, which are found in paragraphs 3 and 4. While describing the construction and life-cycles of the skin, however, the writer manages to present this information in an eloquent, graceful manner. The author uses great imagery throughout, but it is particularly striking in the description of how the skin repairs itself—"the brigade breaks into a charge, fanning out laterally across the wound, racing to seal off the defect." Such an entrancing description captures the reader's imagination. The author manages to present information in an eloquent, graceful manner, and even has a humorous tone when in line 48 the author says, "Hurrah for stratified squamous epithelium." I say hurrah to this great writer.

While the author of passage 1 clearly intended for this essay to entertain and inspire, the author of passage 2 had a different purpose: to inform. This becomes apparent in the first paragraph of the selection in which the author supplies copious facts and figures pertaining to the skin. This is information more typical of a technical piece of writing.

Further proof that the writer of Passage 2's paramount goal was to inform is supplied by the author's style throughout the essay. By using straightforward, unornamented sentence construction, the author's tone in this passage is clinical and objective. It is clear from sentences such as those in paragraphs 3 and 4 that are devoted strictly to description and explanation of the skin's construction and behavior that the writer's intent was entirely to inform the audience of the nature of the human skin.

In conclusion, both passages are very well written and stylized, but each is very different in presentation and effect upon the reader. It is clear that the author of Passage 1 intended to entertain as well as inform, while Passage 2's writer sought only to inform, and cared very little whether or not the reader was entertained or not.

STUDENT B'S RESPONSE TO QUESTION TWO

Who knew that two passages on skin could be so different? Passage 1 is amusing and poetic, and its purpose is to entertain, and as a second thought, educate. Passage 2, however, is just about education. These two passages reaveal their overall purposes with the use of language, rhetorical devices, and style.

The language used in Passage 1 is very poetic and descriptive, with some medical jargon thrown in. This is shown in the exclamation, "Hurrah for stratified squamous epithelium!" Passage 2, on the other hand, uses mostly simple language or straight medical terminology. The reader of Passage 1 is to be entertained and maybe learn something. The reader of Passage 2 is to be educated.

Passage 2 also uses no literary devices, a fact that contributes to its cold, clinical tone. In sharp contrast, Passage 1 uses similes, imagery and personification to illustrate the skin's importance and the biological processes it undergoes.

Perhaps the biggest difference between the two passages is the style. Passage 1 is very poetic and makes the skin seem like a very beautiful thing, and the skin cells seem very heroic. Passage 2 is reminiscent of a biology textbook, and just delivers the facts in a cold, monotonous way. When I imagine these passages being read out loud, the first passage is accompanied by an interpretive dance and music, and is performed on stage. Passage 2 is being read by a boring teacher in front of a sleepy class. Through the use of language, literary devices, and style, both passages achieve their very different purposes in very different ways. "Hurrah for stratified squamus epithelium!" It sure beats "Each square centimeter has 6 million cells, 5,000 sensory points, 100 sweat glands, and 15 sebaceous glands." Ick.

STUDENT C'S RESPONSE QUESTION TWO

Essays get written through the perspective of the author. Although this is no surprise, what is amazing is that so many essays can be written about the same thing. In these two essays about skin, you can see two very different ways of talking about the same thing. Passage 2 is your run of the mill scientific essay. Passage 1, however, manages to take the same topic, skin, and romanticize it in an almost poetic essay.

Passage 2 serves to inform and educate. This is evident from the beginning with all the details—"20% of the body weight, 100 sweat glands, 5,000 sensory points, and 15 sebaceous glands." There's nothing romantic there; this author gets right to the point.

Passage 1 speaks almost fondly of the skin. The diction in this passage is full of emotion, and the author sounds almost enthusiastic as he writes. Lots of imagery is used and even a bible allusion. This is truly a more poetic presentation than the straightforward (boring) Passage 2.

Overall, the possibilities for an essay are endless. It's all up to the author. These two passages show how two people can write very differently on the very same topic. Passage 1 almost inspires the reader while Passage 2 educates (or puts the reader to sleep).

COMMENTARY ON STUDENT A'S RESPONSE

Student A has responded to the double passage in block format. That is, she discusses one passage and then discusses the other passage. Overall, she is successful with her response. She does not discuss all the stylistic devices that make the first passage sing. Instead, she has focused on those that seem to have impressed her the most, using examples from the text and more than a touch of her own voice as well. The mention of baklava and the skin as delectable as a dessert is a nice touch.

Also, her personal aside about "Hurrah to the writer," might be considered by some as too much, but she seems to be celebrating the writer (Richard Selzer) as much as the writer celebrates skin.

Just as the second passage slows down and is more objective, so too is Student A's response. She correctly discusses the informative, objective nature of the second passage in her own informative, objective manner. Perhaps inadvertently, the student's own writing parallels the shift between the two passages.

Readers would have no trouble awarding this response with a 7, and I am sure that many would also vote for a score of 8. This would not be an 8 that's almost a 9 but an 8 just a bit better than a 7. Remember, each number of the scoring guide can have within it a great variety of responses that garner the same score. Think of the difference between a B- and a B+. One score is a squeak above a C, while the other score is just shy of an A. In either case, 7 or 8, Student A has done a more than adequate job of responding to the prompt and the two passages.

COMMENTARY ON STUDENT B'S RESPONSE

This response is a 5. There's no doubt about it. Student B understands the passage. She says all the right things; it's just that she says too much but doesn't show us enough. Her identification of some of the stylistic devices is accurate; it's just that she does not do enough with what she says.

It is the last paragraph of Student B's response that makes this a 5 and not a 4. There is just enough personal reaction here to give us a real sense of her understanding of the passages and their intent. This is a student response that readers wish the student could rewrite for a higher grade. The potential is evident, but the essay does not have enough depth to reach beyond a score of a 5.

COMMENTARY ON STUDENT C'S RESPONSE

At first you might think that this is a 4 response. Reread the description of a 4 paper, then read the description for a 3. This paper has some 4 characteristics but is truly less perceptive than needed. It seems that Student C understands the most obvious differences between the impact of the two passages, but there is uncertainty in what he says. He uses the qualifier *almost* as if he's just taking a stab at a response rather than being sure of what he wants to say.

Student C's response to this question would be scored a 3.

ESSAY QUESTION THREE: SANDY KEMPNER LETTER

ANALYSIS OF ESSAY QUESTION THREE

This charming but heart-wrenching letter from Vietnam is a poignant antiwar testimonial. Students need to pay particular attention to Sandy's word choice, for the connotations of many of his words carry a very strong message.

Like many young men in that war, he wasn't sure exactly what he was doing or how he even got where he was. Nevertheless, he "soldiers" on with his duties. One of these more pleasant duties is writing to his beloved family. His subtle criticism is well hidden within an impressive presentation of descriptive images. You have a lot to look at in this short correspondence but should find it accessible. Most of you will have at least something to say about it.

SCORING GUIDE FOR QUESTION THREE

9   Essays meet all of the criteria for 8 papers and, in addition, are especially full or apt in their analysis or demonstrate particularly impressive composition skills.

8   Essays successfully analyze the rhetorical and stylistic strategies the letter employs to convey the writer's attitude about the Vietnam War and Sandy's part in it. They refer to the passage directly or indirectly and explain convincingly how specific strategies, such as imagery, tone, and figurative language, contribute to an understanding of the narrator's attitude. Their prose controls a wide range of effective writing but is not flawless.

7   Essays fit the description of 6 essays but employ more complete analysis or demonstrate a more mature prose style.

6   Essays adequately analyze the stylistic devices the letter employs to reveal the narrator's attitude about the war in Vietnam and his part in the action. They refer to the passage directly or indirectly, and they recognize the narrator's attitude and how he conveys it by utilizing strategies such as choice of detail, tone, and figurative language. A few lapses in diction or syntax may be present, but generally the prose of 6 essays is clear.

5   Essays analyze Sandy's rhetorical techniques, but the development of how these techniques work or the understanding of Sandy's attitude is limited or too simplistic. These essays may treat techniques superficially or develop ideas about the narrator's attitude inconsistently. A few lapses in diction or syntax may appear, but the prose in these essays usually conveys the writers' ideas adequately.

4   Essays inadequately respond to the task of the prompt. They may misrepresent the narrator's attitude or analyze rhetorical strategies inaccurately or with little understanding of how these strategies reveal Sandy's attitude toward the war. Often the prose of these essays suggests immature control over organization, diction, or syntax.

3   Essays meet the criteria for the score of 4 but are less perceptive about how rhetorical strategies convey attitude or are less consistent in controlling the elements of writing.

2   Essays are unsuccessful in analyzing how stylistic strategies convey the narrator's attitude about the war in Vietnam and his part in the war. These essays tend to pay little or cursory attention to the specific features of the letter, and they may generalize or simplify attitude and tone. They may simply paraphrase or comment on the passage without analyzing technique. The prose of 2 papers often reveals consistent weaknesses in writing, such as a lack of development or organization, grammatical problems, or a lack of control.

1 Essays earning a score of 1 meet the criteria for the score of 2 but are especially simplistic in their discussion or weak in controlling elements of language

STUDENT A'S RESPONSE TO QUESTION THREE

In class this year we read <u>The Things They Carried</u> by Tim O'Brien, which led to an exploration of a lot of different so-called war-related literature. Overall, I found most of it to be subtle and not so subtle war protest literature. This letter by Sandy, describing his numerous experiences in Vietnam, is no exception. He conveys a cynical and resentful attitude toward the situation he is in. He utilizes humor, vivid imagery, sarcasm, and other rhetorical devices to tell his family, and subsequently the rest of us, about the true nature of war.

People have been writing about war for centuries—the early Greeks and Romans spoke of war. War is present in many of Shakespeare's historical plays and he mentions it also in <u>Hamlet</u> and <u>Macbeth</u>. Many poets have written about war as well. A famous war poem that made a big impression on me is "Dulce Et Decorum Est" (World War I think). The powerful imagery in that poem sure stirred my anti-war feelings. In the last century or so anti-war books such as <u>Johnny Got His Gun</u> and <u>On the Beach</u> and <u>Hiroshima</u> have made powerful anti-war statements. Of course, the movie industry has done its part as well with classics such as Failsafe and MASH. Sandy's letter from Vietnam fits right in with all of these classics. With not-so-subtle imagery and undeniable sarcasm, this letter exposes us once again to the travesty of war.

In his greeting, Sandy reveals that he is homesick and has much affection for his family—using their pet names. When he begins his letter, he tries to keep things light—possibly not wanting to worry his family. However, by mentioning the recent maneuvers as an "abortion" we are quickly apprised of Sandy's bitterness over the futility of what they are doing. As he relays his recent adventures, we quickly see that this was definitely no "walk in the sun." In fact, his tone is angry, with only a few details, we are quickly able to understand the grueling nature of his missions. The abundant use of negatives emphasizes even more pessimistic feelings about what he is doing, (and likewise) what America is doing. "No word," "no chow," and "no heels" express how ineffectual they are being. I can almost hear him add "no sense" as well. The reader is sucked into his frustration as he talks about blisters, torn clothing, jungle rot, and forced marches. How can we not empathize with him?

He tries to lighten things with a bit of comic relief about meals of peanut butter and coffee, but soon we realize that a daily diet of this is as bad as blisters and forced marches. Soon, however, even this attempt at humor is replaced by more frustration when he talks about his squadron's inability to effectively do much against the VCs. In fact, he implies that Charley seems not to have a care in the world until he sees the Americans. An inconsequential firefight settles nothing. The power of his description—the ridiculous battle with the snipers, expending $50,000 to no effect; throwing everything but the

Missouri at the enemy—shows just how hopeless his situation is. All their efforts seem to have accomplished he says, almost as an aside, was to wake up a sleeping Marine sentry. (Perhaps if he had not been sleeping, there would have been no cause for a battle?)

By the end of the letter, Sandy may have realized that he has revealed too much of his emotion, frustration, and even fear. He attempts a lighter mood by comparing the squadron to Indian Scouts. Instead of well-trained soldiers, however, it sounds like he's with a group of inept Cub Scouts who don't know what they are doing or even why they are doing it. Instead they manage to kill innocent bystanders and torch (innocent) houses. By now anyone reading this letter wants to scream and shout against such absurdity. The driving rain seems to be a metaphor for the driving futility of it all. Through his attempted humor, raw emotion, incredible imagery, clever sarcasm, and total frustration, Sandy's short letter to his family is an outstanding example of anti-war sentiment. His last words are the most poignant, "I'm afraid" are his last words. The ultimate futility of it all, however, is my knowing that barely two months later, this sensitive, young man, just trying to do his duty, was killed. Dulce Et Decorum Est Pro Patria Mori. What a travesty.

STUDENT B'S RESPONSE TO QUESTION THREE

Sandy Kempner uses several stylistic and rhetorical techniques in this letter to his family. His tone is sarcastic and angry, and he uses humor, understatement, self-pity, and incredibly strong imagery to make his anti-war statement.

At first this seems like a simple letter to his family. The nicknames he uses imply a strong affection for them. Soon, however, he becomes more serious, telling them about an "abortion" known as Operation Jackson. This is a well-chosen word, for what they were doing in Vietnam seemed to be all for nothing. He lists a number of sensations that show the severity of his mission. Sandy includes a number of negatives to emphasize the ineffectiveness of all their attempts. His diction is simple, but he makes it clear how bad things are as he talks about things like blisters and jungle rot.

He tries to use ironic humor as he tells his family about Marine Corps cuisine. Of course, cuisine is hardly an appropriate word for peanut butter and coffee. This just emphasizes his disgust with the whole operation. His squad has no luck with the VCs—it seems like he's telling a story, though, and he talks about the confrontation with the snipers as if he were describing some video game. In 1966, it would have been something like Pac Man. Even $50,000 dollars worth of ammunition, and everything but the kitchen sink (or the Missouri), the soldiers were unable to accomplish anything.

Finally he refers to his squadron as Indian Scouts—an apt metaphor. They seemed as ineffective as children running around in the dark not knowing what to do. He uses understatement when he mentions that they were "very successful"—of course, success was killing innocent people and burning a few shacks—not much to brag about, that's for sure.

Sandy's letter is more than just a correspondence to his family. It is truly a statement that relates the horrors of war and his hopeless situation and the futility of their situation in Vietnam.

COMMENTARY ON STUDENT A'S RESPONSE

Student A has obviously done some reading and apparently has at least a mild interest in war-related literature. In this instance, his additional interest and knowledge has aided his response. However, successful responses by students are often written by students who would not have had such a convenient reading background.

The prompt asks the student to analyze stylistic and rhetorical devices that are present in this letter from Vietnam and how these devices reveal the writer's attitude toward his situation. In addition, the student must consider the value of this letter as a passage of antiwar sentiment. Looking at the scoring guide, this student has written an 8 essay. In fact, it may also garner some 9s from readers. Although some may criticize it as lacking extensive analysis, the total understanding of the letter and the techniques the writer has used are clearly evident. In addition, he has integrated this letter within the realm of war literature. He has done this so successfully that there is no need for closer stylistic analysis.

The student's voice is very present in this response—a characteristic of very successful responses. No doubt other literature has also moved this student, and the way he has applied other literature to this piece makes this an exceptional response. The final Latin phrase, which is actually the title of the poem this student particularly liked reading, says it all—how sweet it is to give one's life to one's country—the ultimate irony of the original poem as well as of this letter from Vietnam.

COMMENTARY ON STUDENT B'S RESPONSE

Student B's response is adequate but not as successful as Student A's. She covers the basics and addresses many of the stylistic devices that are found in this letter. She understands how the irony and dark humor help to make this writing far more than just a letter home.

She refers to the strategies both explicitly and implicitly, but her explanation of specifics is limited. The references she makes to specifics in the letter are appropriate but not extensive. This response tends to move through the letter, step-by-step, without a more global view. This response would probably garner a 6 from AP readers. It is more than a 5, for it is neither inconsistent nor uneven. Nor is it particularly weak in composition skills. This is truly an adequate response.

Practice Test 2 Answer Grid

Before taking this Practice Test, find a quiet place where you can work uninterrupted for about three hours. Make sure you have a comfortable desk, several No. 2 pencils, and a few ballpoint pens.

The Practice Test includes a multiple-choice section and a free-response question. Use the answer grid to record your multiple-choice answers. Write the essays on the pages provided; use additional sheets if needed.

Once you start the test, don't stop until you've finished, except for a 10-minute break between the multiple-choice and essay sections. The answer key and explanations follow the test.

Good luck!

1. Ⓐ Ⓑ Ⓒ Ⓓ Ⓔ	19. Ⓐ Ⓑ Ⓒ Ⓓ Ⓔ	37. Ⓐ Ⓑ Ⓒ Ⓓ Ⓔ
2. Ⓐ Ⓑ Ⓒ Ⓓ Ⓔ	20. Ⓐ Ⓑ Ⓒ Ⓓ Ⓔ	38. Ⓐ Ⓑ Ⓒ Ⓓ Ⓔ
3. Ⓐ Ⓑ Ⓒ Ⓓ Ⓔ	21. Ⓐ Ⓑ Ⓒ Ⓓ Ⓔ	39. Ⓐ Ⓑ Ⓒ Ⓓ Ⓔ
4. Ⓐ Ⓑ Ⓒ Ⓓ Ⓔ	22. Ⓐ Ⓑ Ⓒ Ⓓ Ⓔ	40. Ⓐ Ⓑ Ⓒ Ⓓ Ⓔ
5. Ⓐ Ⓑ Ⓒ Ⓓ Ⓔ	23. Ⓐ Ⓑ Ⓒ Ⓓ Ⓔ	41. Ⓐ Ⓑ Ⓒ Ⓓ Ⓔ
6. Ⓐ Ⓑ Ⓒ Ⓓ Ⓔ	24. Ⓐ Ⓑ Ⓒ Ⓓ Ⓔ	42. Ⓐ Ⓑ Ⓒ Ⓓ Ⓔ
7. Ⓐ Ⓑ Ⓒ Ⓓ Ⓔ	25. Ⓐ Ⓑ Ⓒ Ⓓ Ⓔ	43. Ⓐ Ⓑ Ⓒ Ⓓ Ⓔ
8. Ⓐ Ⓑ Ⓒ Ⓓ Ⓔ	26. Ⓐ Ⓑ Ⓒ Ⓓ Ⓔ	44. Ⓐ Ⓑ Ⓒ Ⓓ Ⓔ
9. Ⓐ Ⓑ Ⓒ Ⓓ Ⓔ	27. Ⓐ Ⓑ Ⓒ Ⓓ Ⓔ	45. Ⓐ Ⓑ Ⓒ Ⓓ Ⓔ
10. Ⓐ Ⓑ Ⓒ Ⓓ Ⓔ	28. Ⓐ Ⓑ Ⓒ Ⓓ Ⓔ	46. Ⓐ Ⓑ Ⓒ Ⓓ Ⓔ
11. Ⓐ Ⓑ Ⓒ Ⓓ Ⓔ	29. Ⓐ Ⓑ Ⓒ Ⓓ Ⓔ	47. Ⓐ Ⓑ Ⓒ Ⓓ Ⓔ
12. Ⓐ Ⓑ Ⓒ Ⓓ Ⓔ	30. Ⓐ Ⓑ Ⓒ Ⓓ Ⓔ	48. Ⓐ Ⓑ Ⓒ Ⓓ Ⓔ
13. Ⓐ Ⓑ Ⓒ Ⓓ Ⓔ	31. Ⓐ Ⓑ Ⓒ Ⓓ Ⓔ	49. Ⓐ Ⓑ Ⓒ Ⓓ Ⓔ
14. Ⓐ Ⓑ Ⓒ Ⓓ Ⓔ	32. Ⓐ Ⓑ Ⓒ Ⓓ Ⓔ	50. Ⓐ Ⓑ Ⓒ Ⓓ Ⓔ
15. Ⓐ Ⓑ Ⓒ Ⓓ Ⓔ	33. Ⓐ Ⓑ Ⓒ Ⓓ Ⓔ	51. Ⓐ Ⓑ Ⓒ Ⓓ Ⓔ
16. Ⓐ Ⓑ Ⓒ Ⓓ Ⓔ	34. Ⓐ Ⓑ Ⓒ Ⓓ Ⓔ	52. Ⓐ Ⓑ Ⓒ Ⓓ Ⓔ
17. Ⓐ Ⓑ Ⓒ Ⓓ Ⓔ	35. Ⓐ Ⓑ Ⓒ Ⓓ Ⓔ	53. Ⓐ Ⓑ Ⓒ Ⓓ Ⓔ
18. Ⓐ Ⓑ Ⓒ Ⓓ Ⓔ	36. Ⓐ Ⓑ Ⓒ Ⓓ Ⓔ	54. Ⓐ Ⓑ Ⓒ Ⓓ Ⓔ

PRACTICE TEST 2

Section I: Multiple-Choice Questions

Time—1 hour
Number of questions—54
Percent of total grade—45%

Directions: This section contains selections from prose works with questions on their content, style, form, structure, and purpose. Read each selection. Then read each question, choosing the best of the five responses that follow. Fill in each oval with the correct answer, checking to be sure the number of the question corresponds to the number on the answer sheet.

Questions 1–14. Read the following essay carefully before responding to the questions.

Since the afternoon in 1967 when I first saw Hoover Dam, its image has never been entirely absent from my inner eye. I will be driving down Sunset Boulevard, or about to enter a
Line
(5) freeway, and abruptly those power transmission towers will appear before me, canted vertiginously over the tailrace. Sometimes I am confronted by the intakes and sometimes by the shadow of the heavy cable that spans the
(10) canyon and sometimes by the ominous outlets to unused spillways, black in the lunar clarity of the desert light. Quite often I hear the turbines. Frequently I wonder what is happening at the dam this instant, at this precise intersection
(15) of time and space, how much water is being released to fill downstream orders and what lights are flashing and which generators are in full use and which just spinning free.

I used to wonder what it was about the dam
(20) that made me think of it at times and in places where I once thought of the Mindanao Trench, or of the stars wheeling in their courses, or of the words *As it was in the beginning, is now and ever shall be, world without end, amen.* Dams,
(25) after all, are commonplace: we have all seen one. This particular dam had existed as an idea in the world's mind for almost forty years before I saw it. Hoover Dam, showpiece of the Boulder Canyon project, the several million tons of
(30) concrete that made the Southwest plausible, the *fait accompli* that was to convey, in the innocent time of its construction, the notion that mankind's brightest promise lay in American engineering.

(35) Of course the dam derives some of its emotional effect from precisely that aspect, that sense of being a monument to a faith since misplaced. "They died to make the desert bloom," reads a plaque dedicated to the

(40) ninety-six men who died building this first of the great high dams, and in context the worn phrase touches, suggests all of that trust in harnessing resources, the meliorative power of the dynamo, so central to the early Thirties.
(45) Boulder City, built in 1931 as the construction town for the dam, retains the ambience of a model city, a new town, a toy triangular grid of green lawns and trim bungalows, all fanning out from the Reclamation building. The bronze
(50) sculptures at the dam itself evoke muscular citizens of tomorrow that never came, sheaves of wheat clutched heavenward, thunderbolts defied. Winged Victories guard the flagpole. The flag whips in the canyon wind. The empty
(55) Pepsi-Cola can clatters across the terrazzo. The place is perfectly frozen in time.

But history does not explain it all, does not entirely suggest what makes that dam so affecting. Nor, even, does energy, the massive
(60) involvement with power and pressure and the transparent sexual overtones to that involvement. Once when I revisited the dam I walked through it with a man from the Bureau of Reclamation. Once in a while he would
(65) explain something, usually in that recondite language having to do with "peaking power," with "outages" and "dewatering," but on the whole we spent the afternoon in a world so alien, so complete and so beautiful unto itself
(70) that it was scarcely necessary to speak at all. We saw almost no one. Cranes moved above us as if under their own volition. Generators roared. Transformers hummed. The gratings on which we stood vibrated. We watched a hundred-ton
(75) steel shaft plunging down to that place where the water was. And finally we got down to that place where the water was, where the water sucked out of Lake Mead roared through thirty-foot

GO ON TO THE NEXT PAGE →

penstocks and then into thirteen-foot penstocks
(80) and finally into the turbines themselves.

There was something beyond all that,
something beyond energy, beyond history,
something I could not fix in my mind. When I
came up from the dam that day the wind was
(85) blowing harder, through the canyon and all
across the Mojave, but out at the dam there
was no dust, only the rock and the dam and a
little greasewood and a few garbage cans, their
tops chained banging against a fence. I walked
(90) across the marble star map that traces a sidereal
revolution of the equinox and fixes forever,
the Reclamation man had told me, for all time
and for all people who can read the stars, the
date the dam was dedicated. The star map was,
(95) he had said, for when we were all gone and
the dam was left. I had not thought much of it
when he said it, but I thought of it then, with
the wind whining and the sun dropping behind
a mesa with the finality of a sunset in space.
(100) Of course that was the image I had seen,
always seen it without quite realizing what I
saw, a dynamo finally free of man, splendid at
last in its absolute isolation, transmitting power
and releasing water to a world where no one is.
(105) From "At the Dam" by Joan Didion in
The White Album (1979)

1. The overall tone of this passage can best be
   described as

   (A) regretfully reminiscent.
   (B) philosophically introspective.
   (C) whimsically lighthearted.
   (D) anxiously foreboding.
   (E) hesitantly guileful.

2. The opening sentence serves the purpose of

   I.   illustrating the topic of the essay.
   II. demonstrating that the narrator's
        experience has remained with her.
   III. comparing this experience to an earlier
        one the narrator has had.

   (A) I only
   (B) II only
   (C) II and III only
   (D) I and II only
   (E) I, II, and III

3. Paragraph 2 (lines 19–34) makes reference to
   all of the following EXCEPT

   (A) a national symbol.
   (B) religious allusion.
   (C) foreign terminology.
   (D) regional hyperbole.
   (E) understated importance.

4. Throughout this passage, the narrator uses

   (A) pathos.
   (B) deductive reasoning.
   (C) logic.
   (D) ethos.
   (E) definition.

5. The narrator's view of the dam in contrast to
   her view of the world can best be described as

   (A) mechanistic : human.
   (B) confined : spacious.
   (C) hopeful : damaged.
   (D) optimistic : pessimistic.
   (E) commonplace : significant.

GO ON TO THE NEXT PAGE

6. Lines 72–74, "Generators roared . . . vibrated," have all of the following EXCEPT

(A) imagery.

(B) onomatopoeia.

(C) parallel syntax.

(D) nostalgic description.

(E) simple sentences.

7. The underlying purpose of this passage seems to be to

(A) explain the hypnotic spell the dam seems to have on the narrator.

(B) express the importance and somewhat mystical beauty of the Hoover Dam.

(C) describe the purpose of the dam and the work that went into its construction.

(D) explain how the dam operates and its importance to the Southwest United States.

(E) articulate the narrator's fascination with the dam as well as her reverence for its power.

8. "The star map was, he had said, for when we were all gone and the dam was left" (lines 94–96) reinforces which of the following statements?

(A) " . . . something beyond energy, beyond history . . ."

(B) " . . . muscular citizens of tomorrow. . . ."

(C) "The place is frozen in time."

(D) "We saw almost no one."

(E) "This particular dam had existed as an idea in the world's mind for almost forty years. . . ."

9. In the context of this passage, the phrase "canted vertiginously" (line 6–7) most closely means

(A) aligned fearfully.

(B) presented awfully.

(C) angled dizzyingly.

(D) chanting comfortably.

(E) appearing disgustedly.

10. The first sentence of paragraph 5 (lines 81–83) contains the specific rhetorical device known as

(A) anaphora.

(B) simile.

(C) connotation.

(D) personification.

(E) repetition.

11. As the passage comes to a close, it establishes a feeling that can best be described as

(A) mystifying.

(B) surprised.

(C) baffled.

(D) celebratory.

(E) haunting.

12. The sentence beginning "Nor, even, does energy, the massive involvement with power," (lines 59–60) can be identified as having or being all of the following EXCEPT

(A) a sentence fragment.

(B) alliteration.

(C) apposition.

(D) a compound sentence.

(E) negation.

GO ON TO THE NEXT PAGE

13. The narrator most likely emphasizes the toylike layout of the city in order to stress the idea that

(A) the people of that time had little imagination.

(B) budget restraints kept the city simple in design.

(C) this was a planned city built for a pragmatic purpose.

(D) the city is minimal in contrast to the greatness of the dam.

(E) the bronze sculptures and Winged Victory are more important than the town.

14. Considering the passage, the narrator seems to be amazed by which of the following ideas?

(A) Hoover Dam is truly one of the great wonders of the world.

(B) What it took so many men to build no longer needs any human beings.

(C) Hoover Dam has proven to be truly the salvation of the Southwest.

(D) The Dam is able to convert the water from Lake Mead into energy and power.

(E) Visitors to the Dam can learn history, politics, and physics all in one trip.

GO ON TO THE NEXT PAGE

Questions 15–27. Read the following essay carefully before responding to the questions.

He who lets the world, or his own portion of it, choose his plan of life for him, has no need of any other faculty than the ape-like one of imitation. He who chooses his plan for
(5) himself, employs all his faculties. He must use observation to see, reason and judgment to foresee, activity to gather materials for decision, discrimination to decide, and when he has decided, firmness and self-control to hold to
(10) his deliberate decisions. And these qualities he requires and exercises exactly in proportion as the part of his conduct which he determines according to his judgment and feelings is a large one. It is possible that he might be guided in
(15) some good path, and kept out of harm's way, without any of these things. But what will be his comparative worth as a human being? It really is of importance, not only what men do, but also what manner of men they are that do it.
(20) Among the works of man, which human life is rightly employed in performing and beautifying, the first in importance surely is man himself. Supposing it were possible to get houses built, corn grown, battles fought, causes tried, and
(25) even churches erected and prayers said, by machinery—by automatons in human form— it would be a considerable loss to exchange for these automatons even the men and women who at present inhabit the more civilized parts
(30) of the world, and who assuredly are but starved specimens of what nature can and will produce. Human nature is not a machine to be built after a model, and set to do exactly the work prescribed for it, but a tree, which requires to
(35) grow and develop itself on all sides, according to the tendency of the inward forces which make it a living thing.

It will probably be conceded that it is desirable people should exercise their
(40) understandings, and that an intelligent following of custom, or even occasionally an intelligent deviation from custom, is better than a blind and simply mechanical adhesion to it. To a certain extent it is admitted that
(45) our understanding should be our own: but there is not the same willingness to admit that our desires and impulses should be our own likewise; or that to possess impulses of our own, and of any strength, is anything but a peril
(50) and a snare. Yet desires and impulses are as much a part of a perfect human being as beliefs and restraints: and strong impulses are only perilous when not properly balanced; when one set of aims and inclinations is developed into
(55) strength, while others, which ought to co-exist with them, remain weak and inactive. It is not because men's desires are strong and they act ill: it is because their consciences are weak; there is no natural connection between strong impulses
(60) and a weak conscience; the natural connection is the other way. To say that one person's desires and feelings are stronger and more various than those of another, is merely to say that he has more of the raw material of human
(65) nature, and is therefore capable, perhaps of more evil, but certainly of more good. Strong impulses are but another name for energy. Energy may be turned to bad uses; but more good may always be made of an energetic
(70) nature, than of an indolent and impassive one.

Those who have most natural feeling are always those whose cultivated feelings may be made the strongest. The same strong susceptibilities which make the personal
(75) impulses vivid and powerful, are also the source from whence are generated the most passionate love of virtue, and the sternest self-control. It is through the cultivation of these that society

GO ON TO THE NEXT PAGE →

both does its duty and protects its interests: not
(80) by rejecting the stuff by which heroes are made,
because it knows not how to make them. A
person whose desires and impulses are his own
is said to have a character. One whose desires
and impulses are not his own, has no character,
(85) no more than a steam engine has character.
If, in addition to being his own, his impulses
are strong, and are under the government of
a strong will, he has an energetic character.
Whoever thinks that individuality of desires
(90) and impulses should not be encouraged to
unfold itself, must maintain that society has
no need of strong natures—is not the better
for containing many persons who have much
character—and that a high general average of
(95) energy is not desirable.

In some early states of society, these
forces might be, and were, too much ahead
of the power which society then possessed of
disciplining and controlling them. There has
(100) been a time when the element of spontaneity
and individuality was in excess, and the social
principle had a hard struggle with it. The
difficulty then was to induce men of strong
bodies or minds to pay obedience to any rules
(105) which required them to control their impulses.
To overcome this difficulty, law and discipline,
like the Popes struggling against the Emperors,
asserted a power over the whole man, claiming
to control all his life in order to control his
(110) character—which society had not found any
other sufficient means of binding. But society
has now fairly got the better of individuality:
and the danger which threatens human nature
is not the excess, but the deficiency, of personal
(115) impulses and preferences. Things are vastly
changed since the passion of those who were
strong by station or by personal endowment
were in a state of habitual rebelling against laws
and ordinances, and required to be rigorously

(120) chained up to enable the persons within their
reach to enjoy any particle of security. In our
times, from the highest class of society down
to the lowest, every one lives as under the eye
of a hostile and dreaded censorship. Not only
(125) in what concerns others, but in what concerns
only themselves, the individual or the family
do not ask themselves—what do I prefer? Or,
what would suit my character and disposition:
or, what would allow the best and highest in
(130) me to have fair play and enable it to grow and
thrive? They ask themselves, what is suitable to
my position, what is usually done by persons
of my station and pecuniary circumstances? Or
(worse still) what is usually done by persons
(135) of a station and circumstances superior to
mine? I do not mean that they choose what is
customary in preference to what suits their own
inclination. It does not occur to them to have
any inclination except for what is customary.
(140) Thus the mind itself is bowed to the yoke: they
like in crowds; they exercise choice only among
things commonly done: peculiarity of taste,
eccentricity of conduct, are shunned equally
with crimes: until by dint of not following their
(145) own nature they have no nature to follow: their
human capacities are withered and starved:
they become incapable of any strong wishes
or native pleasures, and are generally without
either opinions or feelings of home growth, or
(150) properly their own. Now this, or is it not, the
desirable condition of human nature?

From Chapter 3: "On Individuality" of
On Liberty by John Stuart Mill (1859)

GO ON TO THE NEXT PAGE

15. The main idea of this passage can best be summarized as which of the following?

    (A) It is best to let the world choose our plan of life.

    (B) If life chooses for us, it is possible that we may be guided in some good path.

    (C) Automatons really could take care of all of our tasks.

    (D) We must be nurtured and grow into our own person, not just copy others.

    (E) We should exercise imitation and employ all our faculties in making decisions.

16. "Human nature is not . . . living thing" (lines 32–37) combines which of the following two stylistic devices?

    (A) Metaphor and personification

    (B) Simile and metaphor

    (C) Personification and hyperbole

    (D) Understatement and hyperbole

    (E) Litote and metaphor

17. Although the narrator encourages us to become ourselves and exercise personal understandings, he also cautions that

    (A) men's desires are often not very strong.

    (B) strong impulses are dangerous because of their energy.

    (C) individual energy can never be anything but good.

    (D) strong impulses are really separate from individual conscience.

    (E) energy must be carefully self-monitored to do good.

18. The sentence "It is not because . . . the natural connection is the other way" (lines 56–61) can be syntactically characterized as containing both a

    (A) run-on sentence and parallelism.

    (B) series of clauses and asyndeton.

    (C) complex sentence and antithesis.

    (D) compound sentence and parenthetical asides.

    (E) compound-complex sentence and antithesis.

19. In paragraphs 2 and 3, the narrator makes all of the following points EXCEPT

    (A) strong impulses and a weak conscience have no natural connection.

    (B) *energy* is a synonym for the concept "strong impulses."

    (C) despite his conscience, man's desires will cause him to act ill.

    (D) one who has character is one whose desires and impulses are his own.

    (E) society does not desire people with strong natures.

20. In this passage, the writer compares society's struggle to "conquer" man's individuality with

    (A) a man copying an ape.

    (B) an emperor fighting a pope.

    (C) desire conquering conscience.

    (D) impulse overriding logic.

    (E) the Popes struggling against the Emperors.

GO ON TO THE NEXT PAGE

21. The stylistic discourse of paragraph 3 (lines 71–95) can best be described as

    (A) hypothetical, idealistic speculation.

    (B) personal reflection and observation.

    (C) internal argumentation.

    (D) emotional diatribe.

    (E) theoretical query.

22. The main point established by paragraph 3 can best be stated as which of the following?

    (A) Man must learn to control his impulses.

    (B) Censorship is the evil that man must avoid.

    (C) Society has overcome the best of man's personal impulses and preferences.

    (D) Society embraces the man who is able to think independently.

    (E) It is important for man not to have in libation contrary to what is customary.

23. Paragraph 4 (lines 96–151) can best be described as

    (A) a diatribe against the power of the Pope.

    (B) a celebration of man's independent spirit.

    (C) a reaffirmation of the conformity of pleasure.

    (D) an argument against man's instinct to please himself.

    (E) a lament over the loss of personal impulses and preferences.

24. The last sentence of paragraph 3 (lines 89–95) contains all of the following syntactical characteristics EXCEPT

    (A) series preceded by a colon.

    (B) loose parallel structure.

    (C) compound-complex structure.

    (D) multiple use of verbs.

    (E) a parenthetical insert.

25. Within the context of the passage, the sentence beginning "Things are vastly changed" (lines 115–121) can best be interpreted as meaning

    (A) people no longer have to fear for their personal security.

    (B) habitual rebellions are no longer a problem in society.

    (C) times have improved the prison situation.

    (D) human nature has been tamed into submission.

    (E) neither the poor nor the rich need worry about insurrection.

GO ON TO THE NEXT PAGE

26. The author of this essay would most likely agree with which of the following statements?

 I. Man must join the ranks of custom in order to get along.

 II. Man has succumbed to the dictates of society's norm.

 III. Society appreciates a man with a strong, energetic nature.

 IV. Indolent and impassive men are easier to manipulate than those with "energy."

(A) I only

(B) II and III only

(C) II and IV only

(D) I, III, and IV only

(E) I, II, and IV only

27. In paragraph 4 (lines 96–151) the author is most concerned that

(A) ultimately people will follow a path of behavior that best suits who they are.

(B) ultimately the Pope has the most power over the disciplining of man.

(C) upper-class society people are more likely to "be themselves" than lower-class people.

(D) social principle has a difficult time in overcoming man's natural tendency toward individuality and spontaneity.

(E) people will sacrifice what is best and natural for what is customary and appropriate.

GO ON TO THE NEXT PAGE

Questions 28–40. Read the following passage carefully before responding to the questions.

Thomas Jefferson believed that to preserve the very foundations of our nation, we would need dramatic change from time to time. Well, my fellow citizens, this is our time. Let
(5) us embrace it.

Our democracy must be not only the envy of the world but the engine of our own renewal. There is nothing wrong with America that cannot be cured by what is right with America.

(10) And so today, we pledge an end to the era of deadlock and drift—a new season of American renewal has begun.

To renew America, we must be bold.

We must do what no generation has had
(15) to do before. We must invest more in our own people, in their jobs, in their future, and at the same time cut our massive debt. And we must do so in a world in which we must compete for every opportunity.

(20) It will not be easy; it will require sacrifice. But it can be done, and done fairly, not choosing sacrifice for its own sake, but for our own sake. We must provide for our nation the way a family provides for its children.

(25) Our Founders saw themselves in the light of posterity. We can do no less. Anyone who has ever watched a child's eyes wander into sleep knows what posterity is. Posterity is the world to come—the world for whom we hold
(30) our ideals, from whom we have borrowed our planet, and to whom we bear sacred responsibility.

We must do what America does best: offer more opportunity to all and demand
(35) responsibility from all.

It is time to break the bad habit of expecting something for nothing, from our government or from each other. Let us all take more responsibility, not only for ourselves

(40) and our families but for our communities and our country.

To renew America, we must revitalize our democracy.

This beautiful capital, like every capital
(45) since the dawn of civilization, is often a place of intrigue and calculation. Powerful people maneuver for position and worry endlessly about who is in and who is out, who is up and who is down, forgetting those people whose
(50) toil and sweat sends us here and pays our way.

Americans deserve better, and in this city today, there are people who want to do better. And so I say to all of us here, let us resolve to reform our politics, so that power
(55) and privilege no longer shout down the voice of the people. Let us put aside personal advantage so that we can feel the pain and see the promise of America.

Let us resolve to make our government a
(60) place for what Franklin Roosevelt called "bold, persistent experimentation," a government for our tomorrows, not our yesterdays.

Let us give this capital back to the people to whom it belongs.

(65) To renew America, we must meet challenges abroad as well at home. There is no longer division between what is foreign and what is domestic—the world economy, the world environment, the world AIDS crisis, the
(70) world arms race—they affect us all.

Today, as an old order passes, the new world is more free but less stable. Communism's collapse has called forth old animosities and new dangers. Clearly America must continue to
(75) lead the world we did so much to make.

While America rebuilds at home, we will not shrink from the challenges, nor fail to seize the opportunities, of this new world.

GO ON TO THE NEXT PAGE ▷

Together with our friends and allies, we will
(80) work to shape change, lest it engulf us.

When our vital interests are challenged, or
the will and conscience of the international
community is defied, we will act—with
peaceful diplomacy whenever possible, with
(85) force when necessary. The brave Americans
serving our nation today in the Persian Gulf,
in Somalia, and wherever else they stand are
testament to our resolve.

But our greatest strength is the power of
(90) our ideas, which are still new in many lands.
Across the world, we see them embraced—
and we rejoice. Our hopes, our hearts, our
hands, are with those on every continent who
are building democracy and freedom. Their
(95) cause is America's cause.

The American people have summoned the
change we celebrate today. You have raised
your voices in an unmistakable chorus. You
have cast your votes in historic numbers. And
(100) you have changed the face of Congress, the
presidency and the political process itself. Yes,
you, my fellow Americans have forced the
spring. Now, we must do the work the season
demands.
(105) To that work I now turn, with all the
authority of my office. I ask the Congress to
join with me. But no president, no Congress,
no government, can undertake this mission
alone. My fellow Americans, you, too, must
(110) play your part in our renewal. I challenge
a new generation of young Americans to a
season of service—to act on your idealism by
helping troubled children, keeping company
with those in need, reconnecting our torn
(115) communities. There is so much to be done—
enough indeed for millions of others who are
still young in spirit to give of themselves in
service, too.

In serving, we recognize a simple but
(120) powerful truth—we need each other. And
we must care for one another. Today, we do
more than celebrate America; we rededicate
ourselves to the very idea of America.

An idea born in revolution and renewed
(125) through two centuries of challenge. An idea
tempered by the knowledge that, but for fate,
we—the fortunate and the unfortunate—
might have been each other. An idea ennobled
by the faith that our nation can summon
(130) from its myriad diversity the deepest measure
of unity. An idea infused with the conviction
that America's long heroic journey must go
forever upward.

And so, my fellow Americans, at the edge
(135) of the twenty-first century, let us begin with
energy and hope, with faith and discipline,
and let us work until our work is done. The
scripture says, "And let us not be weary in
well-doing, for in due season, we shall reap, if we
(140) faint not."

From this joyful mountaintop of
celebration, we hear a call to service in the
valley. We have heard the trumpets. We have
changed the guard. And now, each in our way,
(145) and with God's help, we must answer the call.

Thank you and God bless you all.
Inaugural Address, William Clinton,
20 January 1993

28. This inaugural speech opens using the stylistic
technique of appealing to the audience's
sense of

(A) intelligence.
(B) humor.
(C) patriotism.
(D) sympathy.
(E) empathy.

GO ON TO THE NEXT PAGE

29. "There is nothing wrong with America that cannot be cured by what is right with America" (lines 8–9) sets up a contradiction that is known as

  (A) paradox.

  (B) parallelism.

  (C) oxymoron.

  (D) absurdity.

  (E) allusion.

30. In the statement in lines 33–35, "We must do what America does best: offer more opportunity to all and demand responsibility from all," President Clinton utilizes the stylistic device known as

  (A) apostrophe.

  (B) alliteration.

  (C) epistrophe.

  (D) anaphora.

  (E) allegory.

31. Paragraph 11 (lines 44–50) includes all of the following syntactical characteristics EXCEPT

  (A) a parenthetical statement.

  (B) an independent clause series.

  (C) a participial phrase.

  (D) a compound verb.

  (E) a compound sentence.

32. The best interpretation of the phrase "a government for our tomorrows, not our yesterdays" (lines 61–62) is that it refers to

  (A) looking to the past for guidance in government.

  (B) a government that is based on tradition and values.

  (C) looking to the future for inspiration in government.

  (D) a government that is forward looking and adaptable.

  (E) a government guided by the philosophy of strong leaders.

33. The main stylistic characteristic of paragraph 12 (lines 51–58) is

  (A) alliteration.

  (B) assonance.

  (C) asyndeton.

  (D) parallel syntax.

  (E) simple sentence structure.

34. The phrase "To renew America" is used throughout this passage as

  (A) a reminder to listeners.

  (B) an exhortation and refrain.

  (C) an opportunity to pause and think.

  (D) a demonstration of the lack of speaker ingenuity.

  (E) emphasis for a point.

GO ON TO THE NEXT PAGE

35. The excerpt " . . . we will act—with peaceful diplomacy whenever possible, with force when necessary" (lines 83–85) is an example of the stylistic device known as

   (A) antithesis.

   (B) oxymoron.

   (C) hyperbole.

   (D) zeugma.

   (E) paradox.

36. Considering the passage as a whole, the words "Yes, you, my fellow Americans have forced the spring" (lines 101–103) are best interpreted by which of the following?

   (A) Through force, the American people have had their way.

   (B) America has retaliated in the best way it knows how.

   (C) Through their vote, Americans have created a new season in government.

   (D) Spring is about to blossom in the capital.

   (E) The government needs to have a spring like that the city is experiencing.

37. Lines 89–95 contain all of the following EXCEPT

   (A) alliteration.

   (B) assonance.

   (C) anaphora.

   (D) parallelism.

   (E) ambiguity.

38. Within lines 105–118, "To that work I now turn, . . . to give of themselves in service, too," President Clinton seems to be presenting what challenge?

   (A) Children in America need to become more informed about their government.

   (B) Troubled children in America must keep better company in their communities.

   (C) Everyone must take on part of the load of government by the people.

   (D) The new generation of Americans must reach out to children and adults in their community.

   (E) The new generation and those still young in spirit must do their share in their local communities.

39. Lines 124–133 contain all the following syntactical structures EXCEPT

   (A) fragmented sentences.

   (B) parenthetical insertion.

   (C) delayed subject.

   (D) complex sentence structure.

   (E) parallel structure.

40. Clinton's overall tone within this speech is one of

   (A) optimism and encouragement.

   (B) reference and hope.

   (C) challenge and confrontation.

   (D) supplication and pleading.

   (E) patriotism and pandering.

GO ON TO THE NEXT PAGE

Questions 41–54. Read the following essay carefully before responding to the questions.

Here was my soup. Dinner was being
served in the great dining-hall. Far from being
spring it was in fact an evening in October.
Line Everybody was assembled in the big dining-
(5) room. Dinner was ready. Here was the soup.
It was a plain gravy soup. There was nothing
to stir the fancy in that. One could have seen
through the transparent liquid any pattern
that there might have been on the plate itself.
(10) But there was no pattern. The plate was plain.
Next came beef with its attendant greens and
potatoes—a homely trinity, suggesting the
rumps of cattle in a muddy market, and sprouts
curled and yellowed at the edge, and bargaining
(15) and cheapening and women with string bags
on Monday morning. There was no reason to
complain of human nature's daily food, seeing
that the supply was sufficient and coal-miners
doubtless were sitting down to less. Prunes and
(20) custard followed. And if anyone complains
that prunes, even when mitigated by custard,
are an uncharitable vegetable (fruit they are
not), stringy as a miser's heart and exuding a
fluid such as might run in misers' veins who
(25) have denied themselves wine and warmth for
eighty years and yet not given to the poor,
he should reflect that there are people whose
charity embraces even the prune. Biscuits and
cheese came next, and here the water-jug was
(30) liberally passed round, for it is in the nature
of biscuits to be dry, and these were biscuits
to the core. That was all. The meal was over.
Everybody scraped their chairs back; the swing-
doors swung violently to and fro; soon the hall
(35) was emptied of every sign of food and made
ready no doubt for breakfast next morning.
Down corridors and up staircases the youth of
England went banging and singing. And was
it for a guest, a stranger, to say 'The dinner was

(40) not good,' or to say now that Mary and I are
in her sitting room, 'Could we not have dined
up here alone?' for if I had said anything of the
kind I should have been prying and searching
into the secret economies of a house which to
(45) the stranger wears so fine a front of gaiety and
courage. No, one could say nothing of the sort.
Indeed, conversation for a moment flagged.
The human frame being what it is, heart, body
and brain all mixed together, and not contained
(50) in separate compartments as they will be no
doubt in another million years, a good dinner
is of great importance to good talk. One cannot
think well, love well, sleep well, if one has not
dined well. The lamp in the spine does not light
(55) on beef and prunes. We are all PROBABLY
going to heaven, and Vandyck is, we HOPE,
to meet us round the next corner—that is
the dubious and qualifying state of mind that
beef and prunes at the end of the day's work
(60) breed between them. Happily my friend, who
taught science, had a cupboard where there
was a squat bottle and little glasses—(but there
should have been sole and partridge to begin
with)—so that we were able to draw up to
(65) the fire and repair some of the damages of the
day's living. In a minute or so we were slipping
freely in and out among all those objects of
curiosity and interest which form in the mind
in the absence of a particular person, and are
(70) naturally to be discussed on coming together
again—how somebody has married, another
has not; one thinks this, another that; one has
improved out of all knowledge, the other most
amazingly gone to the bad—with all those
(75) speculations upon human nature and the
character of the amazing world we live in which
spring naturally from such beginnings. While
these things were being said, however, I became

GO ON TO THE NEXT PAGE ▷

shamefacedly aware of a current setting in of its
(80) own accord and carrying everything forward
to an end of its own. The best course, unless the
whole talk was to be distorted, was to expose
what was in my mind to the air, when with good
luck it would fade and crumble like the head of
(85) the dead king when they opened the coffin at
Windsor. Briefly, then, I told Miss Seton about
the masons who had been all those years on
the roof of the chapel, and about the kings and
queens and nobles bearing sacks of gold and
(90) silver on their shoulders, which they shoveled
into the earth; and then how the great financial
magnates of our own time came and laid
cheques and bonds, I suppose, where the others
had laid ingots and rough lumps of gold. All
(95) that lies beneath the colleges down there, I said;
but this college, where we are now sitting, what
lies beneath its gallant red brick and the wild
unkempt grasses of the garden? What force is
behind that plain china off which we dined, and
(100) (here it popped out of my mouth before I could
stop it) the beef, the custard and the prunes?

From *A Room of One's Own* by Virginia
Woolf (1929)

41. In the opening of the passage, the author best
reinforces the overall plainness of the meal by

(A) using simple words.

(B) describing the undecorated plates.

(C) utilizing a succession of simple sentences.

(D) making the soup sound unappealing.

(E) mentioning that her fancy was not stirred.

42. The "homely trinity" and "muddy market,"
(lines 12–13) are mentioned as

(A) an appeal to the common folk who might
read the passage.

(B) an analogy for the beef, attendant greens,
and potatoes.

(C) a simile for the meal being consumed.

(D) an appeal to any reader who might be
religious.

(E) a distraction for readers who find her
description too boring.

43. The main point of the sentence about prunes,
(lines 20–28) is best stated by which of the
following?

(A) Some people's charity is great enough
even to include prunes.

(B) Miser's hearts are often stringy.

(C) Wine and warmth cannot make up for
prunes.

(D) Misers do not have blood in their veins
but prune juice.

(E) If misers gave to the poor they would
enjoy warmth and wine.

44. The water jug was liberally passed around
during the meal because

(A) the prunes were stringy.

(B) the beef was plain.

(C) wine was not offered to drink.

(D) the custard was gooey.

(E) the biscuits were dry.

GO ON TO THE NEXT PAGE

45. "One cannot think well, love well, sleep well, if one has not dined well," lines 52–54, utilizes a syntactical structure (the opposite of anaphora) known as

   (A) juxtaposition.
   (B) epistrophe.
   (C) parallelism.
   (D) conditional contrast.
   (E) juxtaposition.

46. As it is used in line 21, the word "mitigated" can best be defined as

   (A) moderated.
   (B) improved.
   (C) replaced.
   (D) accompanied.
   (E) cancelled.

47. The use of capital letters in the sentence beginning "We are all PROBABLY going to heaven" (lines 55–60) might best be explained as signifying that

   (A) the narrator is suffering a loss of faith.
   (B) the narrator is actually an agnostic.
   (C) we can never be sure who will also be in heaven.
   (D) the narrator is always in a "dubious and qualifying" state of mind.
   (E) beef and prunes can cause us to doubt unnecessarily.

48. The attitude of the narrator toward the meal she experienced can best be described as one of

   (A) horror and revulsion.
   (B) derision and amazement.
   (C) disdain and annoyance.
   (D) aloof superiority.
   (E) disgusted surprise.

49. The phrase " . . . so that we were able to draw up to the fire and repair some of the damages of the day's living" (lines 64–66) can best be interpreted as which of the following?

   (A) We were able to build a fire and repair the logs that were disturbed in the fireplace.
   (B) We were able to draw conclusions as to what had gone wrong in our lives that day.
   (C) We were able to sit by the fireplace and rebuild the banked fire from the day before.
   (D) We were able to sit by the fire and undo the stress of our respective days.
   (E) We were able to sketch the fireplace and the damage done to the room that day.

50. In lines 71–74, the series of clauses connected by commas and semicolons rather than conjunctions demonstrates the syntactical structure of

   (A) polyphrasis.
   (B) periodic sentence.
   (C) simple sentence.
   (D) anaphora.
   (E) asyndeton.

GO ON TO THE NEXT PAGE ➡

51. The best description of the tone in lines 81–86, the sentence beginning "The best course," would be

    (A) hesitant inquiry.
    (B) modest curiosity.
    (C) blatant bragging.
    (D) subtle jibing.
    (E) financial pedantry.

52. The most likely purpose of the story about the masons at another school (lines 86–94) to the end of the passage, is to

    (A) express empathy for the pathetic working environs of her friend.
    (B) display historical background of this institute that she is visiting.
    (C) explore the historical and financial basis of a nearby college.
    (D) criticize her surroundings and let her friend know she's unhappy.
    (E) retaliate for the terrible meal she has recently endured.

53. The most probable overall purpose of this passage is to

    (A) complain about a bad meal eaten in a poor school.
    (B) make sure her friend knows that things are better elsewhere.
    (C) console her friend for having to work under such conditions.
    (D) lament the sad conditions of the school where her friend works.
    (E) make a sociopolitical statement about the inequities within public education.

54. The best description of the type of writing in this passage is

    (A) comparison and contrast.
    (B) argumentation.
    (C) personal reflection.
    (D) political diatribe.
    (E) whimsical narrative.

STOP

Section II

Reading Period—15 minutes
Total Time—2 hours and 15 minutes
Number of questions—3
Percent of total grade—55%

Directions: This section contains three essay questions. For 15 minutes, you may read the essay questions and take notes on the question sheets. After this initial 15-minute reading period, you may begin writing your essays on the paper provided. You may not start writing on the lined paper until after the 15-minute reading period has ended. When you start writing on the three questions, budget your time carefully. Each essay counts as one-third of your total essay score.

QUESTION ONE
(Suggested reading time—15 minutes)
(Suggested writing time—40 minutes)

Directions: The following prompt is based on the accompanying six sources.

This question requires you to integrate a variety of sources into a coherent, well-written essay. *Refer to the sources to support your position; avoid mere paraphrase or summary. Your argument should be central; the sources should support this argument.*

Remember to attribute both direct and indirect citations.

Introduction: Video games have come a long way since Pong. Today, many youths have grown up playing on their video game consoles as much as, or more than, spending time in their backyards or local parks. Like any new medium (as radio and television were in the 20th century), there are many questions as to the long-lasting effect of video games on our culture. How are kids who have grown up playing video games any different from those who have not? What value do video games have for our culture, or are they a direct reflection of our culture? What concerns should we have about video game violence?

Assignment: Read the following sources (including any introductory information) carefully. **Then, in an essay that synthesizes at least three of the sources for support, take a position that defends, challenges, or qualifies the claim that video games have little cultural value and contribute to aggressive, even violent, behavior.**

You may refer to the sources by their titles (Source A, Source B, etc.) or by the descriptions in parentheses.

Source A (Moon)

Source B (Fagan)

Source C (Green and Bavelier)

Source D (Anderson)

Source E (Horsey)

Source F (Dahlen)

GO ON TO THE NEXT PAGE

Source A

Moon, James. "Video Games Today Not Just Child's Play." *Daily Bruin.* October 21, 2003.

The following passage is excerpted from a college daily newspaper.

While some people would dismiss this [video game] "fad" as a glorified waste of time, the influence of this cyber-trained generation will be felt for years to come. Besides the obvious cultural impact, video games represent a misunderstood art form . . . and a valuable educational tool in the study of society . . . video games deserve respect as being more than child's play.

A recent study from the University of Illinois found that two-thirds of college students said they played video games "at least once in a while." . . . Overall, video games are a $10 billion a year industry.

It is this prevalence that allows video games increasingly to be used as a lens through which we can observe human interaction. The major systems are a bastion for social interaction and a common sight in any house in the United States. Any computer game worth its monthly fee connects users to thousands of other players in a fully interactive online world.

This very-human interaction is the focus of new fields of study that combine aspects of communications, sociology, and political science. . . .

A new proposed minor here at UCLA involves observing these "artificial realities," perhaps hoping to gain a glimpse into our anthropological beginnings. This is life imitating art, all while just playing around.

The newest games . . . require years of development and Hollywood-style budgets. . . . The development of these lush environments and seamless animations can be called nothing less than the premier digital art form of the 21st century.

. . . Even with these social [and] aesthetical . . . attributes, to some people video games will always be considered a child's diversion, and "Doom's" greatest influence has been Columbine, and "Counter-strike" is the wasted potential in the world.

But for the rest of us, video games are much more: A social gauge, a technological marvel . . . and even a good time.

Against

GO ON TO THE NEXT PAGE

Source B

Fagan, Kevin. "Video Games: Glorifying Gore Mayhem for Minors." *San Francisco Chronicle.*
July 7, 2002.

The following passage is excerpted from a major daily newspaper.

It's cathartic to have game-art imitate life, the argument goes. Stress-relieving.
Yeah, right.

. . . The plain fact is that yes, vicariously blowing off your aggressions is a good thing.
Like playing sports. Or Pac Man. Or if that's too wimpy, some of the computer spy
adventures.

Plenty of smart people play bang-em-up video games that stop short of sadistic frenzy.
But there have to be limits—the same sorts of limits that make it not OK to let children see
hard-core porn or R-rated gore-fest movies.

. . . Even though there are voluntary ratings in this country for video games . . . don't
fool yourself that children won't get their hands on the most violent computer fantasies
available.

Take, for example, the best-selling video game in America, "Grand Theft Auto III." . . .
you the player romp off to murder and destroy as much as possible, this time in fictional
Liberty City.

. . . Three-fourths of all video gamers in America are younger than 18, he said, with
nearly as many girls playing as boys. And little keeps kids from wrapping their wee fingers
around whatever they want.

"One federal study even showed how four-year-olds were able to buy the most violent
games," [Dr. Christian] Pariseau [of Stanford University] said. "And when they asked eighth-
graders how often their parents checked what games they bought, 89 percent said 'never.'"

More than 3,000 studies have been done over the past 30 years on the effect of violent
media on children and adults, and all but 18 showed the violence has a "significant negative
effect," Pariseau said.

. . . The companies that make games glorifying brutality say lighten up, they're harmless
fun. They twist adult players only if they're a little unhinged anyway.

For

GO ON TO THE NEXT PAGE ⇨

Source C

Green, C. Shawn, and Daphne Bavelier. "The Cognitive Neuroscience of Video Games."
In *Digital Media: Transformations in Human Communication.* Messaris & Humphreys, Eds.
December 1, 2004.

The following passage is excerpted from a chapter in a book on digital media.

Another group that has been shown to benefit from video game training are laparoscopic surgeons. A recent report by Rosser and colleagues (Rosser Jr. et al. January 2004) suggested that video game players may in fact be better laparoscopic surgeons than nongamers. Laparoscopic surgery is a minimally invasive form of surgery. . . . Visual attention, manual dexterity, and hand-eye coordination are of even more importance than in normal open surgery. Rosser and colleagues found that surgeons who played video games more than 3 hours per week committed 37 percent fewer errors, were 27 percent faster at laparoscopic drills, and were 33 percent better at suturing tasks than nonvideo game playing surgeons. . . . the authors found that a surgeon's video game experience is a better predictor of surgical skill than number of years of practice or number of operations completed! The authors suggest that video games could be used as an important "warm-up" for laparoscopic surgeons or that the development of surgeon-specific video games could greatly enhance surgical aptitude.

. . . Video game play has been shown to dramatically enhance visuo-motor skills. In particular, video game players have been shown to possess decreased reaction times, increased hand-eye coordination and augmented manual dexterity. Video game play has also been shown to improve spatial skills such as mental rotation, spatial visualization, and the ability to mentally work in three dimensions,

In addition, video game play has been shown to enhance numerous aspects of visual attention including the ability to divide and switch attention, the temporal and spatial resolution of visual attention, and the number of objects that can be attended. The possibility that video games provide a medium that facilitates learning, and thus promotes changes in performance and brain organization, has led some to propose that video games are the teaching tool of choice of the 21st century.

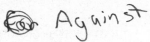 Against

Source D

Anderson, Craig A. "Violent Video Games: Myths, Facts, and Unanswered Questions."
Psychological Science Agenda. 16:5 (October, 2003).

The following excerpts are from an article in a professional psychology association journal.

Myth 1. Violent video game research has yielded very mixed results.

Facts: Some studies have yielded nonsignificant video game effects, just as some smoking studies failed to find a significant link to lung cancer. But when one combines all relevant empirical studies using meta-analytic techniques, five separate effects emerge with considerable consistency. Violent video games are significantly associated with increased aggressive behavior, thoughts, and affect; increased physiological arousal; and decreased prosocial (helping) behavior. Average effect sizes for experimental studies (which help establish causality) and correlational studies (which allow examination of serious violent behavior) appear comparable (Anderson & Bushman, 2001).

Myth 6. There are no studies linking violent video game play to serious aggression.

Facts: High levels of violent video game exposure have been linked to delinquency, fighting at school and during free play periods, and violent criminal behavior (e.g., self-reported assault, robbery).

Myth 7. Violent video games affect only a small fraction of players.

Facts: Though there are good theoretical reasons to expect some populations to be more susceptible to violent video game effects than others, the research literature has not yet substantiated this. That is, there is not consistent evidence for the claim that younger children are more negatively affected than adolescents or young adults or that males are more affected than females. There is some evidence that highly aggressive individuals are more affected than nonaggressive individuals, but this finding does not consistently occur. Even nonaggressive individuals are consistently affected by brief exposures. Further research will likely find some significant moderators of violent video game effects, because the much larger research literature on television violence has found such effects and the underlying processes are the same. However, even that larger literature has not identified a sizeable population that is totally immune to negative effects of media violence.

- - - - - - - -

Anderson, C. A., & Bushman, B. J. (2001). Effects of violent video games on aggressive behavior, aggressive cognition, aggressive affect, physiological arousal, and prosocial behavior: A meta-analytic review of the scientific literature. *Psychological Science, 12,* 353–359.

GO ON TO THE NEXT PAGE

Source E

Horsey, David. "Dr. Frankenstein Creating Little Monsters." *Seattle Post-Intelligencer*. August 1, 2003.

The cartoon below was published in a major daily newspaper.

For

Source F

Dahlen, Chris. "Complicated Games: The Moral Rorschach Test." *Paste.* February/March 2006.

The following passage is excerpted from a bimonthly magazine on music, film, and culture.

Today, many games use a morality system, although they're rarely one-sided. In titles like *Star Wars: Knights of the Old Republic*, you can follow "good" or "evil" paths, and in *Fable*, you even sprout hooves or a halo depending on how truly great or vicious you've become.

. . . The games watch and judge your every move, and tweak your alignment based on how you play . . . video games actually watch what you do when your progress in the game is at stake. Is it faster to take shortcuts, cheat and steal and kill anyone who gets in your way—or is it just more fun?

Of course, some games give you the choice between right and wrong, and then ignore your decision. The ever-controversial *Grand Theft Auto* series bothers people not only because [in the game] you're a criminal, but because you operate in an amoral consequence-free environment: Sometimes you commit a crime and the cops chase you, but often you get away with it. . . . How you feel about it later depends solely on your own conscience.

. . . Does the way you act in a game shape who you are in real life? . . . I firmly believe they can tell you a great deal about who you already are. Whenever I meet people who play exclusively as evil characters . . . I get a little creeped out. As for myself, I've found that I actually behave better in games than I ever do in reality. Normally I cut off other drivers and stiff the tip jar at coffeeshops, but in games, I play by all the rules. . . . I asked a real psychologist what that says about me. "Simple," he answered, "you're a wimp." But that's what makes this kind of freedom so engaging: We find out more about ourselves than we expected.

STOP

QUESTION TWO
(Suggested time—40 minutes)

In this narrative from *Incidents in the Life of a Slave Girl*, "Linda," whose name was actually Harriet Jacobs, comments on her experience of teaching an old male slave (Uncle Fred) how to read and write. Read the passage carefully. Then, write an essay in which you define the attitude the author has toward slavery and toward the double standard under which the white man lives.

There are thousands, who, like good Uncle Fred, are thirsting for the water of life; but the law forbids it, and the churches withhold it. They send the Bible to heathen abroad, and neglect the heathen at home. I am glad that missionaries go out to the dark corners of the earth; but I ask them not to overlook the dark corners at home. Talk to American

Line
(5) slaveholders as you talk to savages in Africa. Tell them it was wrong to traffic in men. Tell them it is sinful to sell their own children, and atrocious to violate their own daughters. Tell them that all men are brethren, and that man has no right to shut out the light of knowledge from his brother. Tell them they are answerable to God for sealing up the Fountain of Life from souls that are thirsting for it.

(10) There are men who would gladly undertake such missionary work as this; but, alas! their number is small. They are hated by the south, and would be driven from its soil, or dragged to prison to die, as others have been before them. The field is ripe for the harvest, and awaits the reapers. Perhaps the great grandchildren of Uncle Fred may have freely imparted to them the divine treasures, which he sought by stealth, at the risk of the prison

(15) and the scourge.

Are doctors of divinity blind, or are they hypocrites? I suppose some are the one, and some the other; but I think if they felt the interest in the poor and the lowly, that they ought to feel, they would not be so easily blinded. A clergyman who goes to the south, for the first time, has usually some feeling, however vague, that slavery is wrong. The

(20) slaveholder suspects this, and plays his game accordingly. He makes himself as agreeable as possible; talks on theology, and other kindred topics. The reverend gentleman is asked to invoke a blessing on a table loaded with luxuries. After dinner he walks round the premises, and sees the beautiful groves and flowering vines, and the comfortable huts of favored household slaves. The southerner invites him to talk with those slaves. He asks

(25) them if they want to be free, and they say, "O, no, massa." This is sufficient to satisfy him. He comes home to publish a "South Side View of Slavery," and to complain of the exaggerations of abolitionists. He assures people that he has been to the south, and seen slavery for himself; that it is a beautiful "patriarchal institution"; that the slaves don't want their freedom; that they have hallelujah meetings and other religious privileges.

(30) What does he know of the half-starved wretches toiling from dawn till dark on the plantations? of mothers shrieking for their children, torn from their arms by slave traders? of young girls dragged down into moral filth? of pools of blood around the whipping post? of hounds trained to tear human flesh? of men screwed into cotton gins to die? The slaveholder showed him none of these things, and the slaves dared not tell of them if he had asked them.

GO ON TO THE NEXT PAGE →

(35)   There is a great difference between Christianity and religion at the south. If a man goes to the communion table, and pays money into the treasury of the church, no matter if it be the price of blood, he is called religious. If a pastor has offspring by a woman not his wife, the church dismisses him, if she is a white woman; but if she is colored, it does not hinder his continuing to be their good shepherd.

(40)   When I was told that Dr. Flint had joined the Episcopal church, I was much surprised. I supposed that religion had a purifying effect on the character of men; but the worst persecutions I endured from him were after he was a communicant. The conversation of the doctor, the day after he had been confirmed, certainly gave me no indication that he had "renounced the devil and all his works." In answer to some of his usual talk, I

(45) reminded him that he had just joined the church. "Yes, Linda," said he. "It was proper for me to do so. I am getting on in years, and my position in society requires it, and it puts an end to all the damed slang. You would do well to join the church, too, Linda."

     "There are sinners enough in it already," rejoined I. "If I could be allowed to live like a Christian, I should be glad."

(50)   "You can do what I require; and if you are faithful to me, you will be as virtuous as my wife," he replied.

     I answered that the Bible didn't say so.

     His voice became hoarse with rage. "How dare you preach to me about your infernal Bible!" he exclaimed. "What right have you, who are my negro, to talk to me about what

(55) you would like and what you wouldn't like? I am your master, and you shall obey me."

     No wonder the slaves sing—

     "Ole Satan's church is here below;

     Up to God's free church I hope to go."

STOP

QUESTION THREE
(Suggested time—40 minutes)

The following passage by Rick Reilly, a humorous sports writer for *Sports Illustrated*, discusses the increasing incidence of sports on Sunday in lieu of religious worship. More specifically, he focuses on parents' involvement in their children's sports. In a well-written essay, analyze Reilly's concerns about children and support, challenge, or qualify his conclusions.

Let Us Play

Another Easter Sunday in the Cathedral. Hushed voices. Amens. People holding hands and praying. At the end, all of them rising as one and screaming, "My God, it's a miracle!" Church?

Line
(5) No. Augusta National. It was Phil Mickelson's win at the Masters.

Sports has nearly swallowed Sunday whole. Every pro sport plays on Sunday. The big day in pro golf and tennis is Sunday. College football started playing bowl games on Sunday. Here's March Madness: 10 NCAA tournament games were played on Sunday. Now more and more youth sports teams are playing on Sunday, when the fields are easier to get and parents are available to drive.

(10) It's that kind of stuff that has really torqued off Pope John Paul II lately. In March he decried the fact that Sundays are losing their "fundamental meaning" to "such things as entertainment and sport." It's not as if he's antijock. The pope was a goalkeeper, skier and kayaker in his day. Hey, he just blessed New England Patriots quarterback Tom Brady's right arm. He's just hacked at the way sport is crowding God right off the list of Sunday

(15) passions.

The first people he might want to crack down on are the Christians themselves. Think he knows that the Santa Clarita (Calif.) YMCA has youth hoops on Sundays? Think the pope would be down on Notre Dame if he knew its softball team will play more games on Sundays in May than on any other day of the week?

(20) He's not the only one who's chapped about sports becoming this country's main religion. Priests and pastors across the country have noticed something lately: God is competing more and more with Sunday sports—and losing. Especially with youth sports.

"It's only happened the last two years," says Rich Cizik of the National Association of Evangelicals. "Coaches never used to schedule games on Sunday."

(25) Says the Reverend Julie Yarborough of Summit (N.J.) Christ Church, "You see kids coming to Sunday school late and their parents coming early to get them for games—if they come at all. Sports is really eating into our time."

Her colleague at Christ Church, the Reverend Charles Rush, knew there was a problem the other day when his 12-year-old acolyte lit the candles at the front of the church

(30) wearing his soccer cleats.

I'll tell you exactly what's going on here: the upping of American youth sports.

GO ON TO THE NEXT PAGE

For some reason overcaffeinated parents feel they have to *keep up* with the Joneses. They used to do it with their cars. Now they do it with their kids. Upping means putting little Justin into not one soccer league but three, not one soccer camp but four.

(35)   Upping also means *playing up*, forcing a kid to play one or even two levels above his age group, so that little Benjamin, age eight, can sit on the 10-year-olds' bench, play three minutes a game and whiff in his only at bat. But, hey, he is playing up!

And upping means *moving up*. The local team isn't high-profile, so little Amber has to switch to an elite team, usually in another town. That means extended drives to and from
(40)   practice plus traveling three or four or six hours to play in tony *invitational* tournaments on weekends. This way parents from far-flung towns can flaunt the status symbol of spending beautiful warm weekends in a freezing ice rink watching 14 mind- and butt-numbing hockey games.

"I admit, we're guilty from time to time," John Burrill, head of the Massachusetts
(45)   Youth Soccer Association, says of playing on Sundays. "We don't feel particularly good about it, but with today's busy schedules Sunday is the only time some of us have to do these things. And if you're going to travel two states away, it doesn't make sense to not play Sunday, too."

Well, religion bosses have decided that they're not going to take it anymore. Spiritual
(50)   leaders in Summit got together recently and appealed for sports leagues to stop scheduling games before noon on Sunday. A meeting between them and area youth coaches is set for May. We'll see who kneels first.

Don't bet on coaches doing the right thing. If they could, they'd have your kids running stairs on Christmas morning. What has to happen is the parents have to start saying no.
(55)   Not to their kids—to their kids' coaches. "I told my boy's coach he wouldn't be playing on Sundays," says Cizik, "and he looked shocked. I said, 'You act like nobody's ever said that to you before.' And he said, 'Honestly? They haven't.'"

I'm with the holy men. Not that I'm the Reverend Lovejoy, but I just feel sorry for these kids who get nothing but organized sports crammed down their gullets 24/7. My
(60)   Lord, even God took a day off.

Kids might weep with joy to get a day off from sports. If they don't spend it at church, maybe they'll spend it getting to know their siblings' names again. Or swing in a hammock without a coach screaming, "Get your hips into it, Samantha!"

Hey, you do what you want. Just remember, when little Shaniqua has two free throws
(65)   to win or lose a game on some Sunday morning, good luck finding somebody who'll answer your prayers.

April 26, 2004

STOP

PRACTICE TEST 2: ANSWER KEY

PASSAGE 1		PASSAGE 2		PASSAGE 3		PASSAGE 4	
1.	B	15.	D	28.	C	41.	C
2.	D	16.	A	29.	A	42.	B
3.	E	17.	E	30.	C	43.	A
4.	A	18.	B	31.	E	44.	E
5.	A	19.	C	32.	D	45.	B
6.	D	20.	E	33.	A	46.	B
7.	E	21.	A	34.	B	47.	E
8.	C	22.	C	35.	D	48.	C
9.	C	23.	E	36.	C	49.	D
10.	A	24.	A	37.	E	50.	E
11.	E	25.	D	38.	E	51.	A
12.	D	26.	C	39.	D	52.	A
13.	C	27.	E	40.	A	53.	E
14.	B					54.	C

ANSWERS AND EXPLANATIONS

SECTION I: MULTIPLE CHOICE

Since the afternoon in 1967 when I first saw Hoover Dam, its image has never been entirely absent from my inner eye. I will be driving down Sunset Boulevard, or about to enter a
Line
(5) freeway, and abruptly those power transmission towers will appear before me, canted vertiginously over the tailrace. Sometimes I am confronted by the intakes and sometimes by the shadow of the heavy cable that spans the
(10) canyon and sometimes by the ominous outlets to unused spillways, black in the lunar clarity of the desert light. Quite often I hear the turbines. Frequently I wonder what is happening at the dam this instant, at this precise intersection
(15) of time and space, how much water is being released to fill downstream orders and what lights are flashing and which generators are in full use and which just spinning free.

I used to wonder what it was about the dam
(20) that made me think of it at times and in places where I once thought of the Mindanao Trench, or of the stars wheeling in their courses, or of the words *As it was in the beginning, is now and ever shall be, world without end, amen.* Dams,
(25) after all, are commonplace: we have all seen one. This particular dam had existed as an idea in the world's mind for almost forty years before I saw it. Hoover Dam, showpiece of the Boulder Canyon project, the several million tons of
(30) concrete that made the Southwest plausible, the fait accompli that was to convey, in the innocent time of its construction, the notion that mankind's brightest promise lay in American engineering.

(35) Of course the dam derives some of its emotional effect from precisely that aspect, that sense of being a monument to a faith since misplaced. "They died to make the desert bloom," reads a plaque dedicated to the
(40) ninety-six men who died building this first of the great high dams, and in context the worn phrase touches, suggests all of that trust in harnessing resources, the meliorative power of the dynamo, so central to the early Thirties.
(45) Boulder City, built in 1931 as the construction town for the dam, retains the ambience of a model city, a new town, a toy triangular grid of green lawns and trim bungalows, all fanning out from the Reclamation building. The bronze
(50) sculptures at the dam itself evoke muscular citizens of tomorrow that never came, sheaves of wheat clutched heavenward, thunderbolts defied. Winged Victories guard the flagpole. The flag whips in the canyon wind. The empty
(55) Pepsi-Cola can clatters across the terrazzo. The place is perfectly frozen in time.

But history does not explain it all, does not entirely suggest what makes that dam so affecting. Nor, even, does energy, the massive
(60) involvement with power and pressure and the transparent sexual overtones to that involvement. Once when I revisited the dam I walked through it with a man from the Bureau of Reclamation. Once in a while he would
(65) explain something, usually in that recondite language having to do with "peaking power," with "outages" and "dewatering," but on the whole we spent the afternoon in a world so alien, so complete and so beautiful unto itself
(70) that it was scarcely necessary to speak at all. We saw almost no one. Cranes moved above us as if under their own volition. Generators roared. Transformers hummed. The gratings on which we stood vibrated. We watched a hundred-ton
(75) steel shaft plunging down to that place where the water was. And finally we got down to that place where the water was, where the water sucked out of Lake Mead roared through thirty-foot

penstocks and then into thirteen-foot penstocks
(80) and finally into the turbines themselves.

There was something beyond all that,
something beyond energy, beyond history,
something I could not fix in my mind. When I
came up from the dam that day the wind was
(85) blowing harder, through the canyon and all
across the Mojave, but out at the dam there
was no dust, only the rock and the dam and a
little greasewood and a few garbage cans, their
tops chained banging against a fence. I walked
(90) across the marble star map that traces a sidereal
revolution of the equinox and fixes forever,
the Reclamation man had told me, for all time
and for all people who can read the stars, the
date the dam was dedicated. The star map was,
(95) he had said, for when we were all gone and
the dam was left. I had not thought much of it
when he said it, but I thought of it then, with
the wind whining and the sun dropping behind
a mesa with the finality of a sunset in space.
(100)   Of course that was the image I had seen,
always seen it without quite realizing what I
saw, a dynamo finally free of man, splendid at
last in its absolute isolation, transmitting power
and releasing water to a world where no one is.
(105)   From "At the Dam" by Joan Didion in
The White Album (1979)

1. B
Although there is a sense of mysticism to this
passage, there is not true anxiety or foreboding,
(D). It is somewhat reminiscent, but not regretful,
(A); it's definitely not lighthearted nor whimsical,
(C). You could never classify it as guileful, although
a bit of the description might be deemed hesitant or
at least unsure, (E).

2. D
This is one of those dreaded Roman numeral
questions. What you have to do is consider all the
choices—which of them is true? Then, consider

the combinations that you are offered as response
possibilities and choose your answer accordingly. In
this case, the opening sentence not only introduces
the topic of the passage but also expresses the
strange haunting the narrator has experienced by
the dam. It does not, however, do any comparing or
contrasting with any other experience.

3. E
The only thing this paragraph does not contain is
any sort of understatement. The national symbol is
self-explanatory. For the religious allusion, see words
in italics. The foreign terminology is *fait accompli*.
The Southwest would exist without the dam; it
just would not exist as it does now, making that
statement an exaggeration, or hyperbole.

4. A
The key word in this question is *throughout*.
Although there is some logic and she does call on
the *expert's* opinion at the dam, providing some
ethos, the reality is that throughout the passage, she
is working with emotion, or pathos.

5. A
This question asks for a comparison or, in this case,
a contrast between the world and the dam. The
world is made of and for people. The dam might
have been created by people, but now that it has
been built, the narrator depicts it as a mechanical
wonder working by itself, perhaps eternally, free of
human interference.

6. D
These lines contain imagery, the sound device
of onomatopoeia, parallel structure, and simple
sentences. However, there is nothing nostalgic about
the description.

7. E
Although you might be tempted to choose (A), this
is a good case for looking at *all* responses before
deciding. Choice (E) most accurately describes the
underlying purpose of the passage.

8.   C

These lines best reinforce the idea that the entire dam is frozen in time. The main fascination for Didion in this passage is the eternality of the dam.

9.   C

Occasionally, the AP English Language and Composition exam will throw a straightforward vocabulary question at you. *Canted* means angled; *vertiginously* means dizzyingly. In her mind's eye, home in California, she sees the dam, causing her to experience instability or unsteadiness. The dam itself is a monstrous structure shored up by an amazing array of oddly angled supports. Just looking at their size and angles would make many observers dizzy.

10.   A

These lines in paragraph 5 repeat the word *something* as the first word of several phrases in succession. While this is definitely a form of repetition, (E), it is most specifically a type of repetition known as anaphora. You will find this and other definitions in the Key Terminology section of this book.

11.   E

The passage closes with "There was something beyond all that, something beyond energy, beyond history, something I could not fix in my mind . . . what I saw, a dynamo finally free of man, splendid at last in its absolute isolation, transmitting power and releasing water to a world where no one is." Joan Didion's closing comments have an eerie and haunting tone about them.

12.   D

This is NOT a sentence at all, so (D) is not possible. Also, the characteristics mentioned by the other choices are present in this fragment.

13.   C

These lines are: "Boulder City, built in 1931, as the construction town for the dam, retains the ambience of a model city, a new town, a toy triangular grid of green lawns and trim bungalows, all fanning out from the Reclamation building." Just as a child might lay out a city with toy houses and cars, so

too did the planners of Boulder Dam lay out the city for the workers who would build this mighty structure. The workers are long gone, but the city has been maintained. Its emptiness reminds the viewer of a toy city, meticulously constructed and left abandoned by its child architect in search of more compelling activities.

14.   B

Didion is amazed by this structure. In this passage, she relates the great energy and manpower it took to build this powerhouse of the Southwest. However, what amazes her most is the "feeling" she has that this dam is so perfectly constructed that there may come a time that man may no longer be around, but the dam, in its self-sufficiency, will continue "transmitting power and releasing water to a world where no one is."

He who lets the world, or his own portion of it, choose his plan of life for him, has no need of any other faculty than the ape-like
Line one of imitation. He who chooses his plan for
(5)   himself, employs all his faculties. He must use observation to see, reason and judgment to foresee, activity to gather materials for decision, discrimination to decide, and when he has decided, firmness and self-control to hold to
(10)   his deliberate decisions. And these qualities he requires and exercises exactly in proportion as the part of his conduct which he determines according to his judgment and feelings is a large one. It is possible that he might be guided in
(15)   some good path, and kept out of harm's way, without any of these things. But what will be his comparative worth as a human being? It really is of importance, not only what men do, but also what manner of men they are that do it.
(20)   Among the works of man, which human life is rightly employed in performing and beautifying, the first in importance surely is man himself. Supposing it were possible to get houses built, corn grown, battles fought, causes tried, and

(25) even churches erected and prayers said, by
machinery—by automatons in human form—
it would be a considerable loss to exchange for
these automatons even the men and women
who at present inhabit the more civilized parts
(30) of the world, and who assuredly are but starved
specimens of what nature can and will produce.
Human nature is not a machine to be built
after a model, and set to do exactly the work
prescribed for it, but a tree, which requires to
(35) grow and develop itself on all sides, according to
the tendency of the inward forces which make it
a living thing.

It will probably be conceded that it
is desirable people should exercise their
(40) understandings, and that an intelligent
following of custom, or even occasionally an
intelligent deviation from custom, is better
than a blind and simply mechanical adhesion
to it. To a certain extent it is admitted that
(45) our understanding should be our own: but
there is not the same willingness to admit that
our desires and impulses should be our own
likewise; or that to possess impulses of our
own, and of any strength, is anything but a peril
(50) and a snare. Yet desires and impulses are as
much a part of a perfect human being as beliefs
and restraints: and strong impulses are only
perilous when not properly balanced; when one
set of aims and inclinations is developed into
(55) strength, while others, which ought to co-exist
with them, remain weak and inactive. It is not
because men's desires are strong and they act ill:
it is because their consciences are weak; there is
no natural connection between strong impulses
(60) and a weak conscience; the natural connection
is the other way. To say that one person's
desires and feelings are stronger and more
various than those of another, is merely to say
that he has more of the raw material of human
(65) nature, and is therefore capable, perhaps of

more evil, but certainly of more good. Strong
impulses are but another name for energy.
Energy may be termed to bad uses; but more
good may always be made of an energetic
(70) nature, than of an indolent and impassive one.

Those who have most natural feeling are
always those whose cultivated feelings may
be made the strongest. The same strong
susceptibilities which make the personal
(75) impulses vivid and powerful, are also the source
from whence are generated the most passionate
love of virtue, and the sternest self-control. It
is through the cultivation of these that society
both does its duty and protects its interests: not
(80) by rejecting the stuff by which heroes are made,
because it knows not how to make them. A
person whose desires and impulses are his own
is said to have a character. One whose desires
and impulses are not his own, has no character,
(85) no more than a steam engine has character.
If, in addition to being his own, his impulses
are strong, and are under the government of
a strong will, he has an energetic character.
Whoever thinks that individuality of desires
(90) and impulses should not be encouraged to
unfold itself, must maintain that society has
no need of strong natures—is not the better
for containing many persons who have much
character—and that a high general average of
(95) energy is not desirable.

In some early states of society, these
forces might be, and were, too much ahead
of the power which society then possessed of
disciplining and controlling them. There has
(100) been a time when the element of spontaneity
and individuality was in excess, and the social
principle had a hard struggle with it. The
difficulty then was to induce men of strong
bodies or minds to pay obedience to any rules
(105) which required them to control their impulses.
To overcome this difficulty, law and discipline,

like the Popes struggling against the Emperors, asserted a power over the whole man, claiming to control all his life in order to control his
(110) character—which society had not found any other sufficient means of binding. But society has now fairly got the better of individuality: and the danger which threatens human nature is not the excess, but the deficiency, of personal
(115) impulses and preferences. Things are vastly changed since the passion of those who were strong by station or by personal endowment were in a state of habitual rebelling against laws and ordinances, and required to be rigorously
(120) chained up to enable the persons within their reach to enjoy any particle of security. In our times, from the highest class of society down to the lowest, every one lives as under the eye of a hostile and dreaded censorship. Not only
(125) in what concerns others, but in what concerns only themselves, the individual or the family do not ask themselves—what do I prefer? Or, what would suit my character and disposition: or, what would allow the best and highest in
(130) me to have fair play and enable it to grow and thrive? They ask themselves, what is suitable to my position, what is usually done by persons of my station and pecuniary circumstances? Or (worse still) what is usually done by persons
(135) of a station and circumstances superior to mine? I do not mean that they choose what is customary in preference to what suits their own inclination. It does not occur to them to have any inclination except for what is customary.
(140) Thus the mind itself is bowed to the yoke: they like in crowds; they exercise choice only among things commonly done: peculiarity of taste, eccentricity of conduct, are shunned equally with crimes: until by dint of not following their
(145) own nature they have no nature to follow: their human capacities are withered and starved: they become incapable of any strong wishes or native pleasures, and are generally without

either opinions or feelings of home growth, or
(150) properly their own. Now this, or is it not, the desirable condition of human nature?

From Chapter 3: "On Individuality" of *On Liberty* by John Stuart Mill (1859)

15. D
The main message of this passage can be borrowed from *Hamlet*: "To thine own self be true." Mill's message, again and again, is that one must develop as one's own person, not copy others or go along with the crowd just because it's an easier route.

16. A
"Human nature is not a machine to be built after a model, and set to do exactly the work prescribed for it, but a tree, which requires to grow and develop itself on all sides according to the tendency of the inward forces which make it a living thing." This question may send you back to the Key Terminology chapter of this book. Refresh your understanding of simile, metaphor, personification, and so on. Sometimes we think we know what something means, but when confronted with it within any sort of literature, we become a bit shaky in our identification.

17. E
To answer this question, you need to look again at paragraph 2 of the passage. You will not have enough time while taking the multiple-choice part of the AP English Language and Composition exam to reread the passage closely, but you should have gleaned two main ideas from the passage. The narrator wants us to become our own person, not copies of something else, no matter how convenient or conventional. The second point, however, is that in developing into our own person, we must maintain our conscience. As a barometer of our actions, we must remain conscious of what we are doing, and we must always be in control of those "energies" that, once unleashed, can lead us into danger.

18. B
Again, you may want to consult Key Terminology. What we have here is a series of clauses *without*

conjunctions (therefore asyndeton in contrast to polysyndeton).

19. C

In actuality, the narrator tells us that if a person listens to his or her conscience, then he will *not* act ill but will act appropriately, even when following his or her own individuality.

20. E

In paragraph 4, the narrator tells us, "The difficulty then was to induce men of strong bodies or minds to pay obedience to any rules which required them to control their impulses. To overcome this difficulty, law and discipline, like the Popes struggling against the Emperors, asserted a power over the whole man, claiming to control all his life in order to control his character—which society had not found any other sufficient means of minding."

21. A

This question asks you to consider the particular mode of discourse of one paragraph, paragraph 3. You have to admit that there is something speculative and wishful about this passage. What the narrator suggests is not necessarily what might happen immediately. Therefore, he is both hypothetical—anticipating what might be—and speculative—anticipating the best-case scenario based upon the moment.

22. C

Again, you are directed to paragraph 3. The main point of this paragraph is that man's innately "wild" energies must succumb to the concept of decorum. Despite the struggle for individuality, society, at least in the narrator's view, has overcome and even squashed any attempts for man to step forward as his own person.

23. E

The last paragraph describes how the rules of society enforce conformity to the detriment of personal freedom and individuality. The tone of the paragraph indicates that the author disagrees with this trend.

24. A

The last sentence of paragraph 3 says, "Whoever thinks that individuality of desires and impulses should not be encouraged to unfold itself, must maintain that society has no need of strong natures—is not the better for containing many persons who have much character—and that a high general average of energy is not desirable." It is not difficult to identify this sentence as not containing a series preceded by a colon.

25. D

"Things are vastly changed since the passion of those who were strong by station or by personal endowment were in a state of habitual rebelling against laws and ordinances, and required to be rigorously chained up to enable the persons within their reach to enjoy any particle of security." The narrator is lamenting the fact that we have all been tamed into submission. No longer does our inner self speak out against being sucked in by the majority.

26. C

Basically, this narrator has just about given up on mankind. We have "gone to the dark side." Men no longer think for themselves and make their own decisions. Instead, man goes with the flow of society and chooses to be indolent rather than harnessing his energy to become himself.

27. E

In the final paragraph, the author is afraid that man will sacrifice everything that makes him an individual, independent person in order to go along with society's mores. Whatever is customary and appropriate is easiest to pursue.

Thomas Jefferson believed that to preserve the very foundations of our nation, we would need dramatic change from time to time. *Line (5)* Well, my fellow citizens, this is our time. Let us embrace it.

Our democracy must be not only the envy of the world but the engine of our own renewal.

There is nothing wrong with America that cannot be cured by what is right with America.

(10) And so today, we pledge an end to the era of deadlock and drift—a new season of American renewal has begun.

To renew America, we must be bold.

We must do what no generation has had (15) to do before. We must invest more in our own people, in their jobs, in their future, and at the same time cut our massive debt. And we must do so in a world in which we must compete for every opportunity.

(20) It will not be easy; it will require sacrifice. But it can be done, and done fairly, not choosing sacrifice for its own sake, but for our own sake. We must provide for our nation the way a family provides for its children.

(25) Our Founders saw themselves in the light of posterity. We can do no less. Anyone who has ever watched a child's eyes wander into sleep knows what posterity is. Posterity is the world to come—the world for whom we hold (30) our ideals, from whom we have borrowed our planet, and to whom we bear sacred responsibility.

We must do what America does best: offer more opportunity to all and demand (35) responsibility from all.

It is time to break the bad habit of expecting something for nothing, from our government or from each other. Let us all take more responsibility, not only for ourselves (40) and our families but for our communities and our country.

To renew America, we must revitalize our democracy.

This beautiful capital, like every capital (45) since the dawn of civilization, is often a place of intrigue and calculation. Powerful people maneuver for position and worry endlessly about who is in and who is out, who is up and who is down, forgetting those people whose (50) toil and sweat sends us here and pays our way.

Americans deserve better, and in this city today, there are people who want to do better. And so I say to all of us here, let us resolve to reform our politics, so that power (55) and privilege no longer shout down the voice of the people. Let us put aside personal advantage so that we can feel the pain and see the promise of America.

Let us resolve to make our government a (60) place for what Franklin Roosevelt called "bold, persistent experimentation," a government for our tomorrows, not our yesterdays.

Let us give this capital back to the people to whom it belongs.

(65) To renew America, we must meet challenges abroad as well at home. There is no longer division between what is foreign and what is domestic—the world economy, the world environment, the world AIDS crisis, the (70) world arms race—they affect us all.

Today, as an old order passes, the new world is more free but less stable. Communism's collapse has called forth old animosities and new dangers. Clearly America must continue to (75) lead the world we did so much to make.

While America rebuilds at home, we will not shrink from the challenges, nor fail to seize the opportunities, of this new world. Together with our friends and allies, we will (80) work to shape change, lest it engulf us.

When our vital interests are challenged, or the will and conscience of the international community is defied, we will act—with peaceful diplomacy whenever possible, with (85) force when necessary. The brave Americans serving our nation today in the Persian Gulf, in Somalia, and wherever else they stand are testament to our resolve.

But our greatest strength is the power of
(90) our ideas, which are still new in many lands.
Across the world, we see them embraced—
and we rejoice. Our hopes, our hearts, our
hands, are with those on every continent who
are building democracy and freedom. Their
(95) cause is America's cause.

The American people have summoned the
change we celebrate today. You have raised
your voices in an unmistakable chorus. You
have cast your votes in historic numbers. And
(100) you have changed the face of Congress, the
presidency and the political process itself. Yes,
you, my fellow Americans have forced the
spring. Now, we must do the work the season
demands.

(105) To that work I now turn, with all the
authority of my office. I ask the Congress to
join with me. But no president, no Congress,
no government, can undertake this mission
alone. My fellow Americans, you, too, must
(110) play your part in our renewal. I challenge
a new generation of young Americans to a
season of service—to act on your idealism by
helping troubled children, keeping company
with those in need, reconnecting our torn
(115) communities. There is so much to be done—
enough indeed for millions of others who are
still young in spirit to give of themselves in
service, too.

In serving, we recognize a simple but
(120) powerful truth—we need each other. And
we must care for one another. Today, we do
more than celebrate America; we rededicate
ourselves to the very idea of America.

An idea born in revolution and renewed
(125) through two centuries of challenge. An idea
tempered by the knowledge that, but for fate,
we—the fortunate and the unfortunate—
might have been each other. An idea ennobled
by the faith that our nation can summon

(130) from its myriad diversity the deepest measure
of unity. An idea infused with the conviction
that America's long heroic journey must go
forever upward.

And so, my fellow Americans, at the edge
(135) of the twenty-first century, let us begin with
energy and hope, with faith and discipline,
and let us work until our work is done. The
scripture says, "And let us not be weary in
well-doing, for in due season, we shall reap, if we
(140) faint not."

From this joyful mountaintop of
celebration, we hear a call to service in the
valley. We have heard the trumpets. We have
changed the guard. And now, each in our way,
(145) and with God's help, we must answer the call.

Thank you and God bless you all.
Inaugural Address, William Clinton,
20 January 1993

28. C
"Thomas Jefferson believed that to preserve the very
foundations of our nation, we would need dramatic
change from time to time. Well, my fellow citizens,
this is our time. Let us embrace it." This opening
paragraph is expecting some empathy, (E), from the
audience, but overall the appeal is to the audience's
patriotism, making (C) the besy answer.

29. A
"Nothing wrong that cannot be cured by what is
right" is enough to make you scratch your head
for a minute. What we have here is a seeming
contradiction that really does make sense, therefore
a paradox.

30. C
Epistrophe is the repetition of a word or words at
the end of two or more successive verses, clauses,
or sentences; "offer more opportunity to all and
demand responsibility from all" demonstrates this
syntactic device.

31. E

This rather short paragraph contains a parenthetical statement ("like every capital since the dawn of civilization"), independent clauses in a series ("who is in and who is out, who is up and who is down"), a participial phrase ("*forgetting* those people who toil"), and a compound verb (*maneuver* and *worry*). What this paragraph does not contain is a compound sentence.

32. D

"A government for our tomorrows, not our yesterdays" is a government that does not rest on prior accomplishments and laurels but is forward thinking and ready to take on new challenges.

33. A

Take a look at these lines. Words starting with the letter *P* are used throughout, which is *alliteration* (the repetition of consonants).

34. B

When a particular line is repeated throughout a poem or piece of prose, it has a stylistic purpose. Often in poetry it is the main message of the poem. Such a repetition is a *refrain* (in music, the chorus). In a speech such as this one, Clinton is strongly emphasizing the idea of renewal. This is known as a refrain.

35. D

A *zeugma* is a linkage of one subject with two or more verbs or, in this speech, a verb with two or more objects or descriptors. ". . . we will act— with peaceful diplomacy . . . with force. . . ." Both peaceful diplomacy and force go back to the verb *act*.

36. C

When you force a flower, you cause it to bloom (change) early, before its normal season. Since it was not spring yet in the capital, when Clinton gave this speech, he says the people (their vote) have forced the spring. In other words, through their vote change has happened and things are going to grow, albeit a bit early in the season.

37. E

If you are unsure of any of the terms offered as choices for this question, go back to Key Terminology and check definitions and examples. *Alliteration* is repetition of consonants; *assonance* is repetition of vowel sounds; *anaphora* is repetition of phrase, clause, or sentence openings; *parallelism* is recurrent structure. All of these are present but not *ambiguity*. There is nothing in these lines wherein multiple connotations are offered, often to confuse or obfuscate meaning.

38. E

Typical of many political speeches of this nature, Clinton is challenging the public—especially the younger generation or those young in spirit—to do their share in the effort to make America a stronger nation.

39. D

You may say that the jumble of sentences (and fragments) found in these lines is truly complex. But here you must ask yourself: Does this sentence represent *complex sentence structure*? No, it does not. A complex sentence is one that has at least one independent clause and one dependent clause. These lines do not represent such a structure.

40. A

This one you should have been able to figure out almost without reading the passage (not a recommended tactic, however). As with most inaugural addresses, Clinton offers encouragement, and he is, of course, optimistic about the future of the United States under his leadership.

> Here was my soup. Dinner was being
> served in the great dining-hall. Far from being
> spring it was in fact an evening in October.
> Everybody was assembled in the big dining-
> *Line* room. Dinner was ready. Here was the soup.
> *(5)* It was a plain gravy soup. There was nothing
> to stir the fancy in that. One could have seen
> through the transparent liquid any pattern
> that there might have been on the plate itself.

(10) But there was no pattern. The plate was plain.
Next came beef with its attendant greens and
potatoes—a homely trinity, suggesting the
rumps of cattle in a muddy market, and sprouts
curled and yellowed at the edge, and bargaining
(15) and cheapening and women with string bags
on Monday morning. There was no reason to
complain of human nature's daily food, seeing
that the supply was sufficient and coal-miners
doubtless were sitting down to less. Prunes and
(20) custard followed. And if anyone complains
that prunes, even when mitigated by custard,
are an uncharitable vegetable (fruit they are
not), stringy as a miser's heart and exuding a
fluid such as might run in misers' veins who
(25) have denied themselves wine and warmth for
eighty years and yet not given to the poor,
he should reflect that there are people whose
charity embraces even the prune. Biscuits and
cheese came next, and here the water-jug was
(30) liberally passed round, for it is in the nature
of biscuits to be dry, and these were biscuits
to the core. That was all. The meal was over.
Everybody scraped their chairs back; the swing-
doors swung violently to and fro; soon the hall
(35) was emptied of every sign of food and made
ready no doubt for breakfast next morning.
Down corridors and up staircases the youth of
England went banging and singing. And was
it for a guest, a stranger, to say 'The dinner was
(40) not good,' or to say now that Mary and I are
in her sitting room, 'Could we not have dined
up here alone?' for if I had said anything of the
kind I should have been prying and searching
into the secret economies of a house which to
(45) the stranger wears so fine a front of gaiety and
courage. No, one could say nothing of the sort.
Indeed, conversation for a moment flagged.
The human frame being what it is, heart, body
and brain all mixed together, and not contained
(50) in separate compartments as they will be no

doubt in another million years, a good dinner
is of great importance to good talk. One cannot
think well, love well, sleep well, if one has not
dined well. The lamp in the spine does not light
(55) on beef and prunes. We are all PROBABLY
going to heaven, and Vandyck is, we HOPE,
to meet us round the next corner—that is
the dubious and qualifying state of mind that
beef and prunes at the end of the day's work
(60) breed between them. Happily my friend, who
taught science, had a cupboard where there
was a squat bottle and little glasses—(but there
should have been sole and partridge to begin
with)—so that we were able to draw up to
(65) the fire and repair some of the damages of the
day's living. In a minute or so we were slipping
freely in and out among all those objects of
curiosity and interest which form in the mind
in the absence of a particular person, and are
(70) naturally to be discussed on coming together
again—how somebody has married, another
has not; one thinks this, another that; one has
improved out of all knowledge, the other most
amazingly gone to the bad—with all those
(75) speculations upon human nature and the
character of the amazing world we live in which
spring naturally from such beginnings. While
these things were being said, however, I became
shamefacedly aware of a current setting in of its
(80) own accord and carrying everything forward
to an end of its own. The best course, unless the
whole talk was to be distorted, was to expose
what was in my mind to the air, when with good
luck it would fade and crumble like the head of
(85) the dead king when they opened the coffin at
Windsor. Briefly, then, I told Miss Seton about
the masons who had been all those years on
the roof of the chapel, and about the kings and
queens and nobles bearing sacks of gold and
(90) silver on their shoulders, which they shoveled
into the earth; and then how the great financial

magnates of our own time came and laid
cheques and bonds, I suppose, where the others
had laid ingots and rough lumps of gold. All
(95) that lies beneath the colleges down there, I said;
but this college, where we are now sitting, what
lies beneath its gallant red brick and the wild
unkempt grasses of the garden? What force is
behind that plain china off which we dined, and
(100) (here it popped out of my mouth before I could
stop it) the beef, the custard and the prunes?
   From *A Room of One's Own* by Virginia
Woolf (1929)

41. C
All these responses seem to reinforce the plainness
of this dreadful meal (described by Virginia Woolf),
don't they? However, the most forceful is the syntax
of the first ten sentences, which are as dreadfully
plain as the meal sounds. If you are not sure, read
them aloud and listen to the short, choppy cadence.
The plainness of her sentences reflects the plainness
of the meal.

42. B
Perhaps you can see the religious overtones with the
word *trinity*, but it is not enough to call this any sort
of religious allusion. Basically, what we have here is a
simple analogy—another way of describing the three
elements that make up the meal: beef, greens, and
potatoes. However, the imagery Woolf chooses to
use does not dress up the plainness of this fare but
only makes it sound worse.

43. A
"And if anyone complains that prunes, even
which mitigated by custard are an uncharitable
vegetable . . . there are people whose charity
embraces even the prune." These lines indicate
that some people are actually charitable enough
to embrace prunes. The narrator is obviously not
among these charitable folk.

44. E
It sounds like the best thing for this meal would be
to drown it all in water. However, Woolf says that

"it is in the nature of biscuits to be dry, and these
were biscuits to the core."

45. B
Epistrophe is the repetition of a word or words at
the end of two or more successive verses, clauses,
sentences, or phrases. The repetition of the word
well within these lines identifies it as an epistrophe.

46. B
Here the narrator is talking about prunes again,
". . . even when mitigated with custard." Apparently,
even custard could neither disguise nor improve
upon the prunes.

47. E
It is not unusual for writers to use capital letters,
italics, or underlining to add emphasis to a passage.
Punctuation can also be used to express tone
or show emotion within a passage, especially in
poetry. In this case, the capital letters emphasize
how negatively this meal has affected her. She is
no longer sure about things she used to know for
certain. "We are all PROBABLY going to heaven,
and Vandyck is, we HOPE, to meet us round the
next corner—that is the dubious and qualifying
state of mind that beef and prunes . . . breed
between them." Although you might be tempted to
choose (D), (E) is the more exact explanation.

48. C
By this point, there can be no doubt—the narrator
not only feels disdain for this poor excuse for a meal,
but she is also annoyed. After all, she is a guest and,
apparently, used to being treated to better fare.

49. D
This sentence must be taken figuratively, not
literally. Now the narrator can be alone with her
friend. They can sit near ("draw up") the fire and
unwind ("repair damages") from their stressful days,
as well as the terrible meal they just endured.

50. E
Asyndeton is the practice of omitting conjunctions
between words, phrases, or clauses. (In contrast,
polysyndeton is when a conjunction is used between
each part of the series.) These terms are a good

example of how prefixes can give you clues as to the meaning of a word. The prefix *a* means without; *poly* means many.

51. A

In this case, the narrator is not too sure how to broach a subject. She seems concerned that her friend must work and live under such dire circumstances, but she does not want to hurt her comrade's feelings, nor it seems, does she want to sound like she is superior to her in any way. Although she is a person who did not hesitate to speak unkindly of her (free) meal, at least shows she is sensitive to the feelings of another person.

52. A

This question goes along with question 51. Again, the narrator is concerned about her friend's rather meager working and living conditions. She is attempting to draw comparisons, perhaps to lure her friend into changing to a more pleasant environment.

53. E

Although you might think that this passage is simply a diatribe against prunes, there is a greater purpose. Woolf is concerned about the gross inequities among institutes of public education. Actually, she was most appalled at the unconscionable conditions inherent in the schooling of young women, in contrast to the luxuries inherent in the educating of males, in the early 1900s. Nevertheless, as with most essays, writers often have far more than one agenda for us to unearth within their words.

54. C

This is a question concerning mode or identifying what type of writing best describes this essay. "Personal reflection" is the best response among the choices offered. You might think that there is more to this essay than simple reflection, but remember that your response is limited to the choices you are offered.

ESSAY QUESTION ONE: VIDEO GAMES

ANALYSIS OF ESSAY QUESTION ONE

Students may have some strong reactions to this question, which makes it a very accessible prompt. The danger here lies in students pushing their passion concerning the subject past the point of simple subjectivity to unsubstantiated ranting. Be careful not to fall into this trap. It's a trap that leads to a lower-half score!

The claim that video games are useless and incite violence is one teenagers have probably heard many times, either from parents or on the news. With so many teens growing up playing video games, almost every test taker reading these sources will have an opinion going into the reading of the prompt. (Here's a strategy hint that might help you: Make the best argument, which might not always be the argument you believe in. See what you are given and play your cards to your advantage.)

In reading the sources provided, you can see that the sources are pretty well split down the middle concerning where they stand on the issue. James Moon (Source A) definitely denies the claim in the assignment (what did you expect from a college student?), citing the artistic merits of video games as well as the social interaction they offer. Kevin Fagan (Source B) notes the kind of gore and violence available in video games, especially those accessible to younger players who are monitored neither by stores that sell M-rated (mature) games indiscriminately nor by parents who don't care. The Green and Bavelier piece is a gold mine for writers denying the claim—video games make for better surgeons! Video games are the educational tool of the future! This clinical article will provide some very good points of support. Source D is a myth buster article from the American Psychological Association. Most of these entries will support the claim given—all pretty solid. The David Horsey cartoon is an obvious jab at the value of video games—the Frankenstein's monster allusion is one that most teens will recognize. The Chris Dahlen article is one of the more interesting excerpts in that it addresses some of the moral choices that gamers must make—Do I choose to be good or evil? Do I do the right thing or what feels "fun" in this alternate reality?

With all this material, it might be a good strategy for writers to qualify the claim. The way the claim is written (as a sort of two-parter) allows for this. The best strategy here might be to refute the idea that video games are useless while supporting (as the research does) the idea that video games can contribute to aggressive and even violent behavior.

SCORING GUIDE FOR QUESTION ONE

9 Essays earning a score of 9 meet the criteria for essays that are scored an 8 and, in addition, are especially sophisticated in their argument and synthesis* of cited sources or impressive in their control of language.

8 **Effective**
Essays earning a score of 8 effectively take a position that defends, challenges, or qualifies the claim that video games have little cultural value and contribute to aggressive, even violent,

behavior. They successfully support their position by synthesizing and citing at least three sources. The writer's argument is convincing, and the cited sources support the writer's position. The prose demonstrates an ability to control a wide range of the elements of effective writing but is not flawless.

7 Essays earning a score of 7 fit the description of essays that are scored a 6 but are distinguished by more complete or more purposeful argumentation and synthesis of cited sources or a more mature prose style.

6 Adequate

Essays earning a score of 6 adequately take a position that defends, challenges, or qualifies the claim that video games have little cultural value and contribute to aggressive, even violent, behavior. They adequately synthesize and cite at least three sources. The writer's argument is generally convincing and the cited sources generally support the writer's position, but the argument is less developed or less cogent than in essays earning higher scores. Though the language may contain lapses in diction or syntax, generally the prose is clear.

5 Essays earning a score of 5 take a position that defends, challenges, or qualifies the claim that video games have little cultural value and contribute to aggressive, even violent, behavior. They support their position by synthesizing at least three sources, but their arguments and their use of cited sources are somewhat limited, inconsistent, or uneven. The writer's argument is generally clear, and the sources generally support the writer's position, but the links between the sources and the argument may be strained. The writing may contain lapses in diction or syntax, but it usually conveys the writer's ideas adequately.

4 Inadequate

Essays earning a score of 4 inadequately take a position that defends, challenges, or qualifies the claim that video games have little cultural value and contribute to aggressive, even violent, behavior. They attempt to present an argument and support their position by synthesizing and citing at least two sources but may misunderstand, misrepresent, or oversimplify either their own argument or the cited sources they include. The link between the argument and the cited sources is weak. The prose of essays scored a 4 may suggest immature control of writing.

3 Essays earning a score of 3 meet the criteria for the score of 4 but demonstrate less understanding of the cited sources, less success in developing the author's position, or less control of writing.

2 Little Success

Essays earning a score of 2 demonstrate little success in taking a position that defends, challenges, or qualifies the claim that video games have little cultural value and contribute to aggressive, even violent, behavior. They may merely allude to knowledge gained from reading the sources rather than citing the sources themselves. These essays may misread the sources, fail to present an argument, or substitute a simpler task by merely responding to the question tangentially or by summarizing the sources. The prose of essays scored a 2 often demonstrates consistent weaknesses in writing, such as a lack of development or organization, grammatical problems, or a lack of control.

1 Essays earning a score of 1 meet the criteria for the score of 2 but are especially simplistic or weak in their control of writing or do not cite even one source.

0 Essays earning a score of 0 are on-topic responses that receive no credit, such as those that merely repeat the prompt.

— Essays earning a dash (–) are blank responses or responses that are completely off topic.

*For the purposes of scoring, *synthesis* refers to combining the sources and the writer's position to form a cohesive, supported argument and accurately citing all sources.

STUDENT A'S RESPONSE TO QUESTION ONE

The sun is shining outside. The public library is open. Habitat for Humanity is looking for volunteers to help raise money to build homes for Hurricane Katrina victims. So what do you want to do? How about this: You can "romp off to murder and destroy as much as possible" (Source B). Huh? Oh, you want to play Grand Theft Auto—the video game? In a world where there is so much more—more to do, more to learn, more to see, more to be—why do people waste their time on video games? I don't know. I can only agree with the claim that video games have little cultural value and can even contribute to aggressive and violent behavior.

Video games have about as much cultural value as television does. They are harmless as light entertainment, but as with anything, moderation and parental guidance are suggested. It seems that more and more video games of a violent nature have found their way into the hands of children. In a San Francisco Chronicle article by Kevin Fagan, Dr. Christian Pariseau noted some pretty startling statistics. He said, "One federal study even showed how 4-year-olds were able to buy the most violent games. . . . And when they asked eighth-graders how often their parents checked what games they bought, 89 percent said 'never.'" If these were movie ratings, the equivalent would mean that 4-year-olds are regularly watching and even buying hard-core pornography. This can't be good.

Furthermore, studies have shown that even though much had been published to the contrary, "high levels of violent video game exposure have been linked to delinquency, fighting at school and during free play periods, and violent criminal behavior" (Source D). It's true that not everyone who plays video games is exposed to such "high levels of violent video game exposure," but considering the fact that "a recent study from the University of Illinois found that two-thirds of college students said they played video games 'at least once in a while,'" some of that majority are going to be pretty regular players (Source A).

The moral maelstrom gets deeper as players can take on "evil" roles and carry out the kinds of crimes and gore-fests reserved for the sensationalist local news shows. In an industry that is making $10 billion a year, they aren't about to water down their best sellers (Source A). So what concerns do video game companies have about borderline psychopaths who get their jollies by cyber-blasting away cyber heads? They say "lighten up, [the video games are] harmless fun. They twist adult players only if they're a little unhinged anyway" (Source B). That makes me feel better already. Not.

Chris Dahlen writes, "Whenever I meet people who play exclusively as evil characters . . . I get a little creeped out."

David Horsey got it right in his political cartoon. The video game companies will continue to develop games that appeal to the lowest common denominator (or should I say "demonizer?"—note the little monster being created). All in the name of entertainment and profit . . . and fun!

STUDENT B'S RESPONSE TO QUESTION ONE

The future is technology. Those who embrace it will be the new trail blazers of the cyber age. Those who choose to avoid it or criticize it will be left (perhaps literally) in the dust. The way we do things today centers around the technology that is available to us. We shop on the Internet, we make calls on cell phones, we eat meals that are scientifically enhanced, and we play games on computers. The games we play are the realms of new possibility and train us for the work of tomorrow. Video games have great cultural worth and the naysayers who complain about video game violence can't see the forest for the trees.

Video games will be the future training for the jobs and careers of tomorrow. Today, video games are used as flight simulators and for training in NASA. Granted, these are pretty complicated games, but they train for skills that cannot be simulated any other way. In fact, video games may soon find their way into the medical field. A recent report suggested that video game players may in fact be better laparoscopic surgeons than nongamers (Source C). A researcher named Rosser found out that "surgeons who played video games more than 3 hours per week committed 37 percent fewer errors, were 27 percent faster at laparoscopic drills, and were 33 percent better at suturing tasks than nonvideo game playing surgeons" (Source C). It's kind of ironic that by playing a game where you might be shooting down people on a screen, you could also be improving your skills to save lives. But that is the wonder of technology.

Video games can save us in other ways. In a world where we are becoming strangers to each other on the street, cyber communities take the place of the old neighborhood. James Moon notes that "any computer game worth its monthly fee connects users to thousands of other players in a fully interactive online world." That's right, thousands! Moon continues by writing, "The major systems are a bastion for social interaction." The new social aspects of video gaming are fast becoming the new communities in which we play. Before long there may even be cyber country clubs!

Another neat thing about video games is that they give a person a chance to find out more about himself. "Games give you the choice between right and wrong" (Source F). The real world has built-in limits and parameters. I may never be able to be president or stand at the plate in the World Series or travel to another world, but in video games, I can. And more importantly, I can see how I would act in these roles. One gamer describes his own experience: "I've found that I actually behave better in games than I ever do in reality. Normally I cut off other drivers and stiff the tip jar at coffeeshops, but in games, I play by all the rules" (Source F).

So what's all the fuss about with violence in video games? Turn on the news every day and what do you see? Video games have much more promise than we give them credit for. They are the future and the future is now.

COMMENTARY ON STUDENT A'S RESPONSE

Student A scores in the 8 range with a paper that is crystal clear in its position and effectively and seamlessly (and masterfully) synthesizes elements from four of the sources provided.

The strength of Student A's piece is her strong sense of voice—there is ample evidence of a person thinking behind the writing. Her writing is not only informative but entertaining as well. You can sense a "yeah, right" tone in her final statement as well as her other attacks on the video game industry. Phrases like "Not." And "get their jollies" are intended to let the reader in on the critical smirk. Also, some pearls like "moral maelstrom" and "gore-fest" and the play on words with denominator/demonizer show that the writer has a command of language and intends to use her pen as a sword when it comes in handy.

The introduction is a great example of juxtaposing incongruent ideas—the possibility of doing positive good in the world with self-improvement and charitable deeds is in stark contrast to the scene of violent crime that is *Grand Theft Auto*. Also, establishing a first-person presence with a strong and identifiable voice sets the tone for the rest of the response.

She might have done more with the political cartoon as a source. As it is, she already effectively used the minimum number required.

COMMENTARY ON STUDENT B'S RESPONSE

Student B does an adequate job of defending video games and is able to effectively synthesize the sources that help his argument the most. He would likely score a 6 for his effort because he does show some fuller development of his ideas, but nothing really stands out to earn him a higher score. Certainly, he doesn't have the voice that Student A's paper has, but he does march through the issues he wants to cover, although perhaps with too much dependency on the sources. It would have been nice to see Student B draw out more of his own ideas rather than using the source material as the hinge on which his writing turns.

His transitions are predictable, and his organization and focus are rock-solid. He really shines when he writes, "The real world has built-in limits and parameters. I may never be able to be president or stand at the plate in the World Series or travel to another world, but in video games, I can." This phrasing may elevate his score with some readers, especially if they remember his nice parallel structure in the introduction.

ESSAY QUESTION TWO: "LINDA'S" NARRATIVE

ANALYSIS OF ESSAY QUESTION TWO

You should have little trouble responding to this prompt and passage. By now, you have studied several similar passages in high school literature and history classes. It is reminiscent of the work of Frederick Douglass or George Washington Carver. What is unique about this passage, however, is not just what Linda says about slavery but her discussion of the hypocrisy of the slave owners themselves and the so-called Christians of that time.

The passage opens with Linda's frustrations over the fact that so many slaves are thirsting for knowledge, longing to learn to read and write, but they are forbidden to pursue such learning. Immediately, she presents her argument: white missionaries will go to darkest Africa to spread the Word and to distribute Bibles—Bibles the slaves in the South are forbidden to read. She begs these missionaries to look to the dark corners of home to "save their brethren."

Briefly, she concedes that a few brave souls have tried to help the slaves, but only at great risk. She hopes that perhaps Uncle Fred's great-grandchildren will have the right to these treasures that he has been denied.

In paragraph 4, Linda's diatribe really begins. Her challenge is straightforward: "Are doctors of divinity blind, or are they hypocrites?" That is the crux of her argument. From there, she cites many instances of the double standard of the South. She describes the false front that many slave owners present to the outside world, and she reveals the horrors that are barely hidden behind "benevolent patriarchy."

Finally, she concludes that Christianity and religion are two very different things in the South. When she refuses to join the church because her master directs her to, he loses his temper. She responds with the powerful lines:

"Ole Satan's church is here below;
Up to God's free church I hope to go."

SCORING GUIDE FOR QUESTION TWO

9   Essays meet all of the criteria for 8 essays and, in addition, are especially full or apt in their analysis or demonstrate particularly impressive composition skills.

8   Essays successfully analyze stylistic strategies the passage employs to convey the writer's attitude toward slavery and the double standard under which the white man lived during the time of Southern slavery. They refer to the passage directly or indirectly and convincingly define the attitude the narrator has toward slavery and her attitude toward the slave owner's double standard. Their prose controls a wide range of effective writing but is not flawless.

7   Essays fit the description of 6 essays but employ more complete analysis or demonstrate a more mature prose style.

6   Essays adequately analyze the writer's attitude toward slavery and the double standard under which the slave owners lived. They refer to the passage directly or indirectly, and they recognize the narrator's attitude and how she conveys it through her language. A few lapses in diction or syntax may be present, but generally the prose of 6 essays is clear.

5   Essays adequately analyze the writer's attitude about the double standard of the Southern white slave owners. They refer to the passage directly or indirectly, and they recognize the narrator's attitude. These essays may convey their thoughts superficially or develop ideas about the narrator's attitude inconsistently. A few lapses in diction or syntax may appear, but the prose in these essays usually conveys the writers' ideas adequately.

4   Essays inadequately respond to the task of the prompt. They may misrepresent the writer's attitude or analyze rhetorical strategies inaccurately or with little understanding of how these strategies reveal her attitude toward the double standard. Often the prose of these essays suggests immature control over organization, diction, or syntax.

3   Essays meet the criteria for the score of 4 but are less perceptive about how rhetorical strategies convey attitude or are less consistent in controlling the elements of writing.

2   Essays are unsuccessful in analyzing how stylistic strategies convey the writer's attitude about the double standard under which Southern white slave owners lived. These essays tend to pay little or cursory attention to specific features, and they may generalize or simplify attitude and tone. They may simply paraphrase or comment on the passage without analyzing technique. The prose of 2 essays often reveals consistent weaknesses in writing, such as a lack of development or organization, grammatical problems, or a lack of control.

1   Essays meet the criteria for the score of 2 but are especially simplistic in their discussion or weak in controlling elements of language.

STUDENT A'S RESPONSE TO QUESTION TWO

We have learned about the horrors of slavery from several fine writers such as Fredrick Douglas, Sojourner Truth, and Harriet Tubman. This essay, from "Incidents in the Life of a Slave Girl," gives us more background, and maybe more information than we'd like to read about. But I think there's more to her passage than just relating her experiences as a slave. What she is really talking about in this passage is man's incredible capacity for hypocrisy.

Hypocrisy is a term from the Greeks, originating with Hippocrates. Over the centuries, however, it has developed into the skill of human beings to say one thing and to do another. Literature is full of famous hypocrites—Brutus in Julius Caesar, Holden Caulfield in Catcher in the Rye are just two. Former President Clinton is another, as are many politicians, because of their personal and public lives.

I think about the man in the church parking lot after services on Sunday who becomes irate because some little old lady cuts in front of him. Wasn't he just professing love and Christianity? In our neighborhood a respectable lawyer and town councilman was recently arrested and convicted of beating his wife and abusing his children. The entire Catholic priest scandal is another sign of hypocrisy as well. In fact, within religion we could probably find a number of hypocrites. Personally, I think people who blow up abortion clinics, and often hurt and even kill those inside, because they are pro-life are hypocrites as well.

The slave owner in Linda's world presented a loving, caring "patriarchal" front to the world, while behind the scenes horrors were taking place that we cringe to read about. The slaves will not, dare not, speak up for they or their loved ones would be punished.

Linda's main point is the contrast between Southern religion vs. Southern Christianity. Her slave owner joined the church because it was the appropriate thing to do. It was good for his standing in the community, and he "pays money into the treasury of the church." After services, however, he might go home and punish a slave who is hiding a book, even the Bible. Negro slaves in the south counted for nothing. No one cared if a white man took a slave girl to bed. Even if that man was an important person in the community, everyone just looked the other way. In fact, slaves were considered less important than the "heathens" in the jungle where the church sends missionaries and bibles. How twisted is that? Where did those white people think their slaves came from?

Hypocrisy is all around us, and if we are not careful, we may also get caught in its trap— either as victim or (let's hope not) victimizer. Perhaps Linda is right: "Ole Satan's church _is_ here below."

STUDENT B'S RESPONSE TO QUESTION TWO

This narrator is a very angry young woman who seems to have every right to be angry. In a combination of personal narration and reflection, she eloquently reveals her very strong feelings toward the double standard under which the Southern white man lives.

She opens calmly enough—she relates her efforts to teach an old negro slave, known as Uncle Fred, to read. Immediately, however, she shows the dichotomy in thinking—it's against the law for slaves to learn to read or write. On the other hand, missionaries from churches in the

South go to deepest Africa carrying the words of religion and providing Bibles for the natives to read. What she says they ought to be preaching is that it is wrong to traffic in slavery, that everyone should have the right to learn, and they will answer to God for not treating everyone the same. Immediately the narrator sets up her central idea of the ultimate paradox of the double standard.

She concedes that there are some who might take up the "at home" missionary work (paragraph 2), but those people are few and often do so at risk of their lives. She hopes that some day this will be possible, but it is not to be now.

COMMENTARY ON STUDENT A'S RESPONSE

This is an interesting essay, truly an upper-half response, a 7; let's take a look at what Student A has done.

This student has internalized the inherent message of the original passage. In the introduction, this essay mentions other writers, not unlike Linda, such as Frederick Douglass or Harriet Tubman. This is a good comparison. She draws on these other writers who were former slaves to tell us that the experiences of slavery have been discussed (and obviously studied) before. Then the student moves to her main point: "man's incredible capacity for hypocrisy."

She does not return to the original passage until the second-to-last paragraph. In the meantime, however, Student A talks about mankind's propensity for hypocrisy. How many people live lives of duplicitous thinking—whether it be in a church parking lot or in the White House. This student obviously understands the frustrations that Linda is trying to express. What we see on the surface is not necessarily what is really going on.

She returns to the original passage with the discussion of Southern religion versus Southern Christianity. The student's points are well made, but the outrage expressed by the two rhetorical questions should have been expressed in well-supported statements rather than questions flung into the air. Rhetorical questions are not a recommended presentation of information. Sometimes they are effective early in an essay if they are eventually answered. Then they become the focus point of the composition. Placed near the end, however, they weaken this response. Therefore, what might have been an 8 response would more likely receive a 7.

Student A has more than adequately answered this question. Her composition skills are strong. Probably if she had more time to analyze the composition, she would recognize that her own anger was interfering with the most successful presentation of her ideas.

COMMENTARY ON STUDENT B'S RESPONSE

This response is clearly a lower-half response. Although this writer shows that she can write, there is little analysis, and the tasks of the prompt have not all been addressed.

Unfortunately, sometimes students run out of time when they are responding to AP English Lanuage and Composition questions. It is imperative that you get used to writing within a 40-minute time period for each response. If you take a few minutes more on one response, you have a few minutes less on the next.

It is unfortunate for Student B that she did not take more time to develop this response. She clearly understands the passage and the tasks of the prompt. However, her response is abbreviated. Her main points are compacted into the short middle paragraph. She touches on the narrator's anger and even refers to the "dichotomy" of thinking in the South. She tells us everything hurriedly with no analysis or attempt at support from specific evidence. This is unfortunate. Her thoughts and her understanding of the passage seem adequate, but the presentation of these views is less than adequate. Due to the lack of development, this is more of a 3 response than even a 4.

ESSAY QUESTION THREE: RICK REILLY'S "LET US PLAY"

ANALYSIS OF ESSAY QUESTION THREE

Rick Reilly has been a writer for *Sports Illustrated* for some time. He has also been voted National Sportswriter of the Year nine times. He often uses humor in discussing various sports issues, many of them controversial in nature.

This passage has two aspects to it. At first, it seems that it will be a discussion of religion versus sports. He takes a few good jabs at how sports is now a 24/7 thing, often leaving little time for religion. With a few jabs at Notre Dame and the YMCA, he gets his point across. Nevertheless, he implies that balance and moderation are really key to the issue.

His main concern, however, is found in this statement: "I'll tell you exactly what's going on here: the upping of American youth sports." This is the crux of his argument.

It starts with the Sunday concern—practices and even games on what used to be considered a day of rest. From there, however, he widens his complaint to include the intensity of kids and sports and pressure and parents and even coaches. He does not go into great detail; however, his message is clear. Sundays or any days—kids need time to be kids. Parents need to back off and pull back on the pressure they are putting on youngsters to perform—whatever day of the week it is.

This argument is one that you should have a lot to say about. If you have not experienced what Reilly is referring to personally, you are certainly aware of it through your friends and classmates.

SCORING GUIDE ESSAY QUESTION THREE

9   Essays meet all of the criteria for 8 essays and, in addition, are especially full or apt in their analysis or demonstrate particularly impressive composition skills.

8   Essays successfully analyze the writer's attitude about Sunday sports and parents and their children's sports. They refer to the passage directly or indirectly and convincingly clarify Reilly's attitude about how parents are interfering with their children's sports.

Their own arguments are effective while demonstrating a wide range of writing skills, though they may not be flawless.

7 Essays fit the description of 6 essays but employ more complete analysis or demonstrate a more mature prose style.

6 Essays adequately analyze Reilly's attitude about sports on Sundays and sports and children. They refer to the passage directly or indirectly and effectively explain Reilly's concerns and, subsequently, respond with their own opinion. Their prose may demonstrate minor lapses in diction or syntax, but the 6 response usually conveys the writer's ideas adequately.

5 Essays analyze the writer's attitude about sports on Sunday and parents and sports. They refer to the passage directly or indirectly, and they recognize the narrator's position and respond accordingly. However, they may superficially analyze or respond to the narrator's position inconsistently. A few lapses in diction or syntax may appear, but the prose in these essays satisfactorily conveys the writers' ideas.

4 Essays inadequately respond to the task of the prompt. They may misrepresent Reilly's attitude or inaccurately analyze his position, or they may generalize or simplify his attitude. Their response to Reilly's stance may often suggest immature control over organization, diction, or syntax.

3 Essays meet the criteria for the score of 4 but are less perceptive about the narrator's attitude or respond to the argument with less consistent control of the elements of writing. They may respond to only part of Reilly's message.

2 Essays are unsuccessful in analyzing Reilly's attitude about Sunday sports and parents and their children's sports. These pay little or cursory attention to the specifics of Reilly's concerns, and they may overgeneralize, or oversimplify, his attitude. They may simply paraphrase or comment on the passage without developing their own responses. The prose of 2 papers often reveals consistent weaknesses in writing, such as a lack of development or organization, grammatical problems, or a lack of control.

1 Essays meet the criteria for the score of 2 but are especially simplistic in their discussion or weak in controlling elements of language.

STUDENT A's RESPONSE TO QUESTION THREE

Rick Reilly is a well-known sports writer. Often his pieces are cleverly presented arguments in favor or against one thing or another. This passage is no exception. At first he seems to be talking about sports versus religion. He makes some very good points, and he catches the reader's attention with his clever comments about the Pope and Notre Dame, YMCA (church affiliated) Sunday sports, and so on. Some of what he says is certainly true, and he uses a humorous tone rather than coming across as super critical. The truth is, however, that today we have more sports than ever, and more people are involved in organized sports—both children as well as adults. There are only so many baseball fields, basketball courts, and hockey rinks to play on. In the United States we are committed to a five-day workweek, and in the winter, in many states it is dark way too early to do much after school. Consequently, someone has to do some playing or practicing on Sundays. It's a matter of common sense. Even before organized sports were so popular, I imagine that many neighborhood pick-up games took place on Sunday afternoons. As long as everyone is given time to attend religious services, and accommodations are made for those who must miss practices, compromise can be the solution.

However, this is not the main point of Reilly's piece. It just provided the clever title and attention getter. What he seems most concerned about is the way that over-ambitious parents are ruining sports for their children. Having been a little league player myself as well as an assistant T-ball coach, I know what Reilly is saying.

Almost every year the news carries a story about an irate father punching out a coach or an over-zealous mother attacking another mother at junior's soccer game. When I coached T-ball I actually felt sorry for some of the kids. They never had an unorganized day just to be a kid. It seems that many children are so super-scheduled, they don't even know how to entertain themselves. I remember one 8 year old, Tommy, who told me that Friday night was the only night he did not have to play a sport or take a lesson of some kind. He said Fridays were when he went to his big brother's high school football games in the fall and basketball games in the winter. What kind of life is that for a child?

Way too much pressure is put on some kids way too soon. Some teams require players to try out. Parents are so intent on their little all-star making the team, they fail to see what damage they are doing. What ought to be an enjoyable learning experience becomes a life-or-death situation. For instance, my T-ball team had a little girl named Karla. When she was practicing with her teammates and her parents weren't around, she was a great player for a 6-year-old. Whenever we had a game, however, her father was constantly screaming at her to do this or that, to hold the bat a certain way, to keep her eye on the ball, etc. Every time he was there, her performance was terrible. He squashed all her talent and enjoyment. Often she would be in tears by the end of a game, which made her father even more upset with her.

This parent pressure is not just with little kids, either. I've seen it among the parents of many guys I have played sports with. The saddest thing was a buddy of mine, a few years ahead of me, on the football team. He was a great player, and was offered a terrific scholarship at a big 10 university. His dad was ecstatic. Bill chose to put off college and joined the Army, instead. You'd think his father would be proud to have a patriot son. No, his father just about disowned him. Bill had visions of doing his patriotic duty; his father had visions of a million-dollar pro contract down the line.

Maybe Rick Reilly should not cross out "Pray" in the title of his article. I think we need a bit of prayer to help parents see what they are doing to their kids. Instead of learning the basics of sportsmanship, getting exercise, and having a good time, children are being driven. As Reilly says, even God took a day off. Maybe it's time for parents to do the same thing and give the kids a break.

STUDENT B'S RESPONSE TO QUESTION THREE

Sunday afternoon football is as American as Mom and apple pie. Rick Reilly points out perhaps sports may be superseding religion. More specifically, for some people sports is their religion. There's nothing wrong with sports any day of the week as long as people keep it in perspective.

The movie Chariots of Fire demonstrates the sports and religion controversy. Although I cannot remember much of the film (our track coach showed it to us), I remember that one of the runners would not participate in competition if it fell on Saturday, the Jewish Sabbath. Although he might have been a world-class runner, religion was more important than sports. Others are able to find a happy medium. They may attend service very early on Sunday, or very late or even on Saturday evening. There's nothing wrong with sports on Sunday as long as everything is kept in perspective. Wearing soccer cleats to Mass, however, is a bit much.

Even the SAT exam has alternate testing days to accommodate religious beliefs. Most people can find a compromise. The important thing is that if Sundays have to be used for practice, that the times are later in the day, and personal religious beliefs and restrictions would never hurt a player who might have to miss sports on that day.

Reilly says a similar balance must be found by parents of future all-stars. They have ruined sports for their kids by pushing them too soon and making everything way more serious than it ought to be. Instead of playing through their children, maybe these parents need to get off their duffs in the sidelines and find a sports activity of their own before they turn off their children toward sports forever.

Have you ever walked by a Little League field in the summer time? What do you hear? Not the cheering of the crowd or the laughter and excitement of the young players, what you hear are parents screaming at their kids to do better, to run faster, to throw more accurately and disputing calls made by umpires and referees against their child, and complaining to coaches that their child isn't getting enough playing time. This is the focus of the passage by Rick Reilly, writer for "Sports Illustrated."

STUDENT C'S RESPONSE TO QUESTION THREE

Rick Reilly is right; we are putting sports before God and we will be sorry.

What has happened to the concept of a day of rest? It used to be that Sundays (or other days for other religions) were for church and family. Now church and family are taking a second place to sports.

Instead of coming home from services and having a nice dinner with the family, dads come home from church and sit down with the TV remote. In the meantime, junior is off to practice some sport or another.

Places like Notre Dame and the YMCA should know better than to have practice or games on Sundays. After all, these are religious places. If a catholic college can't even keep Sundays for God, what sort of example does that present to everyone else?

Parents need to take a stronger stand about this situation. They need to just say "no" when practices or games are scheduled for Sundays. If coaches can't work around God, then maybe kids should be finding something else to do. Some parents are so wrapped up in their kids' sports that they are the ones who ought to be playing. Maybe the kid would rather stay home and read a book, or even go to Sunday school.

Although Mr. Reilly tries to impart a bit of humor into his argument, he has made some strong points. Unfortunately, the people and parents who ought to pay attention are probably too busy driving their kids to practice to even read what Reilly has written.

COMMENTARY ON STUDENT A'S RESPONSE

Obviously, this student understands the implications of Rick Reilly's passage. He shows good perception and understanding of the double messages in the piece. First, he discusses the issue of sports on Sundays. As he says, accommodation and compromise have to be the solution. Then, he tackles the main issue.

Student A uses examples from his own experience for his essay. First, he discusses situations with little children and the pressures parents sometime place on them. He follows this discussion with the story about an older friend of his whose father wanted a player, not a patriot.

This essay is well executed and effectively responds to all elements of the prompt. The student refers to the passage both directly and indirectly, as he efficiently explains Reilly's messages and intentions. This student has a strong control of prose, and his writing is interesting and effective. Student A weaves personal observations into his analysis well, which lends veracity to the Reilly piece while enhancing the reader's interest in the student's composition.

This is a successful response, deserving a score of 8. Although the essay is not without a few weak spots, this student has been very successful in responding to the tasks of the prompt, understanding the dual nature of Reilly's original passage, and communicating those ideas well.

COMMENTARY ON STUDENT B'S RESPONSE

This sample scored a 5; it adequately responds to the prompt. It clearly identifies what the student sees as Reilly's message, but it doesn't look closely enough at Reilly's passage. This student puts too much emphasis on the idea of Sunday sports and much less on the issue of parents and children and sports. Although both ideas are mentioned, they are done so inconsistently, and that is what makes this paper a 5 instead of a 6.

The issues about sports on days of religious importance are well covered. However, when he gets to the second issue, Student B does more summarizing than analyzing. There is a lecturing tone at the end of the third paragraph, but he doesn't go very far with his ideas. The final paragraph demonstrates some originality and reveals more of the voice of the student writer, but again, he doesn't do enough with it.

As the scoring guide for a 5 paper states: "They may analyze superficially or develop ideas about the narrator's attitude inconsistently"—precisely what this paper has done.

COMMENTARY ON STUDENT C'S RESPONSE

This student has fallen into a dangerous trap with her response—she is lecturing, not analyzing. Not only is she lecturing, but she is speaking in broad generalizations, waving around banners, beliefs, and placards while substantiating little of what she says.

No matter how strongly you feel about a topic, keep the rules of rhetorical argument in the forefront of your mind as you respond. Don't point fingers and make accusations. Develop an argument and support your ideas with details and evidence, not just with knee-jerk reactions.

This essay is also incomplete. Nowhere does this student discuss the other aspect of Rick's complaint—children, parents, and sports. Because this essay is unsuccessful in analyzing the strategies Reilly uses to display his attitude toward Sunday sports and fails to address parents and children and organized sports, this essay has earned the score of 2. Some might vote for a 3 because the writing itself is okay, but the thinking is shallow. The essay pays only cursory attention to all the features, and the author tends to generalize and oversimplify Reilly's attitude.

Part Five

RESOURCES

GRAMMAR REFERENCE GUIDE

SENTENCE STRUCTURE

Be sure to know this basic material.

RUN-ON SENTENCES

When a sentence consists of more than one clause (a group of words that contains a subject and a verb), those clauses must be joined properly. It is never acceptable to hook two clauses together with a comma, as the "sentence" below does. That's called a **run-on sentence.**

Wrong: Nietzsche moved to Basel in 1869, he planned to teach classical philology.

There are a number of acceptable ways to fix a run-on.

Correct: Nietzsche moved to Basel in 1869; he planned to teach classical philology.

Also correct: Nietzsche planned to teach classical philology; therefore, he moved to Basel in 1869.

Also correct: Nietzsche moved to Basel in 1869, and he planned to teach classical philology. (The word *and*, like *or*, *for*, *but*, *nor*, and *yet*, is what's called a *coordinating conjunction*.)

Also correct: Because Nietzsche planned to teach classical philology, he moved to Basel in 1869. (The word *because*, like *although*, *if*, *though*, etc., is what's called a *subordinating conjunction*.)

Also correct: Nietzsche, who planned to teach classical philology, moved to Basel in 1869. (The word *who*, like *which*, *where*, *whom*, *that*, and *whose*, is what's called a *relative pronoun*.)

SENTENCE FRAGMENTS

Every sentence must contain at least one complete independent clause. If there is no independent clause at all, or if what's supposed to be the independent clause is incomplete, you've got a **sentence fragment.**

Wrong: While most people, who have worked hard for many years, have not managed to save any money, although they are trying to be more frugal now.

This sentence fragment consists of nothing but subordinate clauses. One of the subordinate clauses must be made into an independent clause.

Correct: Most people, who have worked hard for many years, have not managed to save any money, although they are trying to be more frugal now.

Also correct: While most people, who have worked hard for many years, have not managed to save any money, they are trying to be more frugal now.

SUBJECT-VERB AGREEMENT

Remember, in English, a subject and its verb must **agree** in number and person. **Number** refers to whether a subject (or a verb) is singular or plural. **Person** refers to first person (*I, we*), second person (*you*), and third person (*he, she, it, one, they*).

INTERVENING PHRASES

When the subject of a sentence is followed by a phrase (a group of words that does not have a subject and verb) or relative clause, the words are not part of the subject. They simply add information about that subject.

Learn to recognize groups of words that can come between the subject and verb!

1. **Relative clauses**, which contain important information about the subject of another clause, are often placed between a subject and verb. (The previous sentence contains a relative clause.)

    Wrong: John Clare, *who during the mid-nineteenth century wrote many fine poems on rural themes,* were confined for decades to an insane asylum.

The subject is *John Clare*, which is singular, but the verb is *were*, which is plural. The fact that the relative clause ends with a plural noun (*themes*) might distract you from the fact that the subject and verb don't agree.

    Correct: John Clare, who during the mid-nineteenth century wrote many fine poems on rural themes, *was* confined for decades to an insane asylum.

2. **Appositives** often come between a subject and a verb. Appositives are nouns, pronouns, or noun phrases that are placed next to nouns to describe them further.

    Wrong: Prince Charles, *an avid proponent of sustainable farming practices and restoring native animal and plant breeds,* have converted his own land to organic agriculture.

Correct: Prince Charles, an avid proponent of sustainable farming practices and restoring native animal and plant breeds, *has* converted his own land to organic agriculture.

Relative clauses and appositives are sometimes set off from the rest of the sentence by commas. When this is the case, it's a dead giveaway that those words are not part of the subject. That makes checking for subject-verb agreement much easier; just ignore the words set off by commas and concentrate on the subject and the verb.

3. The **prepositional phrase** is an all-time favorite.

   Wrong: Wild animals *in jungles all over the world* is endangered.

   Correct: Wild animals in jungles all over the world *are* endangered.

Prepositional phrases, and some relative clauses and appositives, are not set off by commas. It's harder to recognize intervening phrases and clauses when they're not set off by commas, but if you remember to check each sentence carefully for such things, you'll be able to pick them out anyway.

COMPOUND SUBJECTS

When two nouns or groups of nouns are joined by *and*, they're called a **compound subject** and are therefore plural.

Correct: *Ontario and Quebec* contain about two-thirds of the population of Canada.

Some connecting phrases may look as though they should make a group of words into a compound subject—but they don't result in a compound subject.

Wrong: George Bernard Shaw, as well as Mahatma Gandhi and River Phoenix, were vegetarians.

And is the only connecting word that results in a compound and plural subject. The following words and phrases do not create compound subjects:

along with	*as well as*
together with	*besides*
in addition to	

Correct: *George Bernard Shaw*, as well as Mahatma Gandhi and River Phoenix, *was* a vegetarian.

Wrong: Neither Thomas Jefferson nor Alexander Hamilton were supportive of Aaron Burr's political ambitions.

When words in the subject position are connected by *either . . . or* or *neither . . . nor*, the verb agrees with the last word in the pair. If the last word is singular, the verb must be singular. If the last word is plural, the verb must be plural.

Correct: Neither Thomas Jefferson nor *Alexander Hamilton was* supportive of Aaron Burr's political ambitions.

Correct: Neither Thomas Jefferson nor *the Federalists were* supportive of Aaron Burr's political ambitions.

Both . . . and is the only pair that always results in a plural subject.

Correct: *Both* Thomas Jefferson *and* Alexander Hamilton *were* unsupportive of Aaron Burr's political ambitions.

UNUSUAL SENTENCE PATTERNS

When you're checking for subject-verb disagreement, remember that the subject doesn't always appear before the verb.

Wrong: Dominating the New York skyline is the Empire State Building and the Chrysler Building.

The subject of this sentence is a compound subject, *the Empire State Building and the Chrysler Building*. The verb should be plural.

Correct: Dominating the New York skyline *are* the Empire State Building and the Chrysler Building.

SUBJECTS THAT ARE NOT NOUNS OR PRONOUNS

An entire clause can serve as the subject of a sentence. When used as a subject, a clause always takes a singular verb.

Whether the economy will improve in the near future *is* a matter of great concern.

Infinitives and gerunds can be used as subjects. Remember that they're singular subjects.

To err is human.

Rollerblading is dangerous.

See the section on verbs for more on infinitives and gerunds.

MODIFICATION

Adjectives and adverbs aren't the only modifiers. Phrases and even relative clauses can act as modifiers in a sentence.

Waiting to regain enough strength to eat, a cheetah, which expends most of its energy in the chase, must rest beside its prey.

Waiting to regain enough strength to eat is a phrase that describes the cheetah, as does the relative clause *which expends most of its energy in the chase*. The phrase *beside its prey* modifies the verb *rest*.

English depends heavily on word order to establish modifying relationships. In other words, most modifiers attach themselves to the first things they can get their hands on in the sentence, sometimes resulting in a different meaning than the writer intended.

INTRODUCTORY MODIFIERS

Wrong: Sifting the sand of a river bed, gold was discovered by prospectors in California in 1848.

A modifying phrase that begins a sentence refers to the noun or pronoun immediately following the phrase. But if we apply that rule here, the sentence says that the *gold was sifting sand*. See the problem? The author apparently meant to say that the prospectors were sifting sand. There are several ways to correct the sentence so that it expresses the intended meaning.

Correct: Sifting the sand in a river bed, prospectors discovered gold in California in 1848.

Also correct: Prospectors, sifting the sand in a river bed, discovered gold in California in 1848.

Also correct: Gold was discovered by prospectors, who were sifting the sand in a river bed, in California in 1848.

In all three cases, the phrase or clause directly precedes or follows the noun it describes.

DANGLING MODIFIERS

A modifying phrase or clause should clearly refer to a particular word in the sentence. A modifying phrase or clause that does not sensibly refer to any word in the sentence is called a **dangling modifier.** The most common sort of dangler is an introductory modifying phrase that's followed by a word it can't logically refer to.

Wrong: Desiring to free his readers from superstition, the theories of Epicurus are expounded in Lucretius's poem *De rerum natura*.

The problem with this sentence is that the phrase that begins the sentence seems to modify the noun following it: *theories*. In fact, there is really nowhere the modifier can be put to make it work properly and no noun to which it can reasonably refer (*Lucretius's*, the possessive, is functioning as an adjective modifying *poem*). Get rid of dangling constructions by clarifying the modification relationship or by making the dangler into a subordinate clause.

Correct: Desiring to free his readers from superstition, Lucretius expounded the theories of Epicurus in his poem *De rerum natura*.

Now the phrase *desiring to free his readers from superstition* clearly refers to the proper noun *Lucretius*.

OTHER MODIFIERS

In correcting some of those misplaced introductory modifiers, we move the modifier to a position inside the sentence rather than at the beginning. This is perfectly acceptable, but remember that modifying phrases inside a sentence can also be misplaced.

Wrong: That night, they sat discussing when the cow might calve in the kitchen.

The problem here is the phrase *in the kitchen*, which seems to refer to where the cow might have her calf. What the author probably meant to say is the following correct sentence:

Correct: That night, they sat in the kitchen discussing when the cow might calve.

This sentence is correct because the phrase comes directly after the word it modifies: the verb *sat*.

Wrong: As a young man, the French novelist Gustave Flaubert traveled in Egypt, which was a fascinating experience.

It's not that *Egypt* itself was a fascinating experience, but that traveling there was fascinating.

Correct: Traveling in Egypt as a young man was a fascinating experience for the French novelist Gustave Flaubert.

PRONOUNS

Always try to locate the antecedent of a pronoun (that is, the word to which the pronoun refers). Most of the pronoun problems you'll encounter will result from a problem in the relationship of the pronoun and its antecedent.

PRONOUN REFERENCE

A pronoun must refer clearly to one and only one antecedent.

1. Watch out for sentences in which pronouns refer to indefinite antecedents, paying particular attention to the pronoun *they*. (Avoid references to some vague *they*.)

   Wrong: They serve meals on many of the buses that run from Santiago to Antofagasta. (Who are *they*?)

   Better: Meals are served on many of the buses that run from Santiago to Antofagasta.

   Note: It's quite all right to use *it* like this:

   It seldom rains in Death Valley.

2. Sometimes a sentence is structured so that a pronoun can refer to more than one thing, and as a result, the reader doesn't know what the author intended.

Wrong: Pennsylvania Governor William Keith encouraged the young Benjamin Franklin to open his own printing shop because he perceived that the quality of printing in Philadelphia was poor. (*Which* man perceived that the quality of printing in Philadelphia was poor?)

Pronouns are assumed to refer to the nearest reasonable antecedent. Nonetheless, it is best to avoid structural ambiguity of the sort that occurs in this sentence.

Better: Because *he* perceived that the quality of printing in Philadelphia was poor, Pennsylvania Governor *William Keith* encouraged the young Benjamin Franklin to open his own printing shop. (*Keith* perceived that the quality of printing was poor.)

Better: Because the young *Benjamin Franklin* perceived that the quality of printing in Philadelphia was poor, Pennsylvania Governor William Keith encouraged *him* to open *his* own printing shop. (In this version, *Franklin* is the one who perceived that the printing was poor.)

3. Sometimes it's easy to see what the author meant to use for the antecedent, but when you examine the sentence more closely, that antecedent is nowhere to be found. Correct the problem either by replacing the pronoun with a noun or by providing a clear antecedent.

Poor: The proslavery writer A. C. C. Thompson questioned Frederick Douglass's authorship of *The Narrative*, claiming that he was too uneducated to have written such an eloquent book.

What's the antecedent of *he*? It should be the noun *Frederick Douglass*, but the sentence contains only the possessive form *Douglass's*. As a rule, avoid using a possessive form as the antecedent of a personal pronoun.

Better: The proslavery writer A. C. C. Thompson questioned whether Frederick Douglass actually wrote *The Narrative*, claiming that *he* was too uneducated to have written such an eloquent book.

ODDBALL PROBLEMS

Here are two oddball pronoun reference problems to watch out for.

DO SO

Wrong: It is common for a native New Yorker who has never driven a car to move to another part of the country and have to learn to do it.

Better: It is common for a native New Yorker who has never driven a car to move to another part of the country and have to learn to *do so*.

ONE AND YOU

When we give advice to others or make general statements, we often use the pronouns *one* and *you*: "You should brush your teeth every day"; "One never knows what to do in a situation like that."

It is never acceptable to mix *one* and *you*, or *one* and *yours*, or *your* and *one's* in a sentence together.

Wrong: One shouldn't eat a high-fat diet and avoid exercise and then be surprised when you gain weight.

Correct: *One* shouldn't eat a high-fat diet and avoid exercise and then be surprised when *one* gains weight.

Also correct: *You* shouldn't eat a high-fat diet and avoid exercise and then be surprised when *you* gain weight.

Also, never use *one* or *one's* to refer to any antecedent except *one*.

Wrong: A person should leave a light on in an empty house if one wants to give the impression that someone is at home.

Correct: A *person* should leave a light on in an empty house if *he or she* wants to give the impression that someone is at home.

Also correct: *One* should leave a light on in an empty house if *one* wants to give the impression that someone is at home.

Also correct: *One* should leave a light on in an empty house if *he or she* wants to give the impression that someone is at home.

PRONOUN AGREEMENT

Always use singular pronouns to refer to singular entities and plural pronouns to refer to plural entities. First, identify the antecedent of a given pronoun; don't allow yourself to be distracted by a phrase that comes between the two.

Wrong: A cactus will flower in spite of the fact that they receive little water.

Correct: A *cactus* will flower in spite of the fact that *it* receives little water.

Wrong: The number of people with college degrees is many times what they were last summer.

Correct: The *number* of people with college degrees is many times what *it* was last summer.

Note: *The number* is always singular. (The number of cookies he ate *was* impressive.) *A number* is always plural. (A number of turkeys *were* gathered outside the shed.)

PRONOUN CASE

One type of pronoun problem you can't catch by looking at the relationship between a pronoun and its antecedent is wrong case.

	Subjective Case	**Objective Case**
First Person:	*I, we*	*me, us*
Second Person:	*you*	*you*
Third Person:	*he, she, it, they, one*	*him, her, it, them, one*
Relative Pronouns:	*who, that, which*	*whom, that, which*

WHEN TO USE SUBJECTIVE CASE PRONOUNS

1. Use the subjective case for the subject of a sentence.

    She is falling asleep.

2. Use the subjective case after forms of *to be*.

    It is *I*.

3. Use the subjective case in comparisons between the subjects of understood verbs.

    Gary is taller than *I* (am).

WHEN TO USE OBJECTIVE CASE PRONOUNS

1. Use the objective case for the object of a verb.

    I called *him*.

2. Use the objective case for the object of a preposition.

    I laughed at *her*.

3. Use the objective case after infinitives and gerunds.

    Asking *him* to go was a big mistake.

4. Use the objective case in comparisons between objects of understood verbs.

    She calls you more than (she calls) *me*.

There probably won't be many times when you are in doubt as to which case of a pronoun is correct. However, the following hints may prove helpful.

When two or more nouns or pronouns are functioning the same way in a sentence, determine the correct case of any pronoun by considering it separately:

Beatrice and (*I* or *me*) are going home early.

Without *Beatrice*, should the sentence read: *Me am going home early* or *I am going home early*? *I am going*, of course, so *Beatrice and I are going home early*.

A common mistake in the use of relative pronouns is using *who* (subject case) when *whom* (object case) is needed, or vice versa. If you tend to confuse the two, try the following system.

Scholars have disagreed over (*who* or *whom*) is most likely to have written *A Yorkshire Tragedy*, but some early sources attribute it to Shakespeare.

1. Isolate the relative pronoun in its own clause: *who/whom is most likely to have written* A Yorkshire Tragedy.

2. Ask yourself the question: Who or whom wrote *A Yorkshire Tragedy*?

3. Answer with an ordinary personal pronoun: *He* did. (If you are a native speaker of English, your ear undoubtedly tells you that *him did* is wrong.)

4. Since *he* is in the subjective case, we need the subjective case relative pronoun: *who*. Therefore, this sentence should read as follows:

Scholars have disagreed over *who* is most likely to have written *A Yorkshire Tragedy*, but some early sources attribute it to Shakespeare.

VERBS

Here are some important terms and concepts to review before you read this section:

Verb: A word that expresses an action or a state of being.

Verbal: A word that is formed from a verb but is not functioning as a verb. There are three kinds of verbals: *participles*, *gerunds*, and *infinitives*.

It is important to realize that a verbal is not a verb, because a sentence must contain a verb and a verbal won't do. A group of words containing a verbal but lacking a verb is not a sentence.

Participle: Usually ends in *-ing* or *-ed*. It is used as an adjective in a sentence.
Let *sleeping* dogs lie.
It is difficult to calm a *frightened* child.
Peering into his microscope, Robert Koch saw the tuberculosis bacilli.

Gerund: Always ends in *-ing*. It is used in a sentence as a noun.
Skiing can be dangerous.
Raising a family is a serious task.
I was surprised at his *acting* like such a coward.

Note from the third sentence that a noun or pronoun that comes before a gerund is in the possessive form: *his*, not *him*.

Infinitive: The basic form of a verb, generally preceded by *to*. It is usually used as a noun but may be used as an adjective or an adverb.

Winston Churchill liked *to paint*. (Infinitive used as a noun.)

The will *to conquer* is crucial. (Infinitive used as an adjective—modifies the *will*.)

Students in imperial China studied the Confucian classics *to excel* on civil service exams. (Infinitive used as an adverb—modifies *studied*.)

VERB TENSE

You need to be familiar with both the way each tense is used individually and the ways the tenses are used together.

PRESENT TENSE

Use the present tense to describe a state or action occurring in the present.

> Congress *is debating* about health policy this session.

Use the present tense to describe habitual action.

> Many Americans *jog* every day.

Use the present tense to describe "general truths"—things that are always true.

> The earth *is* round and *rotates* on its axis.

PAST TENSE

Use the simple past tense to describe an event or state that took place at a specific time in the past and is now over and done with.

> Hundreds of people *died* when the *Titanic* sank.
>
> Few people *bought* new cars last year.

There are two other ways to express past action:

> Bread *used to* cost a few cents per loaf.
>
> She *did say* she would be on time.

FUTURE TENSE

Use the future tense for intended actions or actions expected in the future.

> The 22nd century *will begin* in the year 2101.

We often express future actions with the expression *to be going to*:

> I *am going to move* to another apartment as soon as possible.

The simple present tense is also used to speak of future events. This is called the **anticipatory future.** We often use the anticipatory future with verbs of motion such as *come, go, arrive, depart*, and *leave*:

> The senator *is leaving* for Europe tomorrow.

We also use the anticipatory future in two-clause sentences when one verb is in the regular future tense:

> The disputants will announce the new truce as soon as they *agree* on its terms.

PRESENT PERFECT TENSE

Use the present perfect tense for actions and states that started in the past and continue up to and into the present time.

Hawaii *has been* a state since 1959.

Use the present perfect for actions and states that happened a number of times in the past and may happen again in the future.

Italy *has had* many changes in government since World War II.

Use the present perfect for something that happened at an unspecified time in the past. Notice the difference in meaning between the following two sample sentences.

Present Perfect: Susan Sontag *has written* a critical essay about Leni Riefenstahl. (We have no idea when—we just know she wrote it.)

Simple Past: Susan Sontag *wrote* a critical essay about Leni Riefenstahl in 1974. (We use the simple past because we're specifying when Sontag wrote the essay.)

PAST PERFECT TENSE

The past perfect tense is used to represent past actions or states that were completed before other past states or actions. The more recent past event is expressed in the simple past, and the earlier past event is expressed in the past perfect.

After he came to America, Vladimir Nabokov translated novels that *he had* written in Russian while he was living in Europe.

Note the difference in meaning between these two sentences:

The Civil War *had ended* when Lincoln was shot. = *The war was over by the time of Lincoln's death.*

The Civil War *ended* when Lincoln was shot. = *The war ended when Lincoln died.*

The first sentence is historically accurate.

FUTURE PERFECT TENSE

Use the future perfect tense for a future state or event that will take place before another future event.

By the time the next election is held, the candidates *will have debated* at least once. (Note that the present tense form [anticipatory future] is used in the first clause.)

SEQUENCE OF TENSES

When a sentence has two or more verbs in it, you should always check to see whether the tenses of those verbs correctly indicate the order in which things happened. As a general rule, if two things happened at the same time, the verbs should be in the same tense.

Wrong: Just as the sun rose, the rooster crows.

Rose is past tense and *crows* is present tense, but the words *just as* indicate that both things happened at the same time. The verbs should be in the same tense.

Correct: Just as the sun *rose*, the rooster *crowed*.

Also correct: Just as the sun *rises*, the rooster *crows*.

When we're talking about the past or the future, we often want to indicate that one thing happened or will happen before another. That's where the past perfect and the future perfect come in.

Use the past perfect for the earlier of two past events and the simple past for the later event.

Wrong: Mozart finished about two-thirds of the *Requiem* when he died.

Putting both verbs of the sentence in the simple past tense makes it sound as if Mozart wrote two-thirds of the *Requiem* after dying. If we put the first verb into the past perfect, though, the sentence makes much more sense.

Correct: Mozart *had finished* about two-thirds of the *Requiem* when he *died*.

Use the future perfect for the earlier of two future events.

Wrong: By the time I write to Leo, he will probably move.

The point the author is trying to get across is not that Leo will move when he gets the letter, but that by the time the letter arrives, he'll be living somewhere else.

Correct: By the time I write to Leo, he *will* probably *have moved*.

When you use a participial phrase in a sentence, the action or the situation that phrase describes is assumed to take place at the same time as the action or state described by the verb of the sentence.

Wrong: *Being* a French colony, Senegal is a Francophone nation.

This implies that Senegal is still a French colony. We can make the information in the participial phrase refer to an earlier time than does the verb by changing the regular participle to what's called a **perfect participle.** The way to do it is to use *having + the past participle*.

Correct: *Having been a French colony*, Senegal is a Francophone nation.

You can do the same thing with infinitives by replacing the regular infinitive with *to have + the past participle*.

I'm glad *to meet you.* (I'm glad to be in the process of meeting you right now.)
I'm glad *to have* met you. (I'm glad now that I met you earlier today, last week, or whenever.)

SUBJUNCTIVE MOOD

Subjunctive verb forms are used in two ways.

The subjunctive form *were* is used in statements that express a wish or situations that are contrary to fact.

> I wish I *were* a rich man. (But I'm not.)
> If I *were* you, I wouldn't do that. (But I'm not you.)

The **subjunctive of requirement** is used after verbs such as *ask, demand, insist,* and *suggest*—or after expressions of requirement, suggestion, or demand. A subjunctive verb of requirement is in the base form of the verb: the infinitive without *to*.

> Airlines insist that each passenger *pass* through a metal detector.
> It's extremely important that silicon chips *be made* in a dust-free environment.

CONDITIONAL SENTENCES

Conditional sentences are if-then statements.

> *If* you go, *then* I'll go, too.

We use conditional sentences when we want to speculate about the results of a particular situation. There are three types of conditional sentences.

Statements of fact: There is a real possibility that the situation described in the *if* clause really happened, or is happening, or will happen.

> If Vladimir Putin resigns, there will be unrest in Russia.
> If John Milton met Galileo, they probably discussed astronomy.

Contrary to fact: The situation in the *if* clause never happened, so what is said in the *then* clause is pure speculation.

> Blaise Pascal wrote that if Cleopatra's nose had been shorter, the face of the world would have changed.
> Alexander the Great said, "If I were not Alexander, I would want to be Diogenes."

Future speculation: Some conditional sentences speculate about the future but with the idea that the situation in the *if* clause is extremely unlikely to happen.

> If Shakespeare's manuscripts were to be discovered, the texts of some of his plays would be less uncertain.

PARALLELISM

Remember, when you express a number of ideas of equal importance and function in the same sentence, you should always be careful to make them all the same grammatical form (that is, all nouns, all adjectives, all gerunds, all clauses, or whatever). That's called **parallel structure** or **parallelism.**

COORDINATE IDEAS

Coordinate ideas occur in pairs or in series, and they are linked by conjunctions such as *and*, *but*, *or*, and *nor*, or, in certain instances, by linking verbs such as *is*.

Wrong:	To earn credits, an American college student can take up folk dancing, ballet, or study belly dancing.
Correct:	To earn credits, an American college student can take up *folk dancing*, *ballet*, or *belly dancing*.

Note that once you begin repeating a word in a series like the following, you must follow through:

Wrong:	A wage earner might invest her money in stocks, in bonds, or real estate.
Correct:	A wage earner might invest her money *in* stocks, *in* bonds, or *in* real estate.
Also correct:	A wage earner might invest her money *in* stocks, bonds, or real estate.

This principle applies equally to prepositions (*in*, *on*, *by*, *with*, etc.), articles (*the*, *a*, *an*), helping verbs (*had*, *has*, *would*, etc.), and possessive pronouns (*his*, *her*, etc.). You must either repeat the preposition, helping verb, or whatever in front of each element in the series or include it in front of only the first item in the series.

CORRELATIVE CONSTRUCTIONS

There is a group of words in English called **correlative conjunctions.** They are used to relate two ideas in some way. Here's a list of them:

both . . . and

either . . . or

neither . . . nor

not only . . . but also

You should always be careful to place correlative conjunctions immediately before the terms they're coordinating.

Wrong:	Isaac Newton not only studied physics, but also theology.

The problem here is that the author intends to coordinate the two nouns *physics* and *theology* but makes the mistake of putting the verb of the sentence (*studied*) after the first element of the construction (*not only*), in so doing destroying the parallelism. Note that the solution to an error like this is usually to move one of the conjunctions.

Correct: Isaac Newton studied not only *physics* but also *theology*.

Compared or Contrasted Ideas

Frequently, two or more ideas are compared or contrasted within the same sentence. Compared or contrasted ideas should be presented in the same grammatical form.

Certain phrases should clue you in that the sentence contains ideas that should be presented in parallel form. These phrases include *as . . . as* and *more (or less)* x *than* y.

Wrong: Skiing is as strenuous as to run.

Correct: *Skiing* is as strenuous as *running*.

Wrong: Skiing is less dangerous than to rappel down a cliff.

Correct: *To ski* is less dangerous than *to rappel* down a cliff.

To Be

In certain cases, sentences with forms of *to be* must be expressed in parallel form.

Wrong: To drive while intoxicated is risking grave injury and criminal charges.

When an infinitive is the subject of *to be*, don't use a gerund after the verb, and vice versa. Pair infinitives with infinitives and gerunds with gerunds.

Correct: *To drive* while intoxicated is *to risk* grave injury and criminal charges.

Note that we wouldn't change both words to gerunds in this sentence because it wouldn't sound idiomatic.

COMPARISONS

A sentence that makes a comparison must do two things: it must be clear about what is being compared, and it must compare things that can logically be compared. A sentence that makes an unclear or illogical comparison is grammatically unacceptable.

Unclear Comparisons

Sometimes it isn't clear what the author is trying to compare.

Wrong: Byron admired Dryden more than Wordsworth.

There are two ways to interpret this sentence: that Dryden meant more to Byron than Wordsworth did or that Byron thought more highly of Dryden than Wordsworth did. Whichever meaning you choose, the problem can be cleared up by adding more words to the sentence.

Correct: Byron admired Dryden more than *he did* Wordsworth.

Also correct: Byron admired Dryden more than *Wordsworth did.*

ILLOGICAL COMPARISONS

Sometimes what the author meant to say is clear enough, but what the author meant to say is not what he or she ended up saying.

Wrong: The peaches here are riper than any other fruitstand.

This sentence is comparing *peaches* to *fruitstands*, even though that's clearly not the intention of the author. We can correct it so that we're comparing peaches to peaches by inserting the phrase *those at.*

Correct: The peaches here are riper than *those at* any other fruitstand.

Now the pronoun *those* is standing in for *peaches*, so the sentence is accurately comparing things that can be reasonably compared: the peaches here and some other peaches.

Incomplete comparisons like this one are normally corrected by inserting a phrase like *those of, those in, those at, that of, that in,* and *that at.*

Incomplete comparisons can also be corrected by use of the possessive.

Wrong: Many critics considered Enrico Caruso's voice better than any other tenor. (This is comparing a voice to a person.)

Correct: Many critics considered Enrico Caruso's voice better than *any other tenor's.* (Note that this is a shortened version of *Many critics considered Enrico Caruso's voice better than any other tenor's voice.*)

The second sort of incomplete comparison occurs when one thing is being compared to a group it is a part of. This error is corrected by inserting either the word *other* or the word *else.*

Wrong: Astaire danced better than any man in the world.

This is wrong because he couldn't have danced better than himself.

DIG A LITTLE DEEPER

When you see a comparative expression such as *like, as, more than, unlike, less than, similar to,* or *different from,* it should remind you to ask yourself two questions about the comparison in the sentence: Is it clear? Is it logical?

Correct: Astaire danced better than any *other* man in the world.

COMPARATIVE FORMS

The comparative form is used when comparing only two members of a class, and the superlative for three or more.

Loretta's grass grows *more vigorously* than Jim's.
Loretta's grass grows the *most vigorously* of any in the neighborhood.

Of Buchanan and Lincoln, the *latter* was *taller*.
Of McKinley, Roosevelt, and Taft, the *last* was *heaviest*.

IDIOM

Sometimes the right way to say something isn't a matter of grammar but is a matter of **idiom**: an accepted, set phrase or usage that's right for no other reason than that's just the way we say it.

Most of what we call *idioms* are groups of words that are used together to convey a particular meaning, and many "idiom errors" result from substituting an unacceptable word—usually a preposition—for a word that is always part of the idiom.

Wrong: Brigitte Bardot has joined an organization that is concerned in preventing cruelty to animals.

The adjective *concerned* is followed by either *about* or *with*, either of which would be idiomatic here. But the expression *concerned in* simply isn't idiomatic—we just don't say it that way.

Correct: Brigitte Bardot has joined an organization that is *concerned with* preventing cruelty to animals.

Also correct: Brigitte Bardot has joined an organization that is *concerned about* preventing cruelty to animals.

There are so many possible idiom errors of this kind that we can't list them all.

ELLIPSIS

An **ellipsis** is the omission of words that are clearly understood. Ellipsis is perfectly acceptable as long as it's done properly—in fact, we do it all the time. Not many people would make a statement like this:

I've seen more movies this year than you have seen movies this year.

Instead, we would automatically shorten the statement to this much more concise and natural sounding one:

I've seen more movies this year than you have.

In the following sentence, ellipsis is properly used:

The Spectator was written by Addison and Steele.

This is a shorter way of saying:

The Spectator was written by Addison and by Steele.

It's all right to leave the second *by* out of the sentence because the same preposition appears before *Addison* and before *Steele*; you need to use it only once.

Now watch what happens when ellipsis is improperly used.

Wrong: Ezra Pound was interested but not very knowledgeable about economics.

This is wrong because the preposition that's needed after the word *interested* (*in*) is not the same as the preposition that follows the word *knowledgeable* (*about*).

Correct: Ezra Pound was *interested in* but not very *knowledgeable about* economics.

Wrong: London always has and always will be the capital of the United Kingdom.

This is wrong because the verb form that's needed after *has* is not the same as the one that's needed after *will*, so both must be included.

Correct: London *always has been* and *always will be* the capital of the United Kingdom.

NEGATIVES

You will probably run across at least one item that tests your ability to recognize the difference between idiomatic and unidiomatic ways to express negative ideas. You already know that a double negative is a no-no in standard written English. You wouldn't have any trouble realizing that a sentence such as "I don't want no help" is unacceptable. But the incorrect negatives you will probably see on the exam won't be quite that obvious.

The obviously negative words are *neither, nobody, nor, nowhere, never, none, not, no one,* and *nothing.* But don't forget that *barely, rarely, without, hardly, seldom,* and *scarcely* are also grammatically negative.

You'll find problems with these words where sentences connect two or three negative ideas. Read through the following example sentences carefully:

There were *neither* threats *nor* bombing campaigns.

There were *no* threats *or* bombing campaigns.

There were *no* threats *and no* bombing campaigns.

There were *no* threats, *nor* were there bombing campaigns.

These are the most common idiomatic ways to join two negative ideas. If you can remember these patterns, you can probably eliminate many wrong answers that in some way violate these idiomatic patterns.

Wrong: When Walt Whitman's family moved to Brooklyn, there were no bridges nor tunnels across the East River.

The phrase *no bridges nor tunnels* is just not idiomatic—it contains a double negative. The sentence can be rewritten to correct the problem in several ways.

Correct: There were *no bridges or tunnels* across the East River.

Also correct: There were *neither bridges nor tunnels* across the East River.

Also correct: There were *no bridges and no tunnels* across the East River.

Another situation in which negatives can cause problems is in a series. Words like *no*, *not*, and *without* must follow the same rules as prepositions, articles, helping verbs, etc.

Wrong: After the floods in the Midwest, many farmers were left without homes, businesses, and huge bills to replace all they had lost.

When a preposition, such as *without* in this sentence, is used in front of only the first member of a series, it's taken to refer to all three members of the series. Here, that causes the sentence to say that the farmers were left without homes, without businesses, and without huge bills to replace what they had lost, which makes no sense. There are several ways to rewrite the sentence so that it makes sense.

Correct: After the floods in the Midwest, many farmers were left *without* homes, *without* businesses, and *with* huge bills to replace all they had lost.

Also correct: After the floods in the Midwest, many farmers were left *with no* homes, *with no* businesses, and *with* huge bills to replace all they had lost.

Also correct: After the floods in the Midwest, many farmers were left *with no* homes, *no* businesses, and huge bills to replace all they had lost.

GUIDE TO USAGE AND STYLE

To write an effective essay, you need to do three things:

1. Be concise.
2. Be forceful.
3. Be correct.

An effective essay is concise: it wastes no words. An effective essay is forceful: it makes its point. And an effective essay is correct: it conforms to the generally accepted rules of grammar and form.

The following pages break down the three broad objectives of concision, forcefulness, and correctness into 16 specific principles. Don't panic! Many of them will already be familiar to you. And besides, you will have many chances to practice in the exercises we provide.

Principles 1 through 4 aim primarily at the first objective: concise writing; principles 5 through 10 aim primarily at the second objective: forceful writing; and principles 11 through 16 aim primarily at the third objective: grammatically correct writing. For a thorough understanding of the third of these objectives, though, you should consult the Grammar Reference Guide.

The principles of concise and forceful writing are generally not as rigid as the principles of grammatically correct writing. Concision and forcefulness are matters of art and personal style, as well as common sense and tradition. But if you are going to disregard a principle, we hope you will do so out of educated choice.

BE CONCISE

The first four principles of good writing relate to the goal of expressing your points clearly in as few words as possible. Each principle represents a specific way to tighten your writing.

PRINCIPLE 1: AVOID WORDINESS

Do not use several words when one will do. Wordy phrases are like junk food: they add only fat, not muscle. Many people make the mistake of writing phrases such as *at the present time* or *at this point in time* instead of the simpler *now*, or *take into consideration* instead of simply *consider*, in an attempt to make their prose seem more scholarly or more formal. It does not work. Instead, their prose ends up seeming inflated and pretentious. Don't waste your words or your time.

Wordy: I am of the opinion that the aforementioned managers should be advised that they will be evaluated with regard to the utilization of responsive organizational software for the purpose of devising a responsive network of customers.

Concise: We should tell the managers that we will evaluate their use of flexible computerized databases to develop a customer network.

EXERCISE 1: WORDY PHRASES

Improve the following sentences by omitting or replacing wordy phrases.

1. In view of the fact that John has prepared with much care for this presentation, it would be a good idea to award him with the project.

   _____

2. The airline has a problem with always having arrivals that come at least an hour late, despite the fact that the leaders of the airline promise that promptness is a goal that has a high priority for all the employees involved.

   _____

3. In spite of the fact that she only has a little bit of experience in photography right now, she will probably do well in the future because she has a great deal of motivation to succeed in her chosen profession.

   _____

4. Accuracy is a subject that has great importance to English teachers and company presidents alike.

   _____

5. The reason why humans kill each other is that they experience fear of those whom they do not understand.

   _____

PRINCIPLE 2: DON'T BE REDUNDANT

Redundancy means that the writer needlessly repeats an idea. It's redundant to speak of "a beginner lacking experience." The word *beginner* implies lack of experience by itself. You can eliminate redundant words or phrases without changing the meaning of the sentence. Watch out for words that add nothing to the sense of the sentence.

Here are some common redundancies:

Redundant	Concise
refer back	*refer*
few in number	*few*
small-sized	*small*
grouped together	*grouped*
end result	*result*

Redundancy often results from carelessness, but you can easily eliminate redundant elements when proofreading.

EXERCISE 2: REDUNDANCY

Repair the following sentences by crossing out redundant elements.

1. All these problems have combined together to create a serious crisis.

2. A staff that large in size needs an effective supervisor who can get the job done.

3. He knows how to follow directions, and he knows how to do what he is told.

4. The recently observed trend of spending on credit has created a middle class that is poorer and more impoverished than ever before.

5. Those who can follow directions are few in number.

PRINCIPLE 3: AVOID NEEDLESS QUALIFICATION

Because the objective of your essay is to convince your reader, you will want to adopt a reasonable tone. There will likely be no single, clear-cut "answer" to the essay topic, so don't overstate your case. Occasional use of such qualifiers as *fairly*, *rather*, *somewhat*, and *relatively* and of such expressions as *seems to be*, *a little*, and *a certain amount of* will let the reader know you are reasonable, but overusing such modifiers weakens your argument. Excessive qualification makes you sound hesitant. Like wordy phrases, qualifiers can add bulk without adding substance.

Wordy: This rather serious breach of etiquette may possibly shake the very foundations of the corporate world.

Concise: This serious breach of etiquette may shake the foundations of the corporate world.

Just as bad is the overuse of the word *very*. Some writers use this intensifying adverb before almost every adjective in an attempt to be more forceful. If you need to add emphasis, look for a stronger adjective (or verb).

Weak:	Novak is a very good pianist.
Strong:	Novak is a virtuoso pianist.
	or
	Novak plays beautifully.

And don't try to qualify words that are already absolute.

Wrong	**Correct**
more unique	*unique*
the very worst	*the worst*
completely full	*full*

EXERCISE 3: EXCESSIVE QUALIFICATION

Practice achieving concision by eliminating needless qualification in the sentences below.

1. She is a fairly excellent teacher.

2. Ferrara seems to be sort of a slow worker.

3. You yourself are the very best person to decide what you should do for a living.

4. Needless to say, children should be taught to cooperate at home and in school.

5. The travel agent does not recommend the trip to Tripoli, because it is possible that one may be hurt.

PRINCIPLE 4: DO NOT WRITE SENTENCES JUST TO FILL UP SPACE

This principle suggests several things:

- Don't write a sentence that gets you nowhere.

- Don't ask a question only to answer it.

- Don't merely copy the essay's directions.

- Don't write a whole sentence only to announce that you're changing the subject.

If you have something to say, say it without preamble. If you need to smooth over a change of subject, do so with a transitional word or phrase rather than with a meaningless sentence. If your proofreading reveals unintentional wasted sentences, neatly cross them out.

Wordy:	Which idea of the author's is more in line with what I believe? This is a very interesting . . .
Concise:	The author's beliefs are similar to mine.

The author of the previous wordy example is just wasting words and time. Get to the point quickly and stay there. Simplicity and clarity win points.

EXERCISE 4: UNNECESSARY SENTENCES

Rewrite each of these multiple-sentence statements as one concise sentence.

1. What's the purpose of getting rid of the chemical pollutants in water? People cannot safely consume water that contains chemical pollutants.

   _____

2. I do not believe those who argue that some of Shakespeare's plays were written by others. There is no evidence that other people had a hand in writing Shakespeare's plays.

   _____

3. Which point of view is closest to my own? This is a good question. I agree with those who say that the United States should send soldiers to areas of conflict.

   _____

4. Frank Lloyd Wright was a famous architect. He was renowned for his ability to design buildings that blend into their surroundings.

   _____

5. A lot of people find math a difficult subject to master. They have trouble with math because it requires very precise thinking skills.

   _____

BE FORCEFUL

The next group of principles aim at the goal of producing forceful writing. If you follow these principles, your writing will be much more convincing to the reader.

PRINCIPLE 5: AVOID NEEDLESS SELF-REFERENCE

Avoid such unnecessary phrases as "I believe," "I feel," and "in my opinion." There is no need to remind your reader that what you are writing is your opinion.

Weak: I am of the opinion that air pollution is a more serious problem than the government has led us to believe.

Forceful: Air pollution is a more serious problem than the government has led us to believe.

Self-reference is another form of qualifying what you say—a very obvious form. One or two self-references in an essay might be appropriate, just as the use of qualifiers like *probably* and *perhaps* can be effective if you practice using them *sparingly*. Remember: Practice is the only sure way to improve your writing.

EXERCISE 5: NEEDLESS SELF-REFERENCE

Eliminate needless self-references in these sentences.

1. I do not think this argument can be generalized to most business owners.

   _____

2. My own experience shows me that food is the best social lubricant.

   _____

3. Although I am no expert, I do not think privacy should be valued more than social concerns.

   _____

4. My guess is that most people want to do good work but many are bored or frustrated with their jobs.

   _____

5. I must emphasize that I am not saying the author does not have a point.

   _____

PRINCIPLE 6: USE THE ACTIVE VOICE

Using the passive voice is a way to avoid accountability. Put verbs in the active voice whenever possible. In the active voice, the subject performs the action (e.g., we write essays). In the passive voice, the subject is the receiver of the action, and the performer of the action is often only implied (e.g., essays are written).

You should avoid the passive voice EXCEPT in the following cases:

- When you do not know who performed the action: *The letter was opened before I received it.* (For example, see the last sentence of the above paragraph.)

- When you prefer not to refer directly to the person who performs the action: *An error has been made in computing this data.*

Passive: The estimate of this year's tax revenues was prepared by the General Accounting Office.

Active: The General Accounting Office prepared the estimate of this year's tax revenues.

EXERCISE 6: UNDESIRABLE PASSIVES

Replace passive voice with active wherever possible.

1. The politician's standing in the polls has been hurt by recent allegations of corruption.

    _____

2. The bill was passed in time, but it was not signed by the president until the time for action had passed.

    _____

3. Advice is usually requested by those who need it least; it is not sought out by the truly lost and ignorant.

    _____

4. The minutes of the city council meeting should be taken by the city clerk.

    _____

5. The report was compiled by a number of field anthropologists and marriage experts.

    _____

PRINCIPLE 7: AVOID WEAK OPENINGS

Try not to begin a sentence with *there is*, *there are*, or *it is*. These roundabout expressions usually indicate that you are trying to distance yourself from the position you are taking.

EXERCISE 7: WEAK OPENINGS

Rewrite these sentences to eliminate weak openings.

1. It would be unwise for businesses to ignore the illiteracy problem.

    _____

2. It would be of no use to fight a drug war without waging a battle against the demand for illicit substances.

    _____

3. There are many strong points in the candidate's favor; intelligence, unfortunately, is not among them.

    _____

4. It has been decided that we, as a society, can tolerate homelessness.

    _____

5. There seems to be little doubt that Americans like watching television better than conversing.

    _____

BE SPECIFIC

The essay topics you're given will not be obscure. You will be able to come up with specific examples and concrete information about the topics. Your argument will be more forceful if you stick to this information.

PRINCIPLE 8: AVOID NEEDLESSLY VAGUE LANGUAGE

Don't just ramble on when you're writing. Choose specific, descriptive words. Vague language weakens your writing because it forces the reader to guess what you mean instead of concentrating fully on your ideas and style.

Weak:	Brown is highly educated.
Forceful:	Brown has a master's degree in business administration.
Weak:	She is a great communicator.
Forceful:	She speaks persuasively.

Notice that sometimes, to be more specific and concrete, you will have to use more words than you might with vague language. This principle is not in conflict with the general objective of concision. Being concise may mean eliminating unnecessary words. Avoiding vagueness may mean adding necessary words.

EXERCISE 8: NEEDLESSLY VAGUE LANGUAGE

Rewrite these sentences to replace vague language with specific, concrete language.

1. Water is transformed into steam when the former is heated up to 100°C.

   _____

2. The diplomat was required to execute an agreement that stipulated that he would live in whatever country the federal government thought necessary.

   _____

3. The principal told John that he should not even think about coming back to school until he changed his ways.

   _____

4. The police detective had to seek the permission of the lawyer to question the suspect.

   _____

5. Thousands of species of animals were destroyed when the last ice age occurred.

   _____

PRINCIPLE 9: AVOID CLICHÉS

Clichés are overused expressions that may have once seemed colorful and powerful but are now dull and worn out. Time pressure and anxiety may make you lose focus; that's when clichés may slip into your writing. A reliance on clichés will suggest you are a lazy thinker. Keep them out of your essay.

Weak: Performance in a crisis is the acid test for a leader.

Forceful: Performance in a crisis is the best indicator of a leader's abilities.

Notice whether or not you use clichés. If you do, ask yourself if you could substitute more specific language for the cliché.

EXERCISE 9: CLICHÉS

Make the following sentences more forceful by replacing clichés.

1. Beyond the shadow of a doubt, Jefferson was a great leader.

   _____

2. Trying to find the employee responsible for this embarrassing information leak is like trying to find a needle in a haystack.

   _____

3. The military is putting all its eggs in one basket by relying so heavily on nuclear missiles for the nation's defense.

   _____

4. Older doctors should be required to update their techniques, but you can't teach an old dog new tricks.

   _____

5. A ballpark estimate of the number of fans in the stadium would be 120,000.

   _____

PRINCIPLE 10: AVOID JARGON

Jargon includes two categories of words that you should avoid. First is the specialized vocabulary of a group, such as that used by doctors, lawyers, or baseball coaches. Second is the overly inflated and complex language that burdens many students' essays. You will not impress anyone with big words that do not fit the tone or context of your essay, especially if you misuse them.

If you are not certain of a word's meaning or appropriateness, leave it out. An appropriate word, even a simple one, will add impact to your argument.

Weak: The international banks are cognizant of the new law's significance.

Forceful: The international banks are aware of the new law's significance.

Wrong: The new law would negatively impact each of the nations involved.

Correct: The new law would hurt each of the nations involved. (*Impact* is also used to mean *affect* or *benefit*.)

QUOTING CLICHÉS

Putting a cliché in quotation marks to indicate your distance from it does not strengthen the sentence. If anything, it just makes weak writing more noticeable.

WRITE LIKE A READER

As you come across words you are unsure of, ask yourself, "Would a reader in a different field be able to understand exactly what I mean from the words I've chosen?" "Is there any way I can say the same thing more simply?"

The following are commonly used jargon words:

prioritize	*parameter*
optimize	*time frame*
utilize	*input/output*
finalize	*maximize*
designate	*facilitate*
bottom line	

EXERCISE 10: JARGON

Replace the jargon in the following sentences with more appropriate language.

1. We anticipate utilizing hundreds of paper clips in the foreseeable future.

   _____

2. Education-wise, our schoolchildren have been neglected.

   _____

3. Foreign diplomats should always interface with local leaders.

   _____

4. There is considerable evidentiary support for the assertion that Vienna sausages are good for you.

   _____

5. In the case of the recent railway disaster, it is clear that governmental regulatory agencies obfuscated in the preparation of materials for release to the public through both the electronic and print media.

   _____

BE CORRECT

Correctness is perhaps the most difficult objective for writers to achieve. The complex rules of standard English usage can leave you feeling unsure of your writing and more than a bit confused. Just think of this section, together with the Grammar Reference Guide, as helping you to improve the details of good writing. If this information begins to overwhelm you, stop and take a break. You need time to absorb.

Do the exercises and then compare your answers to ours. Make sure you understand what the error was in each sentence. Use what you learn in this section to help you proofread your practice essays; later, return to your practice essays and edit them. Better yet, ask a friend to edit them, paying special attention to correctness.

BUT REMEMBER

The most important lesson you can take from this section is how to organize your thoughts into a strong, well-supported argument. Style and grammar are important but secondary concerns. Your readers will *not* mark you down for occasional errors common to first-draft writing.

PRINCIPLE 11: AVOID SLANG AND COLLOQUIALISMS

Slang terms and colloquialisms can be confusing to the reader, because these expressions are not universally understood. Even worse, such informal writing may give readers the impression that you are poorly educated or arrogant.

Inappropriate: He is really into gardening.
Correct: He enjoys gardening.

Inappropriate: She plays a wicked game of tennis.
Correct: She excels in tennis.

Inappropriate: Myra has got to go to Memphis for a week.
Correct: Myra must go to Memphis for a week.

Inappropriate: Joan has been doing science for eight years now.
Correct: Joan has been a scientist for eight years now.

With a little thought you will find the right word. Using informal language is risky. Play it safe by sticking to standard usage.

EXERCISE 11: SLANG AND COLLOQUIALISMS

Replace the informal elements of the following sentences with more appropriate terms.

1. Cynthia Larson sure knows her stuff.

   _____

2. Normal human beings can't cope with repeated humiliation.

   _____

3. If you want a good cheesecake, you must make a top-notch crust.

   _____

4. International organizations should try and cooperate on global issues like hunger.

   _____

5. The environmentalists aren't in it for the prestige; they really care about protecting the yellow-throated hornswoggler.

   _____

PRINCIPLE 12: USE COMMAS CORRECTLY

When using the comma, follow these rules.

A. Use commas to separate items in a series. If more than two items are listed in a series, they should be separated by commas; the final comma—the one that precedes the word *and*—is optional. Never use a comma after the word *and*.

Correct: My recipe for buttermilk biscuits contains flour, baking soda, salt, shortening, and buttermilk.

Correct: My recipe for chocolate cake contains flour, baking soda, sugar, eggs, milk and chocolate.

B. Do not place commas before the first element of a series or after the last element.

Wrong: My investment advisor recommended that I construct a portfolio of, stocks, bonds, commodities futures, and precious metals.

Wrong: The elephants, tigers, and dancing bears, were the highlights of the circus.

C. Use commas to separate two or more adjectives before a noun; do not use a comma after the last adjective in the series.

Wrong: I can't believe you sat through that long, dull, uninspired, movie three times.

Correct: I can't believe you sat through that long, dull, uninspired movie three times.

D. Use commas to set off parenthetical clauses and phrases. (A parenthetical expression is one that is not necessary to the main idea of the sentence.)

Correct: Gordon, a writer by profession, bakes an excellent cheesecake.

The main idea is that Gordon bakes an excellent cheesecake. The intervening clause merely serves to identify Gordon; thus, it should be set off with commas.

Correct: The newspaper that has the most insipid editorials is the *Daily Times*.

Correct: The newspaper, which has the most insipid editorials of any I have read, won numerous awards last week.

In the first of these examples, the clause beginning with *that* defines which paper the author is discussing. In the second example, the main point is that the newspaper won numerous awards, and the intervening clause beginning with *which* gives additional information.

E. Use commas after introductory participial or prepositional phrases.

Correct: Having watered his petunias every day during the drought, Harold was very disappointed when his garden was destroyed by insects.

Correct: After the banquet, Harold and Martha went dancing.

F. Use commas to separate independent clauses (clauses that could stand alone as complete sentences) connected by coordinate conjunctions such as *and*, *but*, *not*, *yet*, etc.

Correct: Susan's old car has been belching blue smoke from the tailpipe for two weeks, but it has not broken down yet.

Note: Make sure the comma separates two *independent* clauses, joined by a conjunction. It is incorrect to use a comma to separate the two parts of a compound verb.

Wrong: Barbara went to the grocery store, and bought two quarts of milk.

EXERCISE 12: COMMAS

Correct the punctuation errors in the following sentences.

1. It takes a friendly energetic personality to be a successful salesperson.
2. I was shocked to discover that a large, modern, glass-sheathed, office building had replaced my old school.
3. The country club, a cluster of ivy-covered whitewashed buildings was the site of the president's first speech.
4. Pushing through the panicked crowd the security guards frantically searched for the suspect.
5. Despite careful analysis of the advantages and disadvantages of each proposal Harry found it hard to reach a decision.

PRINCIPLE 13: USE SEMICOLONS CORRECTLY

When using a semicolon, follow these rules.

A. Use a semicolon *instead of* a coordinate conjunction such as *and*, *or*, or *but* to link two closely related independent clauses.

Wrong: Whooping cranes are an endangered species; and they are unlikely to survive if we continue to pollute.

Correct: Whooping cranes are an endangered species; only 50 whooping cranes reside in New Jersey today.

Correct: Whooping cranes are an endangered species, and they are unlikely to survive if we continue to pollute.

B. Use a semicolon between independent clauses connected by words like *therefore*, *nevertheless*, and *moreover*.

Correct: Farm prices have been falling rapidly for two years; nevertheless, the traditional American farm is not in danger of disappearing.

EXERCISE 13: SEMICOLONS

Correct the punctuation errors in the following sentences.

1. Morgan has five years' experience in karate; but Thompson has even more.

   _____

2. Very few students wanted to take the class in physics, only the professor's kindness kept it from being canceled.

   _____

3. You should always be prepared when you go on a camping trip, however you must avoid carrying unnecessary weight.

   _____

PRINCIPLE 14: USE COLONS CORRECTLY

When using a colon, follow these rules.

A. In formal writing, the colon is used only as a means of signaling that what follows is a list, definition, explanation, or concise summary of what has gone before. The colon usually follows an independent clause, and it is frequently accompanied by a reinforcing expression like *the following*, *as follows*, or *namely* or by an explicit demonstrative like *this*.

Correct: Your instructions are as follows: read the passage carefully, answer the questions on the last page, and turn over your answer sheet.

Correct: This is what I found in the refrigerator: a moldy lime, half a bottle of stale soda, and a jar of peanut butter.

Correct: The biggest problem with America today is apathy: the corrosive element that will destroy our democracy.

B. Be careful not to put a colon between a verb and its direct object.

Wrong: I want: a slice of pizza and a small green salad.

Correct: This is what I want: a slice of pizza and a small green salad. (The colon serves to announce that a list is forthcoming.)

Correct: I don't want much for lunch: just a slice of pizza and a small green salad. (Here what follows the colon defines what "don't want much" means.)

C. Context will occasionally make clear that a second independent clause is closely linked to its predecessor, even without an explicit expression like those used previously. Here, too, a colon is appropriate, although a period will always be correct also.

Correct: We were aghast: the "charming country inn" that had been advertised in such glowing terms proved to be a leaking cabin full of mosquitoes.

Correct: We were aghast. The "charming country inn" that had been advertised in such glowing terms proved to be a leaking cabin full of mosquitoes.

EXERCISE 14: COLONS

Edit these sentences so they use colons correctly.

1. I am sick and tired of: your whining, your complaining, your nagging, your teasing, and, most of all, your barbed comments.

   _____

2. The chef has created a masterpiece, the pasta is delicate yet firm, the mustard greens are fresh, and the medallions of veal are melting in my mouth.

   _____

3. To write a good essay, you must: practice, get plenty of sleep, and eat a good breakfast.

   _____

PRINCIPLE 15: USE HYPHENS AND DASHES CORRECTLY

When using a hyphen or a dash, follow these rules.

A. Use the hyphen with the compound numbers twenty-one through ninety-nine and with fractions used as adjectives.

Correct: Sixty-five students constituted a majority.

Correct: A two-thirds vote was necessary to carry the measure.

B. Use the hyphen with the prefixes *ex*, *all*, and *self* and with the suffix *elect*.

Correct: The constitution protects against self-incrimination.

Correct: The president-elect was invited to chair the meeting.

C. Use the hyphen with a compound adjective when it comes before the word it modifies but not when it comes after the word it modifies.

Correct: The no-holds-barred argument continued into the night.

Correct: The argument continued with no holds barred.

D. Use the hyphen with any prefix used before a proper noun or adjective.

Correct: They believed that his activities were un-American.

E. Use a hyphen to separate component parts of a word to avoid confusion with other words or to avoid the use of a double vowel.

Correct: The sculptor was able to re-form the clay after the dog knocked over the bust.

Correct: They had to be re-introduced, since it had been so long since they last met.

F. Use the dash to indicate an abrupt change of thought. In general, however, formal writing is best when you think out what you want to say in advance and avoid abrupt changes of thought.

Correct: To get a high score—and who doesn't want to get a high score?—you need to devote yourself to prolonged and concentrated study.

EXERCISE 15: HYPHENS AND DASHES

Edit these sentences so they use hyphens and dashes correctly.

1. The child was able to count from one to ninety nine.

2. The adults only movie was banned from commercial TV.

3. It was the first time she had seen a movie that was for adults-only.

4. A two thirds majority would be needed to pass the budget reforms.

5. The house, and it was the most dilapidated house that I had ever seen was a bargain because the land was so valuable.

PRINCIPLE 16: USE THE APOSTROPHE CORRECTLY

When using an apostrophe, follow these rules.

A. Use the apostrophe with contracted forms of verbs to indicate that one or more letters have been eliminated in writing.

Full Forms:

you are	*it is*	*you have*	*the boy is*
Harry has	*we would*	*was not*	

Contracted:

you're	*it's*	*you've*	*the boy's*
Harry's	*we'd*	*wasn't*	

Incorrect:	You're chest of drawers is ugly.
Incorrect:	The dog hurt it's paw.
Correct:	Your chest of drawers is ugly.
Correct:	The dog hurt its paw.

B. Use the apostrophe to indicate the possessive form of a noun.

Not Possessive:

| the boy | Harry | the children | the boys |

Possessive Form:

| the boy's | Harry's | the children's | the boys' |

| **Correct:** | Ms. Fox's office is on the first floor. (One person possesses the office.) |
| **Correct:** | The Foxes' apartment has a wonderful view. (There are several people named Fox living in the same apartment. First you must form the plural, then add the apostrophe to indicate possession.) |

C. The apostrophe is used to indicate possession only with nouns; in the case of pronouns, there are separate possessives for each person and number.

my, mine	our, ours
your, yours	your, yours
his, his	their, theirs
her, hers	
its, its	

The exception is the neutral *one*, which forms its possessive by adding an apostrophe and an *s*.

EXERCISE 16: APOSTROPHES

Edit these sentences so they use apostrophes correctly.

1. The presidents limousine had a flat tire.
2. You're tickets for the show will be at the box office.
3. The opportunity to change ones lifestyle does not come often.
4. The desks' surface was immaculate, but it's drawers were messy.
5. The cat on the bed is hers'.

YOUR OR YOU ARE?

One of the most common errors involving use of the apostrophe is using it in the contraction *you're* or *it's* to indicate the possessive form of *you* or *it*. When you write *you're*, ask yourself whether you mean *you are*. If not, the correct word is *your*. Similarly, are you sure you mean *it is*? If not, use the possessive form *its*. You spell *his* or *hers* without an apostrophe, so you should spell *its* without an apostrophe.

ANSWERS TO EXERCISES

ANSWERS TO EXERCISE 1: WORDY PHRASES

1. Because John has prepared for this presentation so carefully, we should award him the project.

2. Flights are always at least an hour late on this airline, though its leaders promise that promptness is a high priority for all its employees.

3. Although she is inexperienced in photography, she will probably succeed because she is motivated.

4. Accuracy is important to English teachers and company presidents alike.

5. Humans kill each other because they fear those whom they do not understand.

ANSWERS TO EXERCISE 2: REDUNDANCY

1. These problems have combined to create a crisis.

2. A staff that large needs an effective supervisor.

3. He knows how to follow directions.

4. The recent trend of spending on credit has created a poorer middle class.

5. Few people can follow directions.

ANSWERS TO EXERCISE 3: EXCESSIVE QUALIFICATION

1. She is a good teacher.

2. Ferrara is a slow worker.

3. You are the best person to decide what you should do for a living.

4. Children should be taught to cooperate at home and in school.

5. The travel agent said not to go to Tripoli, because one may be hurt. (Saying *it is possible that one may be hurt* is an example of redundant qualification, because both *possible* and *may* indicate uncertainty.)

ANSWERS TO EXERCISE 4: UNNECESSARY SENTENCES

1. People cannot safely consume water that contains chemical pollutants.

2. No evidence suggests that Shakespeare's plays were written by others.

3. The United States should send soldiers to areas of conflict.

4. The architect Frank Lloyd Wright was famous for his ability to design buildings that blend into their surroundings.

5. A lot of people find math difficult because it requires very precise thinking skills.

ANSWERS TO EXERCISE 5: NEEDLESS SELF-REFERENCE

1. This argument cannot be generalized to most business owners.

2. Food is the best social lubricant.

3. Privacy should not be valued more than social concerns.

4. Most people want to do good work, but many are bored or frustrated with their jobs.

5. The author has a point.

ANSWERS TO EXERCISE 6: UNDESIRABLE PASSIVES

1. Recent allegations of corruption have hurt the politician's standing in the polls.

2. Congress passed the bill in time, but the president did not sign it until the time for action had passed.

3. Those who need advice least usually request it; the truly lost and ignorant do not seek it.

4. The city clerk should take the minutes of the city council meeting.

5. A number of field anthropologists and marriage experts compiled the report.

ANSWERS TO EXERCISE 7: WEAK OPENINGS

1. Businesses ignore the illiteracy problem at their own peril.

2. The government cannot fight a drug war effectively without waging a battle against demand for illicit substances.

3. The candidate has many strong points; intelligence, unfortunately, is not among them.

4. We, as a society, have decided to tolerate homelessness.

5. Americans must like watching television better than conversing.

ANSWERS TO EXERCISE 8: NEEDLESSLY VAGUE LANGUAGE

1. When water is heated to 100°C, it turns into steam.

2. The diplomat had to agree to live wherever the government sent him.

3. The principal told John not to return to school until he was ready to behave.

4. The police detective had to ask the lawyer for permission to question the suspect.

5. The last ice age destroyed thousands of animal species.

ANSWERS TO EXERCISE 9: CLICHÉS

1. Jefferson was a great leader.

2. Trying to find the employee responsible for this embarrassing information leak may be impossible.

3. The military should diversify its defense rather than rely so heavily on nuclear missiles.

4. Older doctors should be required to update their techniques, but many seem resistant to changes in technology.

5. I estimate that 120,000 fans were in the stadium.

ANSWERS TO EXERCISE 10: JARGON

1. We expect to use hundreds of paper clips in the next two months.

2. Our schoolchildren's education has been neglected.

3. Foreign diplomats should always talk to local leaders.

4. Recent studies suggest that Vienna sausages are good for you.

5. Government regulatory agencies lied in their press releases about the recent railway accident.

ANSWERS TO EXERCISE 11: SLANG AND COLLOQUIALISMS

1. Cynthia Larson is an expert.

2. Normal human beings cannot tolerate repeated humiliation.

3. If you want a good cheesecake, you must make a superb crust.

4. International organizations should try to cooperate on global issues like hunger.

5. The environmentalists are not involved in the project for prestige; they truly care about protecting the yellow-throated hornswoggler.

ANSWERS FOR EXERCISE 12: COMMAS

1. It takes a friendly, energetic personality to be a successful salesperson.

2. I was shocked to discover that a large, modern, glass-sheathed office building had replaced my old school.

3. The country club, a cluster of ivy-covered whitewashed buildings, was the site of the president's first speech.

4. Pushing through the panicked crowd, the security guards frantically searched for the suspect.

5. Despite careful analysis of the advantages and disadvantages of each proposal, Harry found it hard to reach a decision.

ANSWERS FOR EXERCISE 13: SEMICOLONS

1. Morgan has five years' experience in karate; Thompson has even more.

2. Very few students wanted to take the class in physics; only the professor's kindness kept it from being canceled.

3. You should always be prepared when you go on a camping trip; however, you must avoid carrying unnecessary weight.

ANSWERS TO EXERCISE 14: COLONS

1. I am sick and tired of your whining, your complaining, your nagging, your teasing, and, most of all, your barbed comments.

2. The chef has created a masterpiece: the pasta is delicate yet firm, the mustard greens are fresh, and the medallions of veal are melting in my mouth.

3. To write a good essay, you must do the following: practice, get plenty of sleep, and eat a good breakfast.

ANSWERS TO EXERCISE 15: HYPHENS AND DASHES

1. The child was able to count from one to ninety-nine.

2. The adults-only movie was banned from commercial TV.

3. It was the first time she had seen a movie that was for adults only.

4. A two-thirds majority would be needed to pass the budget reforms.

5. The house—and it was the most dilapidated house that I had ever seen—was a bargain because the land was so valuable.

ANSWERS TO EXERCISE 16: APOSTROPHES

1. The president's limousine had a flat tire.

2. Your tickets for the show will be at the box office.

3. The opportunity to change one's lifestyle does not come often.

4. The desk's surface was immaculate, but its drawers were messy.

5. The cat on the bed is hers.

WORD ROOTS

Knowing roots of words can help you in two ways. First, instead of learning one word at a time, you can learn a whole group of words that contain a certain root. They'll be related in meaning, so if you remember one, it will be easier for you to remember others. Second, roots can often help you decode an unknown word. If you recognize a familiar root, you can get a good enough idea of the word's meaning.

A, AN—not, without
amoral, atrophy, asymmetrical, anarchy, anesthetic

AB, A—from, away, apart
abnormal, abdicate, ablution, abnegate, absolve, abstemious, abstruse, annul, avert

AC, ACR—sharp, sour
acid, acerbic, exacerbate, acute, acrimony

AD, A—to, toward
adhere, adjacent, adjunct, admonish, adroit, adumbrate, accretion, accelerate, alleviate, aspire, assail, assonance, attest

ALI, ALTR—another
alias, alienate, inalienable, altruism

AM, AMI—love
amorous, amicable, amiable, amity

AMBI, AMPHI—both
ambiguous, ambivalent, ambidextrous, amphibious

AMBL, AMBUL—walk
amble, ambulatory, perambulator, somnambulist

ANIM—mind, spirit, breath
animal, animosity, unanimous, magnanimous

ANN, ENN—year
annual, annuity, biennial, perennial

ANTE, ANT—before
antecedent, antediluvian, antiquated, anticipate

ANTHROP—human
anthropology, philanthropy

ANTI, ANT—against, opposite
antidote, antithesis, antacid, antagonist, antonym

AUD—hear
audio, audience, audition

AUTO—self
autobiography, autocrat, autonomous

BELLI, BELL—war
belligerent, bellicose, antebellum, rebellion

BENE, BEN—good
benevolent, benefactor, beneficent, benign

BI—two
bicycle, bisect, bilateral, bilingual, biped

BIBLIO—book
Bible, bibliography, bibliophile

BIO—life
biography, biology, amphibious, symbiotic, macrobiotics

BURS—money, purse
reimburse, disburse, bursar

CAD, CAS, CID—happen, fall
accident, cadence, cascade, deciduous

CAP, CAPT, CEPT, CIP—take, hold, seize
capable, capacious, captivate, deception, intercept,
inception, anticipate, emancipation

CAP, CIP—head
captain, decapitate, precipitate, recapitulate

CARN—flesh
carnal, carnage, incarnate

CED, CESS—yield, go
cease, cessation, incessant, cede, precede, accede

CHROM—color
chrome, chromatic, monochrome

CHRON—time
chronology, chronic, anachronism

CIDE—murder
suicide, homicide, regicide, patricide

CIRCUM—around
circumference, circumlocution, circumspect,
circumvent

CLIN, CLIV—slope
incline, declivity, proclivity

CLUD, CLUS, CLAUS, CLOIS—shut, close
conclude, reclusive, claustrophobia, cloister, preclude,
occlude

CO, COM, CON—with, together
coeducation, coagulate, coalesce, coerce, collateral,
commodious, complaint, concord, congenial,
congenital

COGN, GNO—know
recognize, cognition, diagnosis, agnostic, prognosis

CONTRA—against
controversy, incontrovertible, contravene

CORP—body
corpse, corporeal, corpulence

COSMO, COSM—world
cosmopolitan, cosmos, microcosm, macrocosm

CRAC, CRAT—rule, power
democracy, bureaucracy, autocrat, aristocrat

CRED—trust, believe
incredible, credulous, credence

CRESC, CRET—grow
crescent, crescendo, accretion

CULP—blame, fault
culprit, culpable, inculpate, exculpate

CURR, CURS—run
current, concur, cursory, precursor, incursion

DE—down, out, apart
depart, debase, debilitate, defamatory, demur

DEC—ten, tenth
decade, decimal, decathlon, decimate

DEMO, DEM—people
democrat, demographics, demagogue, epidemic

DI, DIURN—day
diary, quotidian, diurnal

DIA—across
diagonal, diatribe, diaphanous

DIC, DICT—speak
abdicate, diction, indict, verdict

DIS, DIF, DI—not, apart, away
disaffected, disband, disbar, distend, differentiate,
diffidence, diffuse, digress, divert

DOC, DOCT—teach
docile, doctrine, doctrinaire

DOL—pain
condolence, doleful, dolorous, indolent

DUC, DUCT—lead
seduce, induce, conduct, viaduct, induct

EGO—self
ego, egoist, egocentric

EN, EM—in, into
enter, entice, encumber, embroil, empathy

ERR—wander
erratic, aberration, errant

EU—well, good
eulogy, euphemism, eurythmics, euthanasia

EX, E—out, out of
exit, exacerbate, excerpt, excommunicate, elicit, egress,
egregious

FAC, FIC, FECT, FY, FEA—make, do
factory, facility, benefactor, malefactor, fiction, fictive,
rectify, vilify, feasible

FAL, FALS—deceive
infallible, fallacious, false

FERV—boil
fervent, fervid, effervescent

FID—faith, trust
confident, diffidence, perfidious, fidelity

FLU, FLUX—flow
fluent, affluent, superfluous, flux

FORE—before
forecast, foreboding, forestall

FRAG, FRAC—break
fragment, fracture, refract

FUS—pour
profuse, infusion, effusive, diffuse

GEN—birth, class, kin
generation, congenital, homogeneous, ingenious,
engender

GRAD, GRESS—step
graduate, gradual, retrograde, ingress, egress

GRAPH, GRAM—writing
biography, bibliography, epigram

GRAT—pleasing
grateful, gratitude, gratuitous, gratuity

GRAV, GRIEV—heavy
grave, gravity, aggrieve, grievous

GREG—crowd, flock
segregate, gregarious, aggregate

HABIT, HIBIT—have, hold
habit, cohabit, habitat, inhibit

HAP—by chance
happen, haphazard, hapless, mishap

HELIO, HELI—sun
heliocentric, heliotrope, aphelion, perihelion, helium

HETERO—other
heterosexual, heterogeneous, heterodox

HOL—whole
holocaust, catholic, holistic

HOMO—same
homosexual, homogenize, homogeneous, homonym

HOMO—man
homo sapiens, homicide, bonhomie

HYDR—water
hydrant, hydrate, dehydration

HYPER—too much, excess
hyperactive, hyperbole, hyperventilate

HYPO—too little, under
hypodermic, hypothermia, hypochondria

IN, IG, IL, IM, IR—not
incorrigible, insomnia, interminable, incessant,
ignorant, ignominious, ignoble, illicit, illimitable,
immaculate, immutable, impertinent, improvident,
irregular

IN, IL, IM, IR—in, on, into
invade, inaugurate, incandescent, illustrate, imbue,
immerse, implicate, irrigate, irritate

INTER—between, among
intercede, intercept, interdiction, interject

INTRA, INTR—within
intrastate, intravenous, intramural, intrinsic

IT, ITER—between, among
transit, itinerant, transitory, reiterate

JECT, JET—throw
eject, interject, abject, trajectory, jettison

JOUR—day
journal, adjourn, sojourn

JUD—judge
judge, judicious, prejudice, adjudicate

JUNCT, JUG—join
junction, adjunct, injunction

JUR—swear, law
jury, abjure, perjure, jurisprudence

LAT—side
lateral, collateral, unilateral

LAV, LAU, LU—wash
lavatory, laundry, ablution, antediluvian

LEG, LEC, LEX—read, speak
legible, lecture, lexicon

LEV—light
elevate, levitate, levity, alleviate

LIBER—free
liberty, liberal, libertarian, libertine

LIG, LECT—choose, gather
eligible, elect, select

LIG, LI, LY—bind
ligament, oblige, religion, liable, liaison, lien, ally

LING, LANG—tongue
lingo, language, linguistics, bilingual

LITER—letter
literate, alliteration, literal

LITH—stone
monolith, lithograph, megalith

LOQU, LOC, LOG—speech, thought
eloquent, loquacious, colloquial, circumlocution,
monologue, dialogue

LUC, LUM—light
lucid, elucidate, pellucid, translucent, illuminate

LUD, LUS—play
ludicrous, allude, delusion

MACRO—great
macrocosm, macrobiotics

MAG, MAJ, MAS, MAX—great
magnify, magnanimous, magnate, magnitude, majesty,
master, maximum

MAL—bad
malady, maladroit, malevolent, malodorous

MAN—hand
manual, manuscript, manifest

MAR—sea
submarine, marine, maritime

MATER, MATR—mother
maternal, matron, matrilineal

MEDI—middle
intermediary, medieval, mediate

MEGA—great
megaphone, megalomania, megaton, megalith

MEM, MEN—remember
memory, memento, memorabilia, reminisce

METER, METR, MENS—measure
meter, thermometer, commensurate

MICRO—small
microscope, microorganism, microcosm, microbe

MIS—wrong, bad, hate
misunderstand, misapprehension, misconstrue,
mishap

MIT, MISS—send
transmit, emit, missive

MOLL—soft
mollify, emollient, mollusk

MON, MONIT—warn
admonish, monitor, premonition

MONO—one
monologue, monotonous, monogamy

MOR—custom, manner
moral, mores, morose

MOR, MORT—dead
morbid, moribund, mortal, amortize

MORPH—shape
amorphous, anthropomorphic, morphology

MOV, MOT, MOB, MOM—move
remove, motion, mobile, momentum, momentous

MUT—change
mutate, mutability, immutable, commute

NAT, NASC—born
native, nativity, cognate, nascent, renascent,
renaissance

NAU, NAV—ship, sailor
nautical, nauseous, navy, circumnavigate

NEG—not, deny
negative, abnegate, renege

NEO—new
neoclassical, neophyte, neologism, neonate

NIHIL—none, nothing
annihilation, nihilism, antinihilist

NOM, NYM—name
nominate, nomenclature, nominal, synonym,
anonymity

NOV—new
novelty, innovation, novitiate

NOX, NIC, NEC, NOC—harm
obnoxious, internecine, innocuous

NUMER—number
numeral, numerous, innumerable, enumerate

OB—against
obstruct, obdurate, obsequious, obtrusive

OMNI—all
omnipresent, omnipotent, omniscient, omnivorous

ONER—burden
onerous, exonerate

OPER—work
operate, cooperate, inoperable

PAC—peace
pacify, pacifist, pacific

PALP—feel
palpable, palpitation, palpation

PAN—all
panorama, panacea, pandemic, panoply

PATER, PATR—father
paternal, paternity, patriot, compatriot, expatriate

PATH, PASS—feel, suffer
sympathy, antipathy, pathos, impassioned

PEC—money
pecuniary, impecunious, peculation

PED, POD—foot
pedestrian, pediment, quadruped, tripod

PEL, PULS—drive
compel, compelling, expel, propel, compulsion

PEN—almost
peninsula, penultimate, penumbra

PEND, PENS—hang
pendant, pendulous, suspense, propensity

PER—against, destruction
perfidious, pernicious, perjure

PER—through, by, for, throughout
perambulator, percipient, perfunctory, pertinacious

PERI—around
perimeter, periphery, perihelion, peripatetic

PET—seek, go toward
petition, impetus, impetuous, petulant, centripetal

PHIL—love
philosopher, philanderer, philanthropy, philology

PHOB—fear
phobia, claustrophobia, xenophobia

PHON—sound
phonograph, megaphone, phonics

PLAC—calm, please
placate, implacable, placid, complacent

PON, POS—put, place
postpone, proponent, juxtaposition, depose

PORT—carry
portable, deportment, rapport

POT—drink
potion, potable, potability

POT—power
potential, potent, impotent, potentate, omnipotence

PRE—before
precede, precipitate, premonition, preposition

PRIM, PRI—first
prime, primary, primordial, pristine

PRO—ahead, forth
proceed, proclivity, protestation, provoke

PROTO—first
prototype, protagonist, protocol

PROX, PROP—near
approximate, propinquity, proximity

PSEUDO—false
pseudoscientific, pseudonym

PYR—fire
pyre, pyrotechnics, pyromania

QUAD, QUAR, QUAT—four
quadrilateral, quadrant, quarter, quarantine

QUES, QUER, QUIS, QUIR—question
quest, inquest, query, querulous, inquisitive, inquiry

QUIE—quiet
disquiet, acquiesce, quiescent, requiem

QUINT, QUIN—five
quintuplets, quintessence

RADI, RAMI—branch
radiate, radiant, eradicate, ramification

RECT, REG—straight, rule
rectangle, rectitude, rectify, regular

REG—king, rule
regal, regent, interregnum

RETRO—backward
retrospective, retroactive, retrograde

RID, RIS—laugh
ridiculous, deride, derision

ROG—ask
interrogate, derogatory, arrogant

RUD—rough, crude
rude, erudite, rudimentary

RUPT—break
disrupt, interrupt, rupture

SACR, SANCT—holy
sacred, sacrilege, sanction, sacrosanct

SCRIB, SCRIPT, SCRIV—write
scribe, ascribe, script, manuscript, scrivener

SE—apart, away
separate, segregate, secede, sedition

SEC, SECT, SEG—cut
sector, dissect, bisect, intersect, segment, secant

SED, SID—sit
sedate, sedentary, supersede, reside, residence

SEM—seed, sow
seminar, seminal, disseminate

SEN—old
senior, senile, senescent

SENT, SENS—feel, think
sentiment, nonsense, consensus, sensual

SEQU, SECU—follow
sequence, sequel, subsequent, consecutive

SIM, SEM—similar, same
similar, verisimilitude, semblance, dissemble

SIGN—mark, sign
signal, designation, assignation

SIN—curve
sine curve, sinuous, insinuate

SOL—alone
solo, solitude, soliloquy, solipsism

SOL—sun
solar, parasol, solarium, solstice

SOMN—sleep
insomnia, somnolent, somnambulist

SON—sound
sonic, consonance, sonorous, resonate

SOPH—wisdom
philosopher, sophistry, sophisticated, sophomoric

SPEC, SPIC—see, look
spectator, retrospective, perspective, perspicacious

SPER—hope
prosper, prosperous, despair, desperate

SPERS, SPAR—scatter
disperse, sparse, aspersion, disparate

SPIR—breathe
respire, inspire, spiritual, aspire, transpire

STRICT, STRING—bind
stricture, constrict, stringent, astringent

STRUCT, STRU—build
structure, obstruct, construe

SUB—under
subconscious, subjugate, subliminal, subpoena

SUMM—highest
summit, summary, consummate

SUPER, SUR—above
supervise, supercilious, superfluous, insurmountable, surfeit

SURGE, SURRECT—rise
surge, resurgent, insurgent, insurrection

SYN, SYM—together
synthesis, sympathy, symposium, symbiosis

TACIT, TIC—silent
tacit, taciturn, reticent

TACT, TAG, TANG—touch
tact, tactile, contagious, tangent, tangential, tangible

TEN, TIN, TAIN—hold, twist
detention, tenable, pertinacious, retinue, retain

TEND, TENS, TENT—stretch
intend, distend, tension, tensile, ostensible, contentious

TERM—end
terminal, terminus, terminate, interminable

TERR—earth, land
terrain, terrestrial, extraterrestrial, subterranean

TEST—witness
testify, attest, testimonial, protestation

THE—god
atheist, theology, apotheosis, theocracy

THERM—heat
thermometer, thermal, thermonuclear, hypothermia

TIM—fear, frightened
timid, intimidate, timorous

TOP—place
topic, topography, utopia

TORP—stiff, numb
torpedo, torpid, torpor

TORT—twist
distort, extort, tortuous

TOX—poison
toxic, toxin, intoxication

TRACT—draw
tractor, intractable, protract

TRANS—across, over, through, beyond
transport, transgress, transient, transitory, translucent

TREM, TREP—shake
tremble, tremor, trepidation, intrepid

TURB—shake
disturb, turbulent, perturbation

UMBR—shadow
umbrella, umbrage, adumbrate, penumbra

UNI, UN—one
unify, unilateral, unanimous

URB—city
urban, suburban, urbane

VAC—empty
vacant, evacuate, vacuous

VAL, VAIL—value, strength
valid, valor, ambivalent, convalescence, avail

VEN, VENT—come
convene, intervene, venue, convention, adventitious

VER—true
verify, verity, verisimilitude, verdict

VERB—word
verbal, verbose, verbiage, verbatim

VERT, VERS—turn
avert, convert, revert, incontrovertible, divert, aversion

VICT, VINC—conquer
victory, conviction, evict, evince, invincible

VID, VIS—see
evident, vision, visage, supervise

VIL—base, mean
vile, vilify, revile

VIV, VIT—life
vivid, vital, convivial, vivacious

VOC, VOK, VOW—call, voice
vocal, equivocate, invoke, avow

VOL—wish
voluntary, malevolent, benevolent, volition

VOLV, VOLUT—turn, roll
revolve, evolve, convoluted

VOR—eat
devour, carnivore, omnivorous, voracious

INDEX

A

active reading, 10–11
active voice, 318–19
allegory, 96
alliteration, 96
allusion, 96
anaphora, 96
annotations, 110, 115–16, 158–59
answers, predicting, 12
anticipatory future tense, 303
antithesis, 96
aphorism, 96
apostrophe (rhetorical device), 96
apostrophes (punctuation), 328–29
appeals to authority, emotion, or logic, 96
appositives, 294–95
argumentation/persuasion
  questions, 145–48, 153
assonance, 96
asyndeton, 96
attitude, 96
audience, in rhetoric, 160
authority, appeals to, 96

B

begging the question, 97
breathing, 27
buffer period before bed, 26

C

canon, 97
chiasmus, 97

claims, 97
clauses, relative, 294
clichés, 320–21
colloquialisms, 97, 323
colons, 326–27
commas, 324–25
comparative forms, 310
comparison and contrast
  defined, 97
  ideas, 308
    questions, 148, 149, 152
comparisons, 308–10
compound subjects, 295–96
conceit, 97
conciseness, in writing, 313–17
conditional sentences, 306
conjunctions, correlative, 307–8
connotation, 97
consonance, 97
context, in rhetoric, 160
contrary to fact, in conditional sentences, 306
control, taking, 18–20
conventions, 97
coordinate ideas, 307
corrections, in essays, 17
correctness, in writing, 322–29
correlative conjunctions, 307–8
countdown to test, 29–30
cramming, 9, 14
critical reading, 15, 110–11
critical words, 11
critiques, 97

D

dangling modifiers, 297
dashes, 328
deductive reasoning, 97
dialects, 98
diction, 98
didactic writing/speech, 98
discourse, modes of, 100
Discover, Define, and Develop (3-D approach), 155–65
documentation and citation questions, 124
"do so," as phrase, 299
double negatives, 311, 312
Douglass, Frederick
    Narrative of the Life of Frederick Douglass, an American Slave excerpt, 126–27
    Narrative of the Life of Frederick Douglass, an American Slave excerpt, questions about, 127–29
dramatic irony, 99

E

easy questions, 11, 15
8-6-4-2 scoring guide, 142–43
    See also scoring guides
elegies, 98
elimination, process of, 13
ellipsis, 310–11
emotion, appeals to, 96
epistrophe, 98
epitaphs, 98
errors, in essays, 17
essay questions
    corrections in response, 17
    length of response, 16–17
    mistakes in response, 17
    organizing response to, 16
    overview, 4
    prompt types, 144–51
    scoring guide and prompts, 152–55
    scoring guide overview, 142–43
    success strategies, 14–18
    3-D approach (Discover, Define, and Develop), 155–65
    tips, 141–42

triage, 18–19
ethos, 98
eulogies, 98
euphemisms, 98
exam. *See* test
EXCEPT questions, 11
exercise, 25–26
exposition, 98
extended metaphors, 98

F

fact, in conditional sentences, 306
fees, test, 6
figurative language/figures of speech, 99
flashbacks, 99
food and drink, during test, 20, 30
forcefulness, in writing, 317–22
future perfect tense, 304, 305
future speculation, in conditional sentences, 306
future tense, 303

G

genres, 99
gerunds, 296, 302
grade reports, 5
grammar reference guide, 293–312
    comparisons, 308–10
    ellipsis, 310–11
    modifiers, 296–98
    negatives, 311–12
    parallel structure, 307–8
    pronouns, 298–302
    sentence structure, 293–94
    subject-verb agreement, 294–96
    verbs, 302–6
gridding, 12–14
guessing, 5, 12, 13

H

hard questions, 119
homilies, 99
How-What approach, 111–14
hyperbole, 99
hyphens, 327–28

I

ideas
    compared/contrasted, 308
    coordinate, 307
idiom, 310
if-then statements, 306
illogical comparisons, 309–10
imagery, 99
inductive reasoning, 99
inference, 99
infinitives, 296, 302–3, 305
intervening phrases, 294–95
introductory modifiers, 297
irony, 99
isocolons, 100
isometric exercise, 26–27, 28
"its" *versus* "it's," 329

J

jargon, 100, 321–22
juxtaposition, 100

K

Keller, Helen
    passage by, 156–57
    passage by, annotations of, 158–59
    passage by, discussion of, 159–60
    passage by, sample essay responses to,
        161–65

L

language
    figurative, 99
    vague, 320
legibility, 17–18
Lincoln, Abraham
    "Second Inaugural Address," 112–13
    "Second Inaugural Address," How-What
        approach to, 113–14
    "Second Inaugural Address," sample
        annotations on, 115–16
listing, 16
litote, 100
logic, appeals to, 96
loose sentences, 100

M

main idea questions, 120–21
meaning and purpose questions, 122
metaphors, 98, 100
metonymy, 100
mistakes, in essays, 17
modes of discourse, 100
modifiers, 296–98
mood, 100, 306
multiple-choice questions
    about, 117–18
    applying strategies, 125–29
    overview, 4
    reading, 118–19
    success strategies, 10–14
    triage, 18
    types, 120–24

N

*Narrative of the Life of Frederick Douglass, an
    American Slave* (Douglass)
    excerpt, 126–27
    excerpt, questions about, 127–29
narratives, 100
negatives, 311–12
Nightingale, Florence
    passage by, 103–4
    passage by, questions about, 104–7

O

objective case pronouns, 301–2
"one," as pronoun, 300
onomatopoeia, 100
openings, weak, 319
order of questions, 11, 12
oxymorons, 101

P

pacing yourself, 9, 11, 14
paradoxes, 101
parallel structure, 101, 307–8
paraphrasing, 19
participles, 302, 305
passive voice, 318–19
past participles, 305

past perfect tense, 304, 305
past tense, 303, 305
pathos, 101
pens and pencils, for test, 12, 17, 29
perfect participles, 305
periodic sentences, 101
personification, 101
phrases
 intervening, 294–95
 prepositional, 295
 wordy, 314
plan of attack, developing, 19
point of view, 101
predicting answers, 12
preparation tips, test, 27–28
prepositional phrases, 295
present perfect tense, 304
present tense, 303, 305
process of elimination, 13
prompt types, essay, 144–51
 argumentation/persuasion, 145–48
 comparison/contrast, 148, 149
 prose analysis, 144–45
 synthesis, 148–51
pronouns, 298–302
prose, 101
prose analysis questions, 144–45, 152
purpose/intention, in rhetoric, 160

Q
qualifiers, 315–16
questions
 argumentation/persuasion, 145–48, 153
 comparison/contrast, 148, 149, 152
 decoding, 14–15
 documentation and citation, 124
 easy, 11, 15
 EXCEPT, 11
 hard, 119
 main idea, 120–21
 meaning and purpose, 122
 order of, 11, 12
 prose analysis, 144–45, 152
 rhetoric, 121
 rhetorical, 101

rhetorical mode, 123
 skipping, 13
 structure and organization, 122–23
 triage, 18–19
 See also essay questions; multiple-choice
  questions; synthesis essay questions
quotes, 16

R
reading
 active, 10–11
 annotations, sample, 115–16
 critical, 15, 110–11
 essay prompts and passages, 15
 How-What approach, 111–14
 importance of, 109
 multiple-choice questions, 118–19
 for understanding, 109–16
realism, 101
reasoning
 deductive, 97
 inductive, 99
rebuttal/refutation, 101
redundancy, 314–15
references
 outside, 17
 to specific lines or words, 11
refutation, 101
registration, test, 5
relative clauses, 294
requirement, subjunctive of, 306
resources, additional, 6
retelling, 16
retrospection, 99
rhetoric, 101, 159–60
rhetoric questions, 121
rhetorical mode questions, 123
rhetorical questions, 101
roots, word, 335–41
rubrics. *See* scoring guides
run-on sentences, 293

S
sarcasm, 102
satire, 102
schedule for last week before test, 29–30

scoring guides
    argumentation/persuasion questions, 153
    comparison/contrast questions, 152
    essay questions, generally, 142–43, 162
    prose analysis questions, 152
    synthesis essay questions, 154–55
scoring overview, 5, 9
"Second Inaugural Address" (Lincoln)
    How-What approach to, 113–14
    sample annotations, 115–16
    text, 112–13
self-reference, needless, 317–18
semicolons, 325–26
sentence fragments, 293–94
sentences
    conditional, 306
    loose, 100
    patterns, unusual, 296
    periodic, 101
    run-on, 293
    structure of, 293–94
    unnecessary, 316–17
simile, 102
situational irony, 99
skipping questions, 13
slang, 323
speaker, in rhetoric, 160
statements of fact, in conditional sentences, 306
strengths, identifying your, 22, 23–24
stress management, 20–28
    breathing, 27
    during test, 28
    exercise, 25–26
    identifying your strengths and weaknesses, 22–24
    isometric exercise, 26–27, 28
    preparation tips, 27–28
    sources of stress, 21–22
    visualizing success, 24–25
structure and organization questions, 122–23
style, 102
    See also usage and style
subject, in rhetoric, 160
subjective case pronouns, 301–2
subjects, compound, 295–96
subject-verb agreement, 294–96

subjunctive mood, 306
subjunctive of requirement, 306
success strategies, 7–30
    countdown to test, 29–30
    essay questions, 14–18
    multiple-choice questions, 10–14
    score requirements, 9
    stress management, 20–28
    taking control, 18–20
    test requirements, 9–10
    using book as resource, 8–9
symbolism, 102
synecdoche, 102
syntax, 102
synthesis essay questions
    about, 148–51
    quotes, 16
    reading period, 14, 18–19
    scoring guide, 154–55

T
tense, verb, 303–5
terminology, key, 95–107
    about, 95
    applying, 103–7
    terms, 96–102
test
    approaching as a whole, 18–20
    countdown to, 29–30
    fees, 6
    food and drink during, 20, 30
    pens and pencils for, 12, 17, 29
    preparation tips, 27–28
    registration, 5
    requirements of, 9–10
    stress management during, 28
    structure overview, 3–4
    watches/timepieces for, 20, 29
    water during, 20, 30
test booklets, marking up, 13, 19, 20
themes, 102
3-D approach (Discover, Define, and Develop), 155–65
time management, 12, 14, 20
"to be," forms of, 308

tone, 102
triage, 18–19

U

unclear comparisons, 308–9
usage and style, 313–29
   conciseness, 313–17
   correctness, 322–29
   forcefulness, 317–22

V

vague language, 320
verbal irony, 99
verbals, 302–3
verbs, 294–96, 302–6
verb tense, 303–5
visualizing success, 24–25
voice, 102, 318–19

W

watches/timepieces, for test, 20, 29
water, during test, 20, 30
weaknesses, identifying your, 22–23
"who" *versus* "whom," 302
wordiness, 314
word roots, 335–41
words, critical, 11
writing, successful, 143

Y

"you," as pronoun, 300
"your" *versus* "you're," 329

Z

zeugma, 102